Victorian Celebrity Culture and Tennyson's Circle

Also by Páraic Finnerty
EMILY DICKINSON'S SHAKESPEARE

Victorian Celebrity Culture and Tennyson's Circle

By

Charlotte Boyce
Senior Lecturer in English and American Literature, University of Portsmouth, UK

Páraic Finnerty
Senior Lecturer in English Literature, University of Portsmouth, UK

and

Anne-Marie Millim
Research Associate in Multilingual Literature, University of Luxembourg

To Alix,

With very best wishes,

Charlotte

To Alix,

Thank you for asking
me to sign this

all my very
best,

Páraic

palgrave
macmillan

First published 2013 by
PALGRAVE MACMILLAN

Palgrave Macmillan in the UK is an imprint of Macmillan Publishers Limited, registered in England, company number 785998, of Houndmills, Basingstoke, Hampshire RG21 6XS.

Palgrave Macmillan in the US is a division of St Martin's Press LLC, 175 Fifth Avenue, New York, NY 10010.

Palgrave Macmillan is the global academic imprint of the above companies and has companies and representatives throughout the world.

Palgrave® and Macmillan® are registered trademarks in the United States, the United Kingdom, Europe and other countries.

ISBN 978–1–137–00793–3

This book is printed on paper suitable for recycling and made from fully managed and sustained forest sources. Logging, pulping and manufacturing processes are expected to conform to the environmental regulations of the country of origin.

A catalogue record for this book is available from the British Library.

A catalog record for this book is available from the Library of Congress.

Typeset by MPS Limited, Chennai, India.

Contents

List of Figures

Acknowledgements

This book emerges out of a project on 'Tennyson's Celebrity Circle: Cultural Interactions of the Isle of Wight' that was undertaken by the authors at the University of Portsmouth between 2010 and 2011 and supported by the Higher Education Innovation Fund (HEIF). We are very grateful for the financial help we received from HEIF and, subsequently, from the Centre for Studies in Literature (CSL) at the University of Portsmouth.

Our researches have taken us to a number of libraries, museums and archives across the UK and the assistance we've received from the staff at these institutions has proved invaluable. Our special thanks go to the Tennyson Research Centre, Lincoln, and Grace Timmins, in particular; the Watts Gallery, Surrey; the National Portrait Gallery, particularly Bryony Millan; the Victoria and Albert Museum; the British Library; Glasgow University Library Special Collections; Portsmouth Central Library; Portsmouth University Library; the National Library of Wales, particularly Emyr Evans; and Cardiff University Library Special Collections, particularly Alison Harvey.

This project has also involved a number of very enjoyable visits to the Isle of Wight and we'd like to thank the many people there who welcomed us so warmly and supported our research. Special mention goes to the Isle of Wight Heritage Service, particularly Sheila Caws; Dimbola Museum and Galleries/the Julia Margaret Cameron Trust; the Freshwater Tennyson Society; Bob Cotton; Brian Hinton; John Holsburt; Elizabeth Hutchings; Rebecca Fitzgerald; Martin Beisly; and Verrall Dunlop.

We would like to thank the National Portrait Gallery, London (G. F. Watts Archive) for permission to quote from Watts's correspondence and the Houghton Library, University of Harvard, for permission to quote from Edward Lear's diaries.

Finally, huge thanks go to our friends and colleagues at the Universities of Portsmouth and Luxembourg, and to our partners and families, for their ongoing support.

Introduction

Charlotte Boyce, Páraic Finnerty and Anne-Marie Millim

In 'A Counterfeit Presentment', a short story published in *Household Words* in 1858, an author, Edgar Sweetwort, who used to write under the pseudonym Hydrophobius, describes the process whereby, after publishing a collection of letters and a book of poems under his own name, he becomes a public figure. At first, he takes great pleasure in the praise and criticism he receives in the 'weekly critical organs' and 'channels of public instruction', and in being a 'literary lion', invited to the kind of fashionable social gatherings that typically facilitated the worship of the distinguished and the great.[1] Within three months, he has become a recognisable figure, of whom passers-by in the street say, 'There he is! That's Sweetwort! – Hydrophobius, you know!', presumably because (as was often the case for Victorian authors) a print or engraving of his portrait is in cultural circulation. His new status, however, generates a 'public demand' for a more exact 'photographic portrait', which Sweetwort instantly resists, owing to personal misgivings about the 'peculiar character' of his face and head. The remainder of the story outlines his gradually increasing 'persecution' by commercial photographers who want to make money by selling his image to publishers, illustrated newspapers and periodicals, or to print shops via manufacturers of *cartes de visite*, the miniature portraits that came into fashion in the late 1850s.[2] These photographers send daily petitioning letters, visit him, and even use 'real or presumed ties of family and kindred' as a means of gaining access to him and convincing him to pose for them. Sweetwort's stand-off ends when one formidable photographer explains 'in the tone of a policeman' that he has an order for 'two thousand copies of [Sweetwort's] portrait, for home consumption, and fifteen hundred for exportation' and that if he does not agree to sit for a photograph an image of a prize-fighter, 'Bill Tippets – the

1

Lambeth Phenomenon', will be sold to the public as if it were a genuine representation of the camera-shy author.[3] The story ends with the author acquiescing, and the next day he finds himself in a 'glass cage', composing his 'countenance according to the imperious instructions of the relentless photographer'. Having once been a happy man with his privacy 'strictly preserved', Sweetwort is now embroiled in the workings of an all-powerful Victorian celebrity culture, in which mass media turn people into commodities, prioritising profit over authenticity and the uniqueness of the individuals they claim to venerate.[4]

The 'portrait mania' to which Sweetwort is subjected makes him feel as if the 'shadow of the abominable instrument', the camera, is cast across his daily life and he grows paranoid that a 'detestable lens' waits for him 'in the street', 'lurking for [him] in bye-lanes, and under cover of the trees in the open meadows'.[5] This experience corresponds with the paranoia and sense of personal entrapment that Leo Braudy describes as the common features of fame in Western culture from the mid-eighteenth century onwards.[6] Without using the word 'celebrity', Sweetwort's story confirms, as recent scholarship has, that many of the discourses, practices and conditions associated with twentieth- or twenty-first-century celebrity culture were already in place in the nineteenth century.[7] Public recognition was already an industrialised, institutionalised and commercialised process that normalised and legitimised the desire for cultural visibility, along with the idea and existence of identifiable figures whose function it was to circulate within an expanding and pervasive mass media and mass market. The 'combination of renown, visibility, and fascination with a personality' that is highlighted in Sweetwort's story is a result of what most critics, following Braudy, agree was a 'democratisation' of fame, which 'proliferated in Western Europe by the early eighteenth century as print media developed and as people of high birth lost their monopoly over distinction'.[8] The appreciation of talent or achievement metamorphosed into an obsession with the biographies, private lives and physical appearances of the famous, an obsession catered for by the commercial circulation of artefacts associated with these personalities. In turn, these commodities created and maintained an illusionary relationship between public figures and their admirers, manufacturing identities and 'forms of consciousness' for celebrated figures as well as for their devotees.[9]

What has not yet been fully explored, but is evident in the story of Sweetwort, is that by the mid-Victorian period there existed not merely reluctant celebrities, but hounded ones. This is confirmed by the article 'Celebrity: Its Pains and Penalties', published in *The Sixpenny Magazine* in 1862, whose descriptions bluntly present the celebrity as the slave of 'the most tyrannical of masters', the insatiable public, encouraged and enabled by a highly organised press.[10] The article advises men such as Sweetwort to hide their talent or avoid accomplishing exceptional feats, for being a 'Lion' means 'you no longer belong to yourself; your person, your gestures, your words, your name, have become public property'. The celebrity is exhausted and tormented by admiring crowds, which treat his every appearance in public as an 'event' and reiterate the 'latest sayings of the celebrated Mr. So and So'.[11] The press's sole aim, according to the article, is to facilitate this ever-closer relationship by intruding into the celebrity's private life and attempting to penetrate his or her mystery. The press is there not only to reveal things about the celebrity that not even a family member or closest friend would know, but to publicise his or her every public move, so that 'at every post-house [he or she] must run the gauntlet of a crowd of idlers and sight-seers'. The author concludes by suggesting that he would rather be a 'crossing sweeper, a cab driver, or an omnibus cad' than a 'celebrated man', and hopes that if it is his 'sad destiny' to be admired it happens after he is dead. The essayist's preference is for the traditional 'fame' associated with posthumous reputation rather than the immediate 'celebrity' that is facilitated and driven by the mass media and marketplace.[12]

If Lord Byron was the first literary celebrity to experience the 'pains and penalties', as well as the pleasures and benefits, of personal distinction, owing to the intimate relationship that he established with his audience (a relationship bolstered by industrialised print culture), then Alfred Tennyson was the first celebrity poet to become known as much for his hatred of this obsessive, fanatical pursuit of acclaimed figures as for his work.[13] To a large extent, from 1850 onwards, his poetry, life, personal identity and consciousness were all shaped by the intrusiveness practised, naturalised and normalised by his admirers and the press. In the 1830s, when Tennyson began publishing his works, poetry was a culturally marginal genre; however, for him, as for his Romantic precursors, poor sales and being misunderstood by one's contemporaries were markers of distinction, as true genius and exceptional originality could only be appreciated by posterity.[14] Instead of seeking the vulgarity of immediate fame or recognition, Tennyson told one hostile critic, in 1834, that he 'prefer[red] vegetating in a very quiet garden where I neither see or hear anything of the great world of literature'.[15] Yet Tennyson also actively sought to distinguish himself through careful self-promotion and self-publicity in an increasingly saturated marketplace in order to make a living as a writer and secure the opportunity of lasting fame.[16]

Despite his criticisms of commercially orientated and aggressively mar-keted periodicals and annuals, for instance, he published frequently in these volumes during the 1830s and 1840s, ensuring a wide readership for his poetry and his eventual status as the nation's favourite poet.[17] At this time, Tennyson avoided Byronic self-revelation in his work, and was greatly admired for his ballads, narrative verse and, in particular, his dramatic lyrics (later called dramatic monologues) – poems that offered psychological portraits of others rather than of himself.[18] This liter-ary recognition translated into celebrity, however, when he published his most personal and heartfelt poem, *In Memoriam A. H. H.*, in 1850, which he later had to emphasise was 'not an actual biography'.[19] The poem's commercial and critical success helped him to secure the Poet Laureateship in the same year, making him one of the most famous writers in Britain, on a par with Charles Dickens.[20] *In Memoriam* enjoyed such success not only because it tapped into Victorian cultural anxie-ties about the place of faith and the status of mourning in an age of science and religious scepticism, but also because it allowed each reader to identify with and participate vicariously in the journey of the elegy's speaker, which ends in the reconciliation of 'the silent "deep self" to the self that speaks and reacts with the world'.[21] Rather than denying readers access to himself by writing impersonal, dramatic lyrics, Tennyson now expressed his genuine, seemingly unmediated feelings of despair, doubt and loss in the aftermath of the death of his beloved friend, Arthur Henry Hallam. The sense of sincerity and authenticity commonly iden-tified in the poem derived in part from the fact that it was written by the formerly reticent Tennyson. This self-dramatising poem inaugurated a new relationship of intimacy between Tennyson and his readers, offer-ing them access to the mind and personality of a man whom many already regarded as a great poet.[22] In a manner similar to Sweetwort, who gave up his anonymity, Tennyson, in revealing his 'true' self (albeit through a poem that was initially published anonymously), moved from being an admired writer to a celebrity whose name had commercial and cultural power.

The Byromania of the early nineteenth century was now replaced by a new enthusiasm for the moral, traditional and domestic propriety that Tennyson represented: as one critic, in 1859, suggested, everyone had become 'Tennysonian'.[23] Having found a confessional self-portrait in *In Memoriam*, his readers began to search his earlier and subsequent work for similar revelations of the private man behind the now public figure. An obliging media and marketplace also began to facilitate his admirers' desire to get close to him through information in newspapers, periodicals, memoirs and biographies; through engravings, prints, photographs and caricatures; and through consumer goods, such as pens, calendars (like the one shown on the cover of this book) and even pills to relieve constipation, apparently endorsed by him.[24] Tennyson was bombarded by requests from fans who wanted him to read their poems and send them autographs; from editors who wanted to publish his poems, knowing that they would bolster the reputation and sales of their periodicals and newspapers; from publishers who offered extravagant amounts of money so that he would publish with them; and from artists and photographers who wanted him to pose for them.[25] Put simply, Tennyson became a brand name that could generate immense sales for the once unmarketable genre of poetry and increase the value of any products associated with him, which in turn expanded his cultural reputation and visibility.[26] While some admirers regarded the cultural artefacts produced by and about Tennyson as tokens of a (quasi-)personal relationship with the poet, others were spurred on by these commodities to seek ever-closer connections with him. Tennyson became one of the most sought-after men in Britain as his admirers pursued opportunities to scrutinise his face and body for clues to his interiority or true selfhood, to solve the mystery of their fascination with his allure. In the first years after he received the Laureateship, his home in Twickenham was bombarded with uninvited visitors; in 1851, when he met the Brownings while holidaying in Paris, he spoke of his desire 'to escape from the dirty hands of his worshippers', and to be in a location where he could be 'quite private'.[27] On his return to Britain, Tennyson began to plan his retreat from the celebrity-obsessed world of London, and, in 1853, he relocated with his family to Freshwater, a remote region of the Isle of Wight. Ironically, this decision transferred some of the features of mainland celebrity culture to this idyllic, rural location, transforming it into a tourist attraction and focal point for press attention.

Tennyson's fans were not the only ones to follow him to Freshwater, however. Another, less objectionable consequence of the Laureate's retreat from literary London was the gradual establishment of a colony of celebrities around his Isle of Wight home. As the poet and dramatist Sir Henry Taylor (a regular visitor to Freshwater) noted in his *Autobiography*, celebrity has magnetic effects: 'Where one celebrated man sets up his rest, there will always be other celebrities coming and going'.[28] Among the famous guests to have visited Farringford, Tennyson's Freshwater home, were the Pre-Raphaelite artist John Everett Millais, the American poet Henry Wadsworth Longfellow, the

Italian revolutionary Giuseppe Garibaldi and the royal consort, Prince Albert. So relentless was the stream of celebrity visitors, Anne Thackeray Ritchie (herself a well-known author) observed in a letter to her friend Walter Senior that 'everybody [in Freshwater] is either a genius, or a poet, or a painter or peculiar in some way, poor Miss Stephen says is there *nobody* common-place?'[29]

As well as making Freshwater a place of pilgrimage for the great men and women of his age, Tennyson's presence encouraged fellow celebrities to relocate there on a permanent basis, resulting in the creation of a tight-knit, mutually supportive community of like-minded artists and intellectuals. Among its members were Julia Margaret Cameron, one of the pioneers of Victorian artistic photography, who would later find fame from her portraits of the Laureate and illustrations of his work, and George Frederic Watts, the best-known and best-respected English painter of the period. According to Cameron's son, Hardinge, it was Tennyson's 'irresistible' aura that prompted his family's move to 'Dimbola' (a property adjoining the Farringford estate) in 1860, an explanation seconded by Cameron's husband, Charles, in an unpublished poem:

> No idle motive hath my will inclined,
> But such as well might sway an earnest mind,
> Such as to all may gladly be confessed
> To dwell united near the chosen nest,
> And hear the Nightingale that sings unseen
> In the dark ilex, on the flowr'y green
> That carpets Farringford's muse-haunted scene.[30]

The friendship between Tennyson and the Camerons had first grown up amidst another 'muse-haunted scene': Julia Margaret's sister Sara Prinsep's literary and artistic salon at Little Holland House, London. Every Sunday, Prinsep (a renowned lioniser) would host a gathering of poets, painters, intellectuals and men of science, typically involving croquet, strawberries and cream, music, dinner and 'much delightful conversation'.[31] The 'fixed star in the Little Holland House firmament' was the painter Watts, 'England's Michelangelo' or 'Signor' to his circle, who lived and had his studio there.[32] When the Prinseps' lease of the property came to an end, Watts decided to follow the Tennysons and Camerons to Freshwater where he built a villa known as 'The Briary' to accommodate himself and his entourage, thus consolidating the village's community of creative celebrities.

Critics have consequently portrayed Freshwater in the 1860s and 1870s as 'Little Holland House-by-sea', a pastoral offshoot of cosmopolitan celebrity culture.[33] For those who participated in and chronicled the activities of the Freshwater circle, however, there were notable differences between the two clusters of celebrity. The soirées at Little Holland House, perhaps inevitably, blurred the boundaries between public and private; they were self-consciously fashionable events at which to see and be seen, as much as occasions for refined conversation among intimates. Notices of the coterie's activities, and the arrival and departure of illustrious guests, were frequently reported in the society, literary or fine-art gossip pages of not only metropolitan but also provincial newspapers.[34] Though Freshwater was not immune from such press attention, its relatively secluded location meant that gatherings at Farringford and Dimbola (in the form of dinners, balls and private theatricals at Cameron's home theatre) took on a much more private and homely character than their London-based equivalents. Highlighting the distinction, the essayist Wilfrid Ward recalled that, at Freshwater,

> the actual conversation was real, wide in its range, and often excessively interesting. It went beyond the mere snatches of serious conversation which one hears at a London dinner party ... If Tyndall, or Browning appeared on the scene it was not merely that we saw great men as one might see them at a large evening party. We heard them talk, and not formally or for display, but in undress. They 'let themselves go' to a degree rarely if ever possible in London society. We were at leisure and the trammels of convention were banished. In London the wings of the immortals are clipped.[35]

Owing to their liberated informality and lack of pretension, Ward concluded, the celebrity gatherings at Freshwater came 'nearer to realizing the purpose and ideal of a French *salon* than any social group ... in England'.[36]

Unlike the salons of Paris, however, the Freshwater circle was distinctly non-urban in setting. This was an essential part of its appeal; where Ward fetishised the circle's philosophical dissimilarity to London society, Ritchie, in her reminiscences, saluted its geographical distance, describing Freshwater as a 'green and sunshiny little republic', 'quiet and self-contained, completely out of the world, and yet at the same time in touch with its larger interests'.[37] Rural remoteness was repeatedly constructed as a boon to the creativity of those who dwelt there. Charles Cameron's representation of Tennyson as a 'Nightingale' in the poem cited earlier, for instance, implies that the Laureate was more at home amongst the 'flowr'y green' of Farringford, where his poetic imagination thrived 'unseen', than in literary London. Ritchie, likewise, suggested that the natural beauty of the Isle of Wight enabled Tennyson not only to write poems but to '[live] them'.[38] Significantly, a kind of synaesthesia emerges in retrospective accounts of Freshwater in the 1860s and 1870s.[39] The memories of those who lived and stayed there are typically tied to a range of sights, sounds and smells: 'beds of turquoise forget-me-not'; 'the wood-pigeons, and the blackbirds and their note'; 'the sea beating against the rocks'; 'the scent of sweetbriar'; and the 'rainbow words' of Watts, vivid 'like the magical colours on his palette'.[40] These vibrant sense-impressions – visual, audible, olfactory – merge and combine to construct Freshwater as a sensory 'Eden', a haven of creative productivity.[41]

Of course, by inspiring the literary and artistic outputs of its illustrious residents, the pastoral seclusion of Freshwater served, ironically, to heighten their cultural and commercial currency. For Cameron, this was something to be desired, but for Tennyson and Watts, whose attitude to celebrity was rather more ambivalent, it was an unwelcome consequence of their retreat from London life. In spite of their disparate views on contemporary celebrity, however, the three worked diligently to fortify each other's fame. As Edmund Gosse suggested, the 'splendid exclusive society which circled, more or less, round Tennyson ... lived in a radiance of mutual admiration'.[42] Watts and Cameron sought to immortalise the Laureate in their painted and photographic portraits – images that helped to forge Tennyson's public image, while simultaneously augmenting the artistic reputations of their producers. Cameron took inspiration from Tennyson's poems in the composition of her 'fancy subjects', and claimed that Watts's technical advice and general encouragement gave her 'wings to fly with'.[43] Watts's painterly technique, meanwhile, influenced Tennyson's poetry, providing inspiration for the lines in *Idylls of the King* in which Elaine pictures Lancelot's face.[44]

The creative core of the Freshwater circle was also supported by those on its periphery. If, as Watts suggested, 'circles imply centres', they also denote an outer circumference that bounds and provides definition.[45] Among those orbital figures to have shaped and reinforced the reputation of Tennyson, Cameron and Watts were Edward Lear, Charles Lutwidge Dodgson (Lewis Carroll), William Allingham and Anne Thackeray Ritchie, along with a raft of friends, family members and less well-known reminiscers; all, collectively, contributed to the mythology of the Freshwater circle. This book seeks to explore, but also to interrogate, that mythology: to examine critically the strategies by which members of the circle sought to construct, and sometimes deflect, their celebrity status, and the (often self-interested) role played by those on its periphery. Like the Freshwater celebrities, the authors of this study have interdisciplinary interests, encompassing literary and biographical criticism, visual culture and cultural history; the chapters in this book therefore consider a wide range of artefacts of Victorian celebrity, from poems, paintings and photographs, to biographies, autobiographies, and articles and illustrations from the periodical press.

As well as focusing on the group of people who encircled the Tennysons in Freshwater, this book highlights the reach and extent of Tennyson's sphere. With its multiple, concentric, permeable layers, Tennyson's circle has an almost Dantesque feel (though without the hellish connotations): extending out from the innermost, familial level are a series of different regions containing close family friends; acquaintances and fans; virtual or actual tourists; and readers, some of whom would never see the poet, but still felt an affective connection with him. Directly and indirectly, Tennyson's profile as the reluctant and hounded celebrity meant that for his admirers at each level there was an etiquette that needed to be followed and performed to show suitable deference to this most private of men. These protocols differentiated Tennysonian devotees from their more frenzied Byronic counterparts, while simultaneously distinguishing Tennyson's respectful, like-minded and unobtrusive enthusiasts from his invasive and invading ones. The following chapters explore the relations and movements between these circles of intimacy: the various processes of screening and vetting that were prerequisites for entry into Tennyson's private life, and also the steps by which a disciple might fall from grace. In other words, this book explores not only the branding of Tennyson as a celebrity but also the way this fashioned and constructed the identities of his admirers.

Examining the innermost and outmost levels of Tennyson's circle, the first chapter of this book investigates the role of the press in catering to and consciously reinforcing the public interest in the Laureate not only as an artist, but also as a private person. It focuses on the virtual tours of Tennyson's residences, including his gardens, grounds and interiors, that were published in the Victorian press and enjoyed immense popularity between the 1860s and 1890s. Catering to the cultural desire to fuse with Tennyson through seeing his homes, such articles functioned as intermediaries between the author and his audience, providing and selling the 'illusion of intimacy' and the promise of getting to know him '*in* his habitat, in those spaces that reflected and shaped his "true" self'. While scholars have investigated touristic appropriations of Abbotsford, the home of Sir Walter Scott, and Haworth Parsonage, the residence of the Brontës, this study is the first to focus on the cultural significance attributed to Farringford, Aldworth and their surroundings during the nineteenth century. Disentangling the complicated conflict between the desire to know and the respect of privacy, Charlotte Boyce highlights journalists' strategies of legitimising their interest and establishing a sense of distinction for themselves and their readers. Through allowing readers virtual visits to Farringford and Aldworth, periodicals constructed a simulacrum of intimacy that was designed to give bio-geographical insight into the poet's inspiration while rendering literal contact unnecessary. Owing to the diversity of their depictions of the Laureate's domestic sphere, Tennyson's public celebrity identity was flexible, epitomising different ideas simultaneously. Yet, Boyce argues, the multiple narrative strategies through which the Laureate's homes were presented to the public imagination were constructed not only to provide knowledge to readers, but also to create mystery: importantly, Tennyson's branded identity within the celebrity marketplace depended on the maintenance of an aura of ineffability.

The next two chapters consider the ways in which members of the Freshwater circle, who were lifelong friends of the Tennysons, engineered their own celebrity status in relation to the Laureate's. Two of these intimates, G. F. Watts and Julia Margaret Cameron, carefully managed their fame and became major Victorian celebrities in their own right, while the other, Edward Lear, ignored the cultural mechanisms for controlling public reputation. Juxtaposing Watts's compliant performance of the role of the professional artist with Lear's more rebellious enactment of the social outsider, Chapter 2 examines how the self-presentation of the celebrity affected his or her public reception. While Watts was the artist-in-residence at Little Holland House between 1851 and 1871, where both his works and his celebrity persona of the 'Signor' enjoyed prominent exposure to London's elite, Lear disliked the practices of lionism and excluded himself from the very places where wider success, fame and fortune were arbitrated and produced. The very different strategies of self-fashioning that the two artists displayed are also manifested in, and communicated to the public by, their individual responses to the culture of publicity: Watts's inventory of important cultural figures entitled *Hall of Fame* and Lear's *A Book of Nonsense* exhibit diametrically opposite constructions of the emulable.

Whereas Watts's catalogue of portraits, for the most part, comprises pictorial renditions of the members of the elitist social circle he frequented, Lear's 'Old Persons' portraits celebrate and empathise with those individuals who 'are or dare to be different'. Ironically, Páraic Finnerty shows, despite Lear's confident championing of 'unselfconsciousness', he was disappointed about the lack of public recognition for his work (compared to that received by Watts), demonstrating that he had internalised his culture's equation of celebrity status with talent. Since Watts and Lear present such different celebrity identities, it follows that Farringford, the secluded, yet well-populated celebrity salon on the Isle of Wight, occupied a different place in each man's consciousness. For Watts, it functioned as the extension of Little Holland House, while Lear deplored the atmosphere of adulation that reigned around Tennyson. Despite the contrived nature of the fan-behaviours that dominated many interactions at Farringford, Finnerty argues, Tennyson's retreat also represented a space in which controversial human relationships were not only tolerated, but could thrive. Watts took his much younger wife Ellen Terry to Freshwater, where Lear was able to cultivate his passionate friendship with Franklin Lushington. This chapter reveals that the celebrity apparatus did not simply dictate behaviours, but that the individual artist, through conscious strategies of self-fashioning, might influence his or her reception by a contemporary and a posthumous audience.

Like Chapters 1 and 2, Chapter 3 insists that celebrity identities are by no means 'inexorable or fixed', but are moulded by fans and critics, as well as by celebrities themselves. Among the members of the Freshwater circle, the pioneering photographer Julia Margaret Cameron distinguished herself through her 'keen embracement of the celebrity apparatus' and the ease, cunning and enthusiasm with which she exploited its mechanisms in order to sell her work and establish herself as an artist. Through her photographs, Cameron actively helped to construct other members of the Freshwater circle as celebrities. Claiming that her work superseded the verisimilitude of the ubiquitous *carte de visite* by capturing the ineffable essence of her subjects, she fostered proximity between them and the audience. Her work, as Boyce shows, also served a memorialising function; she aimed to immortalise her sitters by making 'visible the inner greatness, or essential nobility from which fame implicitly stemmed'. Significantly, Cameron's investment in the celebrity status of her subjects was fundamental to her own. While the quality of her work surely attracted attention, the fact that it depicted celebrities no doubt raised its appeal. But more importantly, Boyce argues, Cameron made use of her celebrity contacts to craft a public persona for herself as an artist, thus engaging in 'self-promotion by proxy'. Cameron perfectly understood the practical 'relationship between dissemination, promotion and sales', but her work also commented on the 'ideological values' inherent in the celebrity apparatus and reacted to (as well as influenced) cultural ideas about fame that portrayed it either as the 'natural consequence of inherent "greatness"' or as the result of hard work. In order to construct herself as a celebrity-artist, Cameron had to both defy and comply with the gendered codes of propriety characteristic of Victorian culture, and skilfully negotiate competing demands for self-assertion and self-effacement.

Developing the themes of the previous chapters, the next two contrast the experiences of those with privileged and exclusive access to Tennyson with the experiences of those who failed to, or never could have, such intimacy. In both her chapters, Anne-Marie Millim delineates the intense suspiciousness of the invasive lionism of the unknown masses of readers that pervaded Victorian culture throughout the latter half of the nineteenth century. Focusing on the diaries of the writer, photographer and academic Lewis Carroll, who will be called Charles Dodgson, and the Irish poet William Allingham, Chapter 4 firstly shows that these diarists' constant fear of potential accusations of lionism encouraged their possessive attitude towards Tennyson, as well as their desire to establish themselves as legitimate fans. Consciously reacting to societal prejudice against fandom, Dodgson and Allingham kept justifying the propriety of their admiration of Tennyson within their diaries, even when they had successfully made the acquaintance of the poet. Secondly, the chapter provides an important and timely investigation of the subjective structures of fandom by examining the place that Tennyson and Farringford occupy in both diaries. It shows that Dodgson and Allingham sincerely longed for a substantiation of their connection with Tennyson, but were constantly afraid of being identified as lionisers, particularly during their encounters with Julia Margaret Cameron, whose authority as the organiser of the Freshwater celebrity circle questioned their legitimacy as Tennyson's peers. This chapter stands as a corrective of critical accounts that dismiss mass-produced memorabilia, such as *cartes de visite*, as meaningless commodities and that tend to portray Dodgson as the epitomic lioniser. It reveals the ways in which these men employed their diaristic writings as private museums in which to collect, relive and cherish their experiences of and reactions to Tennyson's poetry, image and person, demonstrating that the poet was deeply ingrained within their subjective and creative consciousness.

Chapter 5 shows that despite Hallam Tennyson's efforts to control the celebrity apparatus that threatened to divulge and commercialise his late father's image and person through editorial, rhetorical and literary techniques, *Alfred Lord Tennyson: a Memoir by His Son* (1897) represents a springboard for the poet's friends and acquaintances to establish themselves as celebrities in their own right. Through extending his biographical persona to a group of invited reminiscers, composed of Tennyson's friends and colleagues, Hallam establishes a clear boundary between legitimate admirers and unwanted, invasive readers, officially instating a separatist hierarchy of fandom. In order to create privacy within and through this publicly available document, Hallam and his co-biographers anticipate and consciously suffocate the readers' inquisitiveness. The *Memoir* must therefore be seen as a rigorously calculated multi-author biographical project that was designed to stifle, rather than to satisfy the public's curiosity. Millim's analysis of their rhetorical ploys, such as their feigned reluctance to biographise, their insistence on their duty to exclude others and their strategy of inscribing their oblivion into their reports, reveals that Hallam and many of his contributors used their exposure as official biographers as an opportunity to create celebrity status for themselves. By considering the mechanics of exclusion that operate within and through the different types of textual commemoration that make up Hallam's text – excerpts from friends' diaries, letters and reminiscences, as well the series of 'supplementary', free-standing reminiscences at the end – this chapter highlights the textual and ideological constructedness of the *Memoir*. It exposes the autobiographical aspects of biography and thus questions the *Memoir*'s commonly accepted legitimacy as an informational reference text, providing much-needed insight into the fabrication, not only of celebrity, but also of fandom.

The final chapter argues that *Idylls of the King* represents Tennyson's own literary exploration of the realities of his celebrity and the workings of a coterie of famous men and women that resembles that of the Freshwater circle. While Tennyson's Arthurian epic has been abundantly discussed by literary critics, this chapter constitutes the first study to read it as a commentary on Victorian celebrity culture by highlighting the parallels between the societal environment in which Tennyson functioned and the one he constructed for his Arthurian characters. The central concept of *Idylls*, Finnerty argues, is the replication of celebrity identities – while the poem sets out to celebrate the uniqueness of Arthur, it really gives precedence to the 'replica-kings', who initially publicise the King's original aura, but then, paradoxically, expose the flaws of the 'Arthurian brand'. Camelot reflects the 'strategies of intrusion and invasion', the structures of 'ritualised admiration' and the anxieties connected to fame and disfame that distinguish Victorian culture. The characters' eagerness to improve their own status through increasing their knowledge of and proximity to extraordinarily talented, visible and/or scandalous figures mirrors fans' desire for the possession of a celebrity's auratic essence. Vivien's espionage of Guinevere and Lancelot thus echoes the 'psychological vampirism' inherent in Victorian journalists' interviewing and reportage practices, while Elaine's worship of Lancelot's shield recalls the desire to fuse with the idolised person that is at the basis of the craze for autographs and souvenirs. Describing the psychological effects of the 'dissolution of the distinction between public and private life', *Idylls* reveals Tennyson's intimate awareness of the identity-building mechanisms underlying celebrity culture, and his rejection of prescriptive behavioural labels that limit celebrities and fans in their ability to invent themselves.

Notes

1. [John Hollingshead], 'A Counterfeit Presentment', *Household Words*, 18 (1858), 71–72 (p. 71), in *ProQuest British Periodicals* <http://www.proquest.co.uk> (accessed 12 April 2013).
2. See John Plunkett, 'Celebrity and Community: the Poetics of the Carte-de-Visite', *Journal of Victorian Culture*, 8 (2003), 55–79.
3. [Hollingshead], p. 72. For one possible historical source for the story, see Joss Marsh, 'The Rise of Celebrity Culture', in *Charles Dickens in Context*, ed. by Sally Ledger and Holly Furneaux (Cambridge: Cambridge University Press, 2011), pp. 98–108 (p. 106).
4. [Hollingshead], p. 71; see Peter Hamilton and Roger Hargreaves, *The Beautiful and the Damned: the Creation of Identity in Nineteenth-Century Photography* (Aldershot: Lund Humphries, 2001), pp. 19–22.
5. [Hollingshead], pp. 72, 71.
6. See Leo Braudy, *The Frenzy of Renown: Fame and Its History* (New York: Vintage, 1997), pp. 8–9, 22–23, 373–74.
7. See Richard Salmon, *Henry James and the Culture of Publicity* (Cambridge: Cambridge University Press, 1997); Richard Salmon, 'Signs of Intimacy: the Literary Celebrity in the "Age of Interviewing"', *Victorian Literature and Culture*, 25 (1997), 159–77; Linda M. Shires, 'The Author as Spectacle and Commodity: Elizabeth Barrett Browning and Thomas Hardy', in *Victorian Literature and the Victorian Visual Imagination*, ed. by Carol T. Christ and John O. Jordan (Berkeley, CA and London: University of California Press, 1995), pp. 198–212; Nicholas Dames, 'Brushes with Fame: Thackeray and the

Work of Celebrity', *Nineteenth-Century Literature*, 56 (2001), 23–51; Lenard R. Berlanstein, 'Historicizing and Gendering Celebrity Culture: Famous Women in Nineteenth-Century France', *Journal of Women's History*, 16 (2004), 65–91; Claire Brock, *The Feminization of Fame, 1750–1830* (Basingstoke: Palgrave Macmillan, 2006); Tom Mole, *Byron's Romantic Celebrity: Industrial Culture and the Hermeneutic of Intimacy* (Basingstoke: Palgrave Macmillan, 2007); *Romanticism and Celebrity Culture, 1750–1850*, ed. by Tom Mole (Cambridge: Cambridge University Press, 2009); Ghislaine McDayter, *Byromania and the Birth of Celebrity Culture* (Albany: State University of New York Press, 2009); Eric Eisner, *Nineteenth-Century Poetry and Literary Celebrity* (Basingstoke: Palgrave Macmillan, 2009); Simon Morgan, 'Celebrity: Academic "Pseudo Event" or a Useful Concept for Historians?', *Cultural and Social History*, 8 (2011), 95–114; Alexis Easley, *Literary Celebrity, Gender, and Victorian Authorship, 1850–1914* (Newark: University of Delaware Press, 2011); *Women Writers and the Artifacts of Celebrity in the Long Nineteenth Century* ed. by Ann R. Hawkins and Maura Ives (Farnham: Ashgate, 2012); Brenda R. Weber, *Women and Literary Celebrity in the Nineteenth Century: the Transatlantic Production of Fame and Gender* (Farnham: Ashgate, 2012).

8. Berlanstein, p. 67.
9. Dames, p. 25. For a discussion of such parasocial relationships, see David Giles, *Illusions of Immortality: a Psychology of Fame and Celebrity* (Basingstoke: Macmillan, 2000), pp. 128–30.
10. 'Celebrity: Its Pains and Penalties', *The Sixpenny Magazine*, 3 (1862), 82–83 (p. 82), in *ProQuest British Periodicals* <http://www.proquest.co.uk> [accessed 4 April 2013]. The article was republished seven months later as 'On Some of the Inconveniences of Celebrity', *The Sixpenny Magazine*, 4 (1862), 260–61 in *ProQuest British Periodicals* <http://www.proquest.co.uk> [accessed 12 April 2013].
11. 'Celebrity: Its Pains and Penalties', p. 83.
12. The distinction between 'fame' and 'celebrity' is a contentious one. Some critics, such as Braudy, consider the two terms to hold discrete meanings, aligning the former with enduring honour and renown, and the latter with short-lived notoriety. Others, such as Weber, argue that 'the difference between fame and celebrity is rather porous, since it is not always clear what constitutes the legendary stuff of fame as distinct from the momentary fluff of celebrity' (Weber, p. 18). The chapters in this book move between these critical models, owing to the contrasting beliefs and ideals of the Freshwater circle; whereas Tennyson, for instance, endorsed the distinction between celebrity and fame in his writing, Cameron's work and lived practices destabilised the boundary between the two.
13. See Mole, *Byron's Romantic Celebrity*; McDayter, pp. 1–28.
14. See Isobel Armstrong, *Victorian Poetry: Poetry, Poetics and Politics* (London: Routledge, 1993); Lee Erickson, *The Economy of Literary Form: English Literature and the Industrialization of Publishing, 1800–1850* (Baltimore: Johns Hopkins University Press, 1996); Andrew Bennett, *Romantic Poets and the Culture of Posterity* (Cambridge: Cambridge University Press, 1999).
15. *The Letters of Alfred Lord Tennyson*, ed. by Cecil Y. Lang and Edgar F. Shannon, Jr, 3 vols (Oxford: Clarendon Press, 1982–90), I (1982), 109.

16. See Alan Sinfield, *Alfred Tennyson* (Oxford: Basil Blackwell, 1986), pp. 154–85; Anna Barton, *Tennyson's Name: Identity and Responsibility in the Poetry of Alfred Lord Tennyson* (Aldershot: Ashgate, 2008).

17. See Kathryn Ledbetter, *Tennyson and Victorian Periodicals: Commodities in Context* (Aldershot: Ashgate, 2007), p. 115.

18. See Andrew Elfenbein, *Byron and the Victorians* (Cambridge: Cambridge University Press, 1995), pp. 169–205.

19. Hallam Tennyson, *Alfred Lord Tennyson: a Memoir by His Son*, 2 vols (London: Macmillan & Co., 1897), I, 304.

20. See Robert Bernard Martin, *Tennyson: the Unquiet Heart* (Oxford: Clarendon Press, 1983), pp. 349–50.

21. Herbert F. Tucker, *Tennyson and the Doom of Romanticism* (Cambridge, MA: Harvard University Press, 1988), p. 389.

22. See Mole, *Byron's Romantic Celebrity*, pp. 59–60, 156; Eisner, p. 24.

23. Walter Bagehot, 'W. Bagehot on the *Idylls of the King*', in *Tennyson: the Critical Heritage*, ed. by John D. Jump (London: Routledge and Kegan Paul, 1967), pp. 215–40 (p. 216).

24. Drawing on John Plunkett's discovery that the first two portraits registered for copyright were of Tennyson, Ledbetter notes that 'public fascination' with Tennyson 'fueled commercial competition for images that would help sell printed product, whether it be books, periodicals, or individual prints' (Ledbetter, p. 144). See also Hamilton and Hargreaves, p. 19.

25. See Ledbetter, pp. 51–53, 59–60. See also *Letters of Alfred Tennyson*, II (1987), 217–19, 247, 252, 272 n.1, 276.

26. See Gerhard Joseph, 'Commodifying Tennyson: the Historical Transformation of "Brand Loyalty"', *Victorian Poetry*, 34 (1996), 133–47 (p. 141). See also Mole, *Byron's Romantic Celebrity*, p. 16.

27. Elizabeth Barrett Browning, *Letters to Mrs. David Ogilvy, 1849–1861* (Quadrangle: New York Times Book Company and The Browning Institute, 1973), p. 46.

28. *Autobiography of Henry Taylor, 1800–1875*, 2 vols (New York: Harper & Brothers, 1885), II, 162.

29. *Letters of Anne Thackeray Ritchie*, ed. by Hester Ritchie (London: John Murray, 1924), p. 126.

30. Cited in Agnes Grace Weld, *Glimpses of Tennyson and of Some of His Relations and Friends* (London and Oxford: Williams & Norgate, 1903), pp. 75, 72. Hardinge Cameron notes that though his father's poem makes the relocation to Freshwater sound like his decision, he was in fact 'hardly ... consulted'; Julia Margaret made the decision while her husband was in Ceylon (Weld, p. 73).

31. M. S. Watts, *George Frederic Watts: the Annals of an Artist's Life*, 3 vols (London: Macmillan and Co., 1912), I, p. 203. For further discussion of the Sunday afternoon gatherings at Little Holland House, see Laura Troubridge, *Memories and Reflections* (London: William Heinemann, 1925).

32. Troubridge, p. 9.

33. See, for instance, Wilfrid Blunt, *'England's Michelangelo': a Biography of George Frederic Watts* (London: Hamish Hamilton, 1975), p. 108 and Caroline Dakers, *The Holland Park Circle: Artists and Victorian Society* (New Haven: Yale University Press, 1999), pp. 147, 246.

34. For example, Tennyson's arrival at Little Holland House with his wife and sons in July 1858 was noted not only in the London newspapers (e.g. 'Mr. Alfred Tennyson', *Morning Post*, 17 July 1858, p. 5, and 'Mr. Alfred Tennyson', *Daily News*, 19 July 1858, p. 4, both in *Gale 19th Century British Library Newspapers* (<http://gale.cengage.co.uk> [accessed 11 April 2013]), but also in the provincial press (e.g. 'Home Miscellany', *North Wales Chronicle*, 24 July 1858, [p. 3], in *Gale 19th Century British Library Newspapers* <http://gale.cengage.co.uk> [accessed 11 April 2013]).

35. Wilfrid Ward, 'Tennyson at Freshwater', *Dublin Review*, 150 (1912), 68–85 (pp. 69–70).

36. Ibid., p. 68.

37. Anne Thackeray Ritchie, 'Reminiscences', in *Alfred, Lord Tennyson and His Friends: a Series of 25 Portraits and Frontispiece in Photogravure from the Negatives of Mrs. Julia Margaret Cameron and H. H. H. Cameron*, ed. by H. H. H. Cameron and Anne Thackeray Ritchie (London: T. Fisher Unwin, 1893), pp. 9–16 (p. 9).

38. Ibid., p. 9.

39. Anne Thackeray Ritchie wrote in 1916, 'an impression remains of brightest colour and animation', *From Friend to Friend*, ed. by Emily Ritchie (London: John Murray, 1919), p. 22.

40. Ritchie, 'Reminiscences', pp. 9–10; Troubridge, p. 23.

41. Ritchie, 'Reminiscences', p. 9.

42. Edmund Gosse, *Books on the Table* (New York: Charles Scribner's Sons, 1921), p. 293.

43. Julia Margaret Cameron, 'Annals of My Glass House', in *Annals of My Glass House: Photographs by Julia Margaret Cameron*, ed. by Violet Hamilton (Seattle and London: University of Washington Press, 1996), pp. 11–16 (p. 16).

44. Alfred Lord Tennyson, *Idylls of the King*, ed. by J. M. Gray (London: Penguin, 1996), pp. 176–77 (ll. 330–35).

45. Quoted in Watts, I, 317.

1
At Home with Tennyson: Virtual Literary Tourism and the Commodification of Celebrity in the Periodical Press

Charlotte Boyce

An 1860 article in the family periodical the *Leisure Hour*, describing a summer ramble around the homes and haunts of famous poets on England's south coast, concluded by encouraging readers to journey to the secluded region of Freshwater on the Isle of Wight. 'Alfred Tennyson has selected this spot for his place of rest, and has shown his fine taste in doing so', the article's author enthused, adding, 'altogether, for sweep and variety of view ... there is nothing at all equal to it in the Isle of Wight, albeit it is at present the most neglected corner; and, as such, I commend it to all tourists'.[1]

The Tennysons would, no doubt, have been horrified by this recommendation. They had moved to Farringford, a house on the outskirts of Freshwater village, in 1853, hoping to find there the peace and privacy that had recently proved elusive in London.[2] Unlike their previous Twickenham home, Farringford was (for the time being, at least) located far beyond the reach of the railways; it was also screened from public view by a mass of dense foliage, causing one visitor to remark, 'I do not remember ever to have found such seclusion as was here possible. It seemed as if every tree that grew had felt a kind of personal responsibility to keep the intruder out'.[3] By the 1860s, however, the tranquillity so coveted by the family was imperilled by the Isle of Wight's status as a fashionable tourist destination – a status bolstered in no small part by the presence of the Laureate himself. His residence on the island was advertised in guidebooks that venerated Farringford as 'a holy shrine' or 'hallowed ground', a must-see attraction for literary pilgrims.[4] In periodicals, too, prospective travellers were tantalised with the possibility of face-to-face encounters with the poet, with articles routinely confiding that the downs above Tennyson's home were the location of his 'favourite nightly walk'.[5] By positioning

Freshwater as, simultaneously, a celebrity haunt and an area of pictur-esque beauty, suitable for 'any tired denizen of our overgrown cities' who 'wants to avoid high prices and a crowd', these publications worked, ironi-cally, to attract the very masses whose absence they avowedly celebrated.[6]

This chapter argues that such contradictions are characteristic of the mass of articles on Tennyson and his homes that appeared in the British and American press during the latter half of the nineteenth century. Positioning these texts as virtual imitations of the Victorian practice of literary tourism, this chapter explores their paradoxical status and aims. I suggest that, though vested with the promise of genuine insight into Tennyson's domestic life and physical surroundings, these articles in fact constructed only a simulated form of intimacy that, nevertheless, rendered literal contact between the poet and his readers unnecessary. Despite their facilitative function, however, these articles had a com-mercial interest in withholding as much as they revealed about the Laureate, for by maintaining his aura of inscrutability, they were able to both stimulate and perpetuate their readers' desire for knowledge.

Virtualising literary tourism

According to one Victorian biographer, Farringford, during the period of Tennyson's residence, 'became one of the most overrun spots in Europe', with 'people lurking about the shrubberies, staring in at [the poet's] windows, and watching him as he walked out of his gates'.[7] This statement is perhaps a little hyperbolic; it is difficult to gauge the actual number of Victorian travellers to Farringford but, given the lack of efficient transportation to Freshwater, it seems unlikely that the house truly challenged the pre-eminence of continental tourist hotspots.[8] Nevertheless, the notion that Tennyson was constantly besieged by hordes of inquisitive holidaymakers gained a kind of valid-ity from its regular reiteration in Victorian print culture. A series of stock anecdotes – souvenir-hunters stripping branches from the tree planted at Farringford by Garibaldi in 1864, tourists spying on the poet as he ate his breakfast – appeared frequently in the periodical press, as well as in the memoirs and reminiscences of authorised visi-tors and guests.[9] Tennyson's semi-paranoiac reaction to these intrusive 'Cockneys', as he and his wife Emily rather contemptuously called them, was also well documented; according to one report, the poet once took alarm at the approach of a flock of sheep while out walking, having mistaken it for an advancing group of tourists.[10] Eventually, Tennyson's frustration with the perceived frequency and audacity of assaults on his privacy at Freshwater, combined with concerns over Emily's health, led him to commission the building of a new home at Blackdown, on the Sussex–Surrey border. Aldworth was completed in 1869 and, from then on, the Tennysons routinely spent the summer months there, only returning to Farringford late in the autumn. Their self-imposed exile from the Isle of Wight was, like their residence there, widely reported, and further contributed to the mythology of the poet as an isolated figure keen to detach himself from his own celebrity.[11]

Whereas uninvited Victorian visitors to Farringford attracted the ire of Tennyson, more recently, the activities of such 'literary tourists' have piqued the interest of scholars. As Nicola J. Watson, among others, has noted, the nineteenth century saw the practice of visiting places associated with specific books and authors develop into a culturally and commercially significant phenomenon. During the period,

> readers were seized en masse by a newly powerful desire to visit the graves, the birthplaces, and the carefully preserved homes of dead poets and men and women of letters; to contemplate the sites that writers had previously visited and written in or about; and eventually to traverse whole imaginary literary territories, such as 'Dickens' London' or 'Hardy's Wessex'.[12]

As well as iconic literary sites and landscapes, of particular interest to Victorian tourists were writers' houses. Harald Hendrix argues that the trend for journeying to celebrated authors' homes reached 'phenomenal proportions in the nineteenth century' as readers increasingly sought to 'go beyond their intellectual exchanges with texts' and make 'some kind of material contact with the author of those texts'.[13] Houses associated with writers such as Wordsworth and Byron became popular stopping-off points on Britain's tourist trail and were invested with a range of idiosyncratic and collectively constituted meanings; loci of the personally significant experiences of individual literary tourists, they also functioned as repositories of broader cultural values. Alexis Easley suggests that Victorian literary tourism worked to bring 'coherence and meaning to modern experience' by constructing a sense of unified national identity and shared cultural heritage.[14] The houses of revered writers, as expressive but semantically mutable media, could be readily integrated into such narratives of nation-building and creative tradition.

Much critical attention has gathered around touristic appropriations of nineteenth-century writers' houses in recent years. The meanings attached to places such as Abbotsford (home to Sir Walter Scott) and

Haworth Parsonage (home to the Brontës), in particular, have been widely analysed.[15] To date, though, very little has been written on either Farringford or Aldworth as objects of Victorian literary tourism, an omission that initially appears surprising. That Victorian tourists sought out Tennyson's houses is indisputable. Moreover, the Laureate's cultural cachet would, one might presume, have rendered his homes eminently assimilable into the kinds of narratives outlined above (making them, by extension, a source of interest to modern-day scholars). A couple of factors set Tennyson apart from the nineteenth-century writers whose houses have tended to receive the most touristic and critical notice, however. Unlike the majority of his literary contemporaries, Tennyson lived until the 1890s and this longevity meant that his residences were not available for adoption as focal points of nostalgic commemoration – architectural monuments to lost literary greatness – for the majority of the Victorian period. Nor have they been constructed as so since; following his death, Tennyson's residences have remained in the hands of either family members or private owners and, in this way, have resisted the process of 'musealisation' (to adopt Polly Atkin's useful term) to which other writers' houses, bought and maintained by literary societies, fellowships and heritage bodies, have been subject.[16]

Yet, if Farringford and Aldworth can tell us little about the 'culture industry' of the twentieth and twenty-first centuries, the commercialisation of literary heritage and the practices of appropriation and memorialisation undertaken by modern-day literary tourists, their representation in Victorian print culture can give us valuable insights into literary tourism as a manifestation of Victorian *celebrity* culture, a relationship that has not always been fully recognised in critical studies to date. The tendency to concentrate on readerly interactions with the homes of dead authors in works such as Watson's and, to a lesser extent, Easley's implicitly positions literary tourism as a practice of posthumous commemoration, obscuring the important ways in which writers' houses became enmeshed in nineteenth-century readers' efforts to achieve quasi-personal relationships with their *living* literary idols. In fact, it was the public's burgeoning fascination with inhabited writers' houses that particularly concerned Victorian commentators. Erin Hazard notes that when literary tourism's urtext, William Howitt's *Homes and Haunts of the Most Eminent British Poets*, was published in 1847, the British press expressed 'fundamental misgivings about [Howitt's] lack of differentiation between living and dead authors and about intrusion on living authors' privacy'.[17] The *Examiner's* review was typical: 'They [Howitt's two volumes] contain too many modern and even living poets ...What we acknowledge to be genuine emotion in the case of Spenser and Dryden, we may suspect to be prying curiosity in those of Wordsworth and Tennyson'.[18]

The reading public appears not to have been troubled by such scruples. By 1863, *Homes and Haunts* had reached its fifth edition and its success had spawned a number of imitative titles in both Britain and America.[19] Its hybridised brand of literary biography, personal reminiscence and travelogue was also beginning to shape the tone and content of celebrity reportage in the periodical press.[20] Departing from the societal focus of traditional gossip columns, series of articles such as the *World's* 'Celebrities at Home', the *Idler's* 'Lions in their Dens' and the *Strand Magazine's* 'Illustrated Interviews' offered readers enticing opportunities to take virtual tours around the symbolically charged domestic spaces of famous Victorians – to observe the celebrity in the privacy of 'his favourite room or study, and surrounded by his *lares* and *penates*', as one journalist rather excitedly put it.[21] Although such articles continued to prompt in certain quarters the kinds of anxieties earlier generated by Howitt's *Homes and Haunts*, their mass appeal was unquestionable and, so ubiquitous had they become by the 1890s, they began to be parodied in comic publications such as *Judy*, which issued its own spoof addition to the genre: 'Lions of the Day in their Dens,' authored by 'Paul Pry, Junior'.[22]

Through their investment in virtual literary tourism, periodicals both fuelled and supported celebrity culture, kindling public interest while performing an essential intermediary function between author and audience. As Tom Mole has ably demonstrated in his study of Romantic celebrity, industrialised print culture formed a vital component of the nineteenth-century celebrity apparatus, but it also had the potential to alienate; overwhelmed by a swelling tide of new publications, 'readers … felt estranged from authors'.[23] 'At Home with' articles in Victorian periodicals worked to alleviate this sense of estrangement by constructing what Mole terms a 'hermeneutic of intimacy': an illusory but nonetheless powerful sense of connection between reader and celebrity founded on the tacit assurance that, through textual engagement, the former might gain special insight into the latter's interior life.[24]

Tennyson's notorious reticence worked, ironically, to heighten the demand for articles promising such intimacy and, consequently, a steady stream of pieces focusing on the Laureate 'at home' emerged in a range of British and American periodicals, from local daily newspapers to highbrow monthly magazines, between the 1860s and 1890s. Tracing the visual and textual strategies by which these articles sought to craft a quasi-personal relationship between Tennyson and his readers, this chapter demonstrates that the illusion of intimacy underlying them responded to and commodified an incipient desire to *locate* the author; to know him not simply through his works, but *in* his habitat, in those spaces that reflected and shaped his 'true' self.

Knowledge and insight were not the only imperatives driving Victorian virtual literary tourism, however. Coexistent with the hermeneutic of intimacy identified by Mole was a counter-discourse of obscurity and mystique. The allure of celebrity, then as now, depended on an aura of ineffability. Periodicals could not afford to disclose too much, particularly as, in Tennyson's case, his reputation (or 'branded identity' to use Mole's term) hinged on his reserve and aversion to acts of intrusion.[25] To appear authentic, but also, importantly, to stimulate readerly desire, 'Tennyson at Home'-type articles needed to maintain an air of reticence while simultaneously feeding the public's appetite for information. In the sections that follow, I interrogate further this structural conflict between intimacy and detachment, disclosure and obfuscation, highlighting the complex dynamics that governed works of virtual literary tourism in the Victorian press.

Legitimising intimacy

Unlike the reminiscers and fans discussed in subsequent chapters, the authors of 'Tennyson at Home' articles in Victorian periodicals tended to have no prior friendship or acquaintance with the poet. The grounds supporting their writings' implicit claims to intimacy were therefore far from secure. So as to obviate potential doubts, journalists deployed a variety of legitimising techniques designed to intimate authority and authenticity. Most evidently, in the case of articles describing actual visits to Farringford or Aldworth, they were careful to assure readers that their accounts were produced with Tennyson's full knowledge and consent. Editor Edmund Yates's preface to the volume edition of *The World*'s 'Celebrities at Home' series stressed that 'in no case has an article been written without the full consent and authority of its subject'.[26] Posthumous pieces, such as V. C. Scott O'Connor's 'Tennyson and his Friends at Freshwater', meanwhile, made clear that the permission of Tennyson's son, Hallam, had been sought and gained.[27]

Articles also took care to forestall accusations of invasiveness or insensitivity. That Tennyson was fiercely protective of his privacy was well known; his frustrations with over-zealous fans were frequently reported in British and American newspapers, while later editions of tourist guides such as *Nelson's Handbook to the Isle of Wight* warned (with little sense of irony) that 'the intrusive curiosity of ill-bred visitors will probably drive the poet from his island retreat'.[28] Given this context, writers were keen to demonstrate that their visits to Tennyson's homes had not provoked the poet's displeasure or caused him any avoidable distress. F. G. Kitton, for instance, in a retrospective account of a visit to Aldworth undertaken in his role as illustrator for the *Graphic*, took pains to distinguish himself from the thoughtless 'strangers who endeavoured to force their presence upon [Tennyson]':

> It was considerately arranged (after permission had been courteously granted) that my visit should be timed so as to cause the least possible inconvenience, and when an artist's presence in the poet's sanctum would not be considered an intrusion. Fortunately, an opportunity quickly presented itself, for just at the period referred to it was announced in the daily press that Tennyson had accepted Mr. Gladstone's invitation to accompany him on a yachting expedition for the benefit of his somewhat declining health. As soon as the date was fixed for this memorable voyage my plans were speedily laid, and an intimation forwarded to Aldworth that I should arrive there on the following day.[29]

Unfortunately, though, the yachting trip was cancelled at short notice, meaning that Tennyson was at home when the illustrator arrived. Signalling further his tact and considerateness, Kitton avers, 'it was with a fluttering heart that I learned that the Laureate was at home, for I had not gone prepared to "beard the lion in his den"; indeed, I felt rather inclined, under the circumstances, to beat a hasty retreat, and defer operations until a more favourable opportunity'.[30] Tennyson's rather grudging acceptance of Kitton's apologetic explanation, in the end, renders such deferral unnecessary; significantly, though, the illustrator's stated willingness to postpone his commission, should Tennyson wish it, serves an important legitimising function in his account, underlining his difference from the unthinking and insensitive mass of literary tourists.

The sense of intimacy finally achieved in Kitton's article is constructed with similar levels of care; it is not asserted immediately, but rather accomplished incrementally in a series of deftly managed representational stages. Tennyson is initially presented as gruff and unreceptive; his tone indicates 'that he experienced some annoyance' from the artist's presence and 'he inquired, rather brusquely, why people were always wanting to sketch his house'.[31] Kitton's deferential behaviour soon brings about a thaw in relations, however: '[Tennyson's] manner changed, and in a genial, courtly manner, so characteristic of the man, he escorted me at once to his favourite sanctum'. Here, the discovery of a shared artistic sensibility helps to ease relations further: 'the constrained character of my position decreased ... when the poet began to show a personal interest in my work by suggesting the best point of view for the sketch; so admirable ... was his artistic judgment that I unhesitatingly adopted the suggestion'.[32] Still, Kitton is careful not to overplay his hand: 'I advisedly refrained from "vexing the poet's soul" by "small talk," or undue conversation of any kind, and I fancy this reservedness gratified my host and predisposed him in my favour'.[33] Kitton's prudence is ultimately rewarded; he is invited to take tea alone with Tennyson and, on his departure from Aldworth, is accompanied through the grounds by a now affable Laureate.

The shift in relations from awkwardness to intimacy mapped here follows a trajectory common in Victorian virtual literary tourism dealing with Tennyson. Journalistic accounts of visits to Tennyson's homes often begin with expressions of dauntedness, owing to the poet's reputation for brusqueness, and tend initially to reinforce the perception of the Laureate as taciturn and aloof. 'The beginning of our interview was not very encouraging', admitted one American correspondent in a piece for the *Sunday Inter Ocean*; 'one can not get intimate with him during the first hour'.[34] However, after proving themselves intellectually worthy of the poet's regard and winning his trust by degrees, the authors of 'Tennyson at Home' articles typically claim to have gained access to another side of Tennyson's character, one that is warm and convivial. A correspondent for *Harper's New Monthly Magazine* declared that he 'discovered treasures of fun and humor in [the poet] before unsuspected'; similarly, *The World*'s piece on 'Mr. Tennyson at Haslemere' affirmed

> if his first impulse is to receive men brusquely, almost rudely, he reads character with wonderful quickness; and when he changes his first unfavourable impression he is not slow to act on the better opinion ... In place of the cynical curve into which habit has settled the lips, a kindly smile will flicker round the mobile mouth, and the eyes will light with a welcome which, more than his words, is a cordial invitation to join him in the pipe of peace.[35]

By emphasising that this kind of friendly behaviour is usually reserved for Tennyson's 'charmed circle' or 'cherished friends', 'At Home with' articles neatly insinuate the exceptionality of the reception accorded to their authors, consolidating the overall impression of intimacy.[36]

Such articles also endeavour to transfer a sense of distinction onto the reader, who, Richard Salmon notes, constitutes an '(absent) presence' in much Victorian celebrity journalism.[37] Through a process of textual re-enactment and the adoption of a range of interpellative techniques, works of virtual literary tourism create a narrative space for the reader that collapses geographical and temporal distance and 'facilitates [his/her] sense of being present upon [the] intimate occasion' of the journalist's visit.[38] An 1868 article on Farringford in the San Francisco *Daily Evening Bulletin*, for instance, opens with an invitation to 'come with me to it away from the sooty, grimy air of London', before co-opting the reader as a kind of virtual travelling companion: 'Crossing by express train the breezy downs of Surrey and the chalky fields of Hampshire … we alight at Southampton, and speed on a fleet steamer 12 miles to the Isle of Wight'.[39] In an 1887 piece on 'Tennyson at Home', meanwhile, American critic Geoffrey Quarles encourages readers to imagine being greeted by Tennyson in his 'sanctum sanctorum' at Aldworth: 'Most likely he shifts a clay pipe into his left hand that he may grip you with his right … As the conversation warms his puffs come thick and fast'.[40] Together with confidential asides, these seductive gestures create a sense of immediacy and inclusivity, effectively aligning the reading subject with the privileged position claimed by the writer.[41]

Concomitant with this process of assimilation is a repudiation of those 'ordinary stranger[s]' who made real, as opposed to textual, pilgrimages to Tennyson's homes.[42] By ventriloquising Tennyson's well-known opinions on touristic intrusions on his privacy, articles made concerted efforts to dissociate themselves (and their readers) from the uninvited visitors the poet so bitterly disparaged. Grant Allen's 1892 piece on 'Tennyson's Homes at Aldworth and Farringford', for instance, opens with a Tennysonian fulmination against the 'new-fangled railway which has burst rudely in upon [Freshwater's] seclusion to disturb its charms', before turning to the fabled effrontery of American tourists:

> I am not one of those who would pry upon the privacy of a great man with impertinent questions to fill up an article; but rumour has it that the American tourist, descending year by year in the holiday season upon the Isle of Wight with inquisitive opera-glass, made it necessary for the bard to hurry away betimes with each returning spring to the Hampshire moorlands.[43]

American author M. D. Conway goes further in his article for *Harper's New Monthly Magazine*, representing his compatriots as celebrity-baiting huntsmen: 'Sundry Americans have recorded … the success with which they have waylaid and got an eye-shot at a new species of game to be found exclusively in this region – namely, the Poet Laureate'. Continuing with this metaphor of predation, Conway attests that, while walking across the downs at Freshwater,

> I ... knew I was near the much-hunted poet by seeing one of his natural enemies. He would, no doubt, have professed to be only going to and fro seeking to devour the views of the island, but the muzzle of his fatal instrument was already prepared and pointed to a spot where the famous man loves to walk – a cliff on the verge of his own manor, overlooking the grandeurs of Freshwater Bay. But, alas for the solitude he came to seek at Farringford! he startles a curious eye lurking in every bush, and doesn't know when he returns from his walk how many copies of him have been snatched by the remorseless nitrate.[44]

Catering for a curiosity that they simultaneously denounce, articles such as these are founded on an underlying hypocrisy. Yet, by adopting Tennyson's own discourse on railways, Americans and photographers, they manufacture a sympathetic alignment between themselves, their readers and the poet which partially masks such troubling contradictions.

They also set in place a discriminatory logic that serves to legitimise their collective existence. What is striking in each of the accounts discussed above is the subtle distinction made between the text's own readers (who are endorsed as Tennyson's genuine admirers) and the unthinking, vulgar mass of tourists who are drawn to the Poet Laureate and his home simply because of his celebrity. In each example, the inquisitive and unsophisticated Victorian tourist is implicitly positioned as one of 'them', not 'us'. James Buzard points out that this discriminatory logic has long been a feature of touristic discourse: often contrasted with the figure of the independent and discerning 'traveller', the 'tourist' has tended to be characterised in Western cultures as the boorish and thoughtless consumer of inauthentic experiences. The need to distinguish the self from this much-maligned cultural stereotype gives rise to what Buzard labels 'snobbish "anti-tourism"', an 'exemplary way of regarding one's own cultural experiences as authentic and unique, setting them against a backdrop of always assumed tourist vulgarity, repetition, and ignorance'.[45] With their emphasis on exclusivity, legitimacy and authenticity, 'Tennyson at Home' articles can be seen to participate in this anti-touristic impulse.

They also negotiate the contradictions and ironies inherent in anti-tourism. Just as 'anti-tourists wanted to show a uniquely meaningful relationship with visited places, but ... were wary of exerting any of the transformative force so visibly and clumsily wielded by tourists and the industry they fostered', so a certain type of literary fan longed for privileged access to the Laureate and his homes, but shrank from the idea of encroaching directly on his private life.[46] Virtual literary tourism in middle-class periodicals ostensibly resolved this predicament by furnishing readers with the *simulacrum* of intimacy – a textually constructed sense of closeness that circumvented the need for actual contact. By virtue of their very 'virtuality', then, 'Tennyson at Home' articles conferred on readers a kind of cultural distinction that differentiated them from 'literal' tourists. Experiencing Tennyson's homes textually, rather than by visiting in person, implied a sympathetic affinity with the poet, but also, importantly, a cerebral connection; as the following section of this chapter demonstrates, readers of virtual literary tourism were constructed as particularly cultured and perceptive, able to detect in descriptions of Farringford, Aldworth and their surroundings meanings and allusions unavailable to those who physically journeyed there.

Tell-tale topography

A salient feature of 'Tennyson at Home' articles is their deployment of detailed topographical description. *The World*'s 'Mr. Tennyson at Haslemere', for instance, spends four pages outlining the physical features of the surrounding area before moving on to discuss Aldworth itself; a similar amount of geographical exposition can be found in Allen's 1892 piece in the *English Illustrated Magazine*. This preoccupation with locality can be explained in a number of ways. Most straightforwardly, it enabled readers to visualise accurately the landscape surrounding Tennyson's homes and thus to experience, virtually, the views enjoyed by actual tourists. It also helped to consolidate the idea that reader-tourists were privy to a more exclusive form of access to the poet's homes than their 'real-life' counterparts. *The World*, for instance, took pains to emphasise Aldworth's geographic 'hiddenness', observing that

> Nothing of the house but the chimney-tops or the gables and pinnacles of the highest windows can be seen from any point near at hand. A belt of dense foliage and undergrowth hardly less impenetrable than stone walls girdles it closely about; and from the outside it is impossible to get any idea of the bright flower-gardens and pleasant glades that lie hidden in the recesses of the hazel-copse.[47]

As Salmon notes, encoded within this description is 'a rhetoric of obstruction': 'the landscape of Haslemere physically prevents ... acts of surveillance' and this serves to 'reinscribe the privileged moment of vision which is constituted by the narrative itself'.[48] A sense of privilege is further affirmed in the article's suggestion that, while travelling through this obscurifying terrain, 'you may perchance meet a fair devotee of the poet, returning from the shrine of her fruitless pilgrimage in a prosaic donkey-cart'.[49] The reference to unsuccessful literary tourism here heightens the sense of exclusivity accorded to *The World's* readers, whose discovery of and entrance to Tennyson's private residence is guaranteed by the revelatory structure of the text.

Perhaps more interesting, though, is the way in which topographical information is presented in periodicals as a kind of textual conduit to Tennyson's work and, by extension, his 'true' self. Articles about Tennyson's homes consistently blend geographic description with quotations from and allusions to his poetry, implying that a meaningful correlation exists between the two. Indeed, poetic quotation sometimes functions as a substitute for individual observation about the scenery surrounding his residences. When seeking to depict Farringford and its environs, periodicals invariably deployed a few staple lines from the poem 'To the Rev. F. D. Maurice' (1855), in which Tennyson invites the godfather of his eldest son to visit his Freshwater home,

> Where, far from noise and smoke of town,
> I watch the twilight falling brown
> All round a careless-ordered garden
> Close to the ridge of a noble down.[50]

The constitutive relationship between landscape and poem, here, is obvious, as it is in 'To Ulysses' (1889) (quoted in O'Connor's 'Tennyson and his Friends at Freshwater'), in which Tennyson contemplates the plants and trees – 'the branching grace / Of leafless elm, or naked lime'; 'My giant ilex keeping leaf'; 'the waving pine which here / The warrior of Caprera set' – that populate his Farringford garden.[51]

However, 'Tennyson at Home' articles also attempted to identify more nuanced examples of geographic influence in the poet's work. O'Connor proposed that in the opening words of *Enoch Arden* (1864) ('Long lines of cliff breaking have left a chasm; / And in the chasm are foam and yellow sands') 'one recognizes a likeness to Freshwater Bay'.[52] William H. Rideing, meanwhile, contested that a selection of lines from *Maud*, 'Sea Dreams' and *Enoch Arden* were inspired directly by the downs adjoining the Farringford estate.[53] Other articles moved beyond the identification of specific locations to consider broader patterns of geographical representation in the Laureate's work. A number of pieces claimed that the type of topographic detail discernible in Tennyson's poetry changed over time, mapping his residential relocations. An article published in *Temple Bar* is typical in its suggestion that a new kind of landscape can be seen to emerge in Tennyson's work following his removal to Freshwater:

> Tennyson's residence in the Isle of Wight extended over some forty years; and its associations and scenery visibly affected his work. The low-lying meadows of the Fen-country [the place of Tennyson's birth], the 'long dun wolds', the reeds and marish-flowers of his earlier poems, were replaced by a sense of the sea, 'in its broad-flung shipwrecking roar', and the wild sea-voices surging below the storm-swept downs of *Rizpah*.[54]

A similar shift in geographical perspective accompanied Tennyson's later move to the undulating terrain of Blackdown, according to *The World*. Its piece on 'Mr Tennyson at Haslemere' suggested that the poet's once 'vague and dreamlike' descriptions of hills and mountainscapes became 'more vividly real and powerfully distinct' following his move to Aldworth.[55]

Although the manifest purpose of bio-geographical readings was simply to point to a causal relationship between Tennyson's physical surroundings and his poetry, they also contributed to the 'hermeneutic of intimacy' fundamental to virtual literary tourism. The liberal use of unattributed quotations from Tennyson's work helped to construct the reader as an already-knowledgeable admirer, familiar with the Laureate's *oeuvre*. By particularising the localities in which individual poems were produced, 'Tennyson at Home' articles promised this erudite imagined-reader special insight into his sources of inspiration and creative processes, along with a deeper, more informed understanding of his works. The article from *Temple Bar*, discussed above, for instance, invites readers to discern in Tennyson's Freshwater poems not only a new type of scenery, but also a significant change in theme and timbre. 'The larger potentialities, the sonorities and splendours of the sea, shaped him to finer issues', it argues, adding, 'it is easy to compare his broader outline, loftier subject, and more intimate human appeal, thenceforward, with the *genre* work of the English Idyls, and the east-country colouring of *In Memoriam*'.[56] The assumption, here and elsewhere, that readers will share in the periodical's appreciation of such nuances once more confers on them a kind of superiority, tacitly positioning them as not just literary but *literate* tourists, possessors of a refined cultural sensibility that elevates them above the ordinary masses and enables them to connect on a profound level with Tennyson's works.

It is worth noting, though, that Tennyson mostly rejected bio-geographical readings of his poems. While he occasionally acknowledged the influence of local landscapes ('I made these lines on the High Down one morning at Freshwater', he wrote of a sea-inspired simile in *Idylls of the King*),[57] he more usually insisted that his depictions of the natural world were wholly attributable to his imaginative power. To the author of a volume entitled *In Tennyson Land: Being a Brief Account of the Home and Early Surroundings of the Poet Laureate and an Attempt to Identify the Scenes and Trace the Influences of Lincolnshire in His Works*, he instructed his son, Hallam, to write, 'My father thanks you for your book. He thinks that however pleasant your volume you have ridden your hobby to death ... All the poems which you quote ... have nothing of Lincolnshire about them and are purely imaginative inventions'.[58] In the same vein, one reminiscer recalled him complaining, 'Why do they give me no credit for any imagination? The power of poetical creation seems totally ignored now'.[59]

Tennyson's protestations were not without grounds; many of the top-ographical identifications asserted in Victorian periodicals are perhaps more expedient than authentic. The seascapes described in *Enoch Arden*, though invariably equated with the Freshwater coast, are in fact fairly generic in character; resembling much of the southern coastline of the British Isles, they might represent anywhere or nowhere. At times, periodicals tacitly acknowledged the tenuousness of the connections they put forward. *The World*'s remark that, 'the Laureate has built himself [at Haslemere], if not "a lordly pleasure-house", at least a mansion of welcome solitude away from the haunts of the crowd', at once identifies Aldworth with the 'Palace of Art' (a poem first published three decades before the house was constructed) and undermines the comparison. The disputed analogy continues in the article's next lines:

> 'A huge crag platform, smooth as burnish'd brass,
> I chose. The ranged ramparts bright,
> From level meadow bases of deep grass,
> Suddenly scaled the light.'

Though not literally descriptive of the height whereon the poet has set his house, [these lines are] at least suggestive of the spirit that ruled its selection – a spirit that is content with no low or mean abode.[60]

With its curious pattern of association and disavowal, this passage indicates that a literal resemblance between poetic and 'real' topography is less important to works of virtual literary tourism than an auratic or 'spiritual' one. Eager to preserve the coherence of their bio-geographical meta-narratives, 'Tennyson at Home' articles implied that discerning readers would recognise the essence, if not the exact features, of the scenery surrounding Tennyson's residences in his poetry, and vice versa.

Readers were also encouraged to perceive in the copious topographic detail on offer aspects of Tennyson's character. Such was the Laureate's assumed affinity with the natural world ('Nature in its various aspects makes up a larger part of this man's life than it does for other people', wrote family friend Anne Thackeray Ritchie), the landscapes he inhabited were held to inform and disclose his very personality.[61] In 'South-Coast Saunterings', Conway insisted that country scenes were fundamental to the poet's being:

> When I have seen the Laureate in London he has always seemed, in dress, manner, and expression, to be out of place, as a wild wood bird might be alighting for a moment in Hyde Park, but dreaming of the forest whose glooms its wing was meant to light up. He is the natural companion of the clouds, the downs, and the breaking waves.[62]

This sentiment is echoed in Allen's account, which suggests that Tennyson's choice of habitat is both an eloquent form of self-expression and an essential component of his literary success:

> [Farringford's] situation in the midst of such typical quiet English scenery seems admirably suited to the most typically English of great English poets ... If Shakespeare ought to have lived (as he did) among the quaintly-gabled streets of Elizabethan London, and Shelley (in dejection) on the Bay of Naples, or among the blue shadowy Euganeans, then surely Tennyson ought to live, as he has lived, among English downs.[63]

For O'Connor, too, it is Freshwater Down that is most 'connected with Tennyson's personality', not simply because of its status as his 'favorite haunt', but also because its character harmonises with, and reveals, the poet's own: like the 'sea-winds' that 'blow free and untrammeled' there, the Laureate, we are told, roams solitarily across the downs' 'undulating summits', 'happily remote from conventional exercises'.[64]

In each of these examples, an organic, triangular relationship emerges between poetry, landscape and Tennyson's 'true' self. Although the poet was not born on the Freshwater coast, or among the steep hills of Blackdown, he is constructed as 'belonging' in and to both places; their geographical features implicitly mirror and shape the contours of his poetry and self. Topographical writing in 'Tennyson at Home' articles presents itself, then, as a palimpsest on which sympathetic readers may perceive the trace of Tennyson's psyche; to read the terrain where the poet dwells and writes, works of virtual literary tourism suggest, is to read his very soul.

Interior insights

If the countryside surrounding Tennyson's homes was invested with special significance then even greater importance was attached to the interior spaces in which he lived and worked. His study, in particular, tended to be represented in periodicals as a secret sanctum steeped in meaning, to which the ordinary tourist had no hope of gaining admittance. 'Access to his study was ... denied to nearly all callers', Kitton noted in his article for the *Gentleman's Magazine*, the 'nearly' in his sentence reminding readers of the exclusive experience to which they were about to gain access by proxy.[65] His claim was not merely an exercise in self-aggrandisement. Comparatively few 'At Home with' articles were able to offer first-hand accounts of the interiors of Farringford or Aldworth; the majority of their authors lacked a personal or professional connection to Tennyson and therefore had to content themselves with describing the external appearance of his residences and their localities, or rehearsing second-hand accounts that were already in the public domain.[66] The relative rarity of journalistic visits *inside* Tennyson's homes served to heighten the 'auratic expectations' loaded onto the poet's domestic space – expectations that works of virtual literary tourism granting interior access were only too willing to meet.[67]

Correspondents' initial observations of Farringford and Aldworth tended to institute an impression of reverence and wonder, characterising the houses' interiors as especially eloquent, capable of conveying (like the landscapes outside them) something of Tennyson's distinctive poetic sensibility, his inner 'essence' and personal history. In her authoritative piece for *Harper's Magazine*, Anne Thackeray Ritchie described Farringford as 'a charmed palace, with green walls without, and *speaking walls* within'; in a later article, another former visitor confirmed, 'every inch of wall space had a tongue, every picture a history'.[68] As Salmon notes, in the 'sanctified space' of the Victorian celebrity author's home 'even the most mundane object might be invested with a unique significance' and venerated accordingly.[69] Thus, alongside their authors' general impressions of awe, 'Tennyson at Home' articles inundated readers with particularised inventories of furnishings and household items, often endowing rather ordinary domestic objects with special revelatory potential.

Although their aim in doing so was to capture the unique aura that ostensibly permeated the poet's homes and belongings, these catalogues of objects were far from individuated; different articles habitually enlisted the same expressive domestic signifiers in support of their readings of Tennyson's living spaces. The profusion of books and journals in the poet's study was, for instance, commonly noted.[70] Though hardly remarkable or unexpected, this apparently trivial detail formed part of a broader strategy by which Farringford and Aldworth were presented as being saturated with 'literariness'. The busts of Dante and Wordsworth that decorated the Laureate's hallway and study were often evoked to suggest his immersion in and inheritance of an illustrious poetic tradition.[71] Recurrent references to his ubiquitous pipe performed a similar role: articles invariably noted that Tennyson's love of tobacco linked him to other great men of letters who were inveterate pipe-smokers, such as the esteemed historian Thomas Carlyle, once again inserting the poet into a noble literary lineage.[72]

As well as aggregating in this way to build coherent narratives, the personal possessions enumerated in 'At Home with' articles could bifurcate into opposing signifying groups to reveal the flexibility of the celebrity identity constructed for Tennyson in Victorian periodicals – his ability to epitomise simultaneously one thing *and* another. For example, a number of articles call attention to the presence of both antique and contemporary objects in his homes in order to present him as a representative of both the past and the present. Aldworth's decor is described as having an 'old-world flavor'; its 'lofty rooms have broad high windows ... delicately-coloured hangings ... and panelled ceilings of darkly-stained wood with moulded ribs and beams'.[73] Its furnishings complement its architecture; as well as 'two oriel windows', Tennyson's study contains various 'antique chairs and tables', including a 'writing-table of carved oak'.[74] This Gothic grandeur conjures up the medievalism of Tennyson's Arthurian poems and constructs the Laureate as a champion of traditional values and a proud cultural past.

However, it also, ironically, reveals his modernity; homes decorated in revivalist style were, for the Victorians, the height of contemporary good taste.[75] In order to indicate further the Laureate's status as a man of his age, several articles emphasise that in Aldworth 'the old blend[s] with the new, as it should': we are informed that the walls are painted in the 'negative tints in which modern decorators delight'; that alongside the 'high-backed chairs, of ancient and uncompromising stiffness … are comfortable lounges'; and that, in Tennyson's study, there is a 'cane-bottomed arm-chair – a modern French type of furniture'.[76]

The systematic codification of Tennyson's private domestic space is not restricted to textual accounts; in accompanying illustrations, too, his interiors are constructed as signifying systems, replete with opposing, though complementary, meanings. Images of his study tend to be particularly semantically full and draw attention, above all, to Tennyson's parallel status as literary lion and private, family man. W. Biscombe Gardner's full-page illustration of the study at Farringford locates the poet's writing desk at its centre and depicts, a little to the right, a large bookcase stacked with neatly arranged volumes (Figure 1.1). However, the image makes clear that this is a private, as well as a professional space; the Tennyson family's wolfhound, Karenina, stretches out relaxedly on the carpet and portraits of friends and pets adorn the walls.[77] In its very construction, the illustration conveys the sense that we are peering into Tennyson's personal domain, usually inaccessible to the public; significantly, an adumbrated archway to the left and partially extended screen to the right narrow the field of vision and place the reader-spectator in an implicitly voyeuristic position.

Kitton's illustration of the study at Aldworth, made for *The Graphic*'s 'Celebrities of the Day' series, is a lot more open in character, creating the impression that the reader-spectator is actually located *inside* the Laureate's room, rather than lingering uncertainly in the doorway (Figure 1.2). Nevertheless, it shares many of the divulgatory signs present in Gardner's image. Once again, the visual tokens of the poet's profession are manifest: an elaborately carved writing-desk dominates the foreground, its surface covered in manuscripts, letters, bottles of ink and writing implements. In keeping with Kitton's later, textual description of the room (and with the general emphasis on the 'literariness' of Tennyson's homes), 'books and magazines, covering shelves and tables, [are] abundant'.[78] As in Gardner's illustration, the family dog is present, representing Tennyson's domestic life, but here a number of other revelatory items are also discernible. In Kitton's image, the study becomes a space of self-fashioning: a pair of terrestrial and celestial globes, on

Figure 1.1 W. Biscombe Gardner, 'Tennyson's Study at Farringford', in Grant Allen, 'Tennyson's Homes at Aldworth and Farringford', *English Illustrated Magazine*, 10 (1892), p. 149
Source: Llyfrgell Genedlaethol Cymru/National Library of Wales

either side of the window, indicate the breadth of Tennyson's intellectual interests, his status as a natural philosopher as well as a poet, while a vase of carelessly arranged flowers denotes his much-cited love of nature.[79] Interestingly, the illustration also envisions the view from the study window eulogised in so many 'At Home with' articles; the unspoilt, rolling landscape, just perceptible through the panes, communicates Kitton's broadly representative opinion that 'surely nothing could be more conducive to poetic thoughts and inspirations' than this 'happily situated ... historic room at Aldworth'.[80]

Perhaps the most striking component of Kitton's illustration, however, is its depiction of the Laureate himself, seated at his desk, half-facing the reader-spectator. He epitomises the professional/private dichotomy that pervades the image, being shown leafing, rather distractedly, through a book with one hand, while stroking the head of his pet hound with the other. He is also, crucially, transformed here into a signifier of his own celebrity identity. Kitton's observation, on meeting

Figure 1.2   [F. G. Kitton], 'Celebrities of the Day – Lord Tennyson, Poet Laureate', *The Graphic*, 22 March 1884, n. p.
Source: Cardiff University Library: Special Collections and Archives

Tennyson, that 'photography had already made his physiognomy familiar,' indicates that a recognisable 'look' was central to the poet's public 'brand'.[81] His distinctive attire and physical appearance (circulated and popularised in photographs, *cartes de visite* and the frontispieces to his works) were generally considered to distil and convey the very essence of his personality: one commentator noted that 'Tennyson ... looks the poet from top to toe', while another remarked that 'the spirit of the man speaks ... plainly in his garb'.[82] Kitton does not deviate from this familiar idea of the poet in his illustration for *The Graphic*, picturing him in typically 'Tennysonian' costume, and bearing the stern expression made famous by existing media, such as J. E. Mayall's and Julia Margaret Cameron's photographs and Thomas Woolner's medallions and bust. The poet's iconic beard is also present, its representative function here both literal and symbolic: according to David Piper, 'portraits of Tennyson fall into two categories ... those before 1857, clean-shaven, and those from 1857 till his death in 1892, bearded', with the latter set of images helping to cement the Laureate's literary reputation by figuring him as a 'venerable ... grand old man'.[83]

Kitton's representation of Tennyson, then, codifies the poet's person, rendering it a reflective signifier of his literary identity. It also commercialises the Laureate's image, making the engraving into a material artefact of celebrity culture. Tellingly, its position as a supplement to the main body of *The Graphic* (it appears on an unnumbered page) encourages it to be consumed as a detachable keepsake – a souvenir that can be removed and treasured by the reader without interrupting the periodical's overall integrity. Its status as collectable is reinforced by the authenticating presence of the poet's signature in facsimile in the margins of the page (Figure 1.2). This parapictorial addendum magnifies the cultural value of the illustration, converting it from merely evocative visual document into desirable commodity.

Yet, the aura of association that suffuses illustrations such as Kitton's and, to a lesser extent, Gardner's cannot satisfy entirely the hankering for knowledge that underpins works of virtual literary tourism. Though rich in revelatory detail, these images contain obfuscations and lacunae that invite additional questioning and stimulate further the desire for information. What is the content of the half-delineated pictures that decorate the Laureate's studies at Farringford and Aldworth? What is their significance to the poet? Which titles fill his bookshelves? What is hidden behind the screen in Gardner's image? From whom is the opened letter on the desk in Kitton's? These missing data are attributable in part to the limitations of verisimilar representation; they are also, however, structurally essential to the 'At Home with' genre. As Salmon suggests, the frequently deployed 'topos of the "secret"' guarantees these articles' perpetuation, 'since it is through the rhetorical imperative of secrecy that the apparently opposing rhetorical imperative of revelation is sustained'. [84] By propagating an infinite aura of mystery, periodicals ensured that there remained always something more to be said about the celebrity at home.

Circulating celebrity, commodifying desire

Writing after the death of Tennyson, Edmund Gosse noted mournfully, 'It is not merely that no person living now calls forth [the] kind of devotion [inspired by Tennyson], but the sentiment of mystery has disappeared. Not genius itself could survive the Kodak snapshots and the halfpenny newspapers'.[85] Such concerns about the relentlessly expositive role of the press were not new; an 1862 article in the *Sixpenny Magazine* on 'Celebrity: Its Pains and Penalties' had half-ironically warned any prospective 'Lions' among its readership to 'dread and shun the gentlemen connected with the public press; for be assured that with whatever veil you may seek to shroud your person, you cannot remain long hidden from their penetrating glance; they have eyes which pierce through all tissues, pens which respect no mystery'.[86] What these admonitions fail to acknowledge, however, is that, while 'At Home with' articles outwardly revelled in their percipience and divulgatory power, they also had a particular interest in maintaining some vestige of celebrity mystique. The sheer volume of articles dealing with celebrities in Victorian periodicals indicates that such material attracted readers and encouraged sales; to puncture completely the aura of mystery surrounding famous figures – to divest them of their supposed extraordinariness – would be to devalue their cultural currency and make redundant a commercially successful line of business.[87] Thus, for every claim to revelatory detail posited in works of virtual literary tourism one finds a concomitant assertion of the intangible and ineffable nature of celebrity.

Interestingly, in the case of Tennyson, it is often the pieces written by those best placed to offer genuine insight into his life that are most cloaked in the language of inscrutability. Anne Thackeray Ritchie, for instance, was a close friend of the Tennyson family and a regular visitor to both Farringford and Aldworth, and yet her reflections on the Laureate for *Harper's Magazine* are intriguingly opaque. She talks of the 'mysterious essence of individuality' that characterises the poet, and her anecdotes invest him with an ethereal, wraithlike quality:

> I have heard of Mr. Tennyson wandering for days together in the glades round about Lyndhurst. Some people once told me of meeting a mysterious figure in a cloak coming out of a deep glade, passing straight on, looking neither to the right nor the left. 'It was either a ghost or it was Mr. Tennyson', said they.[88]

Easley points out that such discourses of haunting and spectrality were regularly deployed in works of literary tourism for, like ghosts, celebrity writers were constructed as 'extant yet never fully materialized', 'absent ... except as they appeared as presences "behind" written texts, buildings or landscapes'.[89]

One of the notable effects of this uncanny 'interplay of presence and absence', according to Easley, is a curious sense of 'enchantment where the supernatural haunt[s] the apprehension of the real'.[90] This is certainly the case in an article written by another of Tennyson's friends, Annie Fields (wife of the American publisher James T. Fields). Her vivid recollection of her first visit to Farringford blurs the boundary between real and imagined worlds, and imbues the poet's home with a magical ambiance. 'The island might have been Prospero's own', she suggests, adding, 'we found ourselves suddenly walking as in a dream, surrounded with the scenery of [Tennyson's] poems'.[91] Her sentiments are echoed in the kind of 'Tennyson at Home' articles that blended reportage with personal reflection, journalism with fandom. Like Fields, Conway figures Tennyson as 'the Prospero of an enchanted isle', while an anonymous female contributor to *Temple Bar*, who visited the poet as a young girl, compares him to 'some great shade evoked from the long past'.[92] The *Boston Daily Advertiser*'s special correspondent, likewise, identifies in Aldworth and its surroundings a fantastical, fairy-tale quality:

> We found the Haslemere air full ... of echoes – echoes of [Tennyson's] poet [*sic*] fancies. ... The soft breeze that came stealing from the misty south seemed to bring on its wings the distant echo of 'the horns of elfland faintly blowing' to the ear of the poet who has thrown the spell of his fancy over all this fair English land.[93]

For 'Galatea', in the Chicago *Daily Inter-Ocean*, meanwhile, Farringford is similarly dreamlike – 'a place that one would linger about, half-fearing to enter, lest the charm should be broken'.[94]

The sense of mystery and unreality constructed in these accounts perpetuates the idea of Tennyson as a numinous, enigmatic figure who can never finally be 'known'. Significantly, the aura of ineffability surrounding him (an aura compounded, ironically, by his own compulsive need for privacy) served to enhance his value in the celebrity marketplace for, as a number of 'At Home with' articles were quick to point out, the scarcity of information about the poet's personal life only increased public demand. The San Francisco *Daily Evening Bulletin* mused that there was 'perhaps no man in England' of equivalent ability 'of whose daily habits, thoughts and actions so little is known'.[95] The London weekly *Truth* concurred, attributing the Laureate's influence and appeal to his relative obscurity: 'Mr. Tennyson is of course a power in society, not the less so because the man (as distinguished from the poet) is so little heard of'.[96] A later article in the New York publication *Frank Leslie's Illustrated Newspaper* reaffirmed the point: 'Great interest centres about the august person of Lord Tennyson but the Poet Laureate is not easily accessible. ... So little is known, therefore, of his daily life, that an article on the subject ... possesses a peculiar interest for admirers of the poet and his poetry'.[97]

Yet, despite this repeatedly professed lack of authoritative information about Tennyson's 'daily life', there was no shortage of articles on the topic of 'Tennyson at Home' in British and American periodicals between the 1860s and 1890s. Owing to the practices of reprinting and recycling entrenched in the provincial and metropolitan presses of both nations, a derivative and circumscribed body of knowledge about the Laureate was in constant circulation. Works of virtual literary tourism quickly became part of a transatlantic trade in print material; following initial publication, 'new' articles (which often simply rehashed information already in the public domain) were picked up by exchange editors, whose job it was to cull content from other publications, and reprinted, wholesale or in abbreviated form, accredited or unaccredited, in newspapers and magazines on both sides of the Atlantic.[98] For instance, within weeks of its appearance in Britain, *The World*'s 'Mr. Tennyson at Haslemere' had rematerialised in both the *St. Louis Daily Globe-Democrat* and the San Francisco *Daily Evening Bulletin*, while *Truth*'s 'Anecdotal Photograph' of the Laureate was disseminated even further afield, re-emerging as 'Tennyson at Home and Abroad' in the *Hawaiian Gazette* less than three months after its original publication.[99]

A curious incident involving the American poet and travel writer, Bayard Taylor, gives some indication of the extraordinary value placed on fresh information about Tennyson's domestic life (however apparently banal) and the subsequent demand for stories detailing visits to his homes in nineteenth-century periodicals. In February 1867, during a tour of Europe, Taylor and his wife visited Farringford, spending an enjoyable couple of days in the Tennysons' company. A few weeks later, Taylor wrote a lively account of the visit in a letter to his friend, Edmund Clarence Stedman, noting at the end, 'Remember, all this is private. I write to you instead of writing in a journal. These are things that I can't publish, yet wish to note as I go along'.[100] His confidential reminiscences were not to remain private for long, however: in December 1868, an extract from Taylor's letter appeared in the New York *Citizen* and was quickly reprinted in a rival newspaper under the headline 'Tennyson at Home: Drinking, Smoking and Reading His Own Poetry'.[101] By January 1869, the (actually far from sensational) story had reached Britain, appearing in regional papers such as the *Derby Mercury*, the *Hull Packet and East Riding Times* and the *Hampshire Telegraph and*

Sussex Chronicle.[102] It soon came to the notice of Tennyson, who wrote in a letter to James Fields, 'If you visit England this year I shall be most happy to see you here ... for I believe you are a man with some reverence for the hearth, not like Mr. Bayard Taylor who being received with open arms ... saw in me not a man but a paragraph'.[103]

In fact, Taylor was not responsible for the publication of the letter and, indeed, was blissfully unaware of its existence in print until a friend charged him with its broadcast in February 1869. Taylor hastily wrote to Fields:

> Five days ago, a friend in New-York said to me: 'I see that you have been publishing an account of your visit to Farringford'. This was the very first intimation I had that anything had appeared. I went instantly to Stedman, who thus explained the matter. He had been indiscreet enough to show the letter to a literary lady, who professed a great interest in Mr. Tennyson as a poet. This lady, without his knowledge, either copied portions, or attempted to reproduce parts of the letter from memory (I suspect the latter), and Stedman was thunderstruck at seeing what purported to be an extract from my letter in print about two months ago. He gave me no information of it – as he ought to have done – hoping that it might not be further copied, and that I might thus be spared a great vexation. I blame him for this, as I should have written instantly to Mr. Tennyson, and my explanation might have reached him before the article appeared in England.[104]

What this intriguing tale of broken confidences, misappropriated memoirs and unauthorised publication serves to highlight is the growing fascination with 'celebrity' in nineteenth-century culture and the indispensability of periodicals to that growth. It also makes clear, from the speed and voracity with which Taylor's anecdote was internationally circulated and consumed, that stories involving Tennyson represented particularly sought-after commodities in the transatlantic economy of print exchange, owing to the fervent readerly desire for insight into his life.

Yet, while acknowledging that the Laureate's celebrity status led to the commodification and transmission of his identity in ways he could not control, it would be a mistake to position him as the passive victim of a rapacious celebrity industry, snared helplessly between readers' insistent demands for ever more information on the one hand, and the moneymaking instincts of avaricious press-men on the other. In reality, 'Tennyson at Home' articles brought mutual, if uneven, benefits to all interested parties. To readers, as this chapter has shown, they brought the promise of intimacy via virtual contact. To publishers, they brought sales.[105] But to Tennyson, too, they brought indirect rewards. Anna Barton notes that, during the nineteenth century, literary identities took on a new commercial significance as more and more

> goods were sold on the basis of a recognized name ... By the end of the century, anthologies ... were organized according to poet, and the poet's name occupied a prominent position at the head of every page. In the bookshops and circulating libraries books were, for the first time, organized according to the name of the author so that the name came to mediate the work within the literary marketplace and customers were more likely to ask for 'the latest work by such and such an author' rather than for this or that particular title.[106]

A recognisable name was, therefore, a 'valuable ... sign', crucial to commercial success. As a sign, however, it was also potentially 'alienable', 'independent from and prior to' the person that it named.[107] By anchoring Tennyson's name to a distinctive and decipherable identity, to concrete places and tangible things, 'Tennyson at Home' articles helped to de-alienate the poet, securing for him a lucratively recognisable public persona.

Tennyson himself was all too aware of the economics of authorship, appreciating that the domestic comforts and material assets he enjoyed were directly dependent on the commercial success of his poetry (Bayard Taylor's fateful letter to Stedman described the Laureate proudly pointing out 'all his newly acquired territory – among the rest a great stretch of wheat-fields bought for him by Enoch Arden').[108] He was also conscious of the financial benefits of exposure in periodicals. As Kathryn Ledbetter has demonstrated in her excellent study, *Tennyson and Victorian Periodicals*, for all the poet's vociferous claims to detest this (supposedly inferior) medium and the attention it brought, at times he 'actively engage[d] the glare of publicity', authorising the publication of at least 62 poems under his name in 32 different titles during his career (often, for not inconsiderable fees).[109] Periodicals brought his work to the attention of a wider and more diverse audience than that which could afford to buy his poetry in volume form; thus Ledbetter argues, 'the poet and the periodical became commodities in cooperative exchange with Victorian society'.[110]

I would contend that 'Tennyson at Home' articles were an ancillary and facilitative component of this process of exchange. Though

Tennyson may not have initiated the publication of such articles in the way he did his poems, their presence in periodicals brought similar reputational benefits, broadening the potential market for his work. It is perhaps unsurprising, then, to find clues to suggest that the poet was tacitly complicit in the appearance of at least some such pieces. Edmund Yates's autobiography underlined the consensual nature of *The World*'s 'Celebrities at Home' series:

> Granting the correctness of Sir Henry Taylor's assertion that 'the world knows nothing of its greatest men', it had always been my idea that an introduction might be acceptable to both parties. The silly idea that any system of espionage would be practised, that admission into houses would be unduly obtained, and that there would be a general disclosure of skeletons in cupboards, was at once set to rest. By the regulations laid down and insisted upon from the first, that no person should be made the subject of one of these articles without his or her consent having been previously obtained, and without full liberty, if they wished it, to inspect the article in proof before it was published – with these safeguards ... it appears to me that, for the historian of the future, these articles will supply a want which must have been keenly felt by the Macaulays and the Froudes.[111]

The fact that certain celebrities, such as Anthony Trollope and John Delane (editor of *The Times*), refused to appear in Yates's series suggests that Tennyson, too, might have declined, had he wished to do so.[112] Equally, it seems improbable that the article illustrated by Kitton for the *Graphic* or Ritchie's piece for *Harper's* would have been printed without explicit permission; Ritchie, in particular, is unlikely to have jeopardised her close friendship with the Laureate by publishing an article about him, however laudatory, without prior consent.

Of course, once 'At Home with' articles had appeared in the public domain, Tennyson could not control the uses to which they were put. Sometimes they were reprinted, selectively and anonymously, in ways that were less than complimentary; unqualified and unverified statements such as 'the poet, in his wrath, raged like mad [at an intrusion into his library]' were often deployed as titillating 'filler' in newspaper columns.[113] Nevertheless, Tennyson's ambivalent interactions with the press, on the whole, paid cultural and commercial dividends. Whether by design or otherwise, the poet's private sanctioning of a small number of sympathetic articles and concomitant public denouncement of celebrity journalism enabled him to gratify his readers' desire for information, while retaining a proper (and profitable) aura of aloofness and mystique. His paradoxical position is mirrored in the 'Tennyson at Home' articles he at once needed and disparaged. As this chapter has demonstrated, such articles were troubled by an enduring status anxiety, making repeated efforts to distinguish themselves from the vulgar crowds who bothered the poet while inevitably re-enacting, and at times intensifying, the touristic gaze they ostensibly repudiated. The contradiction is crystallised in Allen's piece for the *English Illustrated Magazine*: though it closes with the heartfelt plea, 'Leave him undisturbed in his retreat, oh prying race of tourists', the article elsewhere reveals a tacit understanding of the impulse that drove Tennyson's fans to seek 'personal contact with greatness', noting, 'it is better, after all, to mob a divine bard with one's pressing attentions, than to pass one's life blankly and blandly unaware that there exists in the world such a power as literature'.[114] Owing to these complex rhetorical negotiations and ultimately unresolved tensions, works of virtual literary tourism demand to be read as profoundly ambivalent, though nonetheless valuable, artefacts in the history of celebrity. They represent commodities in a transatlantic economy of desire whose internal inconsistencies and uncertainties expose not only Tennyson's contradictory attitude to his fame, but also the competing artistic and commercial demands that circulated around the figure of the celebrity in Victorian culture.

Notes

1. 'A Summer Ramble', *Leisure Hour*, 448 (1860), 476–78 (pp. 477–78), in *ProQuest British Periodicals* <http://www.proquest.co.uk> [accessed 3 April 2013].
2. The Tennysons rented Farringford from November 1853, buying it outright in 1856.
3. H. D. Rawnsley, 'Memories of Farringford', in *Tennyson: Interviews and Recollections*, ed. by Norman Page (Basingstoke: Macmillan, 1983), pp. 60–75 (p. 60). The extension of the Isle of Wight Railway to Freshwater was fiercely resisted by Tennyson: in an 1865 letter to the Duke of Argyll he wrote, 'my whole afternoon was taken up about a railway with which they threaten us here ... I shall not stay if they do bring this terminus close by me'. When the Freshwater, Yarmouth and Newport Railway began work on its new line from Newport to Freshwater in 1888, Tennyson wrote a letter of protest to *The Times*. See *The Letters of Alfred Lord Tennyson*, ed. by Cecil Y. Lang and Edgar F. Shannon Jr, 3 vols (Oxford: Clarendon Press, 1982–90), II (1987), 396 (21 March 1865); III (1990), 385 (20 December 1888).
4. J. W. Hill, *Historical and Commercial Directory of the Isle of Wight* (London: T. Danks, 1879), p. 239; *Briddon's Illustrated Handbook to the Isle of Wight, Containing Everything Necessary to the Tourist* (Ryde: J. Briddon, 1862), p. 65.
5. 'A Summer Ramble', p. 478.

6. Ibid., p. 477.

7. George G. Napier, *The Homes and Haunts of Alfred Lord Tennyson, Poet Laureate* (Glasgow: James Maclehose & Sons, 1892), p. 167.

8. Highlighting the inaccessibility of Freshwater, one traveller wrote, 'The journey from London turns one's thoughts towards eternity. There are expresses as far as Brockenhurst, but there the traveller for the Isle of Wight is shunted on to a branch line, and the rest of the distance is through a country of crabs and tortoises. The train takes a nap of fifteen minutes at Lymington Town, and then softly steals on a quarter of a mile to Lymington Pier, where ancient mariners, who only need pigtails to connect them with Trafalgar, transfer you and your baggage to a prehistoric boat, which creeps across the Solent on the tips of its toes and cautiously lands you at Yarmouth. Still you are far away from Freshwater, reckoning by the clock. Octogenarian porters smile at you and your "boxes", and then have a good, long chat among themselves and with the boat's crew. Later – never sooner – perhaps in the course of an hour, the coach is ready to start, but ... when the coach starts it stops, and starts to stop again to deliver a cabbage here, a newspaper there ... When you reach Freshwater the day is done and you feel that Switzerland might have been nearer' (William H. Rideing, 'Tennyson in the Isle of Wight', *North American Review*, 165 (1897), 701–10 (p. 707), in *Cornell University Library Making of America Collection* <http://ebooks.library.cornell.edu/m/moa/> [accessed 3 April 2013]).

9. See, for instance, the stories about tourists in 'Mr. Tennyson's Garibaldian Tree', *The London Review*, 8 (1864), 406–07 (p. 406), in *ProQuest British Periodicals* <http://www.proquest.co.uk> [accessed 3 April 2013]; 'Tennyson's Home', *New Hampshire Statesman* (Concord, NH), 14 June 1867, column G, in *Gale 19th Century U.S. Newspapers* <http://gale.cengage.co.uk> [accessed 24 February 2012]; V. C. Scott O'Connor, 'Tennyson and his Friends at Freshwater', *The Century*, 55 (1897), 240–68 (p. 250), in *Cornell University Library Making of America Collection* <http://ebooks.library.cornell.edu/m/moa/> [accessed 3 April 2013].

10. 'Tennyson's Aversion to Being Stared At', *Daily Evening Bulletin* (San Francisco, CA), 8 November 1873, column D, in *Gale 19th Century U. S. Newspapers* <http://gale.cengage.co.uk> [accessed 13 March 2012]. The story is also told by W. E. H. Lecky in Hallam Tennyson, *Alfred Lord Tennyson: a Memoir by His Son*, 2 vols (London: Macmillan & Co., 1897), II, 200–01.

11. For reports of Tennyson's self-imposed exile, see, for instance, Geoffrey Quarles, 'Tennyson at Home', *The Sunday Inter Ocean* (Chicago, IL), 27 November 1887, p. 21, in *Gale 19th Century U. S. Newspapers* <http://gale.cengage.co.uk> [accessed 13 March 2012]; 'Tennyson and Sightseers', *Bismarck Daily Tribune* (Bismarck, ND), 13 December 1892, p. 4, in *Gale 19th Century U. S. Newspapers* <http://gale.cengage.co.uk> [accessed 13 March 2012]; Grant Allen, 'Tennyson's Homes at Aldworth and Farringford', *English Illustrated Magazine*, 10 (1892), 147–56 (p. 153).

12. Nicola J. Watson, 'Introduction', in *Literary Tourism and Nineteenth-Century Culture*, ed. by Nicola J. Watson (Basingstoke: Palgrave Macmillan, 2009), pp. 1–12 (p. 3). Perhaps surprisingly, even Tennyson himself seems to have been susceptible to this vogue for literary tourism. In 1867, he invited William Allingham to travel with him to the town of Lyme Regis on the Dorset coast

specifically to see the famous Cobb from which Louisa Musgrove falls and injures herself in Jane Austen's novel *Persuasion*. See *William Allingham's Diary 1847–1889*, ed. by H. Allingham and D. Radford (London: Centaur Press, 2000), p. 156 (23 August 1867). The story is repeated (in slightly embellished form) in John Vaughan, 'Jane Austen at Lyme', *The Monthly Packet*, n.s., 6 (1893), 271–79 (p. 273).

13. Harald Hendrix, 'Epilogue', in *Writers' Houses and the Making of Memory*, ed. by Harald Hendrix (London and New York: Routledge, 2008), pp. 235–43 (p. 236); Harald Hendrix, 'Writers' Houses as Media of Expression and Remembrance: From Self-Fashioning to Cultural Memory', in *Writers' Houses*, ed. by Hendrix, pp. 1–12 (p. 1).

14. Alexis Easley, *Literary Celebrity, Gender, and Victorian Authorship, 1850–1914* (Newark: University of Delaware Press, 2011), p. 21.

15. See, for instance, Nicola J. Watson, *The Literary Tourist* (Basingstoke: Palgrave Macmillan, 2006), pp. 90–127 [Abbotsford and Haworth]; Erin Hazard, '"A Realized Day-Dream": Excursions to Nineteenth-Century Authors' Homes', *Nineteenth Century Studies*, 20 (2006), 13–34 [Abbotsford]; Alison Booth, 'Author Country: Longfellow, the Brontës, and Anglophone Homes and Haunts', *Romanticism and Victorianism on the Net*, Special Issue: Victorian Internationalisms, 48 (2007), DOI: 10.7202/017438ar [Haworth]; Erin Hazard, 'The Author's House: Abbotsford and Wayside', in *Literary Tourism*, ed. by Watson, pp. 63–72; Ann Rigney, 'Abbotsford: Dislocation and Cultural Remembrance', in *Writers' Houses*, ed. by Hendrix, pp. 75–92; and Christine Alexander, 'Myth and Memory: Reading the Brontë Parsonage', in *Writers' Houses*, ed. by Hendrix, pp. 93–110.

16. The rectory at Somersby in Lincolnshire (where Tennyson was born); Chapel House, Twickenham (where Tennyson and Emily lived between 1851–53, now known as 15 Montpelier Row); and Aldworth House are all, at the time of writing, private houses. Farringford was sold by the Tennyson family in the 1940s, when it was converted into a hotel; it is currently undergoing extensive restoration. For a discussion of the process of 'musealisation', see Polly Atkin, 'Ghosting Grasmere: the Musealisation of Dove Cottage', in *Literary Tourism*, ed. by Watson, pp. 84–94.

17. Hazard, 'A Realized Day-Dream', p. 17.

18. Review of *Homes and Haunts of the Most Eminent British Poets*, cited in Hazard, 'A Realized Day-Dream,' p. 17.

19. See Watson, *The Literary Tourist*, p. 9.

20. In this chapter, I follow Kenneth M. Price and Susan Belasco Smith's broad definition of 'periodicals as publications that are issued at intervals that are more or less regular (*Periodical Literature in Nineteenth-Century America*, ed. by Price and Smith (Charlottesville and London: University Press of Virginia, 1995), p. 9). My analysis will focus, in particular, on provincial and metro-politan newspapers, and weekly and monthly magazines.

21. F. G. Kitton, 'Tennyson at Aldworth: a Reminiscence', *Gentleman's Magazine*, 278 (1895), 53–59 (p. 53).

22. 'Paul Pry' considered it his duty to put to celebrities 'a series of those inquiries which in the society interviewer's case are considered pertinent, but in any-body else's impertinent' ('Lions of the Day in their Dens', *Judy*, 12 February 1890, p. 77, in *Gale 19th Century UK Periodicals* <http://gale.cengage.co.uk>

[accessed 3 April 2013]). The fourth 'Lion' to be featured in *Judy*'s spoof series was Tennyson, who is pictured in an accompanying cartoon barricading himself behind a barrage of signs bearing slogans such as 'Go Home!' ('Lions of the Day in their Dens', *Judy*, 19 March 1890, p. 141, in *Gale 19th Century UK Periodicals* <http://gale.cengage.co.uk> [accessed 3 April 2013]). For a discussion of nineteenth-century attitudes to the celebrity interview, see Richard Salmon, 'Signs of Intimacy: the Literary Celebrity in the "Age of Interviewing"', *Victorian Literature and Culture*, 25 (1997), 159–77.

23. Tom Mole, *Byron's Romantic Celebrity: Industrial Culture and the Hermeneutic of Intimacy* (Basingstoke: Palgrave Macmillan, 2007), p. 16.

24. Ibid., pp. 22–23.

25. Ibid., p. 16.

26. Edmund Yates, Preface, *Celebrities at Home*, repr. from *The World*, 3 vols (London: Office of *The World*, 1877–79), I (1877), n. pag.

27. O'Connor states that it is due to 'the present Lord Tennyson['s]... courtesy ... that this article has been written' (p. 249).

28. W. H. Davenport Adams, *Nelson's Handbook to the Isle of Wight* (London: T. Nelson and Sons, 1873), p. 148.

29. Kitton, p. 53.

30. Ibid., p. 55.

31. Ibid.

32. Ibid., p. 56.

33. Ibid., p. 57.

34. C. Sadakichi Hartmann, 'Tennyson at Home', *The Sunday Inter Ocean* (Chicago, IL), 22 November 1891, p. 31, in *Gale 19th Century U. S. Newspapers* <http://gale.cengage.co.uk> [accessed 13 March 2012].

35. M. D. Conway, 'South-Coast Saunterings in England: Saunter V – The Isle of Wight II', *Harper's New Monthly Magazine*, 40 (1870), 523–42 (p. 541), in *Cornell University Library Making of America Collection* <http://ebooks.library. cornell.edu/m/moa/> [accessed 4 April 2013]; Yates, *Celebrities at Home*, I (1877), 27. A similar point was made by the correspondent of the *Truth* in 1879: 'Mr. Tennyson's orders in reference to the admission of visitors are of the strictest kind. He has more than Wordsworth's horror of tourists, and is equally inaccessible to his neighbours ... But Mr. Tennyson can be much more than courteous with a sympathetic person; he can be the most charming of companions. Lounging in a comfortable arm-chair and smoking his pipe – he is a great smoker – the Laureate will talk on any and every subject, and equally well on all' ('Anecdotal Photographs VIII. – The Laureate', *Truth*, 20 February 1879, pp. 234–35 (p. 234)).

36. Yates, *Celebrities at Home*, I (1877), p. 28; Kitton, p. 58.

37. Salmon, 'Signs of Intimacy', p. 160.

38. Ibid., p. 164.

39. 'Home of Alfred Tennyson', *Daily Evening Bulletin* (San Francisco, CA), 13 June 1868, column H, in *Gale 19th Century U. S. Newspapers* <http://gale. cengage.co.uk> [accessed 24 February 2012].

40. Quarles, p. 21.

41. The *New York Times*, for example, implicitly enlists the reader as a knowledgeable and confidential auditor in the following aside: 'Tennyson, as you know, afterward selected another part of the island [the Isle of Wight] for his

residence' ('The Poet's Island Home', *New York Times*, 31 August 1878, p. 5, in *The New York Times Article Archive* <http://www.nytimes.com/ref/member-center/nytarchive.html> [accessed 4 April 2013]).

42. Kitton, p. 55.
43. Allen, pp. 147, 153.
44. Conway, pp. 539, 540.
45. James Buzard, *The Beaten Track: European Tourism, Literature, and the Ways to Culture, 1800–1918* (Oxford: Clarendon Press, 1993), p. 5.
46. Ibid., p.12.
47. Yates, *Celebrities at Home*, I (1877), 24. A similar discourse of 'hiddenness' can be found in descriptions of Farringford, such as Rideing's: 'The house is invisible from the road as well as from the cliffs, and to see it one must either be invited or become a trespasser' (p. 708).
48. Salmon, 'Signs of Intimacy', p. 168.
49. Yates, *Celebrities at Home*, I (1877), 22.
50. 'To the Rev. F. D. Maurice', in *The Poems of Tennyson*, ed. by Christopher Ricks (London: Longmans, Green and Co., 1969), pp. 1022–25 (p. 1023, ll. 13–16).
51. 'To Ulysses', in *The Poems of Tennyson*, ed. by Ricks, pp. 1396–98 (p. 1397, ll. 15–16, 18, 25–26); O'Connor, p. 250.
52. *Enoch Arden*, in *The Poems of Tennyson*, ed. by Ricks, pp. 1129–52 (p. 1130, ll. 1–2); O'Connor, p. 249.
53. Rideing, p. 706.
54. M., 'A Spring Day at Farringford: An Afternoon with Tennyson', *Temple Bar*, 126 (1902), 216–21 (p. 217).
55. Yates, *Celebrities at Home*, I (1877), 23–24.
56. M., pp. 217–18.
57. Note to ll. 688–9 of 'Geraint and Enid' in *The Poems of Tennyson*, ed. by Ricks, pp. 1551–76 (p. 1569).
58. *The Letters of Alfred Lord Tennyson*, III (1990), 410 (5 February 1890).
59. Blanche Warre-Cornish, 'Memories of Tennyson', in *Tennyson: Interviews and Recollections*, ed. by Page, pp. 110–21 (p. 117).
60. Yates, *Celebrities at Home*, I (1877), 23.
61. Anne Thackeray Ritchie, 'Alfred Tennyson', *Harper's New Monthly Magazine*, 68 (1883), 21–41 (p. 38), in *Cornell University Library Making of America Collection* <http://ebooks.library.cornell.edu/m/moa/> [accessed 4 April 2013].
62. Conway, p. 542.
63. Allen, p. 150.
64. O'Connor, p. 244.
65. Kitton, p. 58.
66. The difficulty of gaining admittance to Tennyson's homes is illustrated in an article by Beverly Crump, correspondent for the Milwaukee *Sentinel*. After bribing the housekeeper at Farringford, Crump is permitted to look around the grounds but fails to gain access to the house itself: '[the housekeeper] would not admit me within the walls, even for a fee, as she said it would certainly be found out, as "his lordship was as sharp as a ferret," so I had to be content with looking at the outside'. There is a noticeable shift in the article's tone as it is obliged to move from this lively, first-hand account to dry, derivative information about Farringford's interior and Tennyson's daily

routine (Beverly Crump, 'Lord Tennyson: the Poet-Laureate's Picturesque Home', *The Sentinel* (Milwaukee, WI), 22 January 1888, p. 12, in *Gale 19th Century U. S. Newspapers* <http://gale.cengage.co.uk> [accessed 24 February 2012]).

67. I borrow this phrase from Nick Couldry's essay on fan journeys to modern media locations (Nick Couldry, 'On the Set of *The Sopranos*: "Inside" a Fan's Construction of Nearness', in *Fandom: Identities and Communities in a Mediated World*, ed. by Jonathan Gray, Cornel Sandvoss and C. Lee Harrington (New York and London: New York University Press, 2007), pp. 139–48 (p. 146).

68. Ritchie, pp. 34–35 (my emphasis); M., p. 219.

69. Salmon, 'Signs of Intimacy', p. 166.

70. See, for instance, Ritchie, p. 35, and Rideing, p. 710, on Farringford; and Hartmann, p. 31, and Kitton, p. 56, on Aldworth.

71. See Ritchie, p. 35, and O'Connor, pp. 251, 255.

72. See, for instance, Yates, *Celebrities at Home*, I (1877), 25–26, 28; 'Lord Tennyson', *The Graphic*, 22 March 1884, p. 290; and Kitton, p. 57.

73. Quarles, p. 21; Yates, *Celebrities at Home*, I (1877), 25.

74. Kitton, p. 56.

75. Hartmann, for instance, describes Aldworth's rooms as 'the perfection of luxury and good taste' (p. 31).

76. Quarles, p. 21; Yates, *Celebrities at Home*, I (1877), 25; Kitton, p. 56.

77. Apart from a silhouette of a dog's head, it is difficult to discern the content of the pictures on the walls in Gardner's image. However, according to O'Connor's 'Tennyson and his Friends at Freshwater', the items on display in the study included portraits of Arthur Hallam, Lionel Tennyson and Lady Tennyson (a copy of the well-known painting by G. F. Watts), some framed words by Garibaldi and a sketch by Thackeray (O'Connor, p. 255). As a later article indicated, these objects, which were personally meaningful to Tennyson, could also be interpreted as signifiers of Tennyson's celebrity; for ordinary visitors, outside of his famous circle, 'the portraits, sketches, and drawings which covered the walls' of his Farringford study represented 'mementoes of almost every illustrious name of the nineteenth century' (M., p. 219).

78. Kitton, p. 56.

79. 'Tennyson at Home' articles often constructed the Laureate as an intellectual all-rounder; Rideing, for instance, claims that '[Tennyson] observed not merely with the eye of a poet, but as a man of wide scientific knowledge, and he had much more than a fair acquaintance with geology, botany, and astronomy' (Rideing, p. 705).

80. Kitton, p. 56.

81. Ibid., p. 55. Again, my understanding of the poet's 'brand' here is indebted to Mole's work on Romantic celebrity.

82. Quarles, p. 21; Yates, *Celebrities at Home*, I (1877), 26.

83. David Piper, *The Image of the Poet: British Poets and their Portraits* (Oxford: Clarendon Press, 1982), p. 166. In articles, too, Tennyson's beard is iconified and fetishised; *The World*'s reverent reference to the 'knightly growth fringing his lips' (a quotation from *Morte d'Arthur*) casts the poet as an inherently noble figure in the Arthurian mould (Yates, *Celebrities at Home*, I (1877), 26).

84. Salmon, 'Signs of Intimacy', pp. 167–68.
85. Edmund Gosse, 'A First Sight of Tennyson', in *Tennyson: Interviews and Recollections*, ed. by Page, pp. 124–26 (p. 124).
86. 'Celebrity: Its Pains and Penalties', *The Sixpenny Magazine*, 3 (1862), 82–83 (p. 83), in *ProQuest British Periodicals* <http://www.proquest.co.uk> [accessed 4 April 2013].
87. In his autobiography, Edmund Yates suggested that the long-running 'Celebrities at Home' feature was integral to the overall success of *The World*: 'Undoubtedly one of the most attractive features of *The World* is the series of "Celebrities at Home", of which nearly four hundred specimens have already appeared, and which seems to be practically inexhaustible' (*Edmund Yates: His Recollections and Experiences*, 2 vols (London: Richard Bentley and Son, 1884), II, 330–31).
88. Ritchie, pp. 41, 36.
89. Easley, pp. 51–52.
90. Ibid., p. 51.
91. Annie Fields, 'Tennyson', *Harper's New Monthly Magazine*, 86 (1893), 309–12 (p. 311), in *Cornell University Library Making of America Collection* <http://ebooks.library.cornell.edu/m/moa/> [accessed 4 April 2013].
92. Conway, p. 542; M., p. 219.
93. 'The Surrey Hills: the Scenes around the Home of Tennyson', *Boston Daily Advertiser* (Boston, MA), 13 January 1883, p. 2, in *Gale 19th Century U. S. Newspapers* <http://gale.cengage.co.uk> [accessed 24 February 2012].
94. Galatea, 'Tennyson's Home', *The Daily Inter-Ocean* (Chicago, IL), 4 March 1875, p. 3, in *Gale 19th Century U. S. Newspapers* <http://gale.cengage.co.uk> [accessed 24 February 2012].
95. 'Home of Alfred Tennyson', column H.
96. 'Anecdotal Photographs', p. 235.
97. 'Tennyson at Home', *Frank Leslie's Illustrated Newspaper* (New York), 7 November 1885, p. 190, in *Gale 19th Century U. S. Newspapers* <http://gale.cengage.co.uk> [accessed 24 February 2012].
98. In the case of smaller publications, the job of gleaning content might be performed by the general editor or a member of the reporting staff. For further information on the nineteenth-century culture of reprinting, see Meredith L. McGill, *American Literature and the Culture of Reprinting, 1834–1853* (Philadelphia: University of Pennsylvania Press, 2003) and Ellen Gruber Garvey, 'Scissorizing and Scrapbooks: Nineteenth-Century Reading, Remaking and Recirculating', in *New Media, 1740–1915*, ed. by Lisa Gitelman and Geoffrey B. Pingree (Cambridge, MA and London: MIT Press, 2003), pp. 207–27.
99. See 'Tennyson at Home', *St. Louis Daily Globe-Democrat – Supplemental Sheet* (St Louis, MO), 10 September 1876, p. 11; 'Tennyson at Home', *Daily Evening Bulletin* (San Francisco, CA), 18 September 1876, column C; and 'Tennyson at Home and Abroad', *Hawaiian Gazette* (Honolulu, HI), 14 May 1879, p. 4, all in *Gale 19th Century U. S. Newspapers* <http://gale.cengage.co.uk> [accessed 24 February 2012]. Ellen Gruber Garvey notes that American 'journalists and commentators often remarked on this recirculation of material, not as failure to generate original material, but as a virtue – a mechanism unifying the country. As one journalist asserted,

"A man who reads the daily exchanges of the country may see an idea travel from the Atlantic slope to the Pacific and from the Pacific to the Atlantic as visibly as a train of freight cars runs over the Vanderbilt system"' (Garvey, pp. 212–13).

100. *Selected Letters of Bayard Taylor*, ed. by Paul C. Wermuth (Lewisburg and London: Bucknell University Press/Associated University Presses, 1997), p. 306 (11 March 1867).

101. I have been unable to locate a copy of the original, New York *Citizen* article. A reprinted version can be found in *The Sun* (New York), 28 December 1868, p. 1, in *Chronicling America: Historic American Newspapers* <http://chroniclingamerica.loc.gov> [accessed 4 April 2013].

102. 'A Yankee Visit to Tennyson', *The Derby Mercury*, 20 January 1869, p. 6; 'A Yankee's Visit to Tennyson', *The Hull Packet and East Riding Times*, 22 January 1869, p. 3; 'The Poet Laureate at Home', *Hampshire Telegraph and Sussex Chronicle*, 23 January 1869, p. 7, all in *Gale 19th Century British Library Newspapers* <http://gale.cengage.co.uk> [accessed 3 April 2013].

103. *The Letters of Alfred Lord Tennyson*, II (1987), 514.

104. *Selected Letters of Bayard Taylor*, p. 328 (26 February 1869).

105. And not just sales of periodicals; it is interesting to note that a number of the American articles considered in this chapter first appeared in *Harper's Magazine*, for in 1870 Harper Brothers published a collected edition of Tennyson's poetry.

106. Anna Barton, *Tennyson's Name: Identity and Responsibility in the Poetry of Alfred Lord Tennyson* (Aldershot: Ashgate, 2008), p. 3.

107. Ibid., p. 3.

108. *Selected Letters of Bayard Taylor*, p. 304 (11 March 1867).

109. Kathryn Ledbetter, *Tennyson and Victorian Periodicals: Commodities in Context* (Aldershot: Ashgate, 2007), pp. 52, 2–3.

110. Ibid., p. 6.

111. *Edmund Yates: His Recollections and Experiences*, II, 331.

112. Ibid., II, 232–33, 169.

113. 'Tennyson Enraged', *Rocky Mountain News* (Denver, CO), 17 February 1884, p. 14, in *Gale 19th Century U. S. Newspapers* <http://gale.cengage.co.uk> [accessed 13 March 2012].

114. Allen, pp. 156, 153.

2

'This Is the Sort of Fame for Which I Have Given My Life': G. F. Watts, Edward Lear and Portraits of Fame and Nonsense

Páraic Finnerty

George Frederic Watts and Edward Lear each left posterity visual representations of themselves that reveal much about their respective self-fashioning and self-perceived place in Victorian society. Although Watts did not exhibit his self-portraits until the latter part of his career, they record his determination to transcend his lowly background and inhabit the role of great artist. They also chronicle his innovations and experiments in portraiture, which transformed this art form into a biographically revealing medium.[1] In the very first of these self-portraits, dated 1834, Watts presents himself as a handsome young man with wavy hair and the attire associated with the Romantic poet or Bohemian, and eyes that suggest sensitivity and resolution. In subsequent self-portraits, for example the 1846 *Self-Portrait in Armour* or the 1853 *Self-Portrait (The Venetian Senator)*, Watts poses as the confident artist assured of the dignified and serious nature of his vocation and asserting his place within a European artistic tradition. By the mid-1860s, Watts had already vindicated the ambition, self-aggrandisement and sense of purpose in these early images; his self-portraits from then onwards reflect his position not merely as one of Britain's most esteemed painters and sculptors, but as a world-renowned artist. In contrast, in 1831, at the age of 20, Lear drew his first self-portrait and described what he saw: an unattractive, long-necked, big-nosed, 'half blind' young man.[2] Forty-eight years later, in his poem 'How Pleasant to know Mr Lear!', he again mentions some of these physical features, describing his visage as 'more or less hideous' and his body as 'perfectly spherical', and presents himself as a pleasant, ill-tempered, 'queer', 'crazy old Englishman' living abroad.[3] His correspondence abounds with similar self-caricature in which Lear, typically, depicts himself

53

as an eccentric, odd-looking, bespectacled man, who is frequently travelling somewhere accompanied by a cat or bird, and often carrying his nonsense verse or landscape paintings. These self-deprecating, humorous self-portraits indicate Lear's awareness of his position as a social outsider who has made marginalisation central to his *drôle* and often poignant literary and artistic representations. These illustrations and descriptions perfectly capture and reinforce Lear's situation as the idiosyncratic guest, amusing correspondent and beloved friend of wealthy, aristocratic and influential cultural figures, on whom he continually relied for financial support for his creative pursuits.

Consequently, for most of his life, Lear remained on the peripheries of fame and renown, admired as much for his quirky personality as for his talents as a painter, travel writer and illustrator; whereas Watts, known in his lifetime as 'England's Michelangelo', achieved a level of fame, influence and importance in the visual arts comparable to Tennyson's in literature. Watts received many honours, including one of the earliest Orders of Merit, and became one of the first artists to have retrospective exhibitions in his own lifetime, the earliest of which took place in Grosvenor Gallery in 1881–82. Such was his celebrity that by the end of his life the increasingly reclusive Watts believed that 'in these days too much is written of every one who comes at all before the public', and he envied 'the oblivion that now hides every fact of the life of the man whose name stands first in literature [meaning Shakespeare].'[4] In contrast, the lack of public recognition for his talents disappointed and frustrated Lear, who told Tennyson in June 1855, 'I feel woundily like a spectator, – all through my life – of what goes on amongst those I know: very little an actor'.[5] As was his penchant, Lear transformed his failures into verse, presenting himself in 'Growling Eclogue' (1867) as a painter who 'make[s] large drawings nobody will buy – / [paints] oil pictures which will never dry – / [and writes] new books which nobody will read' (p. 237). It was not until the last decade of his life that Lear finally received literary acclaim for his highly popular nonsense verse; this culminated, in 1886, with John Ruskin placing Lear's *A Book of Nonsense* first on his list of his 'Choice of Books' in the *Pall Mall Gazette*.[6] If Watts, over the course of his lifetime, became a Victorian celebrity, 'observed, brushed up against, talked about, and above all *recognized*', then Lear, in his, remained a 'notable', a man admired and celebrated within a 'circumscribed sphere' that included literary and artistic celebrities.[7] Expanding on this brief comparison, this chapter explores these men's interactions with nineteenth-century mechanisms of fame and celebrity. It examines their respective responses to the cult of personality and culture of publicity, focusing on Watts's *Hall of Fame*, comprising portraits of his most distinguished contemporaries, and Lear's *A Book of Nonsense*, consisting of verbal and visual 'portraits' of unconventional 'Old Persons'. The chapter, then, compares each man's relationship with Tennyson and the Freshwater circle, focusing on the way the Isle of Wight became one of the settings for Lear's passionate friendship with Franklin Lushington, and one of the locations where Watts and the actress Ellen Terry acted out the problems that would eventually end their short-lived marriage.

Faces of fame

In a letter to Henry Bruce, dated 24 February 1855, Lear writes, 'Watts is a man of whom I never heard any one who knew him speak otherwise than in terms of real liking. I have only met him twice, & those twice at dinner ... [but] I should really like to meet him at your house some day'; however, Lear also cautions his friend: 'Watt's [*sic*] drawings are of the most beautiful I ever saw. But you should not compare me to him, even in joke'.[8] While it is not surprising that Lear and Watts occasionally met, as they moved in similar social circles and had many mutual friends and acquaintances, Lear's rebuke of Bruce's presumably well-meant comparison is revealing. The comment indicates that Lear, like his contemporaries, regarded Watts as an important and highly esteemed artist, and that he saw himself as a professional disappointment, despite the admiration he had already received for his ornithological drawings, landscape paintings and illustrated travel books; the latter were so impressive that Lear was invited to give drawing lessons, in 1846, to Queen Victoria. One other reason for Lear's sense of inferiority was that he, unlike Watts, was not a skilled and sought-after portraitist at a time when portraits were in demand among the upper echelons of society, as well as among the middle classes, who commissioned this aristocratically inflected form as a means of reflecting their status, prosperity and self-importance.[9] The increased cultural significance and popularity of portraiture was also the result of a wider cultural preoccupation with memorialisation and charismatic personalities, and the proliferation of engravings, illustrations and, eventually, photographs of distinguished individuals. As Leo Braudy notes, the foundation of fame and celebrity in this period was to 'lure allegiance through the eye' and portraits represented a 'willingness to face the public in order to be recognized and to be identified'.[10] Although Watts often complained about 'the drudgery of portrait-painting' and felt it prevented him from achieving work 'worthy of an artist', throughout his career commercial portraiture offered him a way of making money, which meant he could develop artistically and create other types of artwork.[11] As his reputation grew, Watts grew choosy about whom he painted and became more innovative in this field. Rather than flattering his sitters, as many of his contemporaries did, Watts aimed to create works that would 'be valuable in all times both as faithful records and as works of art', and, in so doing, he reformed and rejuvenated what Marion Harry Spielmann called 'a sadly declining branch of pictorial art'.[12]

During the 1850s, as Watts popularised the idea of honest and accurate portraiture, Lear gave up on what he later called his 'slavy labours at anatomy', despite having enrolled in the Royal Academy, in 1850, to be taken seriously as an artist and properly trained, particularly in the representation of the human form.[13] This renunciation of portraiture meant that for the rest of his life, in order to make a living, Lear had to petition others persistently to exhibit, commission or buy his landscape paintings, which were out of fashion, and his elaborate oil paintings, which could not compete with those of his contemporaries.[14] Lear grew disenchanted by an Academy-orientated art world, which he regarded as 'narrow' and 'rotten', and became equally frustrated by 'the wise public [that] only give commissions for the pictures through the Press that tell the sheep to leap where others leap!'[15] His dislike of the spectacle and practice of lionism, which were so prevalent in the social gatherings and salons of London, meant that he excluded himself from the very places where wider success, fame and fortune were arbitrated and produced.[16] Although he maintained a network of influential friends and acquaintances in England, Lear also resigned himself to a marginal social and cultural position and exacerbated this by a life of continuous travel that culminated in his eventual exile in San Remo.

Nothing confirmed Watts's reputation as a great and distinguished artist more than his close friendship with the accomplished lion-hunter Sara Prinsep.[17] Prinsep, one of the renowned Pattle sisters, and her husband, Thoby, transformed their home, Little Holland House, into a place celebrated for its social gatherings, which attracted some of the period's most important intellectual, literary, artistic and political figures. From 1851 to 1871, Watts was the salon's artist-in-residence, fashioning himself as a bearded, barefooted monk who was reverentially addressed as 'Signor'.[18] Prinsep, a typical lion-hunter, mastered or tamed Watts only to worship and serve him; and Watts, a representative lion, became exhibited as a visual spectacle and object of curiosity for the gratification of the salon's visitors.[19] As one visitor, Lady Constance Leslie, observed, 'The Signor came out of his studio all spirit and so delicate, and received me very kindly ... Signor was the whole object of adoration and care in that house. He seemed to sanctify Little Holland House'.[20] Another guest, Sidney Colvin, recalled that the main attraction of the place was 'the fame and personality of the great artist Watts', who had a 'total lack of, and indeed incapacity for, any manner of pose or pretension'.[21] Of course, Watts did (and was expected to) pose, and visitors left the salon having had a quasi-religious, face-to-face encounter with a mystical artist and with a clear sense of Prinsep's cultural power. The comforts and luxuries of this environment afforded Watts a privileged life in which he produced historical paintings and symbolical ones that used allegory and drew on mythical, literary or biblical subjects to engage with metaphysical questions and contemporary social issues. In his studio at Little Holland House, Watts's works were on constant show and, as a result, were discussed, admired and bought by London's cultural and economic elite. By being a lion for two decades in this environment, Watts gained the support of those who bestowed and withheld cultural authority, which meant that he had the type of high-profile backing that ensured he, unlike Lear, received the validation of the Academy and the press. In the same year, 1867, the Royal Academy elected him as one of its Associates and Academicians, giving him a position from which to influence the development of British art. From the 1870s onwards, as Carol Dakers notes, Watts became one of the celebrity painters of the 'Holland Park circle', whose studio on Melbury Road, Kensington, was visited by the public and press on 'Show Sundays', prior to the annual Royal Academy Summer Exhibition; these attendees came to examine his new works as well as to see his working environment.[22] For similar inquisitive reasons, illustrated magazines and periodicals featured articles that combined engravings or photographs of Watts's works with biographical information about the man and access to his domestic life.[23]

Hall of celebrities

It was in Little Holland House that Watts began working on the collection of incisive portraits of the most eminent figures of the period that later became known as his *Hall of Fame*. The collection is an artistic equivalent to Prinsep's salon, and immortalised many of its visitors.[24] Watts's project and its ideals were frequently publicised, as was the fact that the collection would eventually become his gift to the nation. For example, on 25 May 1861, *The Athenaeum* announced:

> Mr. Watts has expressed his intention to leave to the nation, at his death, the valuable and interesting collection of contemporary portraits he has been for some years, and still is, forming. Among the persons who have sat to him from time to time may be named Mr. Tennyson, Sir John Lawrence, Mr. Layard, Mr. Holman Hunt, the Duke of Argyll, Mr. Gladstone and the Lord Chancellor.[25]

From the beginning, Watts's intention was to document his nation's present-day accomplishments and celebrate those 'great, earnest, sincere and courageous' Britons whose example would 'perpetuate noble and gracious lives'.[26] Seeking to inspire comparable future achievements, this enterprise reflected Watts's belief that art should have social significance and moral purpose and represented his fulfilment of what he regarded as his civic duty.[27] The scheme derived from the contemporary connection between heroism and social improvement, popularised by Thomas Carlyle's *On Heroes and Hero-Worship and the Heroic in History* (1841), and the idea that portraits of pre-eminent writers, artists, politicians, military leaders, social activists and philanthropists offered access to their exceptional personalities, and that these images were, therefore, morally and socially instructive.[28] To offer the nation 'historical records' of its 'worthies', 'individuals whose names will be connected with the future history of the age', Watts sought to ensure these portraits were 'inartificial & true as possible'.[29] Intensively concentrating on the faces and heads of his sitters, Watts aimed to create 'monumental' images, each of which was a 'summary of [a] life' that insisted 'upon the nobilities of the subject'.[30]

Like Carlyle's *On Heroes and Hero-Worship*, which mediated the public's new power to determine value and exceptionality by tempering it with historical precedence, Watts's *Hall of Fame* represents a direct intervention in celebrity culture. This project underlines that, as Juliette Atkinson has shown, hero worship was a 'congested notion' and that although there was 'a broad consensus that the nation would benefit from worshipping great men, there was a distinct lack of agreement about who these great men were'.[31] Watts's project seeks to re-connect public recognition with ability, achievement and value, counteracting a democratisation and adulteration of renown that had now become beholden to the marketplace and media, and their prioritisation of public personality, self-promotion and self-display, as well as their concomitant valorisation of the popular, ephemeral, sensational and scandalous.[32] Like other similar nineteenth-century visual projects such as *Portraits of Men of Eminence* (1863–67), and *Fraser's Magazine*'s 'A Gallery of Illustrious Literary Characters' (1830–38), Watts's *Hall of Fame* was representative of a pervasive 'fascination with social classification and order', and 'the nexus of national mythmaking and hero worship'.[33]

The individuals included in Watts's collection were, in general, contemporaries who corresponded to Carlyle's historical archetypes: the divine, the prophet, the poet, the priest, the man of letters and the king-politician. Unlike Carlyle, however, Watts is predicting and arbitrating which contemporary poets, intellectuals, politicians, military leaders and humanitarians should be remembered by posterity, certain, as he puts it, that 'the place the future would give [them] would be a very high one'.[34] To be asked to sit for Watts became the 'ultimate accolade of Victorian society' because Watts was performatively certifying that his sitter would survive 'in the minds and thoughts of [future generations], undying and imperishable'.[35] Although Watts was interested in 'any man who is known to the public' and insisted on researching each sitter's life before painting him or her, his choices for inclusion in the collection were partial and personal, revealing his own prejudices as well as larger cultural biases.[36] Pointedly, Watts excluded theatrical performers, sports stars, scientists, or those famous for their inimitable dress or personality.[37] He included only one musician, Joseph Joachim, and one novelist, George Meredith, who may have been there because of his poetry. These choices reverse a cultural trend that marginalised poetry in favour of the other arts, and also ignore two of the most famous and influential celebrities of the day, the novelist Charles Dickens and the actor-manager Henry Irving.[38] The implication is that those he excluded, despite having contemporary importance, were not representative heroes deserving everlasting fame. Although Watts painted many notable women of the period, including female celebrities such as Julia Margaret Cameron, Ellen and Kate Terry and Lillie Langtry, he officially included only one, the reformer Josephine Butler, in his fame collection.[39] This decision may be the result of the incompatibility between accepted practices of idealisation in female portraiture and his exacting technique; however, it may equally reflect Watts's attempt to counteract the growing influence of women on British society and the feminisation of fame and celebrity.[40]

Despite its reactionary conservatism, discriminatory intent and auspicious aspirations, Watts's *Hall of Fame* irresistibly participates in the dissemination and mediation of public personalities. By including portraits of John Everett Millais, Dante Gabriel Rossetti, Frederick Leighton and William Morris, Watts, self-interestedly, adds the artist to Carlyle's list of heroic types, as well as catering to a growing popular interest in the lives, personalities and physical appearances of contemporary artists.[41] These portraits, like that of the controversial poet Algernon Charles Swinburne, fed the media's demand for images of the most talked-about figures.[42] Once exhibited, reviewed and reproduced, and eventually photographed, in 1888, by Frederick Hollyer, Watts's portraits could only increase the public profile of his sitters.[43] Of those figures, such as Tennyson, Browning and Carlyle, whose images were already in cultural circulation, Watts provided another image, albeit a more penetrating one that was explicitly connected with posterity. Watts's 'fame' portraits complemented rather than competed with other images such as engravings, photographs or *cartes de visite*, confirming the importance of possessing visual representations of contemporaries whose historical importance was certain.[44] Except while part of an exhibition, then, Watts's 'worthies' were displayed, at first, in Little Holland House; and, from 1876 onwards, in the exhibition space in his Kensington studio known as 'The Little Holland House Gallery', where they could be seen by the public, free of charge, once a week.[45] Such was the level of their exposure that these portraits not only increased Watts's celebrity, but, according to Harry Quilter, writing in *The Times*, in 1882, they would be that upon which 'Mr Watts's future fame [would] chiefly rest'.[46] Watts's privileged access to his society's most prominent individuals not only authorised his right to, on behalf of the nation, immortalise them, but made him the successor to Britain's first celebrity painter, Joshua Reynolds.[47]

Although attempting to connect fame with great social or cultural accomplishments, Watts's *Hall of Fame* was always already a *Hall of Celebrities*. It is not, as Sidney Colvin suggested, in 1867, that Watts taught the public, despite its initial 'apathy', to appreciate portrait-painting, but that he, by providing 'insight into the character', 'feeling[s]' and inner truth of eminent figures, offered a celebrity-obsessed audience what it most desired.[48] In effect, the public was not merely shown what celebrated figures actually looked like up close; Watts was dismantling the distinction between private and public, and promoting and justifying ever-greater access to the famous. Watts's summary of his purpose and method implies that, for him, each portrait was the record of the artist's personal encounter with his famous sitter:

> in portrait-painting, when, while giving my mental faculties full play so as to seize my sitter's intellectual characteristics, I observe equally the physical minutiae. To assist myself, I converse with him, note his turn of thought, his disposition, and I try to find out by inquiry

or otherwise ... his character and so forth; and having made myself master of these details, I set myself to place them on the canvas, and so reproduce not only his face, but his character and nature.[49]

Engaging in a technique that anticipates that of the 'celebrity' interview as it emerged in the latter half of the century, Watts makes public what was once private, captures the immediate presence of his sitters and is interested in searching for their inner thoughts and representing their authentic selves.[50] Like later interviewers, Watts stresses the importance of his intimacy with his subjects, making it a prerequisite for his revelation of their minds, moods, thoughts and souls. Reflecting on his technique, Watts suggests that his portraits visually capture the space where artist and sitters met 'somewhere, somehow, where the barriers of individual self fell away'; here, his sitters 'talked to him as if to their own souls', 'look[ing] upon [him] as nobody', which meant, as one of his friends commented, Watts 'paint[ed] people alone, and with their best thoughts'.[51] As well as characterising the portraits as visual records of intimate interviews, these comments suggest that these pictures present the sitter's self-reflection and solitary contemplation. Watts, having mysteriously disappeared from the proceedings, captures likenesses that are equivalent to visual self-confessions. This associates his style of portraiture with unmediatedness, unselfconsciousness and naturalness rather than with affectation and posing; it also clarifies why, as one contemporary noted, Watts 'like[d] his sitters to move freely about and talk out their heart to him'.[52] By understating his presence and artistry, Watts emphasised the authenticity and artlessness of his portraits and the state of personal privacy that they depicted.

By externally representing the innermost thoughts, feelings and character of his sitters, Watts's portraits are biographically and visually intrusive in a manner that goes well beyond the moral or national benefit used to justify Victorian hero worship and biography.[53] Although flattered by being asked to pose for this national collection, some sitters complained about how Watts made them look, presumably commenting, in doing so, on what he had revealed about their character.[54] Carlyle, who so greatly influenced Watts's ideals of portraiture, told him, 'You have made me like a mad labourer'.[55] Perhaps he recognised, as G. K. Chesterton did, what Watts had captured in this portrait:

> there is a touch of something meagre and exhausted about the figure; upon every line of it is written that pathos that is worth a thousand excuses. The stroke of genius in the picture is the square

and emphatic treatment of the slant forward of the beard and chin; it is worth pages of psychological discussion on Carlyle's only basic fault, the almost pitiful eagerness to scorn.[56]

Similarly, another near contemporary saw in this work 'the direct impression of all the human fervour which dwelt in that most proud and most troubled spirit', suggesting that the 'touch of wildness in the reddish face', the 'intense eyes' and 'the prominent and rather bitter lips' gave the impression of one ready to let 'loose the thunders of his eloquence upon the crimes and follies of his age'.[57] These responses underline the way in which Watts's *Hall of Fame* transformed cultural heroes such as Carlyle into figures associated with self-revelation and self-expression, reversing the Carlylean ideal of the hero as an unself-conscious, self-forgetting individual, who resists public display, is oblivious to audience and has no interest in reputation or public opinion.[58] In this context, Watts's project draws attention to the unmentioned similarities between national 'worthies' and celebrities, and to the manner in which celebrity culture blurs the very types of distinction that Watts and Carlyle attempted to establish between public figures.[59]

Sharply differentiating his portraits from the realism of commercial photography, Watts stressed that he did not endeavour at 'representation[s] exactly like nature', but wanted his images to have 'a poetry and a mystery'.[60] His 1880 essay 'The Present Conditions of Art' clarified this ideal by arguing that 'it is art that corresponds to the highest literature, both in intention and effect, which must be demanded of our artists, poems painted on canvas, judged and criticised as are the poems written on paper'.[61] Denying 'any intention of presenting actual truth', Watts, instead, sought to create portraits that concealed as much as they revealed, infused with, what he called, a 'poetic element' that appealed to humanity's fascination with the 'mysterious' and inexplicable.[62] In this regard, his works are the transference of what he called the 'mesmeric influence possessed by individuals' to 'artistic productions', for he believed that '[w]ithout this quality they will be cold, and not breathing, and will not live always'.[63] Reviewers at the time commended Watts's presentation of his sitters' impenetrability, praising his attempt to avoid reducing individuals to social type and, instead, to connect greatness with uniqueness and mystery.[64] Arthur Symons, for example, writing in the *Fortnightly Review*, in 1900, praised the artist's ability to depict a 'brooding unconsciousness, coming up into the eyes and fixed there in all its restlessness; the inner mystery itself not the explaining away of that mystery'.[65] Such emphasis on these inexplicable qualities, on a variable rather than unchanging self-hood and on an interiority that remains finally unknowable, singular and impenetrable, of course, facilitates celebrity culture's obsessive endeavour to fathom such secret depths, which has been discussed in the previous chapter. Tapping into the notion of celebrities as absent-present figures, Watts's portraits make his distinguished contemporaries available and accessible, on the one hand, and elusive, inexplicable, and unreadable, on the other.[66] These portraits, going further than photographic ones, provided intimacy rather than accuracy; they were marked with traces of the personal and private contact between the artist and his celebrity sitters, and the complex intersubjectivity which that entailed. His portraits are not merely substitutes for personal encounters with the famous; they also validate and encourage the necessity of ever-closer intimacy with such figures.

The non-commercial and altruistic nature of Watts's portraiture, also, distinguished it from *cartes de visite* and commercial photography, when, as one commentator put it, the 'value of the human face was never tested to such an extent as it is at the present moment'.[67] In contrast to these traditional proliferators of celebrity, associated with the ephemerality and transience of what Walter Benjamin character-ises as aura-defying, mechanically reproduced images, Watts's portraits emphasised their uniqueness, historicity and permanence.[68] If having one's photographs for sale in a print-shop window meant celebrity, then, having Watts paint one's portrait ensured one's national and post-humous significance and participation in the much older tradition of fame.[69] It was not always certain, however, where Watts's 'legacy to [his] country' would be displayed, even though the ideals of his project were similar to those of the contemporaneously established National Portrait Gallery, founded in 1856.[70] The founding of a gallery that would include the 'likeness of persons eminent in British history' was force-fully endorsed by Carlyle, who underlined the importance of having the 'bodily likeness' of such personages, a 'sincere' portrait 'made by a faithful human creature, of that Face and Figure, which he saw with his eyes'.[71] Watts used his well-publicised *Hall of Fame* to position himself as just such a 'faithful' painter, anticipating the Gallery's eventual need for 'sincere' representations of contemporary individuals. The Gallery, however, could not exhibit any of Watts's portraits until each sitter's national significance was unquestionably established and he or she had been dead for at least ten years. It is testament to Watts's reputation that, beginning in 1883, the Gallery began accepting his portraits, at first sporadically, and, then, from 1896 onwards, in a more systematic way.

Portraits of the living were placed in storage until they metamorphosed into what one of the Gallery's directors, Lord Aberdare, tellingly categorised as 'portraits of deceased celebrities'.[72] The procedure underlines the fact that although oblivious to exactly where the nation would display their visages, his sitters were being confronted with their own mortality, knowing that the fame they were promised was 'the recompense not of the living, but of the dead'.[73] The nature and name of Watts's project drew explicit attention to portraiture's traditional function as both a means of cultural survival after death and a reminder of death, a *memento mori*.[74] This double function is reinforced by the mysterious absent-present quality that Watts ensured existed (and that contemporaries recognised) in each of his 'fame' portraits; this liminal quality, in addition, visually corresponds to the threshold position occupied by each sitter between living celebrity and posthumous fame.[75]

Hall of nonsense

While the *Hall of Fame* showcases portraits of exemplary figures to inspire comparable achievement and success, Lear's *A Book of Nonsense* overturns these ideals by exploring the pleasures and hazards of social malformation. This book celebrates a type of personal autonomy and independence that derives from or causes social peripherality, while simultaneously hinting at the often painful and frustrating practices of coercion and stigmatisation experienced by those who, like Lear, are or dare to be different.[76] *A Book of Nonsense*, first published in 1846, was an immediate success, going into nineteen editions in Lear's lifetime and establishing nonsense as a literary genre.[77] Instead of being didactic or moralistic, as was often the case with literature aimed at children, the book, as its first page stated, sought to make 'little folks merry' by allowing them to laugh at descriptions of the foolishness of adult figures, as well as to take delight in those who defy social restraints and limitations. Although early editions were published anonymously, from 1861 onwards all editions included Lear's name, so that, as he explained, he could have 'all the credit due to [him], small as that may be'.[78] In his preface to *More Nonsense, Pictures, Rhymes, Botany, Etc.* (1872), the second of his three subsequent books, Lear expresses his delight at his newfound success, but also seeks to quash rumours that suggested he was not the sole author of *A Book of Nonsense*.[79] As an example of such rumours, Lear recounts an incident that happened to him on a train from London to Guildford. During the journey, one of Lear's fellow passengers, on seeing two boys reading *A Book of Nonsense*, remarked, 'all children and parents too ought to be [grateful] to the statesman who has given his time to composing that charming book!' [80] Although other commuters asserted that Edward Lear was the author of the verses, the man insisted that the Earl of Derby wrote the book and that 'There [was] no such a person at all as Edward Lear'.[81] To settle the matter, Lear revealed his identity to his fellow travellers, showing them his hat, handkerchiefs and letters, all of which contained his name, to prove his claim. The preface includes an illustration featuring Lear, in one of his most accurate self-portraits, confronting the sceptical man, who resembles one of the characters from Lear's nonsense verse.[82] Lear reveals what he looks like so as to ensure readers recognise him and to prevent any similar confusion. Moreover, in so far as it concerns the establishment of public identity, the anecdote draws attention to an important, although as yet unexplored, theme of *A Book of Nonsense*, namely, its concern with the construction of notability or localised reputation. In this regard, Lear's verses and their accompanying illustrations are his responses to a culture of heroism typified by Watts's *Hall of Fame*; they uncover contradictions and fault lines in the workings of celebrity culture. His nonsense, however, also replicates his social milieu's reifying tendencies and increasing preoccupation with models of social failure and personal imperfection.

Lear never called the verses in *A Book of Nonsense* limericks, but did refer to them as his 'Old Persons', suggesting the possibility that each verse and illustration combine to create a type of portrait.[83] Typically, these 'portraits' depict an anonymous figure, who is identified as either young or old and sometimes as male or female; and who usually either comes from a particular place, has an unconventional appearance or displays a curious temperament. A majority of these 'portraits', unlike those of Watts, however, do not focus solely on one figure; instead, they describe and visually represent eccentric behaviour and its comic, absurd and, sometimes, unfortunate results, before passing judgement on the case. Whereas Watts's project, in line with celebrity culture more generally, foregrounds personalities rather than accomplishments and conceals the complex process of communal mediation and arbitration, Lear's nonsense reverses this trajectory. If Watts narrows and intensifies portraiture's focus on the faces and heads of the exemplary, Lear widens the focus to visually and verbally locate 'special' individuals within their communities. Each of his 'portraits' shows an often nebulous or absurd activity and its communal consequences and adjudication, all the while underlining the utter incomprehensibility of the 'Old Person' involved. In this regard, as Edward Strachey noted in 1888, Lear's nonsense brings

Figure 2.1   Edward Lear, 'There was an Old Lady of Chertsey', *Nonsense Books* (Boston: Little, Brown, 1888), p. 7

'confusion into order by setting things upside down'; encourages 'all sorts of unnatural, impossible, and absurd, but not painful or danger-ous, combinations'; highlights 'the incongruities of all things within and without us'; and causes a 'discomfiture of Sense by Nonsense'. [84] A representative example of Lear's nonsense portraiture, therefore, depicts the creation of an individual's communal reputation through retrospective hearsay:

> There was an Old Lady of Chertsey,
> Who made a remarkable curtsey;
> She twirled round and round, till she sunk underground,
> Which distressed all the people of Chertsey.

(p. 161)

In this poem, the 'remarkable curtsey' and its distressing consequences are what characterise this 'Old Lady'; the illustration (Figure. 2.1), sup-plementing this description, shows the woman enigmatically smiling as she sinks into the ground and at least one bemused observer among the distressed people of Chertsey. Although frequently showing the perversity and foolishness of such figures, Lear's nonsense implicitly foregrounds the mysteriousness of those willing to disregard decorum and etiquette. Despite the possible distress their actions cause, Lear's 'Old Persons' are champions of unselfconsciousness who inexplicably, obstinately and, occasionally, disastrously, act out their own private compulsions, challenge convention and defy oppressive or stringent rules. As one 1888 reviewer noted:

[a] lasting charm which breathes through the book is the gallant spirit of so many of the characters, and their noble disregard of any of those inconveniences which ensue upon the indulgence of personal eccentricity. ... [The verses] are instances of a great spirit of independence.[85]

Lear's hall of perplexing anti-heroes, unnamed oddballs, misfits and social outsiders, thus, makes idiosyncrasy a badge of valour and unusual physical features, which might otherwise be a cause of shame or feelings of inadequacy, signs of distinctiveness.

In Lear's nonsense, even those who enchant and please others through conventional accomplishments such as lyre playing and dancing are highly ambiguous figures:

> There was a Young Lady of Tyre,
> Who swept the loud chords of a lyre;
> At the sound of each sweep, she enraptured the deep,
> And enchanted the city of Tyre.

> (p. 83)

> There was an Old Person of Filey,
> Of whom his acquaintance spoke highly;
> He danced perfectly well, to the sound of a bell,
> And delighted the people of Filey.

> (p. 361)

All we know about these entertaining personalities is that their activities enrapture and delight. The illustrations to these verses increase the inscrutability of these figures by visually de-centring them: the first image, as well as showing the 'Young Lady', shows the lyre that she plays with a broom; the second presents the 'Old Person' dancing beside a delighted representative of Filey. Whereas Watts foregrounds his careful depictions of the physical appearances of his worthies, making these images conduits to their personalities and inner natures, Lear elucidates the reactions and adjudication of the community or audience rather than the nature of the mysterious, unnamed individuals, who remain indecipherable. Although Watts's works and writings emphasise the importance of preserving and cultivating inscrutability in the representation of cultural heroes, some of Lear's nonsense, perhaps more accurately, highlights the manner in which human mystery exacerbates the traditional conflict between the individual and the community. In this regard, Lear shows that mystifying individuality can frustrate as well as fascinate:

> There was an Old Person of Deal
> Who in walking, used only his heel;
> When they said, 'Tell us why'? – he made no reply;
> That mysterious Old Person of Deal.

(p. 331)

> There was an Old Person of Burton,
> Whose answers were rather uncertain;
> When they said, 'How d'ye do?' he replied, 'Who are you?'
> That distressing Old Person of Burton.

(p. 78)

Combining independence, inexplicability and exceptionality, Lear's figures frequently trouble and perplex those who represent conventionality, consensus and public opinion, referred to in the poems as 'they'. 'They' observe and comment on the eccentricity and peculiarity of the 'Old Persons', sometimes offering help, but often mocking and ostracising them.[86] These powerful arbitrators of correct behaviour, also, occasionally suppress social transgression using violence:

> There was an Old Man of Whitehaven,
> Who danced a quadrille with a Raven;
> But they said, – 'It's absurd to encourage this bird!'
> So they smashed that Old Man of Whitehaven.

(p. 172)

Depicting the earlier moment before the violent attack, the illustration (Figure. 2.2) of this verse shows the smiling man and the bird dancing; this portrait emphasises the danger faced by those who provoke controversy by being 'absurd'. Lear's description of this 'Old Man' being 'smashed' for his eccentricity shows, again, the communal dislike of inexplicable individuality and preference for conformity. Here, Lear points to the incongruous way his society encourages and valorises exceptionality, while simultaneously seeking to curb and shape it; and the manner in which his culture privileges and promotes uniqueness only to censure it. This nonsense identifies the arbitrary, inconsistent and absurd way public identity is established; the establishment of recognition and

Figure 2.2   Edward Lear, 'There was an Old Man of Whitehaven', *Nonsense Books* (Boston: Little, Brown, 1888), p. 44

fame has less to do with honouring individual personalities, and more to do with whether these figures enthral, distress or enrage those with the power to establish, preserve and judge social identity and communal reputation. Viewed in this context, Watts's 'distinguished men' (and other celebrities of the period) are praiseworthy and exceptional only because they are always already exemplary archetypes that reproduce society's standards and conventions. The individuality and distinctiveness Watts commends are merely examples of thinly disguised conformity and uniformity; in contrast, Lear shows that often the truly individualistic figures within a society are ostracised rather than being reputed for their defiant and baffling peculiarity.

The quirks, follies and deformities of Lear's 'Old Persons' may seem antithetical to features of Victorian celebrity, but, in media terms, his portraits of eccentrics from various national and international locations correspond to verbal and visual caricatures in Victorian newspapers and periodicals, which were used to produce and confirm racial and national stereotypes. [87] Lear's texts, however, function differently by blurring the line between normalcy and apartness, showing the omnipresence and universality of foolishness and deficiency, as well as the negative and positive sides of nonconformity, about which Lear knew all too well. Lear's nonsense, therefore, more specifically, is a manifestation of the cultural formation that popularised freak shows; it taps into Victorian culture's growing fascination with physical, mental or behavioural abnormality, and its transformation of 'freaks' into recognisable and much-discussed figures. At this time, as Erin O'Connor notes:

> Deformity stood out in a world increasingly orientated around mechanization and routine. Every freak was unique, irreducible, intractable; freakish flesh was marvelously impractical, totally outside the automated logic of efficiency that molded the bodies of 'normals' into standardized patterns of behavior. Owning themselves by selling themselves, freaks straddled the boundary between body and commodity by marketing their own misshapenness.[88]

The publication of Lear's first book of nonsense coincides with the cultural moment in Britain when defect and deformity had marketability, and monstrosity had become a profession. This offers a new way of thinking about Lear's frequent representations of physical misshapenness, for example, in the following quite typical poem:

> There was an Old Man with a nose,
> Who said, 'If you choose to suppose
> That my nose is too long, you are certainly wrong!'
> That remarkable Man with a nose.

(p. 158)

The illustration (Figure. 2.3) that accompanies this verse is highly ambivalent, presenting as it does other figures, possibly children, who are either using the Old Man's nose as a skipping rope, or being forced to jump out of the way of his enormous nose. Lear's portrait suggests that the Old Man is 'remarkable' and his nose is not 'too long' because the true significance and real consequences of his abnormality remain undecidable. This calls to mind a nineteenth-century culture 'preoccupied with normativity, [in which] the spectacle of human oddity – either on stage or in fiction – presents a puzzle'.[89] Lear's work evokes the reality of a historical moment in which confusing bodies were commodified to produce profit, 'freakery' created a 'volatile interpretative space' that could challenge 'notions of normalcy', and performers in freak shows gained a level of celebrity.[90] The commemoration of the foibles, faults or physical imperfections in

Figure 2.3   Edward Lear, 'There was an Old Man with a Nose', *Nonsense Books* (Boston: Little, Brown, 1888), p. 3

Lear's work, unexpectedly, imitates those mechanisms of celebrity culture that reify unusual individuals, transforming them into objects of spectacle and display.

Picturing Tennyson

In the same way that Lear and Watts offered diverse responses to celebrity culture, they also left very different representations of Tennyson. Lear greatly admired Tennyson's poems and illustrating them became one of the central missions of his life; however, he grew increasingly ambivalent about the poet himself. In contrast, Watts revered Tennyson, honouring and memorialising him in iconic visual works that also became testimonies to the two men's ever-closer personal relationship. In addition, Lear hated the atmosphere of adulation and worship that followed Tennyson to his Freshwater retreat, whereas Watts was a central player in the transference of mainland celebrity culture to the Isle of Wight. Lear first met Tennyson, in June 1849, through their mutual friends the Lushingtons.[91] There is no extant evidence that Lear, who once turned his request to Tennyson for an autograph into an illustrated joke, was ever, strictly speaking, in awe of the poet.[92] In a December 1852 letter to Emily Tennyson, enclosed with a belated wedding gift of his two-volume *Illustrated Excursions in Italy* (1846), Lear made it clear where his passion lay. He tells Emily that the poems bring him pleasure 'quite beyond reckoning' and that 'There have been but few weeks or days within the last 8 years, that I have not been more or less in the habit of remembering or reading Tennyson's poetry'.[93] Having just finished reading Lear's *Journals of a Landscape Painter in Albania & c.* (1851) and greatly admiring its 'beautiful drawings' that showed 'something of the glory of nature', Tennyson publicly acknowledged his approbation in his poem 'To E. L. on his Travels in Greece'.[94] First published in the eighth edition of *The Poems of Alfred Tennyson* (1853), the poem, particularly its first two stanzas, demonstrates the effect of Lear's illustrations on Tennyson:

> Illyrian woodlands, echoing falls
> Of water, sheets of summer glass,
> The long divine Peneïan pass,
> The vast Akrokeraunian walls,
>
> Tomohrit, Athos, all things fair,
> With such a pencil, such a pen,
> You shadow forth to distant men
> I read and felt that I was there. [95]

As recent critics have noted, the poem does not explicitly show Tennyson's actual engagement with the narrative of Lear's journey and, actually, reduces the unsettling and perplexing realities of a foreign expedition to a romanticised vision; this choice reflects Tennyson's own general preference for virtual rather than actual travel.[96] Considering Tennyson's fame at this point, however, this poem publicises (and advertises) Lear's work as not merely a generic travel guide in an already saturated marketplace, but one that contained drawings with the power to convey readers imaginatively, as stanza three asserts, to 'classic ground' and the 'golden age'.

Such admiration surely encouraged and validated Lear's desire, about which he confided to Emily Tennyson, in 1852, to create 'poetic illustrations' of her husband's works which would demonstrate that the poet's

> descriptions of certain spots are as positively true as if drawn from the places themselves, & that his words have the power of calling up images as distinct & correct as if they were written from those images, instead of giving rise to them.[97]

Rather than leaving reminiscences testifying to his intimacy with the poet, as other friends did, Lear left, at the time of his death, over 200 illustrations that demonstrated his painstaking engagement with

Tennyson's poetry. In the same letter, he told Emily that 'no one could illustrate Tennysons [*sic*] landscape lines & feelings more aptly than' him and that others had failed to recognise the poet's 'genius for the perception of the beautiful in landscape'.[98] Unlike other contemporary illustrators who, in general, foregrounded Tennyson's characters, registering the commonplace admiration of the poet's powers of characterisation and his representation of subjective states, Lear's 'Landscape Illustrations of Tennyson' de-personalised the poetry and primarily used human figures to 'suggest the scale and strangeness of some exotic, distant location'.[99] Offsetting another trend, discussed in the previous chapter, Lear's work was not concerned with identifying the topography that inspired Tennyson, but with depicting exotic landscapes that the poet had never seen, yet which his poetry 'call[ed] up' owing to his powerful imagination. Not only was Lear doing something that was original, he was showing his skills as a landscape illustrator by creating art that derived from clear aesthetic principles rather than being produced, like so much of his work, quickly and out of economic necessity.[100] There is no evidence that Tennyson, who usually disliked the illustrations that accompanied his poems, appreciated Lear's work; he, on one occasion, remarked, 'it is the human beings that ought to have the real interest for us in a dramatic picture'.[101] Unfortunately, when a selection of these illustrations was published in a limited edition, in 1889, a year after Lear's death, the reviews were less than favourable; one suggested that the illustrations proved that Lear was 'no great artist' and another hinted that it was Tennyson's agreement to sign each copy of the book which ensured its publication.[102]

As well as illustrating Tennyson's poetry, Lear left verbal reminiscences that picture Tennyson and Freshwater in a specific way. At first, Lear was drawn to Freshwater as a place he associated with seclusion and creativity, and because of his burgeoning friendship with the Tennysons, in particular with Emily. In 1855, he asked Tennyson if there was a 'Pharmouse or a Nin somewhere near you, where there would be a big room looking to the North? – so that I could paint in it quietly, & come & see you & Mrs. Tennyson promiscuously?'[103] Freshwater, for Lear, is the antithesis of, what he goes on to call, 'Anglosaxnland' [Lear's spelling], which puts restrictions on artists and encourages their 'utter idleness'. The letter implies that Lear's time among and dependence on the economic and cultural elite in London has been detrimental to his artistic faculties and left him feeling disgusted at the wasting of his time and talent. Although not strictly speaking one of the 'men of mark or name' whom Anne Thackeray Ritchie remembers visiting Freshwater for 'rest and change from serious preoccupations', Lear, like them, found it restorative, and would have heartily concurred with her comments about Farringford:

> I can hardly imagine Eden itself a sweeter garden, more sunny and serene, than Farringford. From Eden, as we know, there was no sight of the sea, but from Farringford all day long, and by moonlit nights, you may watch the distant waters, beating time to the natural life in the green glades round the Poet's house.[104]

The pleasure Lear derived from his stays at Farringford in the 1850s left him with what he termed 'heavy post-happiness depression' because he liked it 'better than any other place I know'.[105] During these years, the poet and, in particular, his wife became two of the most important people in Lear's life; he tells Emily, in 1856, 'Forgetting you or Alfred or Faringford [*sic*] is always a fiddlededeeism & impossible'.[106] While at Farringford, Lear delighted the family and his fellow guests with performances of the musical settings he had created for Tennyson's poems including 'Edward Gray', 'Tears, Idle Tears' and *Maud*.[107] Lear's recitals even pleased the fastidious poet, who praised them in 'eulogistic terms' and said they 'seem[ed] to throw a diaphanous veil over the word – nothing more'; on hearing Lear perform *Maud*, Tennyson exclaimed 'Lear, you have revealed more of my Maud to myself!'[108] These reminiscences clarify Lear's reputation as being entertaining company and explain why, during his time in England, he was never short of invitations to social gatherings, even if he didn't always accept them.

If, at first, Lear's Freshwater was an Edenic location, he, unlike others, took no delight in its transformation, in the 1860s, into a place where 'there are nothing but poets and painters everywhere' and where such geniuses were conspicuously worshipped and pursued, and, by implication, distracted from their creative endeavours.[109] Lear's diary entries at this time indicate his great sadness and frustration at the way Tennyson and Freshwater became embroiled in the transplantation of aspects of celebrity culture to the island. These changes were epitomised and heralded by the arrival on the island of Julia Margaret Cameron. During Lear's 1860 visit, he complains about the interference of Tennyson's new neighbour, of the way Cameron transformed a 'pleasant & quiet' place into one of 'odious incense palaver & fuss'.[110] After a few days of this commotion, Lear records, 'believe that this is my last visit to Faringford [*sic*]: – nor can I wish it otherwise all things considered'.[111] During later visits Lear is as horrified by the way the island is being spoilt by new houses, a 'monster hotel and the prospect of a railway', as by the fact that 'Pattledom has taken entire possession of the place' and turned Cameron's Freshwater home, Dimbola, into 'Holland-Park-by-the-sea'.[112] In other diary entries from the 1860s, Lear underlined problematic aspects of Tennyson's nature that manifested themselves in his insensitive treatment of others, particularly of his wife and sons.[113] As Ann Thwaite notes, 'Edward Lear's diary is a source of some of the most revealing, uncensored observation of the Tennysons' marriage, as Lear became increasingly worried by the thought of an angelic wife slaving away – as he saw it – for an unappreciative husband'.[114] Lear's comments on his growing animosity towards Tennyson are concomitant with his assertions of his devotion to Emily, whom he regarded as 'certainly one of the most utterly morally perfect women I have yet seen'.[115] One incident that captures Lear's growing dislike of Tennyson also reflects the latter's growing paranoia about, and dislike of, his adoring public's ever-increasing intrusions into his private life. In his diary, Lear notes that while walking on the downs with the poet and their mutual friend Franklin Lushington, Tennyson became 'disagreeably querulous & irritating' 'chiefly because he saw people approaching'; Tennyson forced his friends to change their route to avoid 'his horror – the villagers coming from church'. Lear adds sarcastically, 'Verily this is a wondrous man – of dreamy sweet words'.[116] During later visits, Lear, again, sharply contrasts the poet and his poems; in 1864, he writes, 'I supposed it is the anomaly of high souled & philosophical writings combined with slovenliness, selfishness & morbid folly that prevents my being happy there', and, a year later, concludes 'I would he were his poems'.[117] In these verbal portraits of the poet, Lear, like others, realised that, as Henry James puts it, 'Tennyson is not personally Tennysonian'.[118]

During the period in which Lear grew to dislike his visits to Freshwater, Watts became a frequent visitor there and was a key participant in this atmosphere of adulation, obsequiousness and show that Lear abhorred. The presence of 'Pattledom' in Freshwater had its origins in Tennyson's frequent visits to Little Holland House in the late 1850s, visits which marked the pinnacle of Sara Prinsep's lion-hunting.[119] One observer, Adelaide Sartoris, complained that the salon was a 'menagerie of which Alfred Tennyson is still royal lion and King of beasts', and described the 'ladies of the family all attired like so many rope dancers, in various altitudes of ecstasy about all that they don't understand the first letter of – it's very funny once in a way – but I couldn't go there often now'.[120] It was in this 'Enchanted Palace' that Watts first met Tennyson.[121] Many visitors to the salon regarded the men as comparable figures who were worshipped in a similarly excessive way. Effie Gray and John Everett Millais, for instance, were disgusted by the 'Tennyson and Watts-worship'; Julia Margaret Cameron would, in the same breath, introduce Tennyson as 'the greatest living poet' and Watts as 'the greatest living painter'; and John Ruskin regarded them as the two prized lions in Prinsep's collection.[122] During this period, Watts created his first two portraits of Tennyson, tapping into a growing public demand to see the face of the Poet Laureate, but also the Tennysons' desire to have an accurate image that would counter the erroneous ones already in circulation.[123] The second of Watts's portraits of Tennyson (rather than the first, less pleasing one) would allow, Emily Tennyson told her husband, 'people to see something truer to thee' 'after all the horrible slanders of thy face', and the poet consented to the exhibition and engraving of the painting.[124] In order to capture Tennyson's essence, Watts used his trademark 'interview' style, encouraging the reticent poet to speak about himself. In turn, Watts explained his technique, which the poet incorporated into 'Lancelot and Elaine', the section of *Idylls of the King* he was composing at the time, to describe Elaine's all-encompassing fascination with Sir Lancelot:

> And all night long his face before her lived,
> As when a painter, poring on a face,
> Divinely thro' all hindrance finds the man
> Behind it, and so paints him that his face,
> The shape and colour of a mind and life,
> Lives for his children, ever at its best
> And fullest.[125]

The lines capture Tennyson's growing awareness of being 'the observed of all observers' at Little Holland House and of the level of scrutiny his famous face had begun to receive.[126] Yet, anticipating one aspect of the interpretation of this idyll in Chapter 6, Tennyson's association of Watts with Elaine may hint at the poet's initial, and perhaps correct, view of the painter as a devoted fan rather than a fellow lion. At this time, the two men occupied very different positions outside Little Holland House: while Watts was a respected painter worshipped within an elite circle, Tennyson was a nationally and internationally renowned poet. Despite Watts's devotion to Tennyson, when the poet complained at the salon about the Pre-Raphaelite illustrations for the 1857 Moxon edition of his works, Watts, along with Ruskin, reprimanded him. Watts told Tennyson that 'no good painter could be subservient at all; but must conceive everything in his own way – that no poems ought to be illustrated at all – but if they were – the poet must be content to have his painter in partnership – not a slave'.[127] Defending his own profession, Watts's comment suggests his intention of making his relationship with Tennyson more symmetrical.

During the early 1860s, Watts achieved his goal and the friendship between the two men was visually sealed by a series of portraits: one of Emily, one of Tennyson's sons, Hallam and Lionel and two almost identical portraits of the poet.[128] As a result, when the lease for Little Holland House expired in 1871, Tennyson asked Watts to 'come to Freshwater and live near me at Farringford', and the painter acquiesced, building a house there, the Briary, which was completed in 1873.[129] The iconic 1864 portrait of Tennyson which was included in Watts's *Hall of Fame* is a testament to the painter's unique access to a poet who was becoming increasingly protective of his own privacy and disliked the whole process of sitting for paintings and, often, the resulting images.[130] Like other portraits in the *Hall of Fame*, this one offers an incisive representation of the poet's head and face, but, unusually for one of the paintings in this collection, it also presents a noticeable background of laurel leaves and the sea. While the sea evokes and even publicises the idyllic Freshwater setting that had become so inextricably associated with the poet, the use of laurel leaves may hint at the Freshwater circle's investment in older or classical forms of fame. Watts's Tennyson, then, is not merely a man of contemporary reputation and public celebrity, but the poet who embodies the elusive and mysterious creativity to which the painter aspired. So, whereas Robert Browning is presented as a contemporary man who has written great poetry, Tennyson, as the critic Chesterton notes, has 'a symbolic green and blue of the eternal sea and the eternal laurels. He has behind him the bays of Dante and he is wrapped in the cloak of the prophets'.[131] The image perpetuates and popularises the idea of Tennyson as 'a lordly and conscious bard', who has assumed the 'stately and epic position' of being 'a poet in person, in post and circumstance and conception of life' and of being a 'recognized and public figure'.[132] In other words, Tennyson is already part of the European tradition of great men to which Watts sought to belong; he is the archetypal poet whose exceptionality and excellence, therefore, deserve a special type of appreciation beyond that given to the other figures in this collection.[133] In Tennyson, Watts presumably saw a reflection of his emerging conception of himself as a 'poet-artist' who uses the physical and concrete to symbolise the metaphysical and inexplicable.[134] The portraits also signify Watts's intertwining of his own cultural fate with that of Tennyson and his related wish to protect *his* visual Tennyson from other rival versions. This is evident in an undated letter to Julia Margaret Cameron from this period, in which he thanked her for her photographs of Tennyson; suggesting that some were magnificent, while criticising others, he reminded her, 'Do justice to the noble and beautiful head, the finest you will ever have before your lens'.[135]

In 1891, a year before Tennyson's death, Watts again painted two nearly identical portraits of Tennyson. During the sittings, these two equally famous men spoke about the perils of celebrity, agreeing that personal vulnerability and 'intrusions were but the cost of fame'. To Tennyson's remark, 'I wish I had never written a line in my life', Watts replied, 'Ah, now you would not have made your Arthur speak like that!'[136] Provocatively, the *Daily Graphic* printed an illustration featuring Tennyson posing for Watts entitled 'The Choice and Master Spirits of this Age', which underlined the cultural partnership of the two men.[137] The image represents an intrusion on the intimacy and privacy of these public figures, but also makes visible the type of intimate contact and personal encounter that was central to Watts's technique as a portraitist. After Tennyson's death, when it was proposed that a statue should be created in his honour, Watts underlined his unique credentials for the task, having 'known the poet so well' and having had the 'grand figure of his friend' so often 'visibly before his eyes'.[138] As with his visual representations of other exceptional individuals, his paintings of Tennyson did not merely honour the poet, but also existed to create cultural aspiration and inspire comparable future achievement. In other words, Watts wanted viewers of these images to be transformed from spectators into 'worthies', believing that art, like great poetry, through 'a kind of hypnotism' could elevate the observer and stimulate emulation.[139] Despite mythologising and glorifying Tennyson and his work, Watts encouraged viewers to look past the poet, literally, by placing laurel leaves in the background of his 1864 and 1891 Tennyson portraits. Whereas Lear explicitly looked beyond Tennyson to his inspirational poetry, Watts saw in the poet an embodiment of the celebrity he had already achieved and the posthumous fame he believed lay ahead.

Images of thwarted worship

Tennyson did not only stimulate Lear's and Watts's visual creativity; the lure of the poet and his Freshwater retreat also shaped other aspects of these men's lives and works. One factor that impacted on Lear's friendship with the Tennysons and his love of Farringford was their association with Franklin Lushington. There is undeniable evidence that Lushington was the great love of Lear's life and that this platonic friendship was an important and enduring aspect of both men's lives. To say with certainty that Lear was, or believed himself to be, homosexual, however, represents a departure from available biographical evidence.[140] What is apparent is that Lear's passionate feelings for this man were channelled through his close friendship with Emily Tennyson. Lear first met Lushington in 1849 in Malta, where the latter's brother Henry was Chief Secretary to the government. Several years younger than Lear and Cambridge-educated, Lushington accompanied Lear on his travels to Corinth, Athens, Attica, Thebes, Parnassus and Delphi; they parted in Patras.[141] In one letter written during these travels, Lear describes the colours of Greek spring for his sister Ann: the 'mile of bright scarlet ground, then half a mile of blue or pale pink – but it is difficult for you to realise that the whole earth is like a rich Turkey carpet'.[142] He, then, mentions the way he and Lushington, who are 'equally fond of flowers', 'gather them all day like children, & when we have stuck our hats & coats & horses all over with them – it is time to throw them away, & get a new set'. For a man who preferred travelling alone, it is particularly significant that Lear calls his friend 'the most merry and kind travelling companion', and adds, 'I am very sorry he is obliged to return to England'; in fact, Lear laments that these, 'the most delightful 6 weeks', went 'a great deal too quickly'.[143] If this friendship made these the happiest weeks of Lear's life, then alterations to the dynamics of the relationship in subsequent years caused Lear much sadness and frustration. During visits to the Lushington family's Maidstone home, Park House, in the 1850s, Lear found a silent and taciturn man, a man very different from the exuberant one with whom he had travelled in Greece. It was not that Lushington changed once he landed on English soil, but that his natural reserve was intensified by the extreme sorrow that engulfed his family during this period, events which culminated in the death of his brother Henry in August 1855. Around this time, Lear hinted at his intense feelings for Lushington to another close male friend, Chichester Fortescue, who recorded the following in his diary that autumn: '[Lear] spoke to me more of himself & his secret feelings than he has ever done – showed me a good deal of his great & self-tormenting sensitiveness'.[144] The other person to whom Lear confided about Lushington was Emily Tennyson, who encouraged him to support Franklin during this time of family crisis, despite the inhospitable behaviour of the other Lushingtons.[145] Implicitly comparing his male friendship and her marriage, Emily confessed to Lear about her feelings of loneliness during her husband's frequent trips to London. She further validates the importance of Lear's friendship by telling him, 'I have a dim sad feeling that we must help each other, those who at all understand each other and love each other', and adds, 'you are not to be always "alone" and you must now sympathise prophetically with me'.[146] Seemingly unperturbed by the intensity of Lear's affection for his friend, in October of 1855, Emily invited the two men to Farringford, informing Lear that he must be 'wellest and freshest and happiest'; Lear obliged and during the visit sang his settings to Tennyson's poems for 'two or three hours'.[147]

In a letter to Emily after the visit, Lear compares his time at Farringford with the period he spent in Greece with Lushington; for example, he describes the journey back from Yarmouth to Lymington as the 'most quiet & pleasant' since their journey from 'Lepanto to Patras'.[148] Telling Emily: 'The three or four days 16 October – 20 October 1855 were the best I have passed for many a long day', he presents Freshwater as a paradise of great beauty with 'rare flashes of light' – 'bright blue & green landscape with purple hills, & winding rivers, & unexplored forests, and airy downs, & trees & birds, & all sorts of calm repose'. Unable to stop thinking of Farringford 'at all times & seasons', he plays back certain moments during the visit: 'I see everything – even to the plate of Mushrooms: then Hallam & Lionel come in, – & when they are gone, you, Alfred & Frank begin to talk like Gods together careless of mankind: – & so on, all through the day'. In the company of his favourite poet, the woman he idolised as a saint, and the young man he passionately loved, Lear is transformed into a god among other deities.

The scene and the entire visit seem to suggest that this household, the embodiment of Victorian decorum and respectability, was a cultural space, like many others in the period, which facilitated and validated the compatibility of passionate male friendship and marital domesticity.[149] Developing this notion, Lear imagines growing old near the Tennysons and the Lushingtons, and being able to 'sometimes see by turns Hallam & Lionel's children, & Frank's grandchildren' and having them 'come & see [him]'.[150] Lear's words evoke recurring themes of his nonsense songs and lyrics that reflect his longing for domesticity and intimacy and communal belonging, and his simultaneous desire for detachment, distance and exile.[151] In the same letter, Lear also reminds Emily of his decision to accompany Lushington to Corfu, where Lushington was taking up a post as a judge of the Supreme Court of Justice of the Ionian

Islands, calling it a 'new beginning of life'.[152] A month earlier, however, Lear didn't know what to do because, as he told Holman Hunt, 'The most intimate friend I have in the world is just going to leave England entirely'.[153] On 17 November, three days before his departure for Corfu, Emily reassured Lear, 'You are not alone, Mr. Lear, you cannot be while you can be so much to those so very dear to you, to those to whom so few are anything but the mere outside world. But one would be all, and, in that one cannot be, here is the loneliness'.[154] Although ambiguous, her words, 'that one cannot be', suggest that, from her perspective, his powerful feelings for Lushington, although not sinful or deviant, were causing his loneliness by preventing him from becoming attached to a suitable female companion.[155]

Lear's time in Corfu was one of the lowest points in his life; he felt dejected and totally alone, mainly owing to the growing distance between himself and Lushington, who was very busy with his new appointment. Their relationship further deteriorated and caused Lear much grief and even subsequent visits to Farringford could not, as Emily hoped, relieve his 'sadness' and, certainly, never lived up to the earlier joyous one.[156] During his last visit to Farringford with Lushington, in 1860, Lear used the following lines to encapsulate his sense that their friendship had irrevocably changed: 'We come no more to the golden shore, where we danced in days of old'.[157] Lear repeats these lines on several different occasions between June 1860 and October 1862, as his relationship with and feelings for Lushington became less intense, owing partly to Lushington's marriage in January 1862 and to Lear's realisation after one visit to his friend that 'a fanatical = frantic caring overmuch for those who care little for us, is a miserable folly. And after all ordinary natural pride revolts at selfish coldness'.[158] Although Lear and Lushington remained lifelong friends – Lear acting as a godparent to all of Lushington's children, and Lushington, eventually, acting as executor to Lear's estate – these lines associate the changed nature of their friendship with Lear's unhappiness about the transformation of his Freshwater paradise. In fact, his first use of these lines occurs in the same diary entry in which he laments the arrival of Julia Margaret Cameron to the island. Provocatively, Lear's imagery echoes that of lines from the last stanza of an early poem by Tennyson entitled 'Anacaona', which describes the aftermath of the intrusion and colonisation of an island paradise where the natives are 'never more upon the shore / Dancing at the break of day'.[159]

On 19 October 1864, Lear offered the following summary of recent changes in Freshwater: 'Camerons and Prinseps [are] building everywhere.

Watts in a cottage (not Mrs. W.)'.[160] His comment suggests the topicality of the subject of Watts's recent marriage, on 20 February 1864, to the actress Ellen Terry, who was thirty years his junior. A few weeks after their marriage, in early March, the couple, accompanied by Sara and Thoby Prinsep, visited Freshwater and stayed with the Camerons at Dimbola. At this time in particular, Freshwater offered Watts and his young wife, as it did Tennyson and others, a place of refuge from aspects of urban celebrity culture. Here, they found a sanctuary from the 'ribald speculation' in the press, for whom 'There was something lip-smacking in the idea of quivering old men – and the frail hypochondriac Watts looked even older than he was – violating beautiful children'.[161] If, for Lear, Freshwater symbolised, at first, the brief retrieval of a friendship, and, later, its loss and recollection, then for Watts, it was the location of more than merely thwarted worship. For, once on the island, the isolation of the place italicised problems within his marriage, problems that would culminate seven months later in his being noticeably alone in this idyllic setting, causing the kind of scandal and gossip of which Lear's comment is representative. Within only a few months of the couple's first visit to the island, Watts began attending social gatherings without his wife, and Terry, in turn, frequently ran away from their marital home, Little Holland House. The legal document, which formally separated them on 26 January 1865, cited the reason as 'incompatibility of temper', to which Terry added, later in her memoir, 'Truer still would have been "incompatibility of *occupation*," and the interference of well-meaning friends'.[162]

Yet, the incongruity of the match was apparent from the beginning: attending Watts and Terry's marriage, Lady Constance Leslie recorded the 'painful' contrast between the 'atrabilious bridegroom' and the 'radiant child bride' who danced up the aisle 'on winged feet'.[163] It was to this friend that Watts first revealed his intentions towards Terry: to 'influence, guide and cultivate a very artistic and peculiar nature and to remove an impulsive young girl from the dangers and temptations of the stage'.[164] At first, Terry was happy to acquiesce to Watts's plan because she was delighted that, as she recalls, '[her] face was the type which the great artist who had married me loved to paint' and she felt that 'the stage seemed a poor place when compared with the wonderful studio'.[165] Initially, she also aspired to participate fully in Little Holland House, which she regarded as 'a world full of pictures and music and gentle, artistic people with quiet voices and elegant manners', a 'paradise, where only beautiful things were allowed to come' and '[a]ll the women were graceful, and all the men were gifted'.[166] Her attitude to the salon changed, however. Terry confessed that when she was 'Nelly

Watts', she was '*very* impudent' and was 'heedless of the greatness of great men'; in other words, Terry refused to play the role allotted to her as the submissive and suppliant worshipper of great men.[167] The marriage ended when Watts and Sara Prinsep, one of the 'interfering friends', realised the impossibility of, what he called, 'reconstruct[ing] Nelly's mind, character & habits' and that her exuberance and vivacity, which he described as 'a common habit of hysteria', were not easily controlled.[168]

During their visit to Freshwater, the difference in temperament and age of husband and wife became abundantly clear. Terry found Dimbola, as she would soon begin to find Little Holland House, oppressive and constraining. She remembers it as a place where 'the others', including her husband, seemed 'very old' and where everyone '[sat] indoors noticing' what their most famous visitor, Tennyson, did or said.[169] Terry sharply differentiates the artificiality and surveillance of Dimbola from the unaffectedness and benevolence of Farringford and of Tennyson himself. Emphasising how young she was, Terry says she 'preferred playing Indians and Knights of the Round Table with Tennyson's sons, Hallam and Lionel, and the young Camerons'.[170] Although he also seemed old, for her, Tennyson was the quintessential poet, 'entirely free from romantic airs and graces'; and she contrasts his unaffectedness with Browning's 'fine society manners'.[171] Terry's Tennyson was 'wonderfully simple', yet also gentle and paternal; he was a father-figure with whom she walked over the downs, and who pointed out 'the differences in the flight of the different birds' and taught her 'to recognise the barks of trees and to call wild flowers by their names'.[172] One of Cameron's first great photographs visualises the married couple's separate and divergent experience of Freshwater and captures the mismatched nature of their relationship. The photograph was supposedly taken in the bathroom at Farringford because its wallpaper had a pattern of crosses. Cameron made Terry pose in 'her négligé, one arm across her waist, the other fingering her necklace, showing off her wedding rings', as Veronica Franklin Gould explains, to produce a 'sensual, soulful picture' of a forlorn and innocent young girl.[173] The photograph, which was exhibited under the title *Sadness*, according to J. B. Priestley, presents '[w]oman herself, her soul withdrawn behind those heavy eyelids, the mystery, the challenge, the torment, the solace'.[174] Similarly, Nina Auerbach suggests that this image shows a 'loveable, because betrayed, woman', capturing and creating 'the Ellen Terry who supposedly wept on a staircase on her wedding night, using her to dramatize the narrowing betrayal of power, the strangling of magic and scope, that come when a girl grows up'.[175] Despite Watts's scepticism about photography's ability to depict the essence of a sitter in as complete a way as his portraits, Cameron's photograph reveals Terry's character and thoughts at this time in a direct and uncompromising way. In contrast, his portraits of Terry reveal more about the dynamics of the couple's marriage and about the painter than they do about his wife-muse.

Unlike his portraits in the *Hall of Fame,* in which he aimed to capture the authentic nature of his sitters in art, his paintings of Terry reveal his attempt to mould and fashion her character in reality. The language Watts used about Ellen before they married suggests that he didn't want to represent her in art, but rather to turn her into his work of art, seeking, as he says, 'To make the poor child what I wish her to be'.[176] As Gail Marshall intimates, Watts saw Terry as 'raw material' and assumed 'the right' to re-create her by making her character 'purer and more appropriate to her beauty'.[177] Watts's plan, as Auerbach argues, meant that in his paintings Terry is 'mobile and brilliantly alive as she seems to struggle for more space than the canvas allows' and she represents the doomed nature of 'female vitality'.[178] *Choosing,* his most famous portrait of Terry, shows Watts's attempt to restrain female energy. The painting, completed and exhibited shortly after the couple's return from Freshwater, was highly praised; in his review in *The Times,* Tom Taylor called it 'the loveliest example of colour and the most delicate piece of fancy'.[179] Rather than capturing his subject's essence, the 'painting's allegory' seems to instruct Terry about the necessity of her 'modest renunciation of glory' of the 'showy, scentless camellia', associated with the theatre, vanity and materialism, and her choice of the 'humble but fragrant violets' that symbolise love, innocence and spirituality.[180] Externalising what he regards as Terry's rejection of theatrical celebrity in favour of the fame that goes with being the muse and respectful wife of a great artist, the painting, in itself, confirmed Terry's mature selection. Yet, the title underlines that this painting depicts the process of choosing and the moment before choice, as the subject is both clutching the violets and smelling the camellias. While, on the one hand, the portrait makes Terry's beauty and identity an expression of Watts's mediating and controlling genius, influence and power, on the other, it visualises and thematises deliberation, hesitation and uncertainty. The painting may even evoke something of Watts's early sense of his inability to subdue her 'restless and impetuous nature', but also an initial feeling of guilt for 'spoil[ing]' her life.[181]

This symbolic painting may also reveal something about Watts's own character that his self-portraits do not show. Recent research by Catherine

Robson makes available the possibility that Watts, like other men in the period such as Ruskin and Lewis Carroll, may be using the image of a young girl to reveal something about his innermost nature and primary subjectivity, drawing on a 'general cultural tendency', reflected in popular and literary texts and the visual arts, that used idealised girlhood to symbolise purity, innocence and universal childhood.[182] Through Terry, Watts is reconnecting with a primary identity and lost selfhood, eternally in the moment of choosing, prior to the inevitable choice that demanded his fall into the competitive male world of financial necessity and manly labour.[183] Moreover, the female figure in *Choosing* emblematises Watts's position in his culture as a lionised, feminised and passive figure, who while in Little Holland House 'was not his own man', but Sara Prinsep's; and who, as one observer, George Du Maurier, commented, 'is worshipped till his manliness hath almost departed'.[184] In this context, the flowers in *Choosing* visualise what Wilfrid Blunt calls Watts's career-long vacillation between his desire to produce 'unprofitable "High Art"' and his financial need to 'stoop to vulgar but lucrative portraiture'.[185] Like the girl in *Choosing*, Watts doesn't choose between his options, but picks both: he finds a way of not choosing and thereby pleases patrons, such as Alexander Ionides and Lord and Lady Holland, and supporters such as the Prinseps, as well as finding in his success, particularly in portraiture, a space for his own artistic innovations.[186]

Conclusion

Watts's and Cameron's visual images of Terry and her time among the lions at Little Holland House and Freshwater gave her a public profile that facilitated her rise to international fame when she triumphantly returned to the stage in 1874. As Terry's celebrity grew, stories spread about Watts's impotency and his monstrosity to his young wife.[187] When the pair met in 1882, five years after their divorce, Watts praised her success, but expressed his concern about his own reputation; he told her, 'What success I may have … will be very incomplete and unsatisfactory if you cannot do what I have long been hesitating to ask. If you cannot, keep silence'.[188] Although she would eventually include information about their life together in her memoir, Ellen agreed to protect what she termed his 'striving after real greatness as distinct from mere success'.[189] Terry shows her understanding that although Watts had striven for celebrity in his lifetime, his real 'dream' was of joining the ranks of the worthy and the best on the 'mountain of Fame'; this was, he told his second wife, 'the sort of fame for which I have given my life'.[190] For Watts, as for so many others in Victorian culture, there was no possibility of choosing between the camellias of celebrity and the violets of fame, for the one concept had become embroiled in the other: cultivating and protecting one's celebrity was necessary to secure one's fame. In contrast to Watts, Lear, disliking the celebrity culture that surrounded him in London and later in Freshwater, chose cultural marginalisation.[191] Yet, even though Lear became reconciled to the idea of giving, what he called, 'armless pleasure to a limited number of people', he never lost hope of the possibility that he would be appreciated by a future generation.[192] He was right, as was Emily Tennyson when she wrote the following to him, in 1886:

> However solitary your life has, for many years been, you must not forget that to you is given the precious gift of peopling the lives of many not only of this generation but of generations to come with good & beautiful things & thoughts, to say nothing of your own life of which so many think with a loving admiration very precious to them.[193]

In fact, something else Lear and Watts had in common was that, at the beginning of the twentieth century, the critic G. K. Chesterton predicted their very different cultural fates. In his 'A Defence of Nonsense' (1901), Chesterton acclaimed Lear the 'father of nonsense', suggesting that his work would soon be recognised and praised for its emotional and poetical depths and for the way it provided access to 'another side' of 'intellectual standards and ... trivial definitions'.[194] In his book *G. F. Watts* (1904), however, Chesterton anticipated that the recently deceased artist's great achievements would soon no longer be valued, mainly because they had already come to be associated with an overly idealistic, simplistic and overbearingly moralistic and out-of-date Victorianism.[195] In other words, the qualities that made Watts a Victorian celebrity would cost him, at least until the twenty-first century, his posthumous fame; whereas that which was underestimated by Lear's adult contemporaries – his playful gallery of eccentrics and nonconformists and his construction of a language that balances 'a multiplicity of meaning with a simultaneous absence of meaning' – was finally appreciated by his modernist heirs.[196]

Notes

1. Information in this chapter about Watts's life derives from the following biographical sources: M. S. Watts, *George Frederic Watts: the Annals of*

an Artist's Life, 3 vols (London: Macmillan and Co., 1912); Wilfrid Blunt, *'England's Michelangelo': a Biography of George Frederic Watts* (London: Hamish Hamilton, 1975); Caroline Dakers, *The Holland Park Circle: Artists and Victorian Society* (New Haven: Yale University Press, 1999); Veronica Franklin Gould, *G. F. Watts: the Last Great Victorian* (New Haven and London: Yale University Press, 2004); *G. F. Watts: Victorian Visionary*, ed. by Mark Bills and Barbara Bryant (New Haven: Yale University Press, 2008).

2. See Vivian Noakes, *Edward Lear: the Life of a Wanderer*, rev. edn (Stroud: Sutton Publishing, 2004), p. 20. Information in this chapter about Lear's life derives from the following biographical sources: Noakes, *Edward Lear*; Angus Davidson, *Edward Lear: Landscape Painter and Nonsense Poet* (London: John Murray, 1938); Peter Levi, *Edward Lear* (London: Taylor and Francis, 1995); Susan Chitty, *That Singular Person Called Lear* (Stroud: Tempus, 2007).

3. Edward Lear, *The Complete Nonsense and Other Verse*, ed. by Vivian Noakes (London: Penguin, 2002), pp. 428–29. All subsequent references to this text are taken from this edition and given as page numbers in parentheses in the essay.

4. *Annals*, I, 3.

5. Letter dated 9 June 1855, cited in Noakes, *Edward Lear*, p. 110.

6. See *Selected Letters of Edward Lear*, ed. by Vivian Noakes (Oxford: Oxford University Press, 1988), pp. 276–79.

7. Nicholas Dames, 'Brushes with Fame: Thackeray and the Work of Celebrity', *Nineteenth-Century Literature*, 56 (2001), 23–51 (pp. 33, 28).

8. *Selected Letters*, p. 130.

9. See Paul Barlow, 'Facing the Past and Present: the National Portrait Gallery and the Search for "Authentic" Portraiture', in *Portraiture: Facing the Subject*, ed. by Joanna Woodall (Manchester: Manchester University Press, 1997), pp. 219–38; Louise Lippincott, 'Expanding on Portraiture: the Market, the Public, and the Hierarchy of Genres in Eighteenth-Century Britain', in *The Consumption of Culture, 1600–1800: Image, Object, Text*, ed. by Ann Bermingham and John Brewer (London: Routledge, 1995), pp. 75–88.

10. Leo Braudy, *The Frenzy of Renown: Fame and Its History* (New York: Vintage, 1997), p. 399.

11. *Annals*, I, 208.

12. Cited in Barbara Bryant, *G F Watts Portraits: Fame and Beauty in Victorian Society* (London: National Portrait Gallery, 2004), pp. 19, 23. See also Marcia Pointon, *Hanging the Head: Portraiture and Social Formation in Eighteenth-Century England* (New Haven: Yale University Press, 1997), p. 79.

13. Diary, 8 December 1860. Edward Lear Diaries (MS Eng 797.3). Houghton Library, Harvard University. Item Number 3. See also 'Edward Lear's Diaries: the Private Journals of a Landscape Painter'. <http://www.nonsenselit.org/diaries/> Transcript of Houghton Library MS Eng. 797.3.

14. See Noakes, *Edward Lear*, pp. 164–68. In a diary entry dated 14 January 1880, Lord Derby, Lear's patron, offers an astute commentary of Lear's career: 'in the world, where nothing succeeds like success, he has done himself much harm by his perpetual neediness. An artist who is always asking his friends to buy a picture, & often to pay for it in advance, makes outsiders believe that he cannot know his business: which in Lear's case is certainly far from the truth. But he has been out at elbows all his life, & so will remain to the

last' (cited in Noakes, *Edward Lear*, p. 182). Lear complained that he had to work hard at 'attract[ing] the attention of small Capitalists' and called his paintings 'Tyrants' (*Letters of Edward Lear, Author of 'The Book of Nonsense', To Chichester Fortescue, Lord Carlingford, and Frances Countess Waldegrave*, ed. by Lady Strachey (London: T. Fisher Unwin, 1907), p. 261; Noakes, *Edward Lear*, pp. 164–75.)

15. *Later Letters of Edward Lear, Author of 'The Book of Nonsense', to Chichester Fortescue, Lord Carlingford, Frances Countess Waldegrave and others*, ed. by Lady Strachey (London: T. Fisher Unwin, 1911), p. 107. As Lear jokingly asserted in one letter, 'For the Public, says I, I have no sort of respect not none whatever – for provided pictures are cried up & well hung up – they are safe to be bought – be they by Whistler or anybody else. But the voice of Fashion whether it hissues hout of a Hart Cricket in a Paper, or hout of the mouth of a Duke or a Duchess – ain't by no means the voice of Truth' (*Selected Letters*, p. 251).

16. See Levi, pp. 132–33; Noakes, *Edward Lear*, p. 172; Blunt, p. 72.

17. Elizabeth Barrett Browning was less than flattering about Sara Prinsep's lionising; in 1857, she told her sister: 'To go there and be quiet would be impossible. People tear us to pieces, Robert and me. And if, by shutting the door, we escaped the class represented by Mrs. Prinsep and her peers, we could not refuse to see others who are friends in another sense' (see *Elizabeth Barrett Browning: Letters to her Sister, 1846–1859*, ed. by Leonard Huxley (London: John Murray, 1929), p. 274).

18. See Dakers, pp. 18–40.

19. See Richard Salmon, 'The Physiognomy of the Lion: Encountering Literary Celebrity in the Nineteenth Century', in *Romanticism and Celebrity Culture, 1750–1850*, ed. by Tom Mole (Cambridge: Cambridge University Press, 2009), pp. 60–78.

20. *Annals*, I, 159–60.

21. Sidney Colvin, *Memories and Notes of Persons and Places, 1852–1912* (London: Edward Arnold, 1921), pp. 94, 95.

22. See Dakers, pp. 1–5.

23. For an example of such articles, see D. W., 'The Surrey Home of Mr G F Watts RA', *Illustrated London News*, 29 July 1893, p. 135, in *The Illustrated London News Historical Archive 1842–2003* <http://gale.cengage.co.uk> [accessed 12 April 2013].

24. See Richard Ormond, *G. F. Watts, The Hall of Fame: Portraits of his Famous Contemporaries* (London: National Portrait Gallery, 1975); Leonée and Richard Ormond, *G. F. Watts: the Hall of Fame, Portraits of his Famous Contemporaries* (Compton: Watts Gallery, 2012).

25. 'Fine-Art Gossip', *Athenaeum*, 25 May 1861, p. 700, in *ProQuest British Periodicals* <http://www.proquest.co.uk> [accessed 12 April 2013].

26. *Annals*, I, 247; III, 54. See also *Annals*, I, 113, 248; II, 148–49.

27. Watts's ideas are explicated throughout his writings: see, for example, G. F. Watts, 'The Present Conditions of Art', in Watts, *Annals*, III, 147–90. See John Price, '"Heroism in Everyday Life": the Watts Memorial for Heroic Self Sacrifice', *History Workshop Journal*, 63 (2007), 254–78.

28. See Ormond, *G. F. Watts*, p. 8; Barlow, pp. 224–38; Lara Perry, 'Nationalizing Watts: the *Hall of Fame* and the National Portrait Gallery', in *Representations*

of G. F. Watts: Art Making in Victorian Culture, ed. by Colin Trodd and Stephanie Brown (Aldershot: Ashgate, 2004), pp. 121–33 (pp. 121, 127).

29. Cited in *G F Watts Portraits*, pp. 18, 20.

30. *Annals*, III, 35; II, 164.

31. Juliette Atkinson, *Victorian Biography Reconsidered: a Study of Nineteenth-Century 'Hidden' Lives* (Oxford: Oxford University Press, 2010), pp. 54, 48.

32. Dames, p. 35.

33. Peter Hamilton and Roger Hargreaves, *The Beautiful and the Damned: the Creation of Identity in Nineteenth-Century Photography* (Aldershot: Lund Humphries, 2001), p. 5; Helen Groth, *Victorian Photography and Literary Nostalgia* (Oxford: Oxford University Press, 2003), p. 36. See also Barlow, pp. 221–22.

34. *Annals*, II, 118.

35. Fiona MacCarthy, *William Morris: a Life for our Time* (London: Faber and Faber, 1994), p. 270; William Hazlitt, *Lectures on the English Poets, and the English Comic Writers* (London: George Bell & Sons, 1876), p. 190.

36. Cited in *G F Watts Portraits*, p. 35.

37. For a discussion of the various celebrity types in the period, see *Romanticism and Celebrity Culture, 1750–1850*, ed. by Mole.

38. For a discussion of the marginalisation of poetry, see Lee Erickson, *The Economy of Literary Form: English Literature and the Industrialization of Publishing, 1800–1850* (Baltimore: Johns Hopkins University Press, 1996), pp. 19–48. See also Joss Marsh, 'The Rise of Celebrity Culture', in *Charles Dickens in Context*, ed. by Sally Ledger and Holly Furneaux (Cambridge: Cambridge University Press, 2011), pp. 98–108; Jeffrey Richards, *Sir Henry Irving* (Hambledon: Continuum, 2005), pp. 259–81.

39. According to Watts's wife, '[t]here were four women of mark whom Signor would have liked to include in his series – Mrs. Barrett Browning, whom he never had the good fortune to meet; Mrs. George Lewes (George Eliot), whose portrait he was afraid to attempt, perceiving the difficulty that it would have presented; Miss Florence Nightingale, whose portrait he found he was unable to complete; and Mrs. (Josephine) Butler, for whose heroism he had a deep veneration' (*Annals*, II, 250). See also Perry, p. 130.

40. See Claire Brock, *The Feminization of Fame, 1750–1830* (Basingstoke: Palgrave Macmillan, 2006); *Women Writers and the Artifacts of Celebrity in the Long Nineteenth Century*, ed. by Ann R. Hawkins and Maura Ives (Farnham: Ashgate, 2012).

41. See Julie F. Codell, 'Victorian Artists' Family Biographies: Domestic Authority, the Marketplace and the Artist's Body', in *Biographical Passages: Essays on Victorian and Modernist Biography*, ed. by Jo Law and Linda K. Hughes (Columbia: University of Missouri Press, 2000), pp. 65–108.

42. See Gould, *G. F. Watts*, pp. 98–99, 159–60.

43. See Jim Cheshire, 'Introduction', in *Tennyson Transformed: Alfred Lord Tennyson and Visual Culture*, ed. by Jim Cheshire (Farnham: Lund Humphries, 2009), pp. 8–19 (p. 11).

44. See Perry, p. 122–25.

45. See *Annals*, II, 9–10; Dakers, p. 4.

46. Harry Quilter, 'The Art of Watts', *The Times*, 6 January 1882, p. 8, in *The Times Digital Archive* <http://gale.cengage.co.uk> [accessed 12 April 2012].

47. See Perry, 121–33. See also *Annals*, I, 248; II, 45.

48. Sidney Colvin, 'English Painters and Paintings in 1867', *Fortnightly Review*, 2 (1867), 464–75 (p. 475), in *ProQuest British Periodicals* <http://www.proquest.co.uk> [accessed 12 April 2013].

49. M. H. Spielmann, 'The Works of Mr George F. Watts, R. A. with a complete catalogue of his Pictures', *Pall Mall Gazette*, 22 (1886), 1–32 (p. 13), in *Gale 19th Century British Library Newspapers* <http://gale.cengage.co.uk> [accessed 12 April 2013].

50. See Richard Salmon, 'Signs of Intimacy: the Literary Celebrity in the "Age of Interviewing"', *Victorian Literature and Culture*, 25 (1997), 159–77.

51. *Annals*, I, 114.

52. Cited in *G F Watts Portraits*, p. 36.

53. Atkinson, pp. 47–48.

54. See William Holman Hunt, *Pre-Raphaelitism and the Pre-Raphaelite Brotherhood*, 2 vols (New York and London: Macmillan, 1905–06), II (1906), 123; William Cosmo Monkhouse, *British Contemporary Artists* (New York: Scribner's Sons, 1899), p. 27.

55. *Annals*, I, 248. See Barlow, pp. 232–37.

56. G. K. Chesterton, 'The Literary Portraits of G. F. Watts, R. A.', *The Bookman*, 19 (1900), 80–83 (p. 81), in *ProQuest British Periodicals* <http://www.proquest.co.uk> [accessed 12 April 2013].

57. W. K. West, *G. F. Watts* (London: George Newnes, 1904), p. xxvii.

58. See James Eli Adams, 'The Hero as Spectacle: Carlyle and the Persistence of Dandyism', in *Victorian Literature and the Victorian Visual Imagination*, ed. by Carol T. Christ and John O. Jordan (Berkeley, CA, and London: University of California Press, 1995), pp. 213–32 (p. 215).

59. See also Thomas Carlyle, *On Heroes, Hero-Worship, and the Heroic in History*, ed. by Archibald MacMechan (London: Ginn, 1901), pp. 132, 164.

60. *Annals*, III, 33; I, 206.

61. Watts, 'The Present Conditions of Art', p. 180.

62. Cited in *G F Watts Portraits*, p. 32; *Annals*, II, 177; see also Mary Watts's Diary, 22 August 1891.

63. *Annals*, II, 2.

64. See Colin Trodd, 'Illuminating Experience: Watts and the Subject of Portraiture', in *Representations of G. F. Watts*, ed. by Trodd and Brown, pp. 135–52.

65. Arthur Symons, 'The Art of Watts', *Fortnightly Review*, 74 (1900), 188–97 (p. 189), in *ProQuest British Periodicals* <http://www.proquest.co.uk> [accessed 12 April 2013].

66. See Alexis Easley, *Literary Celebrity, Gender, and Victorian Authorship, 1850–1914* (Newark: University of Delaware Press, 2011), pp. 49–52.

67. A[ndrew] Wynter, 'Cartes de Visite', *Once A Week*, 25 January 1862, pp. 134–37 (p. 135), in *ProQuest British Periodicals* <http://www.proquest.co.uk> [accessed 8 April 2013].

68. See Walter Benjamin, 'A Small History of Photography', in *One Way Street and Other Writings*, trans. by Edmund Jephcott and Kingsley Shorter (London: Verso, 1985), pp. 240–57.

69. See Helmut and Alison Gernsheim, *The History of Photography: From the Earliest Use of the Camera Obscura in the Eleventh Century up to 1914* (London: Oxford University Press, 1955), p. 227.

70. *Annals*, I, 113. For a discussion of the ideals of the National Portrait Gallery in relation to celebrity culture, see Aaron Jaffe, *Modernism and the Culture of Celebrity* (Cambridge: Cambridge University Press, 2005), pp. 171–74.

71. Cited in 'A National Gallery', *The Gentleman's Magazine*, 45 (1856), 367–71 (p. 369), in *ProQuest British Periodicals* <http://www.proquest.co.uk> [accessed 12 April 2013]. In 1853, Carlyle suggested the need for a 'home of all the national Divinities [...] where unconsciously but very veritably, the better parts of the souls of all men might worship' (cited in Charles Saumarez Smith, *The National Portrait Gallery* (London: National Portrait Gallery, 1997), p. 12).

72. *Annals*, II, 46. For a discussion of this process, see Perry, p. 126; Barlow, pp. 219–38.

73. Hazlitt, p. 190.

74. The portrait, like its photographic equivalent, is a 'memento mori'; see Susan Sontag, *On Photography* (New York: Farrar, Straus & Giroux, 1977), p. 15. See also Carol Christ, 'Painting the Dead: Portraiture and Necrophilia in Victorian Art and Poetry', in *Death and Representation*, ed. by Sarah Goodwin and Elisabeth Bronfen (Baltimore: The Johns Hopkins University Press, 1993), pp. 133–51.

75. Interestingly, Watts stressed that he would only paint those who were able to sit for him and refused to paint eminent figures who were deceased (see *Annals*, I, 33–34).

76. For one of the best overviews of Lear's nonsense verse, see Ina Rae Hark, *Edward Lear* (Boston: Twayne Publishers, 1982). See also Jackie Wullschläger, *Inventing Wonderland: the Lives and Fantasies of Lewis Carroll, Edward Lear, J. M. Barrie, Kenneth Grahame, and A. A. Milne* (London: Methuen, 1995); Ann Colley, 'Edward Lear's Limericks and the Reversals of Nonsense', *Victorian Poetry*, 26 (1988), 285–99; Clifton Snider, 'Victorian Trickster: a Jungian Consideration of Edward Lear's Nonsense Verse', *Psychological Perspectives*, 24 (1991), 90–110; Kirby Olson, 'Edward Lear: Deleuzian Landscape Painter', *Victorian Poetry*, 31 (1993), 347–62; Ann C. Colley, 'Edward Lear's Anti-Colonial Bestiary', *Victorian Poetry*, 30 (1992), 109–20.

77. Noakes, *Edward Lear*, pp. 54–58. Lear published three other collections of verse: *Nonsense Songs, Stories, Botany and Alphabets* (1871), *More Nonsense, Pictures, Rhymes, Botany Etc.* (London: Robert John Bush, 1872) and *A Fourth Book of Nonsense Poems, Songs, Botany, Music* (1877).

78. *Letters of Edward Lear*, p. 219.

79. Lear, *More Nonsense*, p. v.

80. Ibid., p. vi.

81. Ibid., p. vii.

82. Hark, p. 22.

83. *Later Letters*, p. 122.

84. [Edward Strachey], 'Nonsense as a Fine Art', *Quarterly Review*, 167 (1888), 335–65 (p. 335), in *ProQuest British Periodicals* <http://www.proquest.co.uk> [accessed 8 April 2013]. For an indication of how Lear's work has been interpreted by other contemporary critics, see Ann C. Colley, *Edward Lear and the Critics* (Columbia, SC: Camden House, 1993), pp. 1–45; 'Mr. Lear's New Nonsense', *The Spectator*, 23 December 1871, pp. 1570–71; Sidney Colvin, 'Review of *More Nonsense, Pictures, Rhymes, Botany, &c.*',

The Academy, 3 (1872), 23–24, in *ProQuest British Periodicals* <http://www.proquest.co.uk> [accessed 12 April 2013]; 'Lear's Nonsense Books', *The Spectator*, 17 September 1887, pp. 1251–52.

85. 'Lear's Book of Nonsense', *The Saturday Review*, 24 March 1888, p. 361, in *ProQuest British Periodicals* <http://www.proquest.co.uk> [accessed 12 April 2013].

86. See Hark, pp. 24–51.

87. See Michael de Nie, *The Eternal Paddy: Irish Identity and the British Press, 1798–1882* (Madison: University of Wisconsin Press, 2004); Martha Banta, *Barbaric Intercourse: Caricature and the Culture of Conduct, 1841–1936* (Chicago: Chicago University Press, 2003), pp. 19–124.

88. Erin O' Connor, *Raw Materials: Producing Pathology in Victorian Culture* (Durham: Duke University Press, 2000), pp. 151–52.

89. Lillian Craton, *The Victorian Freak Show: the Significance of Disability and Physical Differences in 19th-Century Fiction* (Amherst: Cambria Press, 2009), p. 35.

90. Marlene Tromp, with Karyn Valerius, 'Toward Situating the Victorian Freak', in *Victorian Freaks: the Social Context of Freakery in Britain*, ed. by Marlene Tromp (Columbus: Ohio State University Press, 2008), pp. 1–18 (p. 8).

91. See Levi, p. 128.

92. See Charlotte Boyce and Páraic Finnerty, *Tennyson's Celebrity Circle* (Portsmouth: Tricorn Books, 2011), p. 20.

93. *Selected Letters*, p. 115.

94. *The Letters of Emily Lady Tennyson*, ed. by James O. Hoge (University Park and London: Pennsylvania State University Press, 1974), p. 56.

95. *Selected Poems of Alfred Tennyson*, ed. by Christopher Ricks (London: Penguin, 2008), p. 214.

96. See Anna Barton, 'Delirious Bulldogs and Nasty Crockery: Tennyson as Nonsense Poet', *Victorian Poetry*, 47 (2009), 313–30; Richard Cronin, 'Edward Lear and Tennyson's Nonsense', in *Tennyson Among the Poets: Bicentenary Essays*, ed. by Robert Douglas-Fairhurst and Seamus Perry (Oxford: Oxford University Press, 2009), pp. 259–75; Richard Maxwell, 'Palms and Temples: Edward Lear's Topographies', *Victorian Poetry*, 48 (2010), 73–94.

97. *Selected Letters*, pp. 115, 117.

98. Ibid., pp. 117, 116.

99. Ruth Pitman, *Edward Lear's Tennyson* (Manchester: Carcanet, 1988), p. 28.

100. See Maxwell, p. 92.

101. Hallam Tennyson, *Alfred Lord Tennyson: a Memoir by His Son*, 2 vols (London: Macmillan & Co., 1897), I, 381. See Leonée Ormond, 'Tennyson and the Artists', in *Tennyson Transformed*, ed. by Cheshire, pp. 42–61 (p. 45).

102. 'Mr Lear's Drawings', *The Saturday Review*, 31 May 1890, p. 684, in *ProQuest British Periodicals* <http://www.proquest.co.uk> [accessed 12 April 2013]. See also 'Fine-Art Gossip', *Athenaeum*, 2 November 1889, p. 604, in *ProQuest British Periodicals* <http://www.proquest.co.uk> [accessed 12 April 2013]; 'Edward Lear', *Athenaeum*, 2 December 1911, p. 687, in *ProQuest British Periodicals* <http://www.proquest.co.uk> [accessed 12 April 2013]. See also Charles Tennyson, *Alfred Tennyson* (London: Macmillan & Co., 1949), p. 501.

103. Cited in Noakes, *Edward Lear*, p. 110.

104. Anne Thackeray Ritchie, 'Reminiscences', in *Alfred, Lord Tennyson and His Friends: a Series of 25 Portraits and Frontispiece in Photogravure from the Negatives of Mrs. Julia Margaret Cameron and H. H. H. Cameron*, ed. by H. H. H. Cameron and Anne Thackeray Ritchie (London: T. Fisher Unwin, 1893), pp. 9–16 (p. 9).

105. *Letters of Emily Lady Tennyson*, p. 137; cited in Ann Thwaite, *Emily Tennyson: the Poet's Wife* (London: Faber and Faber, 1996), p. 342.

106. *Selected Letters*, p. 138.

107. Noakes, *Edward Lear*, pp. 99–100, 142–43.

108. *The Life and Letters of Sir John Everett Millais,* ed. by John Guille Millais, 2 vols (London: Methuen & Co., 1899), II, 142; Tennyson, *Alfred Tennyson,* p. 441; Edith Nicholl Ellison, *A Child's Recollections of Tennyson* (London: J. Dent, 1907), p. 9.

109. *Letters of Anne Thackeray Ritchie,* ed. by Hester Ritchie (London: John Murray, 1924), p. 127. See also Hester Thackeray Fuller, *Three Freshwater Friends: Tennyson, Watts and Mrs. Cameron* (Newport: Isle of Wight County Press, 1933), p. 24.

110. Diary, 16 June 1860. Edward Lear Diaries (MS Eng 797.3). Houghton Library, Harvard University. Item Number 3. During his 1860 visit, Lear was upset by the commotion and bother that Cameron caused, on 14 July, when she had eight men bring her grand piano from her house to Farringford. See *The Farringford Journal of Emily Tennyson: 1853–1864*, ed. by Richard J. Hutchings and Brian Hinton (Newport: Isle of Wight County Press, 1986), p. 92.

111. Diary, 17 June 1860. Edward Lear Diaries (MS Eng 797.3). Houghton Library, Harvard University. Item Number 3.

112. *Later Letters*, p. 47; Blunt, p. 108. Lear records his surprise at meeting Tennyson in London and finding him 'particularly nice & friendly', adding 'I was wholly wrong in thinking he had got into Pattledom' (Diary, 11 February 1861. Edward Lear Diaries (MS Eng 797.3). Houghton Library, Harvard University. Item Number 4).

113. For a discussion of the deterioration of Lear and Tennyson's relationship, see Noakes, *Edward Lear*, p. 205.

114. Thwaite, p. 284.

115. Cited in Levi, p. 168. See also Diary, 16 June 1860. Edward Lear Diaries (MS Eng 797.3). Houghton Library, Harvard University. Item Number 3; see also *Letters of Edward Lear*, p. 138.

116. Diary, 17 June 1860. Edward Lear Diaries (MS Eng 797.3). Houghton Library, Harvard University. Item Number 3.

117. Diary, 17 October 1864. Edward Lear Diaries (MS Eng 797.3). Houghton Library, Harvard University. Item Number 7; Diary, 11 July 1865. Edward Lear Diaries (MS Eng 797.3). Houghton Library, Harvard University. Item Number 8.

118. *The Letters of Alfred Lord Tennyson*, ed. by Cecil Y. Lang and Edgar F. Shannon, Jr, 3 vols (Oxford: Clarendon Press, 1982–90), III (1990), 164.

119. See *Annals*, I, 169–70.

120. Cited in Gould, *G. F. Watts*, p. 45.

121. *Letters of Alfred Lord Tennyson*, II (1987), 219.

122. Cited in Gould, *G. F. Watts*, p. 45; *Annals*, I, 294; Blunt, pp. 78–79.

123. See *Letters of Alfred Lord Tennyson*, II (1987), 216–19, 247.

124. Ibid., p. 219.

125. Alfred Lord Tennyson, *Idylls of the King*, ed. by J. M. Gray (London: Penguin, 1996), pp. 176–77.

126. *Letters of Alfred Lord Tennyson*, II (1987), 204.

127. Cited in Blunt, p. 79.

128. See Gould, *G. F. Watts*, p. 62; *Letters of Alfred Lord Tennyson*, II (1987), 332.

129. Cited in Gould, *G. F. Watts*, p. 107.

130. Ben Stoker, 'Alfred: Informal Portraits of a Poet', in *Tennyson Transformed*, ed. by Cheshire, pp. 62–67 (pp. 63, 67).

131. G. K. Chesterton, *G. F. Watts* (London: Duckworth, 1904), p. 40.

132. Ibid., pp. 40, 41.

133. *Annals*, II, 164.

134. See Barbara Bryant, 'Invention and Reinvention: the Art and Life of G. F. Watts', in *G. F. Watts: Victorian Visionary*, ed. by Bills and Bryant, pp. 19–49 (p. 35).

135. *Annals*, I, 208.

136. Ibid., II, 160.

137. Repr. in Gould, *G. F. Watts*, p. 243.

138. *Annals*, I, 283.

139. Ibid., p. 174.

140. See Noakes, *Edward Lear*, pp. 115–16; Chitty, pp. 21–22.

141. See Noakes, *Edward Lear*, pp. 82–86.

142. Cited in Noakes, *Edward Lear*, p. 84.

143. Ibid., p. 84. See also Davidson, p. 68.

144. Chichester Fortescue, *And Mr. Fortescue: a Selection from the Diaries from 1851 to 1862 of Chichester Fortescue, Lord Carlingford, K. P. P.* (London: J. Murray, 1958), p. 86.

145. See *Letters of Emily Tennyson*, pp. 78, 80.

146. Ibid., p. 80.

147. Ibid., p. 83; see also *Farringford Journal of Emily Tennyson*, p. 27.

148. *Selected Letters*, p. 133.

149. For a discussion, see Sarah Rose Cole, 'The Recovery of Friendship: Male Love and Developmental Narrative in Tennyson's *In Memoriam*', *Victorian Poetry*, 50 (2010), 43–66.

150. *Selected Letters*, p. 133.

151. See Hark, pp. 49–51, 86–92.

152. *Selected Letters*, p. 134.

153. Cited in Davidson, p. 93.

154. *Letters of Emily Tennyson*, pp. 89–90.

155. During his stay at Farringford in October, Lear played some of his settings to Tennyson's poems and was so admired by one listener, Miss Cotton, that Emily called Lear a 'hero of romance'. She encouraged him to pursue Miss Cotton romantically, and even told him how Miss Cotton had been 'found all pale after a sleepless night, how her companions came and poured into my ear a mighty river of thanks and praises and admiration' (see *Letters of Emily Tennyson*, p. 88). Lear dismissed such admirers, noting, 'we all know about the beautiful blue glass jar – which was only a white one after all, only there was blue water inside it' (cited in Noakes, *Edward Lear*, p. 112).

156. *Letters of Emily Tennyson*, p. 114.
157. Diary, 16 June 1860. Edward Lear Diaries (MS Eng 797.3). Houghton Library, Harvard University. Item Number 3; he quotes these lines in his diary on the following days: 4 August 1860, 26 August 1861, 15 August 1862, 4 September 1862, 5 October 1862. Edward Lear Diaries (MS Eng 797.3). Houghton Library, Harvard University. Item Numbers 3, 4 and 5.
158. Diary, 17 February 1861. Edward Lear Diaries (MS Eng 797.3). Houghton Library, Harvard University. Item Number 4.
159. *Memoir*, I, 58.
160. *Later Letters*, p. 47. See also 'Book review', *London Review of Politics, Society, Literature, Art, and Science*, 27 February 1864, p. 226, in *ProQuest British Periodicals* <http://www.proquest.co.uk> [accessed 12 April 2013]; 'London', *Orchestra*, 14 January 1865, p. 248, in *ProQuest British Periodicals* <http://www.proquest.co.uk> [accessed 12 April 2013].
161. Nina Auerbach, *Ellen Terry: Player in Her Time* (London and Melbourne: J. M. Dent & Sons Ltd., 1987), p. 77.
162. *Ellen Terry's Memoirs*, ed. by Edith Craig and Christopher St. John (London: Victor Gollancz ,1933), p. 46.
163. Ibid., p. 51.
164. Cited in Auerbach, p. 116.
165. *Ellen Terry's Memoirs*, pp. 42, 39.
166. Ibid., pp. 40, 43.
167. Ibid., p. 45.
168. Cited in Veronica Franklin Gould, 'G. F. Watts and Ellen Terry', in *Ellen Terry, Spheres of Influence*, ed. by Katherine Cockin (London: Pickering & Chatto, 2011), pp. 33–47 (p. 39).
169. *Ellen Terry's Memoirs*, p. 45.
170. Ibid., pp. 44–45.
171. Ibid., p. 44.
172. Ibid.
173. Gould, *G. F. Watts*, p. 72.
174. Cited in Gould, 'G. F. Watts and Ellen Terry', p. 38.
175. Auerbach, pp. 96, 99.
176. Cited in Blunt, p. 105.
177. Gail Marshall, *Actresses on the Victorian Stage: Feminine Performances and the Galatea Myth* (Cambridge: Cambridge University Press, 1998), p. 33.
178. Auerbach, pp. 100, 105.
179. Cited in *G F Watts Portraits*, p. 136.
180. Auerbach, p. 103; Blunt, p. 108.
181. Cited in Auerbach, p. 116; *Ellen Terry's Memoir*, p. 47.
182. Catherine Robson, *Men in Wonderland: the Lost Girlhood of the Victorian Gentleman* (Princeton: Princeton University Press, 2001), p. 222.
183. Ibid., pp. 3–4, 31.
184. Auerbach, p. 76; cited in Blunt, p. 80. Interestingly Ruskin suggested that Watts 'with all his power, paints still as weakly as a woman – is essentially a woman – because he paints what he *likes* in defiance of what *is*' (cited in Gould, *G. F. Watts*, p. 110).
185. Blunt, p. 12.

186. However, as Nina Auerbach puts it, '[Watts] was not his own man'; he was the possession of Sara Prinsep, for whom 'owning artists was a finer accomplishment than collecting paintings' (Auerbach, p. 76).

187. Ibid., pp. 119–20.

188. *Ellen Terry's Memoirs*, p. 47.

189. Cited in Auerbach, p. 118.

190. *Annals*, II, 143, 144. Watts appears to have believed that the pursuit of fame was an individualistic struggle, but that its achievement and experience would associate him with and position him in the ranks of the great men (and women) of history. For example, Watts told his wife about a dream he had in which he climbs up the side of the steep 'mountain of Fame' and is, at first, sure that his arduous journey is an unprecedented one. He tells her that he has 'to cut each step that [he] took' and the path closed behind him, 'so that no one could follow'. At the summit, however, he can see the beauty and ethereality of nature in everything around him and hears the voices of those who have made a similar journey and now 'remain there for ever, themselves a part of that great beauty'. Reflecting on his dream, he realises that achieving 'Fame in the greatest sense of the word, [is] all that is worthy of the best endeavour' (see *Annals*, II, 143–44).

191. 'Perhaps after all, the less one stays in places one likes the better – & so one escapes [some] pain. – Therefore, wander' (Diary, 5 April 1861. Edward Lear Diaries (MS Eng 797.3). Houghton Library, Harvard University. Item Number 4).

192. *Selected Letters*, p. 251. See *Letters of Edward Lear*, p. 14; *Later Letters*, p. 91.

193. *Letters of Emily Tennyson*, p. 334.

194. G. K. Chesterton, *The Defendant* (London: E. Brimley Johnson, 1902), pp. 44, 48–49.

195. See Chesterton, *G. F. Watts*, pp. 11–17.

196. Wim Tigges, *An Anatomy of Literary Nonsense* (Amsterdam: Rodopi, 1988), pp. 47. See also Tigges, 47–50, 126–32; William Baker, 'T. S. Eliot on Edward Lear: An Unnoted Attribution', *English Studies*, 64 (1983), 564–66; Hana F. Khasawneh, 'The Dynamics of Nonsense Literature: 1840-1940' (unpublished doctoral thesis, University of Sussex, 2009).

3
'She Shall Be Made Immortal': Julia Margaret Cameron's Photography and the Construction of Celebrity

Charlotte Boyce

In his pioneering 1948 study of the life and work of Julia Margaret Cameron, Helmut Gernsheim recalls the moment when his interest in Cameron's photography was first piqued. While waiting for a train at Brockenhurst in the New Forest in the early decades of the twentieth century, the renowned photo-historian sought shelter in the station waiting-room, where he 'was suddenly struck by familiar faces gazing down from the walls':

> To my astonishment I found no fewer than eleven autographed portraits of famous Victorians by Julia Margaret Cameron. I must admit that I was rather puzzled to see these photographs decorating a dingy railway waiting room, of all places, but a moment later I came across the surprising explanation inscribed on one or two of the photographs.
> *This gallery of the great men of our age is presented to this room by Mrs. Cameron in grateful memory of this being the spot where she first met one of her sons after a long absence of four years in Ceylon. 11th November 1871.*[1]

Cameron's improvised 'gallery of great men' recalls another visual anthology of eminent Victorians put together by a member of the Freshwater circle: painter G. F. Watts's *Hall of Fame* (discussed in Chapter 2). However, whereas Watts's celebrity portraits formed an important part of the National Portrait Gallery's collection at the time Gernsheim was writing, Cameron's were hidden away in the 'dingy railway waiting room' of a small Hampshire village.[2] By the twentieth century, it seems, Cameron's name had slipped from the collective cultural consciousness, as well as from the photographic histories to which a curious Gernsheim subsequently turned for information; significantly, few of the source books he consulted during his researches in the 1940s 'deigned to mention her work at all'.[3]

This fall from recognition is somewhat ironic given the concerted efforts Cameron made during her lifetime to establish a reputation for herself not simply as a photographer, but as an 'artist'. Unlike the male members of her circle, discussed elsewhere in this study, she welcomed public acclaim and engaged unabashedly in strategies of self-promotion, capitalising on the influence and celebrity of her acquaintances and seizing with gusto opportunities to raise her profile. In spite of this keen embracement of the Victorian celebrity apparatus, however, Cameron's conception of and relationship to fame was by no means free from the kinds of contradictions and complexities that characterised Tennyson's and Watts's. As this chapter will demonstrate, the idea of celebrity sponsored within Cameron's portrait photography – that is, celebrity as exalted, timeless and enduring; the corollary of innate greatness and nobility – sits uneasily alongside the more pragmatic understanding of celebrity as a condition conferring material rewards and financial security – a condition that might be achieved through hard work and persistence – revealed in her private writings. What is more, the gendered vision of celebrity suggested by her 'gallery of great men' (it was not without cause that a posthumous collection of her work was titled *Victorian Photographs of Famous Men and Fair Women*) is destabilised by her own active pursuit of personal renown.

The complex gender politics of Victorian celebrity culture have been explored at length in a number of recent studies.[4] As Brenda R. Weber points out, 'the nineteenth century offered a marked rise in opportunities for women to occupy public and celebrated positions' – opportunities that many female writers, artists and performers readily exploited.[5] Nevertheless, women's relationship to celebrity culture was often fraught owing to its disruption of embedded cultural codes and the gendered assumptions around issues such as visibility, professionalism and propriety. As Tom Mole notes, though the doctrine of 'separate spheres' for the genders does not accurately describe the historical reality of the nineteenth century, it does indicate the existence of a 'prescriptive discourse' that encouraged women 'to adjust or excuse' their practices and behaviours in line with established norms.[6] Consequently, celebrity for Victorian women was often a matter of careful management and negotiation between conflicting cultural imperatives. Alexis Easley observes that 'obscurity was required to maintain social respectability, yet women found it necessary to balance privacy with visibility to enhance public interest in their lives and work. Too little exposure could mean invisibility … yet too much exposure could mean being cast aside'.[7] Given this ideologically charged cultural environment, it is perhaps understandable that some women (along with their biographers, family and friends) chose to represent themselves as 'accidental' celebrities whose fame was 'a matter of fate rather than of design, of rewards passively received rather than conquests actively pursued', while others drew attention to their conventional domesticity and femininity in order to present their celebrity in socially acceptable terms.[8]

Maura Ives argues, however, that 'we must not allow such cautionary tales to obscure the *agency* of women … within celebrity culture'.[9] Certainly, the experiences of the Freshwater circle discussed in this book belie the notion that the celebrity infrastructure inhibited women while enabling men.[10] Julia Margaret Cameron does not fit comfortably into the paradigm of the reluctant or self-effacing female celebrity; whereas her male friends Tennyson and Watts publicly eschewed the active pursuit of fame, Cameron was mostly open about her ambitions, candid about her talent and, as Agnes Weld (a niece of the Tennysons) pointed out, 'she refused to be bound by any of the artificialities of modern society life'.[11] Her status as a photographer further distinguished her from the literary women who have been the focus of existing scholarship on the gender politics of Victorian celebrity. When Cameron first took up her camera, photography was still a relatively new art form and had not accrued the kinds of inveterately masculinised values that had long attached to the activities of authorship and portraiture. Indeed, a tentative consensus clustered around the idea that photography might be a medium 'pre-eminently suited for women'; its dependence on so-called 'feminine' skills, such as delicacy, taste and patience, appeased the conservatively minded while, for the emerging women's movement, photography offered unprecedented opportunities for female professionalisation and employment.[12] Therefore, although Cameron's innovative artistic style often brought her into conflict with the conformist ideals of critics and photographic societies, her gender proved no significant barrier to her creative – or commercial – ambitions.

Her privileged social standing, meanwhile, helped both to shield her from accusations of impropriety and to facilitate her photographic career. Born into a leading Anglo-Indian family, Cameron was able to draw upon the connections made available to her by birth and by the advantageous marriages of her six sisters (two of whom married into the English aristocracy). As Coventry Patmore noted in 1866, 'her position in literary and aristocratic society gives her the pick of the most beautiful and intellectual heads in the world'.[13] In particular, the weekly artistic 'salons' hosted by her sister, Sara Prinsep, at Little Holland House proved fertile hunting-ground for celebrity sitters, while, at home in Freshwater, Cameron could avail herself of the ever-replenishing pool of famous friends and acquaintances that eddied around Tennyson. Unsurprisingly, the Laureate himself was, along with Watts, one of Cameron's most frequent (though reluctant) celebrity subjects. In the multiple photographs that she took of these two men, Cameron sought to capture their ineffable genius, the intangible source of their present (and, implicitly, future) fame. As the following sections of this chapter demonstrate, though, her role within the Freshwater circle was much more than that of mere chronicler or lioniser. Through her photographic studies, she played an active part in defining the parameters of Victorian celebrity, while simultaneously forging for herself a celebrity identity that both defied and complied with existing gender codes. Following her death, this identity was appropriated and recast, largely by her female relatives and intimates, in a variety of contradictory (and sometimes self-serving) ways that collectively highlight, as the final section of this chapter shows, the ongoing problematics of female incursions into the public consciousness. Elaborating on Cameron's complex engagements with the Victorian celebrity apparatus – the shifting conceptions of fame vested in her photography, commercial practices, personal correspondence and posthumous legacy – this chapter argues for the inherent mutability of Victorian celebrity, its uncanny ability to morph itself to the changing demands of its participants and their adherents.

Making immortal: photography and celebrity

Although, as Leo Braudy argues, 'the fertile groundwork for the extraordinary advance in visible fame' predated the emergence of modern photography, its popularity as a visual medium in the nineteenth century was integral to the growth of the celebrity industry.[14] By the time Julia Margaret Cameron was presented with her first camera (a gift from her daughter and son-in-law) in 1863, Britain was in the grip of 'cartomania': a collecting craze for miniature mounted photographic portraits, or *cartes de visite*.[15] Philippa Wright points out that, alongside the demand for personal portraits which could be collected in albums and distributed to the sitter's friends and family, 'professional photographers discovered a lucrative market for mass-produced cartes-de-visite of celebrities, and a vibrant industry developed with startling rapidity to meet the huge demand'.[16] This industry encompassed not only well-known commercial photographers, such as J. E. Mayall and Camille Silvy, who provided a steady stream of marketable images, earning themselves up to £400 per 10,000 copies sold, but also wholesalers, such as the London firm Marion & Co., who stocked and distributed an astonishing range of miniature portraits, and retailers, who sold between three and four hundred million *cartes* a year from metropolitan and provincial high streets.[17]

One of the *carte* industry's most significant effects was to democratise access to the celebrity's image. In an 1862 article for *Once a Week*, Andrew Wynter wondered

> how many people there are in London who have actually seen the National Portrait Gallery! ...We question, indeed, if one man in a thousand knows where the effigies of England's departed great are deposited; and even those who seek the whereabouts of the gallery are as likely as not to be disappointed in obtaining admission, for ... the gallery is permitted to be open only three days in the week. ... [Contrast] it with the hundred portrait galleries of great and noted Englishmen to be found in – our shop windows. Wherever in our fashionable streets we see a crowd congregated before a shop window, there for certain a like number of notabilities are staring back at the crowd in the shape of *cartes de visite*. Certainly our street portrait galleries are a great success: no solemn flights of stairs lead to pompous rooms in which pompous attendants preside with a severe air over pompous portraits ... Here, on the contrary, social equality is carried to its utmost limit.[18]

Not only did print shops assemble an egalitarian 'bricolage of images', in which aristocrats and politicians rubbed shoulders with actresses and sportsmen, they also empowered consumers, for, as John Plunkett notes, 'it was through their choices that celebrities were formed'.[19] While portraits of the Royal Family and literary idols enjoyed a fairly constant sale, the marketability of other figures was dependent on the caprices of the buying public and the turn of historical events.[20] Certain *cartes* might 'run like wildfire for a day', in response to a temporary surge in their subjects' newsworthiness, 'and then fall a dead letter' the next.[21] In this way, the *carte de visite* functioned as an effective barometer of Victorian celebrity, charting both the short-lived notoriety of the overnight sensation and the abiding fame of the culturally pre-eminent.

Celebrity *cartes*, and photographic portraits more generally, were valued in Victorian culture for their much-lauded ability to render the sitter as he or she *really* was. In an 1857 essay for the *Quarterly Review*, Lady Elizabeth Eastlake argued that photography

> is the sworn witness of everything presented to her view. ... What indeed are nine-tenths of those facial maps called photographic portraits, but accurate landmarks and measurements for loving eyes and memories to deck with beauty and animate with expression, in perfect certainty, that the ground-plan is founded upon fact?[22]

Owing to its apparently transparent relationship to 'fact', photography was thought to differ from, and enjoy an advantage over, other media. Anne Thackeray, in the *Pall Mall Gazette*, suggested that though 'type, and printers' ink, and paper' may provide a 'record of things as they are', 'a photograph of your friend will, to a certain point, tell you more about him in one minute than whole pages of elaborate description. You see him himself – the identity is there'.[23] Wynter claimed a similar representational superiority for photography over painting, arguing that whereas the artist's style inevitably influences the portrayal of the subject in traditional portraiture, photographs present us with 'the very lines that Nature has engraven on our faces, and it can be said of them that no two are alike'.[24] Photography was fetishised, then, for its realism and its con-comitant ability to render celebrity visages as intimately familiar to the public as those of their own kin. (Indeed, Tennyson famously complained to Julia Margaret Cameron, 'I can't be anonymous by reason of your confounded photographs').[25] The fact that images of celebrities could be collated and displayed in albums alongside those of genuine acquaint-ances helped to elide further the distance and difference between them, transforming the celebrity into a recognisable and knowable entity.

Yet, the value of celebrity portraiture did not derive solely from its claims to verisimilitude, nor from the fantasy of intimacy it helped to sustain. From its earliest inception, photography was invested with a special memorialising power. As Elizabeth Barrett marvelled in an 1843 letter to her friend, Mary Russell Mitford, on the subject of daguerreo-types, 'It is not merely the likeness which is precious ... but ... the fact of the very shadow of the person lying there *fixed for ever*! It is the very sanctification of portraits'.[26] In his presidential address to the Photographic Society in 1855, Sir Frederick Pollock reflected similarly on photography's fixative capability:

> The varied objects to which Photography can address itself, its power of rendering permanent that which appears to be as fleeting as the

shadows that go across the dial, the power that it possesses of giving fixedness to instantaneous objects, are for the purposes of history ... a matter of the greatest importance. It is not too much to say that no individual ... need now perish; but may be rendered immortal by the assistance of Photography.[27]

Pollock's extolment of photography's immortalising power, here, responds to the specific desires and concerns of his age. A year after this address, Earl Stanhope made a speech to the House of Lords urging the formation of a National Portrait Gallery in which images of 'those persons who are most honourably commemorated in British history' might be collected and preserved for the benefit of the nation. (It was noted, with some chagrin, that the French already had such a gallery of 'celebrities'.)[28] The visual memorialisation of eminent figures was embraced by the Victorians as a way of asserting Britain's past and present greatness, and of ensuring the continued recognition of that greatness in the future. That photography might afford prospective generations of historians an invaluable service in this respect was quickly recognised. Wynter meditated that 'if a box or two of [*cartes de visite*] were to be sealed up and buried deep in the ground, to be dug up two or three centuries hence, what a prize they would be to the fortunate finder! ... What would we give to have such pictures of old Pepys, his wife, and Mistress Nip? Yet treasures such as these we shall be able to hand down to our posterity'.[29]

Julia Margaret Cameron was only too aware of photography's value to posterity; she frequently made reference to the eternalising power of her work, coaxing one potential sitter with the words, 'Bid her come, and she shall be made *Immortal*'.[30] It was to the portraits of the eminent poets, artists and scientists who sat before her lens that she most regularly applied this signifier, however.[31] Joanne Lukitsh argues that Cameron perceived herself as 'a witness to human nobility', noting that, in a letter to her close friend and mentor, the eminent astronomer and chemist Sir John Herschel, she wrote of her 'longing' to take his photograph, adding, 'I often think I could ... do a head that would be Valuable to all ages'.[32] She was similarly keen to capture the genius of her friends Tennyson and Watts for the benefit of future generations, producing over twenty portraits of the two between 1864 and 1869. Her conviction of the historical value of these representations is clear from her comments regarding them; she described one portrait of Tennyson as 'a National Treasure of immense value', and another, commonly known as 'The Dirty Monk' (Figure 3.1), as an 'immortal head' and 'a column of immortal grandeur'.[33]

Importantly, Cameron's use of the term 'immortal', here, conveys something more than the simple arresting of the Laureate's image in perpetuity. Like Elizabeth Barrett's description of the daguerreotype process as 'the sanctification of portraits', it implies a kind of consecration. A number of critics have noted that ideas of immortality were in a state of flux in the Victorian age; indeed, Braudy claims that from the eighteenth century onwards 'hope of heaven, hope of immediate fame, and hope of fame in posterity were becoming difficult to distinguish'.[34] In Cameron's work, however, the modern understanding of immortality as 'enduring fame or remembrance' (*OED*) never quite supplants traditional ideas about immortality and divinity; a strong religious tendency runs through both her photography and her written reflections on her

Figure 3.1   Julia Margaret Cameron, photograph of Alfred Tennyson ('The Dirty Monk') (1865), TRC 11

Source: Tennyson Research Centre, Lincolnshire County Council

art. In an album presented in 1864 to her friend and mentor, Watts, she wrote, 'To The Signor to whose generosity / I owe the choicest fruits of / his Immortal genius. / I offer these my first successes / in my mortal but yet / divine! art of Photography'.[35] This short dedication generates a complex range of meanings around the interrelated concepts of fame, genius and immortality. Cameron is careful to position herself as a mere mortal in relation to the great Watts, who is deified as a transcendental genius. Her praise implicitly gestures towards Watts's immortalising skill as an artist, while signalling that, because of this, his present fame will persist through the ages. In her own case, by contrast, Cameron suggests it is to the photographic medium, rather than the all-too-human photographer, that divinity must be assigned.[36] By ascribing the gift of immortalisation to her inanimate camera rather than herself, the neophyte artist modestly avoids claims to personal recognition, while simultaneously positioning her work as theophanic.[37]

Cameron's self-assessments were not always so unassuming. In an 1864 letter to Herschel, she credited herself with a much more active role in the process of photographic commemoration than that of mere operative. Comparing her portraits to those produced by commercial photographers, Cameron expressed her wish that the public might come to 'believe in other than mere conventional topographic photography – map-making and skeleton rendering of feature and form without that roundness and fulness of force and feature, that modelling of flesh and limb, *which the focus I use only can give*'.[38] Her pronouncement draws attention to the representational significance of her idiosyncratic technique: the reference to 'map-making' recalls Lady Eastlake's description of photographic portraits as 'facial maps' (cited above), but whereas Eastlake was endorsing the trend for realistic representation in photography, Cameron implies that it generates merely a perfunctory outline of the person before the lens; only by means of *her* distinctive style – commonly derided as 'out of focus' – can the true essence of the sitter be captured and enshrined.[39]

One of the recognised ironies of Victorian photography was that, as Daniel A. Novak suggests, its heightened realism worked to '*efface* particularity and individuality'.[40] In an 1865 article, Anne Thackeray noted the dreary conventionality of commercial portraiture, poking fun at the means by which photographers attempted 'to give both dignity and repose to their sitters':

> If dignity is desired, the plaster column is brought into requisition; if repose is considered more characteristic, the dining-room chair and

the small and ricketty [sic] table are produced. You are requested to place one elbow on the table, to twist your head violently over one shoulder, to stick out your little finger if you are a lady, to put one hand into your pocket if you are a man ... With the tasteful addition of a vase, or a small bronze statuette of a horse, and a volume negligently placed upon the small table, the composition is complete.[41]

Like her mentor Watts, Cameron rejected outright this troublingly homogenising aesthetic and its deadening obsession with 'detail of table-cover, chair and crinoline skirt'.[42] Her photographs of celebrities are notable for being strikingly visually spare; unencumbered by elaborate scenery or ostentatious costumes, they invite the viewer to focus exclusively on the head of the sitter, which invariably dominates the image.[43] They do not function as forensically detailed phrenological studies, however. Cameron's primary interest was in capturing the 'essence' or spirit of her subjects. As she explained in 'Annals of my Glass House' (her unpublished, unfinished autobiography), 'when I have had such men before my camera my whole soul has endeavoured to do its duty towards them in recording faithfully the *greatness of the inner* as well as the features of the outer man'.[44] In other words, her photography sought to elucidate as well as to immortalise her subjects' celebrity: to make visible the inner greatness, or essential nobility, from which their fame implicitly stemmed. In this way, it can be interpreted as a visual form of the Victorian practice of 'hero worship' discussed in Chapter 2; Cameron's conviction that certain men possessed metaphysical qualities that ensured their place in history contains telling echoes of Thomas Carlyle's idea that 'the History of the world is but the Biography of great men' and that 'we cannot look, however imperfectly, upon a great man, without gaining something by him'.[45]

Fittingly, Cameron's 1867 photographs of Carlyle make evident this heroising propensity. Pictured face-on and in profile (Figure 3.2) against a dark background, Carlyle takes on the aspect of the 'great man' as 'living light-fountain', described in his first lecture on the heroic in history.[46] As Violet Hamilton notes, Cameron's replication of the painterly technique of *sfumato* and clever manipulation of light and shade work to construct Carlyle as a powerful intellect: 'the massive head ... seems to exude an extraordinary light from within, suggesting Cameron's view that Carlyle was a secular prophet, gifted with great insight'.[47] James Eli Adams offers a similar reading, arguing that Cameron's images turn 'the sage of Chelsea into an icon of Thought'.[48] Practically speaking, Carlyle's

Figure 3.2 Julia Margaret Cameron, photograph of Thomas Carlyle (1867), TRC 186
Source: Tennyson Research Centre, Lincolnshire County Council

pensive attitude in these examples can be attributed to Cameron's use of long exposure, which obliged her sitters to keep still for minutes at a time. Yet, as Carol Hanbery MacKay points out, though we may rationally ascribe Carlyle's intently contemplative expression to 'an intense effort to hold the eyes open ... the images that result still depict our sense of meditation and its concomitant state of mind'.[49]

If Carlyle figured as the 'hero as prophet' or 'sage' in Cameron's photography, then Tennyson represented the 'hero as poet', though the distinction between these two types of 'great men' was not always clear-cut.[50] Interestingly, Cameron labelled her 'Dirty Monk' photograph of Tennyson (Figure 3.1) 'a fit representation of Isiah [*sic*] or of Jeremiah', implicitly positioning the Laureate as a modern seer, blessed with divine insight.[51] The portrait also attests to Tennyson's literariness; draped in the sombre cloak of a medieval scribe, he holds prominently in his left hand a leather-bound book.[52] Other Cameron images work in similar ways to construct the Laureate as the 'embodiment of literary genius'.[53] Like Carlyle, Cameron considered Shakespeare to be the type of the 'hero as poet', and so, in a number of photographs, she consciously attempted to represent Tennyson in this mould. In a letter to Blanche Cornish, she described her final photograph of the poet, taken in 1869, as portraying 'very straight eyes, a little drooping eyelids, bearing the weight of thought, a massive brow and an Elizabethan character in the whole man as if he were sharing the Kingdom of the world with Shakespeare – he bearing the burthen and the weight of all this unintelligible world (its Penseroso side) and leaving Shakespeare to sing its Allegro side'.[54] Yet, while deliberately alluding to Tennyson's literary forebears in order to signal his illustrious pedigree, Cameron's photographs also worked to construct an iconic identity for him in his own right. They implicitly promised the kind of radical insight into the man and his work necessarily unavailable to admirers of his literary predecessors. As F. D. Maurice wrote in a congratulatory letter to Cameron,

> Had we such portraits of Shakespeare and of Milton we should know more of their own selves. We should have better commentaries on 'Hamlet' and on 'Comus' than we now possess, even as you have secured to us a better commentary in [sic] 'Maud' and 'In Memoriam' than all our critics have given us or ever will give us.[55]

Implicit in Maurice's claim is the idea that the poet's literary genius saturates, and is identifiable in, his person and that the camera, even more than the paintbrush, is capable of arresting and elucidating this iconicity for posterity.[56]

Cameron's celebrity portraits endeavoured, then, to capture something more than their subjects' own selves; by means of photographic immortalisation, they aimed to depict their sitters as paradigms or 'types' of human greatness.[57] As Margaret D. Stetz points out, in widely circulated images such as 'The Dirty Monk', 'Tennyson inhabit[s] the role not only of the poet laureate, but of the *quintessential* Victorian Poet'.[58] According to MacKay, this typological representational practice results in a persistent 'double vision', whereby we become aware of both the sitter's 'individual self' and 'a divine or transpersonal "meta-self"'.[59] Tellingly, in the letter to Herschel in which she rejected 'conventional topographic photography', Cameron gestured toward this biformity, expressing her desire to 'ennoble photography... by combining *the real and ideal* and sacrificing nothing of Truth by all possible devotion to Poetry and beauty'.[60] The projected combination of apparently contradictory aesthetic codes, here, draws attention to the paradoxes of meaning inherent in Cameron's photographs (as well as in Victorian responses to them). At once 'real' and 'ideal', her portraits promised both to actualise and transcendentalise their illustrious referents.

Cameron frequently annotated her photographs with the words 'From Life' to signal their status as dependable records of specific moments in time (the phrase denoted that she had not retouched the negative to improve her sitter's features or even to remove any scratches or blemishes that might have accidentally marked the plate).[61] Whereas many of her contemporaries advocated retouching and composition, arguing that such practices resulted, ironically, in more naturalistic images, Cameron suggested that her own, unaltered portraits were 'not only From the Life but to the Life'.[62] Her belief in the vivifying power of her photographs was echoed in the comments of her friends and reviewers. An 1893 article in the *Woman's Herald* described a picture of Herschel as 'a living, speaking portrait', while Edith Nicholl Ellison described an 1867 photograph of Tennyson as 'more lifelike to me than any other'.[63] Cameron's great-niece, Laura Troubridge, similarly suggested that her aunt's photographs provided authentic, vivid representations, claiming that, from them, sitters might 'learn more about their own faces than the looking-glass had ever told them'. The revelatory potential Troubridge lauds here is not merely mimetic, however; her subsequent assertion that 'Mrs. Cameron had the real artist's faculty of piercing through the outward structure to the very soul of the individual', implicitly shifts the discursive terrain from the real to the ideal – from the external features of the 'individual' to the transcendental qualities of the 'meta-self'.[64]

Other commentaries on Cameron's work make similar transitions: William Michael Rossetti claimed that 'the surprising and magnificent pictorial photographs of Mrs. Cameron ... well-nigh recreate a subject', but at the same time, 'place it in novel unanticipable lights; aggrandize the fine, suppress or ignore the petty; and transfigure both the subject-matter, and the reproducing process itself, into something almost higher than we know them to be'.[65] Implicit in Rossetti's panegyric, and in Cameron's own reflections on her art, is the notion that idealised representation may deliver a more truthful vision of the celebrity's essence, or being, than the merely lifelike. However, as Rossetti indicates, idealisation is a process with transformative effects. Significantly, when the poet and dramatist Sir Henry Taylor – Cameron's most-photographed celebrity subject – showed some portraits of himself to his wife, her playful response hinted that the images interpolated, rather than reflected, a sense of exalted nobility: 'most of them I think very grand; decidedly grander than anything you have yet written or lived; so I begin to expect great things of you'.[66] Though light-hearted in tone, this piece of wifely teasing points to the possibility that Cameron's idealised celebrity photographs *manufacture* rather than simply capture the greatness of 'great men'. The fact that Cameron's representation of 'the transcendent qualities of intellect and heroism' depended on a fixed set of visual signifiers ('as conventional, in their turn, as the formulaic poses, lighting, and backgrounds of the *carte*', Lukitsh suggests) lends further weight to the suggestion that her photographs constructed, as much as catalogued, Victorian celebrity.[67]

Cameron's photographic portraits cannot be read, then, as neutral documents. Although they putatively operated outside of the commercial framework of the *carte de visite* industry (a claim that will be reconsidered in the following section), they nevertheless invested heavily in the ideological values of the celebrity apparatus, portraying fame as the natural consequence of inherent 'greatness', while eliding their own role in the construction of that greatness. They also appear to have subscribed to the gendered conception of fame implicit in Carlyle's 'great man' theory of history; although Cameron produced many photographs of women, her gallery of celebrities is indubitably, conspicuously male in character. This impression is enhanced by the fact that the few photographs Cameron took of eminent women either are missing (as in the case of Christina Rossetti) or pre-date the period in which their subjects' fame reached its height (in the cases of Ellen Terry and Marie Spartali).[68] The most famous female literary lion of the day, George Eliot, never sat for Cameron, despite having corresponded with her.[69] Cameron's thinking on gender, greatness and renown appears, then, to have chimed with conventional Victorian values; tellingly, in a letter to Sir Henry Taylor, she wrote that while men are great 'thro' genius', women are great 'thro' love ... – that which women are born for'.[70] She is also reputed to have said that 'no woman should ever allow herself to be photographed between the ages of eighteen and eighty', suggesting that she participated, to an extent, in Victorian anxieties about the appropriateness of female self-display.[71] Her seeming endorsement of conservative gender norms is complicated, however, by her indomitable pursuit of personal 'greatness' and her unwavering determination to gain public recognition for her artistic accomplishments. Crucially, Cameron's photography was not simply a vehicle for celebrating and immortalising the great men of her age; it was also the means by which she sought to secure her own enduring fame.

The art of self-promotion

During the Victorian era, the celebrity arena came increasingly to resemble a marketplace. This commercial turn was accompanied by a growing recognition that it was no longer enough to rely on one's innate qualities in order to secure one's lasting fame; some level of engagement with the celebrity apparatus was also required. While (as Chapters 1 and 2 of this book demonstrate) Tennyson and Watts participated reluctantly and covertly in such self-promotional activities, Cameron showed an open willingness to work with (and, at times, manipulate) the commercial infrastructure supporting the celebrity industry. Though she viewed her photography as a 'high art' form, distinct from the moneymaking *carte* trade, and celebrated fame as something noble and exalted – the gift of posterity – she nevertheless appreciated the desirability of present-day renown and its associated material rewards. She therefore marketed herself relentlessly (and coerced others into doing the same), while navigating adroitly the obstacles inevitably faced by female celebrities in Victorian culture.

A close reading of Cameron's autobiographical fragment, 'Annals of my Glass House', reveals the tactical skill with which she negotiated the competing demands placed on famous women, moving dextrously between the poles of self-advertisement and self-effacement. Dwelling on the mixed critical response to her early work, Cameron wrote that while the photographic press was splenetic in its disapproval,

> Artists ... immediately crowned me with laurels, and though 'Fame' is pronounced 'The last infirmity of noble minds', I must confess that when those whose judgement I revered have valued and praised my works, 'my heart has leapt up like a rainbow in the sky', and I have renewed my zeal.[72]

Though unpublished at the time of her death, Cameron's musings reveal a keen awareness of audience; her self-praise is carefully modulated, here, in deference to the likely expectations of her imagined readership. Her acknowledgement of the pleasure derived from the admiration of her peers is presented as a 'confession', a characterisation that signals the need for humility in Victorian female autobiography. Her use of literary quotation and allusion, meanwhile, deflects attention (and agency) away from the writing 'I'. The (not-quite-accurate) citation of Wordsworth's poem, 'My Heart Leaps Up', positions her response to artistic acclaim as one of innocent, instinctual pleasure rather than indulgent self-congratulation.[73] And, though her evocation of a garlanded female artist inevitably recalls the moment in *Aurora Leigh* when the eponymous heroine bedecks herself with an ivy crown, Cameron warily establishes that *her* plaudits are sanctioned by the wider artistic community rather than self-awarded.[74]

The reference to Milton's *Lycidas* generates a rather more complex set of intertextual meanings, however. Most straightforwardly, Cameron draws on Milton's poem in order to disavow an immodest love of fame; this 'last infirmity of noble mind' is not what motivates her creative endeavours, she suggests.[75] Indeed, in common with the speaker of *Lycidas*, Cameron appears to doubt that she has yet reached artistic maturity;[76] her assurance that the early commendation of her peers served only to increase her 'zeal' implies that she has not been content to bask in prematurely bestowed glory, but rather, aware of her inadequacies, has striven constantly to improve. This intimation of sustained effort and application (a theme that recurs throughout the autobiography)[77] subtly alters the tenor of Cameron's reflections, suggesting that any praise she has received for her photography actually represents due reward for hard work. It also forges a secondary strand of affiliation with *Lycidas* for, though Milton's speaker perceives the pursuit of fame as a manifestation of human frailty, he also considers it 'the spur that the clear spirit doth raise /... To scorn delights, and live laborious days'.[78] The ultimate worthiness of such unremitting enterprise is affirmed in the poem by Phoebus, god of the arts, who reminds the speaker that, though life may be short, fame is immortal (a sentiment implicitly shared by Cameron and the Freshwater circle).[79] While appearing to serve the author's strategy of self-deprecation, then, the intertextual relationship with *Lycidas* in 'Annals of my Glass House' in fact gestures toward a more positive interpretation of the quest for fame – a celebration of, as much as an apologia for, Cameron's celebrity.

According to MacKay, such complex patterns of self-assertion and self-effacement are common in nineteenth-century women's autobiographies and represent an important feature of Cameron's memoir, in particular. Noting the use of the third person at the beginning of the 'Annals', MacKay argues that,

> [Cameron] not only denies herself a personal voice in her first sentence, but she negates herself in favor of her work, her apparent

subject, treating it as a published but checkered study in itself: '*Mrs. Cameron's Photography*, now ten years old, has passed the age of lisping and stammering and may speak for itself'. Even the story of her work is ostensibly a 'little history'. Yet in equally typical fashion for women's self voicing, Cameron subtly, perhaps even subversively, starts to build an incremental self-portrait that points up her creative energies.[80]

In fact, a subversive potential can be identified in the initial reference to 'Mrs. Cameron's Photography' critiqued by MacKay, for, as well as a reticent evasion of self, this phrase can be understood as a form of branding, an affirmation of Cameron's distinctive market identity. (Notably, reviews of her work were often titled 'Mrs. Cameron's Photographs' or 'Mrs. Cameron's Photography', indicating that, by the time she wrote the 'Annals', the phrase had gained a degree of cultural and commercial currency.) This sense is compounded in a later aside: Cameron's declaration that the Isle of Wight has furnished her with 'lovely subjects, *as all the patrons of my photography know*', positions her work as a recognisable brand with a defined and active clientele.[81]

That Cameron saw her photography as a commercial as well as an artistic venture, and understood the importance of marketing and self-promotion, is clear from her private letters. Her correspondence with Watts, for instance, is marked not only by the elevated language of artistic appreciation but also pragmatic discussions on increasing saleability: 'because I know you must turn your labour & expense into some pecuniary advantage ... I am sure that you should now turn all your attention to the object of producing pictures free from those defects which are purely the result of careless or imperfect manipulation', Watts counselled, adding, 'it is most especially with reference to the sale of your Photographs that this is so important'.[82] In a series of letters to Sir Henry Cole, founder of the South Kensington Museum, meanwhile, Cameron actively solicited institutional endorsement and exhibition space for her work.[83] Just a day after photographing Cole at Little Holland House in 1865, Cameron sent him a copy of her portfolio, along with a letter indicating that she would be honoured should the Museum agree to display her work.[84] A year later, she wrote to Cole again to enquire about the possibility of staging an exhibition at the South Kensington. Though already confident in the artistic merit of her work, Cameron realised that its installation in a prominent museum would serve not only to advertise but also to publicly legitimise its worth. She was also shrewd enough to realise that public recognition would, in all likelihood, bring with it financial rewards. In an 1868 letter to Cole, she discussed with remarkable frankness her need to secure remuneration as well as critical acclaim for her work, noting that fame without fortune would not help her to meet the cost of educating her sons. The apparently playful tone of her admission masks the seriousness of the monetary situation in which she and her husband found themselves in the 1860s; owing to the repeated failure of the coffee crop on the family's estates in Ceylon, they had little security of income and were often obliged to seek help from relatives and friends.[85] Indeed, in 1869, Cameron turned to Cole once more, imploring him to find space for her work at the South Kensington. The increasingly desperate tone of her entreaties testifies to the growing insecurity of her family's financial situation and draws attention to the economic realities that are often occluded by the spectacle of celebrity. It also indicates that her unremitting pursuit of celebrity sitters (for which she was criticised by Freshwater visitors Edward Lear and William Allingham) was attributable to something more than a mere lionising propensity.

Yet, while Cameron evidently hoped that her photography would generate additional income during this period of crisis, critics such as Gernsheim and Mike Weaver have suggested that her activities may actually have exacerbated her family's distress, for the wet collodion process she favoured required a ready supply of expensive chemicals and, as her 1869 letter to Cole makes clear, her income rarely exceeded her outlay.[86] In this light, it is tempting to go along with Cameron's son Hardinge's suggestion that his mother was 'the least business-like' of his parents, or Anne Thackeray Ritchie's claim that Cameron was too much of 'a true artist in her attitude towards money' to have been a successful businesswoman.[87] To do so, however, would be to disregard the perspicacity with which Cameron viewed Victorian celebrity culture and the indefatigability with which she exploited its mechanisms. Notably, she was one of the first photographers to have consistently copyrighted her work, registering over 500 photographs at Stationer's Hall between 1864 and 1875 (among them twenty-eight portraits of Tennyson, nineteen of Sir Henry Taylor and ten of Watts).[88] Her determination to assert her legal status as the sole creator of these images indicates not only a desire to profit from them financially but also an awareness of the workings of celebrity culture. As Tom Mole points out, 'in order to boost the celebrity individual's visibility over that of other aspirants, the celebrity apparatus turned his or her proper name into a brand name'.[89] Cameron evidently appreciated the importance of establishing a distinctive identity for herself within the 'name-centred society' of

Victorian Britain, for she not only registered her photographs formally but also annotated them with explicit statements of authorship.[90] Even those albums assembled as gifts for her friends were sometimes marked by declarations of creative ownership: 'I have no assistant and the whole process from first to last including the printing is all done by my own hand', Cameron insisted in a handwritten addendum to the album she presented to Herschel in 1864; 'Each picture is registered, and I have to request that these photographs may not be copied. JMC Nov. 64'.[91]

As well as comprehending the legal, commercial and cultural significance of the artist's name within the celebrity marketplace, Cameron seems to have understood the importance of the relationship between dissemination, promotion and sales. Like the commercial photographers whose products she disparaged, she recognised the benefits of using a professional dealer to distribute her work, entering into an agreement with leading London print-sellers, P. & D. Colnaghi & Co., in 1864. Keen to gain critical plaudits, she submitted regularly to national and international photographic exhibitions (often winning medals and honourable mentions), but she also organised (and financed) a series of one-woman shows in private galleries with the aim of generating profits.[92] Furthermore, in an audacious but canny move designed to bring notice of her exhibited works to the widest possible audience – and to counteract negative reviews in the photographic press[93] – she coerced literary and artistic acquaintances into providing positive reviews in mainstream periodicals. In 1865, William Michael Rossetti reported to Frederic George Stephens that 'our good old friend the enthusiastic Mrs. Cameron has been writing to me ... and refers to some of her photographs now at 9 Conduit Street, which she would like me to write about'.[94] Although seemingly reluctant to comply ('I shall be compelled to tell her the simple fact that I have no publication wherein to write about them. ... Perhaps you will considerately regard the task as delegated to you'),[95] Rossetti eventually succumbed to Cameron's badgering, praising her work in an 1866 essay for the *Fine Arts Quarterly Review* and an 1867 article for the *Chronicle*; Stephens, too, accepted his delegated commission, writing a brief, but complimentary report on Cameron's contribution to the Conduit Street exhibition for the *Athenaeum* in 1865.[96]

Other high-profile friends to have admired Cameron's work in print include Coventry Patmore in *Macmillan's Magazine* and Anne Thackeray and William Allingham in the *Pall Mall Gazette*, while members of her circle are also likely to have been responsible for favourable notices in publications such as the *Reader* and the *Intellectual Observer*, as Lukitsh suggests.[97] Though independently produced, these unsigned reviews deployed a similar range of promotional tactics in their discussion of Cameron's work, invariably juxtaposing the elevated language of aesthetic appreciation with the pragmatic commercialism of advertisement as they sought, on the one hand, to construct Cameron as a serious artist and, on the other, to hawk her photographic wares. In order to validate the desirability and artistic value of her works at a time when the status of photography was still a matter of contention (in 1862, one MP had argued in Parliament that 'photography was not a fine art, but a mechanical process'),[98] Cameron's supporters set up a series of comparisons with Renaissance painting and sculpture. Thackeray, for instance, claimed that 'there is one portrait, of WATTS ... which is Holbein-like in its perfection of detail, while another ... for repose and solemn flow of outline puts one in mind of some stately figure of MICHAEL ANGELO'S'.[99] Patmore, similarly, suggested that Cameron's portraits of Tennyson, Taylor and Watts were 'as noble and true as old Italian art could have made them', adding, 'the beauty of the heads in [her] photographs is the beauty of the highest art. We seem to be gazing upon so many Luinis, Leonardos, and Vandykes'.[100] These assertions of artistic value were carefully balanced with practical details about where Cameron's productions could be seen and, more importantly, purchased: Thackeray noted assiduously that Cameron's portfolio could be viewed 'at Messrs. Colnaghis' by anybody who likes to go there'; Patmore dutifully publicised her 1865–66 show at the French Gallery, Pall Mall; while Allingham conscientiously directed readers to her 1868 exhibition at the German Gallery, Old Bond Street.[101]

Further evidence of Cameron's adeptness at self-promotion by proxy can be found in the succession of articles about her work that featured in leading newspapers, such as the *Illustrated London News*, the *Morning Post* and *The Times*. The sequence of notices that appeared in the *ILN* between 1865 and 1873, in particular, bears subtle traces of her influence. On 15 July 1865, the newspaper announced that a new exhibition of Cameron's work was available to view at Colnaghi's.[102] A week later, a second notice appeared, declaring that the paper had 'been requested to state that, to artists', Mrs Cameron's photographs would 'be sold half-price'.[103] By November, the *ILN*'s art correspondent was again plugging Cameron's wares:

About three months back, under the heading 'Art in Photography', we reviewed a series of photographs, by Mrs. Cameron, then, as now, on view at Messrs. Colnaghi's . ... Since that review Mrs. Cameron has produced many larger and still more remarkable works. We are glad to add that the whole of her collection is now being exhibited ... at the French Gallery, Pall-mall. As the collection will only remain open to the public three weeks, we strongly recommend a visit from all interested in a wonderful art ... and we hope to have space next week to notice that portion of the collection which we have not yet reviewed.[104]

The paper was true to its word; an enthusiastic review appeared a week later, followed by an announcement on 9 December that the exhibition at the French Gallery would remain open, free of charge, for an extra fortnight.[105] Some months later, another obliging notice emerged, publicising the Queen's 'warm admiration of Mrs. Cameron's works'.[106] Indeed, so regularly did the *ILN*'s unnamed but persistent informant push for new notices and endorsements of Cameron's photographs that, by 1873, the newspaper was forced to concede, 'we have ... repeatedly acknowledged their rare merits, and need not, therefore, review them anew'.[107]

As well as seeking press attention, Cameron was also willing to exploit her network of celebrity acquaintances to boost her profile and profits. The 'Priced Catalogue' that accompanied her 1868 exhibition at the German Gallery indicates that she was only too aware of the pecuniary worth of her eminent friends; tellingly, she valued her portraits of famous men much more highly than her allegorical studies or 'fancy subjects'. More revealing still, the gradations *within* her portraits' pricing structure suggest an acute understanding of the varying marketability of different sitters.[108] As Sylvia Wolf points out, a photograph of the American poet Henry Wadsworth Longfellow was retailed at half the price of a comparably sized image of Robert Browning, signalling the latter's greater saleability among British consumers.[109] The best known (and most bankable) of Cameron's sitters were represented in multiple images, at multiple price-points, maximising their potential consumer base; for instance, six different portraits of Tennyson were listed, ranging from 7/6 to 21 shillings. The most expensive photographs were those accompanied by a 'genuine autograph', a lucrative supplement acquired through Cameron's continual beleaguering of her famous friends. In 1868 she wrote to Herschel, 'Am I to be pardoned for sending you blank mounts & trusting to your goodness to sign them *when you can.* ... The Photograph of you is to my idea doubled in value by *your* genuine autograph'.[110] Tennyson was an even more frequent target: his niece recalled, 'the more he signed, the more she wanted him to sign; and

I have really pitied my uncle when she has come flying up to Farringford with such a huge sheaf of her photographs of him that she has had to hire a carriage to bring them, and has plumped them down before him, with a selection of new pens, so that he might not have the excuse of not having a pen handy to sign them with'.[111]

Although Cameron's doggedness at times frustrated her Freshwater friends (and Tennyson, in particular), they were mainly supportive of her artistic ambitions, allowing her to benefit from their profile and influence: as well as providing technical advice and encouragement, Watts permitted her to make public his admiration of her work; Allingham, as noted earlier, 'blew the trumpet for it' in the press; while Tennyson used his connections to furnish her with a steady stream of celebrity sitters and, in 1874, invited her to illustrate a new edition of his hugely successful Arthurian epic, *Idylls of the King*.[112] Cameron was quick to perceive the potential financial benefits of such collaboration, noting that '[Gustave] Doré got a fortune for his *drawn* fancy illustrations of these Idylls'.[113] Once again, she set about promoting and publicising her work with gusto; between November and December 1874 she sent a series of letters and telegrams to her friend, Sir Edward Ryan, begging him to use his influence with Sir George Webb Dasent (brother-in-law of John Delane, editor of *The Times*) to get a lavish, six-guinea volume of her *Idylls* photographs noticed in the newspaper. Yet, though indubitably motivated by the prospect of financial reward ('I *hope* to get one single grain of the momentous mountain heap of profits the poetical part of the work brings in to Alfred'), Cameron also sought a less tangible form of remuneration from her involvement in the *Idylls* project.[114] When Tennyson first proposed the idea, she replied, 'Now *you* know, Alfred, that *I* know that it is immortality to me to be bound up with you'.[115] As this response reveals, Cameron's desire for present fortune was never straightforwardly extricable from her desire for enduring fame.

A similarly multifaceted wish to make money while assuring the permanence of her artistic legacy marked her dealings with the Autotype Company in the 1870s. Patented in 1868, autotype was a popular means of photographic reproduction which enabled fade-resistant carbon prints to be produced from original negatives. When the Camerons decided, in 1875, to leave England permanently for Ceylon, Julia wrote to her friend Blanche Warre Cornish:

> I could not bear that all my ten years labour should be forgotten and 'the grace of the fashion of it' perish and pass out of sight and this

I knew was too likely to happen – stored away in an upper locked and barred room ... as all my precious negatives are. Therefore I had most of them autotyped at an expense of two guineas for each negative, consoling my self-reproach for this outlay by thinking that in selling each print for 7s. 6d. I should soon recover my expenses.[116]

Cameron's optimism was misplaced; she quickly became embroiled in 'rather a fierce controversy' with the Autotype Company, having failed to realise that they charged a commission of 40 per cent on every print sold before entering into a contract with them.[117] Critics have viewed this miscalculation as further evidence of her 'wayward business sense'.[118] However, as Wolf argues, Cameron was no naive 'dilettante or dabbler'; her commercial instincts were, in many ways, remarkably prescient and, although her profits were limited, she did make money from her work.[119] More importantly, from the perspective of this study, her entrepreneurial spirit and aptitude for self-promotion demonstrated a clear understanding of the celebrity industry and its status as a marketplace. If Victorian culture attempted to control the form and magnitude of female incursions into the celebrity arena, then Cameron managed to work within and, where necessary, circumvent its strictures. Indeed, it could be argued that she negotiated the celebrity infrastructure with greater dexterity and brio than her male counterparts. Her artistic idealism and instinctive generosity may, at times, have undermined her commercial savvy, but the fact that she saw fame and fortune as mutually reinforcing, and did everything within her power to turn technological advances and the influence of the press to her advantage, indicates her keen appreciation of the workings of the celebrity apparatus and marks her out as a pioneering participant in modern celebrity culture.

Reconstructing Julia Margaret Cameron

If Cameron's embracement of the growing commercialisation of Victorian celebrity serves to distinguish her from the male participants in the Freshwater circle, and from Tennyson in particular, then, in their respective posthumous legacies, this distinction becomes even more pronounced. Despite her commitment to achieving personal renown during her lifetime, Cameron left little biographical material through which she could be appropriated and 'known' as a public figure after her death in Ceylon in January 1879. Her autobiography remained incomplete and unpublished; much of her voluminous correspondence was, by her own wish, destroyed; and relatively few images of her person were in circulation. Those images that did exist, such as the platinum print of her 1852 portrait by Watts, or an 1858 photograph of her with two of her sons, did little to construct her as a celebrated artist, or even an energetic, independent woman, instead figuring her as passive, pious and/or maternal. Little wonder that only seven years after her death a reminiscer writing in the *Photographic News* questioned whether any of the emerging generation would remember Julia Margaret Cameron.[120]

Whereas, as Chapter 5 of this study shows, Tennyson took careful control of his posthumous legacy, charging his son Hallam with the production of an authorised and authoritative *Memoir*, no definitive biography followed Cameron's death. Instead, her story was disseminated as a series of disparate traces, threaded through a variety of fragmented and contingent accounts that invariably shaped their remembrances of her fame to their own ideological interests. This fracturing of perspective is most clearly evident in the divergent ways in which Cameron's biographers framed her activities in relation to her gender. Almost all constructed her as an 'exceptional' woman; however, as Weber suggests, 'exceptionality' could prove a double-edged sword for female celebrities: 'to be branded singular ... was a coded label that might well have read as un-gendered and un-sexed'.[121] Therefore, though many of her extensive network of female relations, keen to mythologise their 'exceptional' matrilineage, emphasised Cameron's disregard for custom and celebrated her trailblazing career, other biographers coupled such observations with reflections on her traditionally 'feminine' virtues – her generosity and devotion to her family – thus staging a return to the conventionally gendered ground they ostensibly impugned.

In the histories of the male participants in the Freshwater circle, for instance, Cameron's celebrity was often minimised, her story reduced to a series of domestic anecdotes. In his 1885 *Autobiography*, Sir Henry Taylor constructed her as a loveable eccentric with a 'genial, ardent ... generous nature', noting her tendency to shower friends with unsolicited gifts ('Indian shawls, turquoise bracelets, inlaid portfolios, ivory elephants, etc.') and to open her home to complete strangers ('One day, I remember, a lady and gentleman and their daughter came to luncheon, and Mrs. Cameron, wishing to introduce them to me, took the liberty of asking them what were their names. She had met them in the steam-boat ... and had invited them without knowing anything about them').[122] These affectionate reminiscences do little to construct Cameron as a celebrity; significantly, Taylor quotes Cameron discussing Tennyson's, rather than her own, attitude to fame and, although he describes her portrait of Herschel as 'one of the greatest triumphs of photography', his anecdotes are mainly concerned with detailing Cameron's idiosyncrasies and the unconventionality of life at her Dimbola home.[123] Mary Seton Watts's 1912 biography of her husband, G. F. Watts, similarly focuses on Cameron's eccentricity, characterising her as a 'unique figure', who 'commanded' over life at Freshwater.[124] Watts does pay some attention to Cameron's achievements as an artist, suggesting that 'she was able to give to her work a poetry and a mystery far removed from the work of the ordinary photographer, far even from that of the very best who have followed her' (as a designer and craftswoman herself, Watts was doubtless aware of the challenges nineteenth-century women faced in gaining widespread critical and artistic recognition).[125] Yet, though laudatory, her recollections are no less selective or shaped to a particular agenda than Taylor's. References to Cameron's lionising of G. F. Watts as 'the greatest living painter', and to her extensive 'correspondence with Signor on the subject of principles of composition', serve primarily to extol the latter by emphasising his artistic genius and role as master to Cameron's student.[126]

Cameron's biography played a similar, subsidiary role in the raft of late-Victorian and Edwardian memoirs of Tennyson. Though an inevitable presence in reminiscences of the Laureate's life at Freshwater, Cameron usually features as the ebullient foil to his more grave and pensive persona. Agnes Weld's *Glimpses of Tennyson and of Some of his Relations and Friends* (1903), Edith Nicholl Ellison's *A Child's Recollections of Tennyson* (1906) and Wilfrid Ward's 'Tennyson at Freshwater' (1912) all position Cameron as the dynamic, driving force behind the community of celebrities that gathered at Freshwater during the 1860s and 1870s while, nevertheless, subjugating her life story to their prevailing interest in the Laureate.[127] This is hardly surprising: in the years following his death, as during his lifetime, Tennyson's name functioned as a beacon, attracting a mass of readers to any publication that bore it. Significantly, even Cameron's son Henry's posthumous collection of his mother's work – *Alfred, Lord Tennyson and his Friends* (1893) – privileged the poet over the photographer in its title.

However, although this volume's 'pictorial biography' focuses predominantly on Tennyson and the 'brotherhood' of poets, painters, thinkers and scientists that congregated around him, its textual front matter is more concerned with commemorating Cameron. Henry Cameron's introduction begins by quoting F. D. Maurice's acclamation of Julia Margaret's work (cited earlier in this chapter), before reproducing a large section of her autobiography in which the 'hurrahs' of her contemporaries are recorded ('Henry Taylor said the picture was as fine as Alfred Tennyson's finest poem'; 'The Laureate has since said of it that he likes it better than any other photograph'; 'Mr. Watts gave me such encouragement that I felt I had wings to fly with').[128] Unlike the male relatives of many nineteenth-century female celebrities, then, Henry Cameron made no attempt to play down his mother's professional status; indeed, during the 1890s, he seems to have taken a keen interest in securing her reputation as an important photographic artist.[129] As well as instigating the publication of *Alfred, Lord Tennyson and his Friends*, he authorised articles on his mother's life and work in the *Windsor* and *Century* magazines, supplying both periodicals with biographical information and permissions for the reproduction of images.[130] This concern for his mother's posthumous legacy was not entirely disinterested, however. Henry Cameron was, in the 1890s, trying to make his own name as an artistic photographer and, in this light, it is interesting to note that the publications he sanctioned often printed notices and examples of *his* work alongside that of his mother. It seems that the retrospective appreciation of Cameron's *oeuvre* facilitated by Henry in late-Victorian print media enabled him, conveniently, to kindle public awareness of his own photography by anchoring himself to his mother's name and locating himself, implicitly, as the inheritor of her creative talent.

Such manoeuvrings by Victorian celebrities' relatives were not uncommon. Family members played an integral role in sustaining their kin's posthumous fame; however, as Ives points out, they could also 'attempt to manipulate that celebrity status by defining (or redefining)' the celebrity's 'life and achievements' to their own ends.[131] In Cameron's case, it was her extensive network of female relatives who sought most persistently to maintain and propagate her memory in their reminiscences and literary writings; in doing so, however, they inevitably (though, perhaps, unconsciously) shaped their representations of her life to their own interests and preconceptions, generating a shifting and contradictory anthology of biographical traces.

For instance, Cameron's niece Isabella (Lady Somerset), a prominent women's rights campaigner, appropriated Cameron as a proto-feminist in the women's press of the 1890s. An unsigned 1891 article in the *Woman's Herald* (a newspaper to which Somerset had strong connections) declared that

An account ... of this wonderful woman, who has surpassed all men, and raised photography to a fine art, will not be without deep interest to women, more especially to those women who are now treading in her steps and taking up the camera as a profession.[132]

Another celebratory piece on 'Julia Cameron and her Work: the Story of a Remarkable Woman' appeared in the *Woman's Herald* in 1893 (the year Somerset took over as editor) while, in 1894, Somerset devoted much of her signed review of Henry Cameron's *Tennyson and his Friends*, in the renamed *Woman's Signal*, to the repetition of admiring anecdotes about her aunt.[133] Owing to her ambition, drive and determined pursuit of photography as something more than just a casual amusement, Cameron proved an ideal exemplar for the Victorian women's movement, which sought to dismantle the stereotype of the 'proper' domestic woman by promoting female activity, employability and independence. However, on account of Cameron's rather traditional gender politics, she could also be constructed in alternative terms. While acknowledging her great-aunt's revolutionary artistic vision, Laura Troubridge, in her 1925 *Memories and Reflections*, suggested that her personal values were much more conventional in character: a devoted wife and mother, who saw her role as 'to serve and bless', Cameron 'cared nothing for the feminist movement and the rights and wrongs of [her] sex', according to Troubridge's narrative.[134]

Contested versions of Cameron's posthumous identity emerged not only between but also *within* the accounts of her female relations. In 1886, Cameron's niece Julia (one of her favourite photographic subjects and the second wife of Leslie Stephen) authored an entry for her aunt in the recently conceived *Dictionary of National Biography*. In doing so, she automatically identified Cameron as exceptional and iconic for, as Henry Matthew points out, relatively few women were given their own entries in the *DNB*, more usually appearing as 'an appendage to men … mentioned only at the end, following the death of the subject of the article, like a vampirish adjunct'.[135] Not only did Stephen's entry carve out a space for Cameron distinct from her husband (who was the subject of a separate article), it also emphasised her professional identity and achievements, defining her as a 'photographer', and listing some of the prizes won during her short career.[136] However, in other respects, Stephen's biography undermined its own construction of Cameron as an autonomous woman and self-determining celebrity. The detailed inventory provided of Cameron's famous friends and sitters (including Carlyle, Taylor, Herschel, Darwin, Tennyson and Browning), on the one hand, implied that she was accepted into the highest echelons of intellectual and artistic society but, on the other, defined her problematically in terms of the men with whom she associated. Additionally, Stephen's catalogue of Cameron's personal attributes contains echoes of the qualities ascribed to the Victorian feminine ideal: Cameron is celebrated as much for her 'philanthropy', 'benevolence', 'genuine sympathy and goodness of heart' as for her role as an eminent photographer.[137]

A similar representational bifurcation marks the writings of Anne Thackeray Ritchie. Although not a blood relation, Ritchie can nevertheless be positioned as a kind of kinswoman to Cameron owing to the intimate connections that existed between their families.[138] Further, she was one of the most assiduous guardians of Cameron's posthumous reputation, contributing a collection of celebratory 'Reminiscences' to *Alfred, Lord Tennyson and his Friends* and a heartfelt essay, 'From Friend to Friend', to *Cornhill Magazine* in 1916 (the essay was later reprinted in a volume of the same title). Both texts worked to construct Cameron as someone who operated outside of the norms of Victorian femininity. According to Ritchie, 'One marked peculiarity in [her] whole family was their respect for their own time; our philistine domestic rule, by which, from the earliest hour in the morning, the women of the house are expected to be at the receipt of custom, to live in public, to receive any casual stranger, any passing visitor, was utterly ignored by them'.[139] As well as granting herself time, Ritchie suggests, Cameron furnished herself at Dimbola with the physical and metaphorical room required to pursue her photographic ambitions; her commandeering of domestic spaces in the service of her art was typical of her tendency to '[allow] herself in life and on paper more space than is usually accorded to other people'.[140] Such assertions of Cameron's 'disregard for ordinary rules' were supplemented, however, by counter-narratives of selfless benevolence and conventional domesticity.[141] Ritchie identified in Cameron a self-abnegating propensity – 'Torch-bearers sometimes consume themselves and burn some of their own life and spirit in the torches they carry' – as well as a nurturing instinct and affiliation with home and hearth: 'After my father's death she brought us [Ritchie and her sister] to her cottage, where fires of hospitality and sympathy were lighted and endless kindness and helping affection surrounded us from her ... all through that cold and icy winter'.[142] As Alison Booth surmises, this kind of return to gendered conventions is one of the paradoxical effects of biographical celebrations of atypical women: 'norms must be restated when exceptions to them are registered'.[143]

The genealogical appropriation and renegotiation of Cameron's identity took a new turn in the writings of her great-niece, Virginia Woolf (daughter of Julia Stephen and niece-by-marriage of Ritchie). In 1926,

Woolf published a selection of her great-aunt's portraiture under the title *Victorian Photographs of Famous Men and Fair Women*. Similar in structure to Henry Cameron's *Tennyson and his Friends*, the book showcased Julia Margaret's sitters in its collection of plates, while focusing on her life and career in two prefatory essays (one by Woolf, the other by Roger Fry). Unlike Henry Cameron's homage to his mother, though, Woolf's work was not based on personal knowledge; her great-aunt had died three years before she was born and so her tribute was necessarily dependent on other sources, which she adapted and reshaped to suit her biographical philosophy and personal ends. Rejecting the Victorian tradition of life-writing as stultifyingly longwinded, Woolf sought instead to capture the *essence* of Cameron's personality in her essay.[144] In doing so, she adopted an ironic distance from her subject, evident in her summary of Cameron's photographic career:

> In 1865, when she was fifty, [Cameron's] son's gift of a camera gave her at last an outlet for the energies which she had dissipated in poetry and fiction and doing up houses and concocting curries and entertaining her friends. Now she became a photographer. ... Boatmen were turned into King Arthur; village girls into Queen Guenevere. Tennyson was wrapped in rugs: Sir Henry Taylor was crowned with tinsel. The parlour-maid sat for her portrait and the guest had to answer the bell.[145]

The sense of amused detachment (and casual concern for fact) manifest in this quotation are also apparent in Woolf's play *Freshwater*, a farce based on the lives of the Freshwater circle, written for and performed by the Bloomsbury Group.[146] In it, Cameron is represented as a Victorian eccentric, who, after ordering that a turkey be killed to provide the wings required for her photograph of a Muse, declares, 'The turkey is happy. ... The turkey has become part and parcel of my immortal art'.[147] In both texts, Woolf's comically exaggerated rendering of her great-aunt suggests a modernist rejection of the outmoded values and excesses of Victorian culture, for which Cameron and her contemporaries are made to stand. This process of inter-generational refutation is undercut, however, by the affinities that emerge between Woolf's biographical project and Cameron's aesthetic ideology. In her essay on 'The New Biography', Woolf stipulates that the biographer should be not a 'chronicler', but an 'artist' with the ability to blend the 'real' and the 'imaginary' – a demand that echoes Cameron's insistence on combining the 'real and ideal' in (bio)photographic portraiture.[148] Furthermore, Woolf's construction of

Cameron as one of a family of 'remarkable' and 'imperious' women in the introduction to *Victorian Photographs* stages a self-interested recuperation of her great-aunt's history and identity; by drawing attention to her iconoclastic pedigree, Woolf implicitly cements her own status as an 'exceptional' woman.

Cameron's legacy was, then, subject to perpetual remodelling by her kith and kin. The interpretative revisions to which her reputation was subject – her shift in status from exemplary modern woman to quaintly eccentric relic of a bygone age – demonstrates Booth's point that biographical writing 'tends to have a very brief shelf life, as later generations need new versions of the past'.[149] It is worth noting, however, that a sense of representational instability does not emerge only from the competing or internally conflicted accounts of Cameron's descendants; it is always already present in Cameron's own writing, photography and lived practices. As this chapter has shown, her self-construction consistently undermined the traditional distinction between 'fame' and 'celebrity' (whereby, as Weber summarises, 'fame stands for the high, celebrity for the low. Fame marks aspiration; celebrity brands ambition'), along with assumptions about the efficacy and extent of female agency within the Victorian celebrity arena.[150] Seeking both immediate commercial success and enduring reputational renown, Cameron identified herself by turns as a photographer, an artist, and a wife and mother.[151] This vacillating understanding of self, in conjunction with the strategically shifting posthumous representations of her life and career, signals the inherent mutability of celebrity identity, the requirement for it to modify and adapt to meet changing cultural ideals and the contradictory demands of the celebrity infrastructure. While Cameron may have sought to arrest and 'immortalise' fame in her portraits of great men, her own history belies the notion that celebrity is inexorable or fixed.

Notes

1. Helmut Gernsheim, *Julia Margaret Cameron: Her Life and Photographic Work* (London: Gordon Fraser, 1975), p. 15.
2. Photographs were not accepted by the National Portrait Gallery during Cameron's lifetime and beyond. In 1926, Roger Fry wrote, 'One day we may hope that the National Portrait Gallery will be deprived of so large a part of its grant that it will turn to fostering the art of photography and will rely on its results for its records instead of buying acres of canvas covered at great expense by fashionable practitioners in paint' (Virginia Woolf and Roger Fry,

Victorian Photographs of Famous Men and Fair Women (London: Hogarth Press, 1926), p. 15).

3. Gernsheim, p. 15.
4. See *Women Writers and the Artifacts of Celebrity in the Long Nineteenth Century*, ed. by Ann R. Hawkins and Maura Ives (Farnham: Ashgate, 2012); Brenda R. Weber, *Women and Literary Celebrity in the Nineteenth Century: the Transatlantic Production of Fame and Gender* (Farnham: Ashgate, 2012); Alexis Easley, *Literary Celebrity, Gender, and Victorian Authorship, 1850–1914* (Newark: University of Delaware Press, 2011); and *Marketing the Author: Authorial Personae, Narrative Selves and Self-Fashioning, 1880–1930*, ed. by Marysa Demoor (Basingstoke: Palgrave Macmillan, 2004).
5. Weber, p. 16.
6. Tom Mole, *Byron's Romantic Celebrity: Industrial Culture and the Hermeneutic of Intimacy* (Basingstoke: Palgrave Macmillan, 2007), p. 5.
7. Easley, p. 12.
8. Weber, p. 4. See also *Women Writers and the Artifacts of Celebrity*.
9. Maura Ives, 'Introduction: Women Writers and the Artifacts of Celebrity', in *Women Writers and the Artifacts of Celebrity*, ed. by Hawkins and Ives, pp. 1–12 (p. 12) (my emphasis).
10. Mole advocates care when undertaking gendered readings of celebrity culture: 'It [the celebrity apparatus] constrained and empowered celebrities of both genders in gender-specific ways, but neither gender had the monopoly on constraint or empowerment' (p. 21).
11. Agnes Grace Weld, *Glimpses of Tennyson and of Some of his Relations and Friends* (London and Oxford: Williams & Norgate, 1903), p. 65.
12. 'Photography as an Employment for Women', *The Englishwoman's Review*, [1 July 1867], pp. 219–23 (p. 219), in *Gale 19th Century UK Periodicals* <http://gale.cengage.co.uk> [accessed 5 April 2013]. Similar claims were made in a number of articles in the Victorian women's press: see, for instance, Adeline Anning, 'A Profession for Women: Photography', *The Woman's Signal*, 7 March 1895, p. 149; and Emily Hill, 'Photography for Women: An Interview with Mrs. Weed Ward', *The Woman's Signal*, 28 April 1898, pp. 259–60, both in *Gale 19th Century UK Periodicals* <http://gale.cengage.co.uk> [accessed 8 April 2013].
13. [Coventry Patmore], 'Mrs. Cameron's Photographs', *Macmillan's Magazine*, 13 (1866), 230–31 (p. 230), in *ProQuest British Periodicals* <http://www.proquest.co.uk> [accessed 8 April 2013].
14. Leo Braudy, *The Frenzy of Renown: Fame and Its History* (New York: Vintage, 1997), p. 450.
15. For a history of 'cartomania,' see Philippa Wright, 'Little Pictures: Julia Margaret Cameron and Small-Format Photography', in *Julia Margaret Cameron: the Complete Photographs*, ed. by Julian Cox and Colin Ford (London: Thames & Hudson, 2003), pp. 81–93 (pp. 82–83); Joanne Lukitsh, 'Julia Margaret Cameron and the "Enoblement" of Photographic Portraiture', in *Victorian Scandals: Representations of Gender and Class*, ed. by Kristine Ottesen Garrigan (Athens, OH: Ohio University Press, 1992), pp. 207–32 (pp. 211–17); and Daniel A. Novak, *Realism, Photography and Nineteenth-Century Fiction* (Cambridge: Cambridge University Press, 2008), pp. 10–11.
16. Wright, p. 82.

17. See Gernsheim, p. 59.
18. A[ndrew] Wynter, 'Cartes de Visite', *Once a Week*, 25 January 1862, pp. 134–37 (pp. 134–35), in *ProQuest British Periodicals* <http://www.proquest.co.uk> [accessed 8 April 2013].
19. John Plunkett, *Queen Victoria: First Media Monarch* (Oxford: Oxford University Press, 2003), p. 174.
20. See 'Cartes de Visite of Celebrities', *The Saturday Review*, 27 September 1862, pp. 371–72 (p. 372), in *ProQuest British Periodicals* <http://www.proquest.co.uk> [accessed 8 April 2013]; and Wynter, p. 136.
21. Wynter, p. 136.
22. [Lady Elizabeth Eastlake], 'Art. V.', *The Quarterly Review*, 101 (1857), 442–68 (p. 465), in *ProQuest British Periodicals* <http://www.proquest.co.uk> [accessed 8 April 2013].
23. [Anne Thackeray], 'A Book of Photographs', *Pall Mall Gazette*, 10 April 1865, pp. 10–11 (p. 10), in *Gale 19th Century British Library Newspapers* <http://gale.cengage.co.uk> [accessed 8 April 2013].
24. Wynter, p. 135.
25. Cited in Gernsheim, p. 35.
26. Elizabeth Barrett, 'Letter to Mary Russell Mitford (1843)', in *The Broadview Anthology of British Literature: the Victorian Era*, ed. by Joseph Black, Leonard Conolly, Kate Flint and others (Peterborough, Ontario: Broadview Press, 2006), p. 381 (my emphasis).
27. Sir Frederick Pollock, '"Presidential Address", Photographic Society (1855)', in *The Broadview Anthology*, ed. by Black, Conolly, Flint and others, p. 381.
28. 'National Portrait Gallery', *Art Journal*, 16 (1856), 99–100 (pp. 100, 99), in *ProQuest British Periodicals* <http://www.proquest.co.uk> [accessed 8 April 2013].
29. Wynter, p. 135.
30. Cited in *Letters of Anne Thackeray Ritchie*, ed. by Hester Ritchie (London: John Murray, 1924), p. 128.
31. Cameron's celebrity sitters included the historian Thomas Carlyle; the musician Joseph Joachim; the scientists Charles Darwin and Sir John Herschel; the artists William Holman Hunt, Valentine Prinsep, William Michael Rossetti and G. F. Watts; the novelist Anthony Trollope; and the poets Robert Browning, Aubrey de Vere, Henry Wadsworth Longfellow, Sir Henry Taylor and Alfred Tennyson.
32. Cited in Lukitsh, 'Julia Margaret Cameron', pp. 227, 228.
33. Cited in Sylvia Wolf, *Julia Margaret Cameron's Women* (New Haven and London: Yale University Press, 1998), p. 216; Julia Margaret Cameron, 'Annals of My Glass House', in *Annals of My Glass House: Photographs by Julia Margaret Cameron*, ed. by Violet Hamilton (Seattle and London: University of Washington Press, 1996), pp. 11–16 (p. 16); Colin Ford, *Julia Margaret Cameron: a Critical Biography* (Los Angeles: J. Paul Getty Museum, 2003), p. 50.
34. Braudy, p. 379.
35. Cited in *Julia Margaret Cameron*, ed. by Cox and Ford, p. 503.
36. Watts, it should be noted, responded in kind, describing a Cameron photograph called 'The Dream' as 'Quite Divine' (M. S. Watts, *George Frederic Watts: the Annals of an Artist's Life*, 3 vols (London: Macmillan and Co., 1912), I, 207).

37. For more on the theophanic character of Cameron's photographs, see Mike Weaver, *Whisper of the Muse: the Overstone Album and Other Photographs by Julia Margaret Cameron* (Malibu: J. Paul Getty Museum, 1986), pp. 15–58.
38. Cited in Gernsheim, p. 14 (my emphasis).
39. Ibid. Cameron's 'out-of-focus' photography has been much discussed in both Victorian and contemporary criticism. Cameron described her initial success with the technique as 'a fluke': 'when focusing and coming to something which, to my eye, was very beautiful, I stopped there instead of screwing on the lens to the more definite focus which all other photographers insist upon' (Cameron, 'Annals', p. 12). For further discussions of Cameron's technique, see two essays by Lindsay Smith: 'The Politics of Focus: Feminism and Photographic Theory', in *New Feminist Discourses*, ed. by Isobel Armstrong (London: Routledge, 1992), pp. 238–62, and 'Further Thoughts on "The Politics of Focus"', *The Library Chronicle of the University of Texas at Austin*, 26 (1996), 13–31.
40. Novak, p. 5.
41. 'A Book of Photographs', p. 11.
42. Cameron, 'Annals', p. 13.
43. Sylvia Wolf notes that Cameron's shift to a larger camera and Dallmeyer Rapid Rectilinear lens in 1866 enabled her 'literally to fill the frame with the head of her sitter, making nearly life-sized heads' (p. 215).
44. Cameron, 'Annals', p. 15 (my emphasis).
45. Thomas Carlyle, *On Heroes, Hero-Worship and the Heroic in History*, ed. by Archibald MacMechan (London: Ginn, 1901), pp. 33, 2.
46. Ibid., p. 2.
47. *Annals of My Glass House: Photographs by Julia Margaret Cameron*, ed. by Violet Hamilton (Seattle and London: University of Washington Press, 1996), pp. 32–4.
48. James Eli Adams, 'The Hero as Spectacle: Carlyle and the Persistence of Dandyism', in *Victorian Literature and the Victorian Visual Imagination*, ed. by Carol T. Christ and John O. Jordan (Berkeley, CA, and London: University of California Press, 1995), pp. 213–32 (p. 218).
49. Carol Hanbery MacKay, *Creative Negativity: Four Victorian Exemplars of the Female Quest* (Stanford: Stanford University Press, 2001), p. 23.
50. See Carlyle, pp. 91, 127.
51. Cameron, 'Annals', p. 16.
52. According to Colin Ford, the book in the photograph 'looms unnaturally large, because of the short focal length of [Cameron's] lens' (Ford, p. 48).
53. Margaret D. Stetz, *Facing the Late Victorians: Portraits of Writers and Artists from the Mark Samuels Lasner Collection* (Newark: University of Delaware Press, 2007), p. 7.
54. Cited in Gernsheim, p. 53.
55. Cited in Raymond Blathwayt, 'How Celebrities Have Been Photographed', *Windsor Magazine*, 2 (1895), 639–48 (p. 648), in *ProQuest British Periodicals* <http://www.proquest.co.uk> [accessed 8 April 2013].
56. Anne Thackeray Ritchie concurred, suggesting that, through her photography, Cameron 'clothed great spirits in the flesh for the admiration of succeeding generations' ('Reminiscences', in *Alfred, Lord Tennyson and his Friends: a Series of 25 Portraits and Frontispiece in Photogravure from the Negatives of Mrs. Julia*

Cameron and H. H. H. Cameron, ed. by H. H. H. Cameron and Anne Thackeray Ritchie (London: T. Fisher Unwin, 1893), pp. 9–16 (p. 11)).

57. See Weaver, p. 26 and Hamilton, pp. 29–30.

58. Stetz, pp. 7–8 (my emphasis).

59. MacKay, pp. 22, 21.

60. Cited in Gernsheim, p. 14 (my emphasis).

61. Cameron wrote to Sir Edward Ryan, 'Lastly as to spots, they must, I think, remain. I could have them touched out, but I am the only photographer who always issues untouched photographs, and artists for this reason, among others, value my photographs' (cited in Gernsheim, p. 76).

62. Cited in Hamilton, p. 31. For a discussion of the practices of retouching and composition in Victorian photography, see Novak, pp. 1–29.

63. 'Julia Cameron and her Work: the Story of a Remarkable Woman', *Woman's Herald*, 6 July 1893, p. 318, in *Gale 19th Century UK Periodicals* <http://gale. cengage.co.uk> [accessed 8 April 2013]; Edith Nicholl Ellison, *A Child's Recollections of Tennyson* (London: J. Dent, 1907), p. 76.

64. Laura Troubridge, *Memories and Reflections* (London: William Heinemann, 1925), p. 35.

65. W[illiam] M[ichael] Rossetti, 'Essays on Art by Francis Palgrave Turner', *Fine Arts Quarterly Review*, 1 (October 1866), 302–11 (p. 310), in *ProQuest British Periodicals* <http://www.proquest.co.uk> [accessed 8 April 2013].

66. *Autobiography of Henry Taylor, 1800–1875*, 2 vols (New York: Harper & Brothers, 1885), II, 163.

67. Lukitsh, 'Julia Margaret Cameron', p. 218.

68. Cox and Ford note that there is documentation to suggest that a photograph of Christina Rossetti was made, but, to date, no print of it has been located ('Introduction', in *Julia Margaret Cameron*, ed. by Cox and Ford, pp. 1–5 (p. 5)). Cameron's photographs of Ellen Terry were taken shortly after her marriage to Watts, by which time she had gained a certain amount of recognition as a child actress, but nothing like the renown she would achieve later in life. Cameron's photographs of the Pre-Raphaelite artist and model Marie Spartali date mainly from 1860s; at this point, Spartali had started her artistic training with William Holman Hunt, but she did not begin exhibiting in prominent venues such as the Royal Academy and Grosvenor Gallery until the 1870s.

69. See Gernsheim, p. 67.

70. Cited in Weaver, p. 30.

71. Cited in Hester Thackeray Fuller, *Three Freshwater Friends: Tennyson, Watts and Mrs. Cameron* (Newport: Isle of Wight County Press, 1993), p. 36.

72. Cameron, 'Annals', p. 13.

73. See 'My heart leaps up when I behold', in *The Complete Poetical Works of William Wordsworth* (London: Edward Moxon, Son, and Co., 1869), p. 54.

74. See Elizabeth Barrett Browning, *Aurora Leigh and Other Poems* (London: Penguin, 1995), p. 34 (Book II, ll. 56–58). Cameron often made reference to being crowned with laurels; see, for instance, her letters to Sir Henry Cole (Henry Cole Correspondence and Papers, 55.BB Box 8, Victoria and Albert Museum, London).

75. John Milton, *Lycidas* in *The Major Works*, ed. by Stephen Orgel and Jonathan Goldberg (Oxford: Oxford University Press, 2003), pp. 39–44 (p. 41, l. 71).

76. Ibid., p. 39 (ll. 1–5).

77. Cameron writes of her 'indefatigable work' at photography, noting that 'its difficulty enhanced the value of the pursuit' and that by 'work[ing] on' at it she has been able to 'reap rich rewards' ('Annals', pp. 11–12).

78. Milton, p. 41 (ll. 70–72).

79. Ibid., p. 41 (ll. 76–84).

80. MacKay, p. 43.

81. Cameron, 'Annals', p. 12 (my emphasis).

82. G. F. Watts, undated letter to Julia Margaret Cameron, G. F. Watts Correspondence, Box 3, National Portrait Gallery, London. In another letter to Cameron, Watts advises, 'for the purposes of sale repetition [of subject] will not do' (undated letter, Watts Correspondence, Box 3, NPG).

83. See Henry Cole Correspondence and Papers, 55.BB Box 8, Victoria and Albert Museum, London. Transcripts of Cameron's letters to Cole are available on the Victoria and Albert Museum website: http://www.vam.ac.uk/content/articles/j/julia-margaret-cameron-and-the-v-and-a/ [accessed 8 April 2013].

84. The South Kensington Museum purchased eighty of Cameron's photographs in August 1865; a month later, she gifted thirty-four more to the institution.

85. Weaver quotes from a letter from Cameron's son-in-law, Charles Norman, to family friend Lord Overstone, in which he describes his wife's family as 'utterly penniless' and requests a loan of £1000 (Weaver, p. 18). According to Anne Thackeray Ritchie, Cameron claimed, 'I myself never felt humiliated at the idea of receiving charities, for I always feel about friendship and love that what it is good to give it is also good to take' (*From Friend to Friend*, ed. by Emily Ritchie (London: John Murray, 1919), p. 27).

86. See Gernsheim, pp. 36–37, and Weaver, pp. 18–21.

87. Hardinge Cameron, cited in Weld, p. 74; Ritchie, *From Friend to Friend*, p. 27.

88. Photographs were (somewhat controversially) included in the Fine Arts Copyright Act (1862). Details of the photographs copyrighted by Cameron can be found at the Public Record Office, London.

89. Mole, p. 16.

90. Anna Barton, *Tennyson's Name: Identity and Responsibility in the Poetry of Alfred Lord Tennyson* (Aldershot: Ashgate, 2008), p. 3. For more on Cameron's annotations to her photographs, see *Julia Margaret Cameron*, ed. by Cox and Ford, pp. 498–99.

91. Cited in Gernsheim, p. 177.

92. For details of Cameron's exhibitions, see the chronology in *Julia Margaret Cameron*, ed. by Cox and Ford, pp. 6–9.

93. Of the initial reviews of her work in the photographic press, Cameron wrote in 'Annals of My Glass House', 'The Photographic Society of London in their *Journal* would have dispirited me very much had I not valued that criticism at its worth. It was unsparing and too manifestly unjust for me to attend to it' ('Annals', p. 13). For more on Victorian reviews of Cameron's work, see Gernsheim, pp. 62–67, and Joanne Lukitsh, *Cameron: Her Work and Career* (Rochester, NY: International Museum of Photography at George Eastman House, 1986), pp. 41–46.

94. *Selected Letters of William Michael Rossetti*, ed. by Roger W. Peattie (University Park, PA: Pennsylvania State University Press, 1990), p. 134 (5 May [1865]).

95. Ibid.

96. See William Michael Rossetti, 'Essays on Art', p. 310, and 'Mrs. Cameron's Photographs', *Chronicle*, 31 August 1867, pp. 546–47; and [Frederic George Stephens], 'Fine Art Gossip', *Athenaeum*, 20 May 1865, p. 690 in *ProQuest British Periodicals* <http://www.proquest.co.uk> [accessed 8 April 2013].

97. See [Patmore], 'Mrs. Cameron's Photographs', pp. 230–31; 'A Book of Photographs', pp. 10–11; [William Allingham], 'Mrs. Cameron's Photographs', *Pall Mall Gazette*, 29 January 1868, p. 10, in *Gale 19th Century British Library Newspapers* <http://gale.cengage.co.uk> [accessed 8 April 2013]; Joanne Lukitsh, 'The Thackeray Album: Looking at Julia Margaret Cameron's Gift to Her Friend Annie Thackeray', *The Library Chronicle of the University of Texas at Austin*, 26.4 (1996), 33–61 (p. 38).

98. *Hansard*, 165 (1862), 1890–91.

99. 'A Book of Photographs', p. 11.

100. [Patmore], 'Mrs. Cameron's Photographs', pp. 230, 231.

101. 'A Book of Photographs', p. 10; [Patmore], 'Mrs. Cameron's Photographs', p. 231; [Allingham], 'Mrs. Cameron's Photographs', p. 10.

102. 'Art in Photography', *Illustrated London News*, 15 July 1865, p. 50, in *The Illustrated London News Historical Archive 1842–2003* <http://gale.cengage.co.uk> [accessed 8 April 2013].

103. 'Fine Arts', *Illustrated London News*, 22 July 1865, p. 71, in *The Illustrated London News Historical Archive 1842–2003* <http://gale.cengage.co.uk> [accessed 8 April 2013].

104. 'Fine Arts', *Illustrated London News*, 11 November 1865, pp. 462–63 (p. 463), in *The Illustrated London News Historical Archive 1842–2003* <http://gale.cengage.co.uk> [accessed 8 April 2013].

105. 'Fine Arts', *Illustrated London News*, 18 November 1865, p. 486; 'Fine Arts', *Illustrated London News*, 9 December 1865, p. 566, both in *The Illustrated London News Historical Archive 1842–2003* <http://gale.cengage.co.uk> [accessed 8 April 2013].

106. 'Fine Arts', *Illustrated London News*, 28 April 1866, p. 411, in *The Illustrated London News Historical Archive 1842–2003* <http://gale.cengage.co.uk> [accessed 8 April 2013].

107. 'Fine Arts', *Illustrated London News*, 27 December 1873, p. 619, in *The Illustrated London News Historical Archive 1842–2003* <http://gale.cengage.co.uk> [accessed 8 April 2013].

108. Cameron's 'Priced Catalogue' is reproduced in *Julia Margaret Cameron*, ed. by Cox and Ford, p. 3, and Wolf, pp. 210–11. That Cameron was directly involved in determining the prices of her photographs is apparent from her handwritten annotations to the catalogue and from an 1865 letter to Jane Senior in which she discusses her reasons for not reducing her prices (cited in Ford, p. 41).

109. Wolf, p. 212.

110. Cited in Wolf, p. 209.

111. Weld, p. 66.

112. *William Allingham's Diary 1847–1889*, ed. by H. Allingham and D. Radford (London: Centaur, 2000), p. 171 (7 February 1868). In an undated letter to Cameron, Watts wrote modestly, 'I do not ... think any observations of mine upon your Photography are worth quoting but you are perfectly welcome of any service I can render' (Watts Correspondence, Box 3, NPG).

113. Cited in Gernsheim, p. 45.
114. Ibid., p. 46.
115. Ibid., p. 42.
116. Ibid., p. 53.
117. Ibid.
118. *Julia Margaret Cameron*, ed. by Cox and Ford, p. 500.
119. Wolf, p. 216.
120. 'A Reminiscence of Mrs. Cameron by a Lady Amateur', *Photographic News*, 1 January 1886, pp. 2–4 (p. 2). There was a brief revival of interest in Cameron in photographic circles in the 1890s, when her work was positioned as an important precursor of *fin-de-siècle* artistic taste. Her 'out-of-focus' technique was much debated by theorist-practitioners such as Henry Peach Robinson and Peter Henry Emerson in the photographic press, with the latter endorsing her vision and devoting the fifth number of *Sun Artists* (a serial committed to promoting 'the artistic claims of Photography') to a study of her life and work. Yet, though predominantly celebratory, Emerson's tribute was ambivalent regarding Cameron's status, tending to position her as a gifted amateur – one who viewed her photographic subjects 'joyfully, as a child' – rather than as 'a great artist'. It also overlooked her moneymaking agenda, situating her in an oppositional relationship to Victorian 'photographers of commerce' (P. H. Emerson, 'Mrs. Cameron', *Sun Artists*, 5 (1890), 33–42 (pp. 40, 37)). As Lukitsh suggests, these revisionary tactics are typical of the way in which the fine art photography movement of the *fin de siècle* constructed Cameron according to its own ends, minimising or ignoring those aspects of her life and work which did not fit with its aesthetic or ideological assumptions (Lukitsh, *Cameron: Her Work and Career*, pp. 77–81).
121. Weber, p. 32.
122. *Autobiography of Henry Taylor*, II, 42, 153–54.
123. Ibid., II, 57. Regarding Tennyson's attitude to fame, Taylor quotes a letter from Cameron in which she writes of the Laureate's feeling of being 'ripped open like a pig' by the press (II, 160).
124. Watts, I, 204, 205.
125. Ibid., I, 206–07.
126. Ibid., I, 294, 207.
127. Weld described Cameron as a 'unique personality ... who seemed to be all the famous women of the French salons of the 18th century rolled into one' (Weld, p. 64); Ellison characterised her as a 'benevolent tyrant', whose home was a social hub, 'the scene of "feasts of intellect"' (Ellison, pp. 71–72); while Wilfrid Ward compared her to 'Madame Récamier', noting 'the essential work of gathering together the interesting people who were to form the Tennyson society ... was Mrs. Cameron's part' (Wilfrid Ward, 'Tennyson at Freshwater', *Dublin Review*, 150 (1912), 68–85 (p. 68)).
128. H. H. H. Cameron, 'Introduction', in *Alfred, Lord Tennyson and his Friends*, ed. by Cameron and Ritchie, pp. 7–8.
129. For more on the domesticisation of nineteenth-century female celebrities' fame by their male relatives, see Katie Halsey, '"Faultless Herself, As Nearly As Human Nature Can Be": the Construction of Jane Austen's Public Image, 1817–1917', and Jennifer Phegley, 'Motherhood, Authorship, and

Rivalry: Sons' Memoirs of the Lives of Ellen Price Wood and Mary Elizabeth Braddon', in *Women Writers and the Artifacts of Celebrity*, ed. by Hawkins and Ives, pp. 33–47 and 189–204.

130. See Blathwayt, p. 645, and V. C. Scott O'Connor, 'Mrs. Cameron, Her Friends, and Her Photographs', *Century Magazine*, 55 (1897), 3–10 (p. 4), in *Cornell University Library Making of America Collection* <http://ebooks.library.cornell.edu/m/moa/> [accessed 8 April 2013].

131. Ives, 'Introduction', p. 5.

132. 'Mrs. Julia Margaret Cameron', *Woman's Herald*, 4 April 1891, pp. 369–70 (p. 369), in *Gale 19th Century UK Periodicals* <http://gale.cengage.co.uk> [accessed 8 April 2013]. Interestingly, the article demonstrates something of Cameron's own instinct for promotion, concluding, 'We have still ... her best portraits, which will survive all time, and can be seen at the Cameron studio in Mortimer-street, where her son, Henry Herschel Hay Cameron, himself a remarkable photographer, now conducts a studio' (p. 370).

133. 'Julia Margaret Cameron and her Work', p. 318; Lady Henry Somerset, 'Books Worth Reading', *The Woman's Signal*, 24 May 1894, pp. 361–62, in *Gale 19th Century UK Periodicals* <http://gale.cengage.co.uk> [accessed 8 April 2013].

134. Troubridge, p. 40.

135. H. C. G. Matthew, *Leslie Stephen and the New Dictionary of National Biography* (Cambridge: Cambridge University Press, 1997), p. 16.

136. Julia Stephen, 'Cameron, Julia Margaret', in *Dictionary of National Biography*, ed. by Leslie Stephen, series 1, 63 vols (London: Smith, Elder, & Co., 1885–1900), VIII (1886), 300.

137. Ibid.

138. Ritchie's father, William Makepeace Thackeray, was a long-standing friend of Cameron, having known her since her girlhood. After Thackeray's death in December 1863, Anne and her sister Harriet (known as 'Minnie') went to stay at 'The Porch' in Freshwater at Cameron's invitation, cementing their close bond. In 1867, Minnie married Leslie Stephen, who, after her death, married Cameron's niece, Julia Duckworth (née Jackson). Ritchie enjoyed a particularly close relationship with the Stephens' daughter (Cameron's great-niece), Virginia Woolf, who called her 'Aunt Anny'.

139. Ritchie, 'Reminiscences', p. 13.

140. Ritchie, *From Friend to Friend*, p. 7. In her 'Annals', Cameron makes nonchalant reference to the domestic upheaval caused by her photography: 'I turned my coal-house into my dark room, and a glazed fowl-house I had given to my children became my glass house! The hens were liberated, I hope and believe not eaten. ... [My] habit of running into the dining room with my wet pictures has stained such an immense quantity of table linen with nitrate of silver, indelible stains, that I should have been banished from any less indulgent household' ('Annals', pp. 12–13).

141. Ritchie, *From Friend to Friend*, p. 5.

142. Ibid., pp. 24, 30.

143. Alison Booth, *How to Make It as a Woman: Collective Biographical History from Victoria to the Present* (Chicago and London: University of Chicago Press, 2004), p. 4.

144. For Woolf's ideas on life-writing, see 'The New Biography' in *Selected Essays*, ed. by David Bradshaw (Oxford: Oxford University Press, 2008), pp. 95–100.

145. Woolf and Fry, p. 6.

146. As Tristram Powell notes in a later edition of *Victorian Photographs*, Woolf's assertions 'were not always strictly accurate'; for instance, it was Cameron's daughter Julia and son-in-law Charles who presented her with her first camera, not her son (Tristram Powell, 'Editor's Note', in Virginia Woolf and Roger Fry, *Victorian Photographs of Famous Men and Fair Women*, ed. by Tristram Powell (London: Hogarth Press, 1973), pp. 21–22 (p. 21).

147. Virginia Woolf, *Freshwater: a Comedy*, ed. by Lucio P. Ruotolo (London: Harcourt, 1985), p. 14.

148. Woolf, 'The New Biography', pp. 97–98.

149. Booth, p. 226.

150. Weber, p. 18.

151. Wolf points out that, in spite of Cameron's established reputation as a photographer, she is listed simply as 'wife' in the 1871 census, 'with no occupation given under the heading "profession"' (p. 216).

4

Personal Museums: the Fan Diaries of Charles Dodgson and William Allingham

Anne-Marie Millim

In its 1896 commemoration of the late Emily Tennyson's life work, the *Athenaeum* particularly commended her skilful diaristic writing and praised her 'power of selecting really luminous points for preservation in her diary'; namely those that 'shed light upon Tennyson's method'.[1] According to the journalist, Emily's talent for daily chronicling distinguishes her record from the great bulk of diaries of the time, which,

> as a rule[,] professing as they do to give portraitures of eminent men, are mostly very much worse than worthless. The points seized upon by the diarist are almost never physiognomic, and even if the diarist does give some glimpse of the character he professes to limn, the picture can only be partially true, inasmuch as it can never be toned down by other aspects of the character unseen by the diarist and unknown to him.[2]

Intriguingly, the author establishes biographising as the principal task of a diary, stipulating that the quality of diaristic writing depends on the diarist's ability to render the 'character' of an eminent figure, rather than his or her own, from the perspective of an omniscient external observer. Disregarding the private endeavour of diaries and deploring their inadequacy to serve as accurate reminiscences, the author establishes diaristic observations as necessarily one-sided and flawed due to the diarist's insuperably subjective stance. The severity of the *Athenaeum*'s dismissal of diaries as reliable biographical sources must, however, be understood as a reaction to the hero-worshipping culture of the nineteenth century rather than as an attempt to set standards for the quality and usefulness of diaristic writing. Criticising reminiscences based on diary entries, and diaries published by authors prone to exaggerate the kindness, wildness, or grumpiness of the poet, the article confounds biographies written in diary-format with diaries that display a biographical interest.

This chapter demonstrates the impact of the Victorian belief in a strict hierarchy of fans on the fan behaviour of the mid-century diarists William Allingham and Charles Dodgson (Lewis Carroll). The fact that these diarists relentlessly justify their own fan behaviour, and constantly re-negotiate their position as fans within Tennyson's circle and the lionising culture that surrounded them, indicates the influence of their culture's separatism. This chapter investigates a constellation of the bio-graphical triad slightly different from the one examined in Chapter 5; namely the changing personae of the diarist as fan, friend and biog-rapher. While scholarship has thus far reduced Allingham's diary to a useful biographical account of Tennyson's eccentricity, I highlight the diarist's reactions to contemporary conventions of fandom, which caused his own status to constantly waver between that of an onlooker, guest and biographer. Critics have tended to stigmatise Dodgson as a lion-hunter, insisting that his fan behaviour and his personal desire for anonymity are irredeemably paradoxical. I extend and correct this read-ing by highlighting the self-fashioning and system-building function of celebrity-worship in the life of the fan and by arguing that 'collecting' involves the cultivation of an intimate, if often imagined, relationship with an admired other, rather than unsympathetic consumption. This chapter demonstrates that fandom naturally involves the narrative and spatial organisation of collected objects and impressions related to celebrities, but that, beyond this cataloguing of the other, it also includes the classification of the individual as either a legitimate reader or an obtrusive fan and thus demands the active positioning of the self within a set of behaviours and values.

Dodgson's and Allingham's diaristic records differ from published reminiscences in their tendency to faithfully include their disappoint-ments about *not* seeing the poet, the latter's quirks and moody spells, as well as their own consequent tiptoeing around him. Although the diaries in question are not wholly private documents, as both clearly exhibit an awareness of a potential reader, their unedited nature reveals the direct experience of the vulnerable fan more so than the self-bolstering success stories of reminiscers do. There are some similarities between the two modes of narration, such as the typical division of the acquaintance process into several stages (admiration of poetry, anticipation, arrival at Farringford, first impressions of the poet, delightful afternoons on the lawn, walks, poetry readings and dramatic farewells), but reminiscences tend to omit vital steps, such as the visitor's scheming to meet Tennyson, his or her active attempts to gain the poet's attention and the difficulties of coping with his rude remarks and rejections. While writers of reminiscences tend to construct sleek monuments of their hero as well as of themselves, stressing their own importance in the poet's life, rather than vice versa, Dodgson's and Allingham's diaries are important documents because they candidly testify to Tennyson's enriching presence in their private lives. In this context, it is important to stress that fan experiences differ greatly: while Allingham was a fan who became a friend, Dodgson remained a fan.

Recent scholarship has altogether dismissed the myth of the reader/fan as a mere consumer, rejecting the lingering idea that fans are an ahistorical mass of mindless followers, driven by the 'collective strategy' of the herd. Instead, they have considered the impact of readers and fans on the artist's creative process and also the emotional aspects of venerating a celebrity. Accordingly, Tom Mole considers celebrity to be 'a cultural apparatus, consisting of the relations between an individual, an industry and an audience'.[3] These three instances influence each other – fans do not blindly adopt the industry's fabrication of the famous individual but do have the choice to make or break a celebrity. Eric Eisner has shown that 'nineteenth-century poetry was crucially shaped by the practices of its star-struck readers and by the affective relationships between reader and writer'.[4] Evidently, fans' lionising behaviour and subjective responses to a celebrity's image, presence and work differed greatly, and surely, the nature of the latter's discipline (acting, writing, painting, etc.) affected those responses. Since 'consumption' is frequently applied to all forms of fandom, I shall not treat each category specifically, but wish to replace the idea of celebrity-worship as primarily utilitarian consumption, a process in which images, texts, objects and persons are swallowed up and nothing is retained, by the concept of the collection, in which 'aesthetic value replaces use value', to use Susan Stewart's terms.[5]

The fact that the Victorians were avid collectors is well known. The countless museums built during the nineteenth century to house and display both exotic and familiar objects are prominent physical manifestations of this 'impulse or spirit that infused the age and many of its projects', as Barbara J. Black has shown.[6] The accumulation of congruent and incongruent objects in various forms such as 'the triple-decker novel; collected works, encyclopaedias and dictionaries [and] phenomena as ordinary as keepsakes, dollhouses [and] rock collections' similarly stems from the desire to implement 'system-building projects' in order to both structure and enjoy the world.[7] Because a museum can be seen as the concretisation of and the stimulus for the Victorians' passion for collecting, for Black, it allows a culture 'to stand outside of itself within itself' and 'to leave the realm of the merely familiar while staying at home'.[8] A *carte-de-visite* album, an autograph book or a diary can similarly cater to a fan's desire to see his or her tastes represented and affirmed and to expand his or her sensory and intellectual environment. The physical and intellectual appropriation of the world inherent in both collecting and celebrity-worship are characteristic of an age shaped by colonialism, scientific discoveries and a new historical consciousness. As Judith Pascoe has demonstrated, the democratisation and popularisation of collecting were decidedly nineteenth-century phenomena as 'opportunities for participating in this activity, directly or vicariously, proliferated'.[9] Collecting was an integral part of nineteenth-century education and 'from an early age children were encouraged to identify objects and effectively "curate" the formation of their own collections' as collaborating scholars Susan M. Pearce, Rosemary Flanders, Mark Hall and Fiona Morton have highlighted.[10]

Victorian fans, like museum-goers, were able to feed their imagination by engaging in parasocial relationships with their idols, who, just like the Elgin marbles, were on public display. The collection of impressions, feelings and ideas inherent in museum and celebrity culture is not merely an economically motivated quantitative amassment, but a world view influenced by the Romantics' belief that the past is an 'idealised lost world, partly salvageable through the recovery and preservation of old objects and documents', as Pascoe has argued.[11] The fan and/or the museum-goer do not simply want to increase their cultural capital, but they wish to render tangible and durable the world of their imagination through collecting objects, writing down impressions and claiming acquaintance with celebrities through pilgrimages to their houses. Considering that periodical editors tended to 'equate magazines to museums or cabinets of collectible objects', it is entirely conceivable to view fan culture with its paraphernalia, such as *cartes de visite*, albums, press cuttings, celebrity interviews and souvenirs, as a fundamental part of the Victorian culture of collection.[12] If a magazine could assume the function and aura of a museum, the diary must be seen as an individual's effort to 'curate' his or her personal collection of memorable experiences and memoranda. Because classifying is inherently linked to collecting, Asa Briggs has shown, it was 'a favourite as well as a necessary Victorian preoccupation, like naming and listing'.[13]

For both Allingham and Dodgson, diaristic inscription was the means through which to translate their fascination with celebrities into a possession, allowing them to prolong the excitement of first-hand contact. In their fan behaviour, the diary functions as a museum to harbour delightful experiences that might also showcase them to potential readers. While it is tempting to think of Dodgson as not only the bigger star, but also the bigger lioniser of the two, his intention to create durable traces of Tennyson's cultural eminence is in fact very similar to Allingham's, differing mostly in the chosen generic medium. Allingham used his diary as the basis of an autobiographical/biographical project, whereas Dodgson 'collected' the distinguished figures of his day by naming them in brief diary entries and appropriating their image in numerous photograph albums. This impulse to collect and keep images, snippets, as well as memories of first-hand contact stems from a desire for emotional and intellectual complementation by an admired person. A fan's attempts to become acquainted with a celebrity, often described as 'hunting', should therefore be seen as acts of 'wooing' him or her into an actual relationship.

Dodgson's and Allingham's diaries document a sincere longing for a relationship with Tennyson (as well as other selected celebrities/ children). In their chronological comprehensiveness, the diaries demonstrate the extensive efforts that Dodgson and Allingham undertook to advance from the passive position of the admiring reader, who '[participates] mentally in the lives of ... characters and personalities' through engaging with the Poet Laureate's works and reviews of it, to actually making his acquaintance. The meetings with Tennyson were carefully engineered through a series of cunning schemes and facilitated by acquaintances. Allingham retrospectively recorded the first encounter in his diary, stating 'that a longing of [his] life had been fulfilled', and Dodgson '[marked] this day with a white stone'.[14] The prominent position that Tennyson occupies in both diaries indicates the authors' intention to give physical presence to the visual and spiritual image they had formed of the poet, based on his published works and press appearances. Many scholars of celebrity have argued that this 'parasocial', unsubstantiated relationship connecting the fan to the celebrity is very similar to an actual relationship, as 'we attribute motives to and develop expectations about the behaviour of parasocial partners'.[15] The diarists' reports of their gradual penetration into the poet's consciousness and, subsequently, his domestic sphere, indeed illustrate that fandom, just like fame, is a '*process* rather than a state of being'.[16] The fans' passage from a relationship with the poet that is, to a large extent, imagined to a bilateral one is accompanied by the emotional transition from personal insignificance to actualisation, which may be reversed at any moment.

Although Allingham's endeavour to befriend Tennyson was much more successful than Dodgson's, both believed that proximity to celebrities benefited them intellectually, artistically and emotionally. The form of these diaries reflects the diarists' fan status: while Allingham (eventually) enjoys the position of a privileged interlocutor, creating lively, meticulous and intimate records of his conversations with Tennyson (and Carlyle), Dodgson's accounts of his encounters with Tennyson and other celebrities remain cursory; often simply list-like and emotionally detached. The apparent formal carelessness of Dodgson's diary has no doubt reinforced his critics' tendency to interpret his strong desire to appropriate and reproduce celebrities' images, through photography, drawing, or the acquisition of their autograph, as the behaviour of an indefatigable lion-hunter.

White stone days: Dodgson's diary

Lewis Carroll biographer John Pudney's assessment of the diary as a 'two-dimensional … massively detailed monument of self-evasion', seems strangely appropriate, yet unfair.[17] Rather than to dismiss Dodgson's unconfessional diaristic writing as guarded, incomplete and therefore hermetic, I propose to 'study what the subject has selected for preservation', as diary critics Wendy J. Wiener and George C. Rosenwald suggest, viewing 'the act of remembrance [as] a choosing, a highlighting, a shaping, an enshrinement' not unlike a collection staged at a museum.[18] Dodgson's diary is characterised by its striking tendency to limit entries to brief summaries of encounters with celebrities and children, often presented in the form of lists, which are punctuated by longer accounts on particularly memorable 'white stone' days. The careful selection of tensely compressed shreds of information underlying Dodgson's diaristic process is gesturally analogous to choosing and photographing subjects and to collecting *cartes de visite* and autographs in its attempt to 'temporarily [move] history into private time'.[19] Stewart's theorisation of everyday objects as reflections of 'longing' helps to demonstrate that Dodgson's diary is not simply a 'gigantic' public 'monument of self-evasion', but rather a private, domestic 'miniature' of self-cultivation. Dodgson's diary, like his photographic albums, indicates a desire to make the appropriated 'souvenir' melt into the 'collection', endeavouring to 'collapse distance' into manageable 'proximity to, or approximation with, the self' and thus to create a 'nexus for all narratives, the place where history is transformed into space, into property'.[20] Diary-writing allowed Dodgson to take possession of pleasurable experiences and persons and to revisit them at leisure.

While critics interested in the work of Lewis Carroll have almost unanimously viewed Dodgson's intense aversion to publicity as irreconcilable with his enthralled interest in encountering contemporary celebrities and in capturing their image and handwriting, a focus on the creative aspects of fandom can rectify this misjudgement. Helmut Gernsheim's formulation of Dodgson's 'paradox' sums up the critical consensus on his ambiguous stance towards celebrity culture:

> he had a horror of being photographed but never tired of pressing others to sit for him; he was fond of collecting *cartes* but to have his own portrait collected was distasteful to him; he was a lion-hunter who hated to be lionised himself; he was a great autograph collector but when he suspected others of writing to him only in order to get his signature he would use script or a typewriter and ask a friend to sign for him.[21]

Despite this apparent inconsistency, Dodgson's behaviour is in no way contradictory: he simply did not consider himself obligated to engage in a compensatory relationship with his subjects/audience and felt no pressure to provide his own image in exchange for taking someone else's – just as the majority of theatregoers would never venture onto the stage themselves. While he could be sure of his own 'fondness' of his subjects and his genuine admiration for the personalities he lionised, he could not himself understand or control the reaction of those in possession of his image. Dodgson's desire to respectfully '[preserve] in perpetuity' the 'likenesses' of his 'dearly beloved' family and child friends, as well as those of the public figures he admired, through various photographic means neither conflicts with, nor does it necessarily relate to, his fear of being at the mercy of a lionising public.[22] As John Plunkett has convincingly argued, 'the familiarity created through celebrity photographs was far from being a wholly benevolent affair'.[23] Since the publication of Mayall's *Royal Album* of 1860, the public was able to respond with a 'voyeuristic *schadenfreude*' to the 'authentic countenances of kings and queens for the first time'.[24] This availability of images and the consequent deconstruction of blind idolatry were certainly illuminating and empowering to the masses, as sovereigns could 'no longer hope to perpetuate their sway by throwing the dust of flattering portraits in the eyes of the multitude'.[25] However, the dispersion of *cartes de visite* meant that the photographed individual was integrated into the household of the Victorian family as 'no drawing-room was considered complete without an album'.[26] Caged into an unknowable context and exposed to the judgement of ever-changing gatherings of visitors, the photographic subject becomes exceedingly vulnerable. If the loss of personal agency represented the 'trauma of commodity capitalism', Tom Mole has observed, then the celebrity experienced it 'in a particularly acute fashion'.[27] The emotional ordeal of the celebrity was not merely caused by the threat of having his or her work misrepresented by an audience, but by that of being physically represented and owned by someone else. The photographed celebrity was thus exposed to an ever-changing congregation of spectators, which implies his or her integration into an unforeseeable number of social constellations.

Dodgson's visits to the Tennysons

Although Dodgson is always mentioned among the famous guests at Farringford, he cannot be seen as a member of the Freshwater circle, as he was neither a regular, nor a particularly welcome visitor of the Tennysons. The process of acquaintance between Dodgson and the Laureate was long and effortful, resulting in sparse interactions between the two that provided little satisfaction to the former aside from a few compliments about his work. In his diary, his personal museum, Dodgson marks the day he encounters Emily, Hallam and Lionel Tennyson (18 September 1857) 'with a white stone', as he does when meeting Alice Liddell on 25 April 1856 and Kate and Ellen Terry on 20–21 December 1864 – events that durably shaped his life.[28] John Pudney insists that the day Dodgson spent with Alice and her siblings 'hit home', not because he was able to capture the children's physical beauty – the photographs 'did not come out' – but because 'he was in love'.[29] While the nature of Dodgson's 'penchant for pre-pubescent girls' must remain a mystery and cannot be addressed in this context, it is important here to stress that he uses the exact same formulation to record the significance of 'becoming excellent friends' with the Liddells and 'having at last accomplished [his] wish' to meet the Terrys, as he does to mark the day he enters the Tennysons' domestic sphere.[30]

For Dodgson, meeting celebrities and children was a system-building activity in that it lent structure and substance to his life as a mathematician. Hoping to establish stimulating and rewarding bilateral relationships, he was as attracted to the wholesome purity of talent as he was to the innocent beauty of childhood; though befriending celebrities proved to be much more difficult for the socially awkward Dodgson than entertaining child friends. Derek Hudson has asserted that Dodgson received emotional, rather than sexual, nurture from his child friends and we may infer that he sought similar affective warmth, as well as intellectual support, from celebrities. Dodgson's first encounter with John Ruskin at Christ Church College on 27 October 1857 is very telling of his hopes for awe-inspiring intellectual prowess:

> At Common Room breakfast met, for the first time, John Ruskin. I had a little conversation with him, but not enough to bring out anything characteristic or striking in him. His appearance was rather disappointing – a general feebleness of expression, with no commanding air, or any external signs of deep thought, as one would have expected to see in such a man.[31]

Whereas the Terrys succeeded in embodying as persons the ideal of genuine grace and lucidity that their stage personae had conjured up, Ruskin's corporeal self failed to radiate the intellectual grandeur that his writings evoked. Dodgson felt let down by Ruskin's demeanour as it did not correspond to the mental picture he had formed. Although he still deemed the day a 'dies notabilis', he was obviously waiting to be awed by the physical characteristics of leadership of 'such a man' and appears harshly disillusioned by the real Ruskin, almost contesting his celebrity status.[32] Dodgson's demand for embodied intellect challenges assumptions of his lionism, proving that he expected guidance rather than spectacular entertainment. As Hudson has explained, in the 1850s, Dodgson did not meet famous people 'on equal terms, as a celebrity, but as a diffident, stammering youth, whose future fame could scarcely have been prophesied'.[33] Despite his strong interest in meeting and photographing celebrities, Dodgson must not be seen as a lurking autograph-hunter, but as an admirer who had to contrive calculated plans in order to approach them.

For Dodgson, meeting Tennyson was an important step to personalise and bilateralise his relationship with the poet through actualisation, as his rating of 'dies mirabilis' indicates.[34] Not only would Tennyson's physical appearance be revealed but Dodgson would also be able to stand out from the mass of fans and enter the poet's consciousness. He is deeply excited when he makes the acquaintance of Emily's sister Mrs Weld in Yorkshire on 18 August, 1857:

> A party came down from the Castle to be photographed, consisting of Mrs. Otter, W. Chaytor, and a Mrs. Weld and her little girl Agnes

Grace; the last being the principal object – Mrs. Weld is sister-in-law to Alfred Tennyson, (I presume sister of Mrs. Tennyson), and I was much interested in talking about him with one who knew him so well.[35]

Starting with an indefinite article, Dodgson creates suspense by gradually adding specificity, culminating with the person most closely associated with Tennyson, who increases his own proximity to the poet. Dodgson photographs Agnes Grace as 'Little Red Riding-Hood' and sends a print 'through Mrs. Weld, for Tennyson's acceptance'.[36] Much like Allingham, whose poetry had paved his way towards the Poet, Dodgson gained Tennyson's attention through his artistic 'gem', as the Tennysons 'pronounced' the photograph.[37]

Having thus gained the Tennysons' artistic approval, which was a common requirement for entry into the social circle, Dodgson seeks to increase the proximity to them even further by visiting Tent Lodge in Cumbria. Concurrently, his culture's contempt of lionising forces him to minimise and detract from his wish for the actualisation of his imagined relationship with Tennyson, even in the privacy of his diary. John Pudney, like many critics, has observed this deliberate de-emphasis of his aim to go see the Tennysons: 'in 1857, on his way back from his only visit to Scotland, he "happened" to find himself in the Lake District, and indeed at Coniston where the Tennysons were staying'.[38] Besides a clear awareness of a potential reader, Dodgson's reticence to disclose his plan to his diary indicates his desire to differentiate himself from the status of the intrusive fan as defined by convention. Documenting and probably feigning indecision, Dodgson presents himself as merely 'intending at least to see Tent Lodge (where Tennyson stays) if not call'.[39] This interest in 'seeing' the house is not motivated solely by an aesthetic or historical curiosity, but by a strong desire to 'experience "in reality" the pleasurable dramas [he has] already experienced in [his] imagination'.[40] Having imagined encountering Tennyson in person and having visualised his presence in the house, the close proximity to Tent Lodge gains magnetic attraction, so that he 'at last [makes] up [his] mind to take the liberty of calling'; a formulation that accentuates the long process of internal debate preceding this decision.[41] As this visit has obvious similarities with invasive tourism, Dodgson somewhat defensively emphasises the propriety of his approach of the poet: 'I sent my card, adding (underneath the name) in pencil "artist of 'Agnes Grace' and 'Little Red Riding-Hood'"'.[42] Dodgson's specification of his writing utensil denotes his satisfaction with his own polite confidence and his pride at the 'strength' of the introduction he was able to craft for himself.[43]

Although Dodgson only met Tennyson five days later, he marks 17 September 'with a white stone'.[44] He was overjoyed at the 'kind' reception by Emily and her sons and probably visualised his integration into the family unit, as his emphasis on the amount of time spent with Emily ('nearly an hour') and the children's attachment to him ('they wanted to come with me when I left') indicates.[45] Dodgson's diary entry of 18 September is remarkable because he consistently foregrounds his respectful behaviour in an attempt to conceal his intense joy at having penetrated the poet's domestic sanctum, at '[getting] leave to take portraits of them' and at Emily's indication that 'it was not hopeless that Tennyson himself might sit'.[46] As if reacting to accusations of lionising, Dodgson adds in modest self-effacement: 'I said I would not request [a sitting], as he must have refused so many that it is unfair to expect it'.[47] Although Dodgson simulates humble solidarity to impress Emily as well as a potential reader, he clearly positions himself above the countless photographers whom Tennyson rejected, as one of the few whose gaze and camera were to receive the poet's aspect directly. Dodgson interprets this advancement into Tennyson's private circumference and the assurance of a sitting as a promise of an affectionate reciprocal relationship.

Dodgson's narrative rendition of his first meeting with Tennyson builds up a suspenseful tension, which indicates that he savoured this moment of initiation and actualisation and wished to preserve it for re-visitation. Reporting the events of his travels and his waiting time at Tent Lodge, he carefully sets the stage for the poet's entrance, which he recounts with a deliberately realistic vividness:

> the door opened, and a strange shaggy-looking man entered: his hair, moustache and beard looked wild and neglected: these very much hid the character of the face. He was dressed in a loosely fitting morning coat, common grey flannel waist-coat and trousers, and a carelessly tied back silk neckerchief. His hair is black: I think the eyes too; they are keen and restless – nose acquiline [*sic*]– forehead high and broad – both face and head are fine and manly. His manner was kind and friendly from the first: there is a dry lurking humour in his style of talking.[48]

The report clearly stages the moment of recognition and the actualisation of the relationship: Dodgson switches from a descriptive past tense and from a sequence of vague indefinite articles to the surprisingly concrete 'is' to render the emergence of Tennyson in the writer's life. During this first meeting at Tent Lodge, Dodgson immediately takes the opportunity to substantiate his imagined relationship with the poet by 'asking meanings of two passages in Tennyson's poems which have always puzzled [him]'.[49] Receiving the privilege of the poet's personal guidance, Dodgson is able to participate in the latter's imagination, which increases the intellectual proximity between them.

Due to the unfortunate loss of four out of thirteen volumes of Dodgson's diaries, we do not have a diaristic account of his first visit to Farringford during the Easter vacation of 1859. Dodgson's letter to his cousin W. E. Wilcox of 11 May, however, reports the reconnection with the Tennysons and shows that the accusations of invasive fandom that he imagines and reacts to in his diaristic writing were in fact levelled at him. Claiming to offer a general 'account of my visit to the Isle of Wight' to his cousin, Dodgson focuses in great detail on his time at the Tennysons'. Part of this account consists of his immediate defence against the allegation of violating the family's privacy: 'Wilfred must have basely misrepresented me if he said that I followed the Laureate down to his retreat, as I went not knowing that he was there, to stay with an old College friend at Freshwater'.[50] Indeed, as Anne Clark writes, Dodgson habitually stayed at Freshwater during his holidays (later preferring Sandown as a recreational spot), a fact that explains his biting insistence on the 'inalienable right of a freeborn Briton to make a morning call', evoking his earlier formulation of taking 'the liberty of calling' at Tent Lodge.[51] Dodgson adamantly maintains he did not hope to meet Tennyson, stressing that his friend Collyns had 'advised [him] that the Tennysons had not yet arrived', and that he 'fully [expected] the answer "no"' when inquiring about the poet, accentuating the 'agreeable surprise' at his unanticipated presence. Before Dodgson can begin to recount his experiences, he feels compelled to call attention to his respectful, dignified approach to the Tennysons, positioning himself against the intruding tourists with whom he has been associated.

At Farringford, Dodgson rejoicingly participates in the poet's consciousness, verbally following the latter's eyes as he directs him around his property. Upon his arrival, Dodgson candidly includes, Tennyson does not recognise him, which he promptly excuses on the basis of the poet being 'too short-sighted to recognise people'.[52] In the account he crafts for Wilcox, Dodgson counteracts his feared irrelevance by assuming the persona of a close friend who knowingly omits depictions of interior decoration, which were typical for first-time visitors and journalistic interviews, such as Edmund Yates's series of articles *Celebrities*

At Home (1877–79), and frequently took the appearance of a 'furniture catalogue'.[53] In the context of the Victorian obsession with celebrities' homes, which Chapter 1 has discussed, Dodgson's 'refusal-to-describe' counters this type of 'ritualised scrutiny', stressing his superiority to celebrity culture.[54] He instead adds descriptors that highlight his own integration into Tennyson's domestic sphere; '[the poet's] little sitting room at the top of the house', for instance, is characterised as the place 'where [Tennyson] of course offered [Dodgson] a pipe', 'the nursery' is where they meet Hallam 'who remembered [Dodgson] more readily than his father had done'.[55] Through recounting these gestures of welcoming acceptance, Dodgson seeks to anchor himself in the house and establish himself as a friend of the Tennysons, who was invited, not invading. While Dodgson subtly exaggerates his integration into the Tennysons' sphere, he cunningly dissimulates his delight at the incorporation of his photographic work among the decorative artwork displayed inside Farringford, which he modestly mentions in a parenthesis: '(... my photographs of the family were hung "on the line", framed in those enamel – what do you call them – cartons?)'[56] Dodgson purposefully detracts from his pleasure at the Tennysons' obvious appreciation of his work by inserting uncertainty concerning an irrelevant issue into this understated aside. At the same time the seemingly unpretentious focus on the elegant frames highlights the Tennysons' careful staging of Dodgson's work, thus affirming his sense of belonging not only among the family friends, but also among the great artists whose work is displayed in the house.

Although Dodgson did not return to Farringford after the summer of 1864, during which he took only two good pictures he was pleased with, he never explicitly expresses disappointment over the fact that the friendship never burgeoned, which can perhaps be related to his increasing devotion to making new child friends at the seaside, especially from the late 1870s onwards. The relationship with Tennyson had been unravelling since his stay in April 1862 when he saw 'hardly anything more of Mr. Tennyson' despite his excellent friendship with Hallam and Lionel.[57] As a consequence of Dodgson's well-documented quarrel with Tennyson about an unpublished poem, contact ceased completely. Nevertheless, the fact that the interactions with the Tennysons, as well as those with the Liddells, stand out in terms of narrative development, contrasting with the many short notes that simply sketched the appearance and character of other child friends, demonstrates that Dodgson envisaged a relationship that combined the thrill of the new and the stability of intellectual companionship.

Allingham's diaries

Allingham's diaristic records are part of an elaborate autobiographical project, in which he sought to render 'the whole texture of [his] life', 'without philosophising' and '[giving] recollections and impressions as simply as may be'.[58] Though he never completed it, Allingham's project aimed to portray his heroes in a lifelike, non-didactic fashion rather than to monumentalise himself; a rare occurrence in the context of Victorian biography's fixation with '[prompting] emulation' and teaching 'lessons about hard work and perseverance'.[59] The narrative style of Allingham's diary alternates between retrospective formal autobiography and the immediacy of diaristic writing. The resulting pastiche offers a vivid picture of the living Tennyson, as well as of Allingham's ongoing adjustments to the poet's eccentricity. As opposed to the glorifying reminiscences by Tennyson's other friends and acquaintances (discussed in Chapter 5), Allingham's diary strictly privileges realistic accuracy over the flattering idealisation of the poet. Although the Irish poet enjoyed a uniquely fortunate position as one of Tennyson's closest friends, Allingham, unlike most reminiscers, did not explicitly portray himself as fundamentally superior to those who were deprived access to Farringford. Nevertheless, he constantly re-negotiated his position as Tennyson's confidant to avert reproaches of intrusive lion-hunting, and competed with fellow visitors at Farringford for Tennyson's affections.

The first meeting between Allingham and Tennyson took place on Saturday, 28 June 1851, when the poet and his wife were living at Twickenham.[60] Long before this 'appointed day', however, Tennyson had been an integral part of Allingham's consciousness.[61] Allingham was not merely a passive reader of Tennyson's work, but he actively created awareness of the poet's work when the latter was still 'an unknown name' by '[preaching] Tennyson' to the clerks when he was a Principal Coast Officer (1846–48), 'reciting bits from *Locksley Hall*' and 'meeting at first a cold reception, but afterwards better acknowledgment'.[62] These poetry recitals, unusual in the context of a customs office, are a symptom of Allingham's 'longing for culture, conversation and opportunity' during these years.[63] Tennyson's work shielded Allingham against the frustrating banality of his life: 'my mind was brimful of love and poetry, and usually, all external things appeared trivial in their relations to it'.[64] Allingham's connection to Tennyson can clearly be seen as parasocial, as 'the quality of the relationship, rather than the quantity of the interaction seems to matter most'.[65]

This parasocial relationship is likely to have grown in intensity because Allingham had few qualified interlocutors who could share his intellectual passions and ambitions. As Sharon Marcus has argued, in Victorian culture, 'friendship between men was believed to promote enlightenment ideals of self-cultivation, sympathetic communion and civic association'.[66] Thus, even before the first meeting, Tennyson occupied a doubly important role for Allingham: while the latter's poetry provided him with intellectual nourishment and encourage- ment, he longed for further self-actualisation as an intimate friend. The jealousy he displays when his status as a leading fan and pro- spective friend is threatened is indicative of his advanced emotional attachment to the poet. When, for instance, on 1 January 1849, in Donegal, Reverend Jos. Welsh and English land agent Wilson stop by his room for a snack, Allingham reports that 'Wilson looked into my Tennyson, and saying "Now that is what I call *stuff*!" began to read out part of Ænone'.[67] Allingham's attachment to 'his' book extends to Tennyson as a poet and person, which explains the rush of irritation with which he reclaims the volume from his rival: 'I said, "Let me look at it", and put the book in my pocket without another word. [Wilson] appeared rather stunned'.[68] As if to console himself after this annoying incident, Allingham seeks to restore the possessive intimacy between himself and his image of Tennyson: 'How Tennyson gives the effect of everything, – enriched with a peculiar glow!'[69] Allingham's shriek of delight communicates his gratitude to Tennyson for gracefully render- ing the universal 'everything', which brightens his personal vision of the world and thus creates emotional proximity between the reader and the writer.

We see that Tennyson's work significantly shaped Allingham's world view and emotional well-being, and thus the poet as an imagined person occupied a crucial position in his thoughts. When in the summer of 1849, Allingham travels to England to investigate the possibilities of starting a literary life in London, he feels titillated by his growing geographical proximity to Tennyson and excitedly screens his environ- ment for traces of his hero. When, on 6 July, at a *table d'hôte*, he spots a 'dark, long-haired, notable looking' man drinking a glass of wine and smoking a cigar, 'a thought flashed – *Could* it be Alfred Tennyson!'[70] This heave of hope is deflated after a brief conversation: 'Tennyson quickly vanished'.[71] Evidently, even before Tennyson was awarded the laureateship, Allingham was familiar with his image, visualised the poet consistently and, most likely, imagined interactions. Longing to see the poet embodied, Allingham eagerly collected and assembled traces of Tennyson, even randomly asking a waiter in Kentish Town whether he had 'heard of a Mr. Tennyson' to maximise his sources of first-hand information.[72] Upon receiving a negative response, Allingham '[tries] another waiter who *had* heard of him, but had never seen him'.[73] Tennyson's presence becomes more traceable when, on 18 August, Coventry Patmore shows Allingham his former house in Hampstead Heath, 'where Emerson and Tennyson sat at his table and liked each other'.[74] Patmore's house, located 'in a sort of crescent with trees before it', becomes an auratic object that is imbued with Tennyson's presence.[75] Seeing, apprehending and writing about the place in which Tennyson interacted with Emerson as if it was a museum allows Allingham to substantiate his purely imagined vision of the living Tennyson and to participate in this bygone scene mentally. In light of Harald Hendrix's observation that writers' houses 'attract those that feel the need to go beyond their intellectual exchanges with texts and long for some kind of material contact with the author', Patmore's abode acquires the status of a secondary shrine, worshipped for temporarily housing Tennyson.[76]

Patmore's anecdotes and possessions document the presence of Tennyson and thus help Allingham to concretise his conception of the poet. The drafts of his poems 'The Storm' and 'The Two Journeys' that Patmore shows Allingham, for instance, bear the physical traces of Tennyson's mental engagement with them: 'Tennyson's mark is on the margin in various places: "+T"'.[77] Like many of his contemporaries, for whom the 'collecting of papers in the author's own hand' had 'a certain element of piety or of sentiment and romance', Allingham is in awe of these MS, as they have been read, touched and annotated by Tennyson.[78] Even their value is exceeded by Patmore's announcement that he has 'in this room perhaps the greatest literary treasure in England – the manuscript of Tennyson's *next poem*'.[79] Rather than criticise Patmore's self-important teasing or deplore not being able to look at the poem, Allingham revels in being in such close proximity to a poem that millions of readers are waiting for. He retrospectively adds that he 'was not even told the title at this time', creating suspense for an anticipated reader by a full stop and then solemnly revealing: 'It was *In Memoriam*'.[80] There is a quiet triumph in Allingham's realisation that, without then knowing it, he once occupied the same room as the manuscript of Tennyson's most important poem. The proximity to this unpublished treasure validates Allingham as a privileged insider in Tennyson's social and intellectual sphere.

For those who got to meet Tennyson in person, the vision of the poet they had fostered in their imagination, often based upon images dispersed by the press and through *cartes de visite*, was incongruent with the poet's actual aspect. Perhaps to detract from the unglamorous awkwardness of their first encounter with Tennyson, reminiscers tend to foreground their grand entry into the charmed grounds of Farringford, usually omitting their first impressions of the poet. In contrast, Allingham, like Dodgson, candidly describes Tennyson as a 'strange' and 'almost spectral figure'.[81] Tennyson's warm welcome transforms the parasocial relationship into a bilateral one, with 'the Great Man [peering] close' at Allingham, reciprocating his gaze and 'shaking hands cordially ... with a profound quietude of manner'.[82] Significantly, Tennyson had also been establishing a parasocial relationship to Allingham, albeit of a less elaborate character than vice versa, when engaging intensely with the latter's poetry: 'He took up my volume of poems, saying, "You can see it is a good deal dirtier than most of the books"'.[83] Being thus acknowledged as a capable poet by Tennyson must have provided immense gratification to Allingham, but aside from recording these facts, he remains silent about his feelings. When Patmore calls, Tennyson tells him: 'You didn't know Allingham was here' and it '[rejoices]' Allingham 'to hear the familiar mention of my name'.[84] Tennyson's comfortable use of Allingham's name proves the latter's integration into the poet's sphere of consciousness.

Allingham's autobiographical project demonstrates that he was acutely aware that his friendship with the Tennysons might be perceived as lion-hunting. He thus insists that his relocation from Ballyshannon to Lymington in Hampshire in early 1863 was determined by 'fortune, not choice', meaning that he did not plan on intruding into the poet's refuge at Farringford.[85] Lymington and Freshwater were conveniently close, so Allingham tried to manage his hopes of becoming a frequent visitor, which is evident in the following scene: '"You will be near Tennyson," said Carlyle [.] "I doubt if I shall see him" I replied, disheartened by a second failure to settle in London, and disinclined for even the best company. "Yes, yes", said C., "you are sure to come together"'.[86] In this retrospective entry, Allingham mimics his own reticence, effecting Carlyle's reassuring response, in order to show his respectful distance from the Tennysons and to stress the extent to which his friendship with them is established and known to others. At times, Allingham, in his overcautious yet determined approach to the Tennysons, seems to perform insecurity in order to legitimise his longing for admission into 'the enchanted realm of Farringford'.[87] His description of his first visit to Freshwater on 3 July 1863 strikingly recalls the accounts given in published reminiscences in that it builds up suspense through his inclusion of the voyage on the 'evening boat' and his walks 'over the bridge' and 'two or three miles of beautiful green-sided roads, spoilt here and there by Forts', leading to Farringford. Surprisingly, he constructs the arrival at the house as an anticlimax, as he 'could not see the house' and 'would not of course enter any gate'.[88] The inclusion of 'of course' into this purposefully anticlimactic narrative suggests that Allingham aims to distinguish his own respectful behaviour from that of pushy tourists. Hiding his excitement as well as his obvious wish to be close to the poet, Allingham insists that he has not 'the faintest thought of presenting myself to him or wish, even, to meet him by chance on his return (he was from home at this time)'.[89] The insecure desire for undeserved proximity that Allingham experiences outside the gates of Farringford is closely related to Tennyson's celebrity status. Allingham feels intellectually and socially unequal to the Poet Laureate and to others he admires, and deplores that he has 'lost the faith I used to have in people's wishing to see me'.[90] This lack of self-confidence indicates that Allingham's bilateral relationship with Tennyson has collapsed back into parasocial one-sidedness, with the fan's position regressing from interlocutor to spectator.

Allingham refuses to bear the pledge of inferiority, however, and, as if to defend himself against societal judgment, stresses his sense of belonging to Tennyson's circle and his right to be well acquainted with Carlyle, Rossetti and Palgrave:

> But I feel a natural bond to him (I say it with humility) and to a very few others, and only in their company am better contented than to be with nature and books. With these persons I feel truly humble, yet at the same time easy. I understand and am understood, with words or without words. It is not the fame that attracts me, it disgusts me rather. Fame has cooled many friendships for me, never made or increased one. Fame is a thing of the 'World,' and the 'World' is a dreadful separator.[91]

With a gentle but decisive 'but', Allingham negotiates a space for himself among his heroes, acknowledging his inferiority by insisting on his 'humility', yet asserting equality. Due to its organicity, he locates the connection he feels between himself and Tennyson, as well as that between himself and selected others, outside the realm of culture, beyond discourse, and hence beyond society's judging gaze. Even though Allingham regards fame as a label obtruded by the intruding world, which splits the bonds between spiritually connected persons through imposing a meritorious and commercial value upon the individual, he reacts to it.

Fan rivalry

Unlike many reminiscers, who publicly insist on the fundamental, insuperable division between Tennyson's 'true' admirers and those presumably going through the motions of fandom for its entertainment value, Allingham is uninterested in situating his relationship to the poet in a macro-societal context. He does respond to conventions of fandom in his diaristic writing, especially when first meeting the poet, but he does so in order to evade accusations of inappropriate invasiveness, rather than to demean others. His accounts are permeated not by his annoyance with anonymous fans, but with his culture's selfish expectation that the celebrity's endlessly giving eminence might compensate for the receiving admirer's shortcomings. In his auto/biographical narrative construction of himself as Tennyson's intellectual companion, his rivalry with other members of Tennyson's entourage takes on a prominent role. While most of them, Julia Margaret Cameron in particular, seem to hinder the development of his friendship with Tennyson, their relative inadequacy as listeners and interlocutors also serves to heighten his own importance in Tennyson's life. Allingham's reports of his interactions with Tennyson thus demonstrate a desire to respect the humanity of the poet by renouncing selfish possessiveness and the simultaneous wish for an exclusive friendship with him.

Although Allingham does not explicitly comment on Tennyson's celebrity status, several of his entries touch upon the poet's position in society. Witnessing the arrival of amateurs' poetry and letters from 'autograph seekers' at Farringford on 21 November 1866, he understands through Tennyson's enervated reaction – 'I should like to sneak out and get a cup of tea by myself' – that fans' pressures and expectations weighed on the poet.[92] Writers of such fan mail hoped to establish educative, validating and inspiring contact with the poet in order to, as Carlyle promised in his 1840 lectures *On Heroes*, improve themselves in different ways: 'Great Men, taken up in any way, are profitable company. We cannot look, however imperfectly, upon a great man, without gaining something by him. He is the living light-fountain, which it is good and pleasant to be near'.[93] Although Tennyson fulfilled precisely this enlightening function in Allingham's life, Allingham refused to view the poet entirely from a utilitarian perspective and did not expect him to have the answers to all sorts of subjective anguish:

T. is unhappy from his uncertainty regarding the condition and destiny of man. Is it dispiriting to find a great Poet with no better grounds of comfort than a common person? At first it is. But how should the case be otherwise? The poet has only the same materials of sensation and thought as ordinary mortals; he uses them better; but to step outside the human limitations is not granted even to him. The secret is kept from one and all of us.[94]

Allingham here deconstructs the premise of celebrity culture, namely the construction of a talented person as an 'indispensable saviour of his epoch', to use Carlyle's terms, or 'one of those beacon-lights of humanity', to use those of *The Saturday Review*.[95] Society venerated the poet as a natural leader, distinguished by his unparalleled insight into the human condition. Many expected Tennyson to give a sense of direction to 'the generation which flourished from 1780 to 1850 [and who] had passed from a period of great national danger to one of great personal perplexity', as Harold Nicholson observed.[96] Autographs, like *cartes de visite* and annotated manuscripts of poems, constituted an extension of the poet to which the public could intimately connect, as my discussion of Dodgson's collection of such items has shown. What united Tennyson's fans was the hope to 'gain' something through interacting with him, be this knowledge, status or even money. Allingham resented the universal responsibility that was attributed to the poet and insisted on the latter's insurmountable, because fundamentally human, ignorance without attacking specific groups.

Although for Allingham, his imagined relationship with Tennyson represented an important source of emotional comfort and intellectual inspiration and ambition, he felt that a consistent focus on Tennyson's poetry could prevent the emotional and social exploitation of the poet for the personal gain of his fans:

I doubt if – – holds poetry in any honour, or poets as such. I sought AT and worshipped him as the well-head of an enchanting river of song: charm of personality and surroundings came in addition, a fine setting to the priceless jewel of his genius. – – I imagine, admires the poetry mainly because she admires and loves the man.[97]

This entry represents one of the only instances in which Allingham directly compares the authenticity of his own admiration for Tennyson and poetry in general to that of another person. Unlike this unnamed female, who seems enthralled by the external glamour surrounding

Tennyson's person, Allingham came to the poet for the reasons he considers legitimate, namely through reading authorised, published poems. Through attentive listening to and devoted fandom of Tennyson, Allingham created a space for himself in the poet's life and remained a regular visitor until his death in 1889.

In his introduction to the published diary, Geoffrey Grigson remarks that for Allingham, Tennyson 'was not a person' but that it was rather 'as if Tennyson was always the Desired Place, half real, half dream'.[98] During the pre-1851 period Allingham was indeed so enchanted by Tennyson's poems that their dreamy atmosphere saturated his otherwise bleak life as an administrator. In the 1860s, although he had made his entrance into the poet's world, Allingham was in awe of Farringford, not only because of its exclusivity but also because of its unearthly beauty, as the entry of 25 June 1865 shows: 'I go to the top of the house alone, have a strong sense of being at Tennyson's, green summer, ruddy light in the sky'.[99] Allingham has undergone an emancipatory evolution since his intimidated paralysis at the gates in 1863 and moves freely about the property. His amazement at being allowed to immerse himself in the glow of Farringford is still palpable in his account of entering Tennyson's sanctuary 'alone'.

It is evident from Allingham's attitudes towards celebrity-worship, as well as his unembellished accounts of Tennyson, that he, unlike the majority of biographers and reminiscers, consistently sought to represent and surround himself with the poet's humanity instead of constructing him as the generous, warm, welcoming and supremely interesting host, who managed to effortlessly combine socialising and poetic work. Rather than praising Tennyson endlessly and thus elevating himself, Allingham depicts the poet's quirks, such as his occasional quarrelsomeness and his domineering superiority, at his own expense, as can be seen in the following anecdote of 22 July 1866:

> After dinner we talk of dreams. T. said, 'In my boyhood I had *intuitions* of Immortality – inexpressible! I have never been able to express them. I shall try some day'.
>
> I say that I too have felt something of that kind; whereat T. (being in one of his less amiable moods) growls, 'I don't believe you have. You say it out of rivalry'.[100]

Questioning Allingham's intellect, talent and truthfulness and insisting on his higher status, Tennyson re-establishes inequality between them, which the former's bold claim had sought to eliminate. When, on 25 August 1867, while the two men are having a beer in Charmouth, Allingham quotes a line of poetry, 'T. (as usual)' reprimands Allingham: '"You don't say it properly" – and repeats it in his own sonorous manner'.[101] For the sake of giving a 'physiognomic' account of the poet's character and behaviour, Allingham faithfully includes Tennyson's slightly denigrating comments but omits his own response to them. He does, however, subtly, and somewhat apologetically, use parentheses to write his responses into the accounts, thus conveying his explanations for the poet's contrariness. In the first case, Allingham relativises the poet's snide comment by implying that, for the most part, Tennyson's moods are 'amiable', and in the second case, the diarist banalises and thus normalises his hero's meliorative suggestion.

While Allingham records his encounters with Tennyson in great detail, he is remarkably reluctant to include simultaneous visitors to Farringford into his accounts. He occasionally acknowledges their presence and at times briefly sketches conversations – 'At dinner: Mr. and Mrs. Bradley of Marlborough, Mr. and Mrs. Butler of Harrow' – but he does so in order to emphasise Tennyson's memorable statements or to shed light on his own relationship with the poet rather than to include the respective visitor. In this often quoted anecdote of 28 December 1863, for instance, Allingham mentions Palgrave in order to introduce the subject of Tennyson's patronising schoolmasterly behaviour: 'A.T. reproves P. for talking so fast and saying "of – of – of – of", etc. He also corrects me for my pronunciation (or so he asserts) of "dew". "There is no *Jew* on the grass!" says he – "there may be *dew*, but that's quite another thing"'.[102] Omitting Palgrave's, as well as his own, reaction to Tennyson's criticism, Allingham normalises and palliates his own slight indignation. Whereas Tennyson reprimands Palgrave, he rectifies the delivery of Allingham's utterances in order to improve it, which establishes the latter as the poet's favoured interlocutor.

Allingham's mentions of simultaneous visitors tend to be quite brief and neutral, but his accounts of Julia Margaret Cameron's presence at Freshwater, much like Edward Lear's (Chapter 2) bear a definite tint of irritation. Many reminiscers foreground Cameron's generosity, creativity and kindness, but Allingham portrays her as an incongruous element that disturbs the perfect harmony and serenity of Farringford. Allingham's entry of 3 October 1863, for example, creates an atmosphere of calm domestic comfort, 'Drawing-room, tea, Mrs. Tennyson in white, I can sometimes scarcely hear her low tones', which is interrupted by 'Mrs. Cameron, dark, short, sharp-eyed, one hears very distinctly'.[103] This snide description of Cameron's restlessness and craving for attention suggests that Allingham is annoyed by the former's eccentricity. Cameron's boundless enthusiasm for socialising and photographing contrasts with Allingham's humble, patient and reticent demeanour as a listener. The dissimilarity in their attitudes to celebrity is evident in Allingham's entry of 24 June 1865, when he, still a shy and insecure visitor, appears at Farringford unannounced, '[hides his] bag' and '[finds] some people in the hay-field and Mrs. Cameron photographing like mad'.[104] The confident determination with which Cameron positions her often famous photographic subjects stands in stark contrast to Allingham's decision to wait, in a passive and cowardly manner, to be invited by Tennyson. Cameron's strong belief in her work as an artist irritates Allingham, who, after a failed attempt, refuses to be photographed by her: 'she thinks it a great honour to be done by her'.[105] As Chapter 3 shows, he does, though, go on to write a positive review of her work in the press, which suggests a willingness to subjugate his personal antipathy in the interest of maintaining the harmony of the wider circle. While Cameron, as the talented wife of a diplomat and a member of the Prinsep family, is firmly integrated in the celebrity circle and, with Emily, partly runs it, Allingham, the customs officer longing to be a professional poet, still does not feel assured of his place in it. He expresses his disapproval of her self-confidence, which to him is unfounded arrogance, again on 10 June 1867, in his account of a shared train journey to Lymington, during which 'she [talks] all the time'.[106]

Allingham constructs Cameron as his effusively chatty counterpart and rival, continuously implying that her privileged social position does not make her Tennyson's favourite. His comment on her tendency to interject 'Hm?' into her conversations makes his irritation obvious: '[she] seldom waits for a reply'.[107] Not only are such pseudo-interrogative utterances gratuitous, but, coupled with an unwillingness to engage with an interlocutor, they become meaningless. In contrast, during the long conversations between Allingham and Tennyson, conducted 'all with the friendliest sympathy and mutual understanding', the poet was able to discuss his ever-troubling anxiety 'to get some real insight into the nature and prospects of the Human Race'.[108] Although Allingham portrays his own participation in these dialogues as marginal, with his role confined to that of an encouraging interviewer and attentive listener, he nevertheless maintains that 'T. is the most delightful man in the world to converse with, even when he disagrees'.[109] Allingham here stresses the bilateral nature of his interactions with the poet, constructing himself as Tennyson's confidant, who does not just talk at the poet, but 'converses with' him. Allingham gets the impression that Tennyson indeed prefers his conversational style to Cameron's when, on the way to her house, he confides: 'Mrs. C. (using the initial, as he often does) is so gushing!'[110] This criticism of Cameron's effusiveness, Allingham writes, was 'presently justified' by her 'fervent' assurance that F. Walker's 'soul' was at Tennyson's 'feet'.[111] Much to Allingham's delight, Tennyson provocatively responds: 'I hope his soles are at his own feet!'[112] The poet's brusquely playful sarcasm suggests Cameron's misestimation of her interlocutor's interests, providing another, certainly satisfying, example of her ineptitude as Tennyson's friend to Allingham. The diaristic inscription of these rivalries serves to affirm Allingham's importance in Tennyson's most intimate circle without his having to utter self-complacent and therefore critical reminiscences about other members of that circle.

Allingham's autobiographical project functions as a written museum that allows for the preservation and re-visitation of personal memories, but also accommodates potential readers by acquainting them with aspects of Tennyson not otherwise accessible. Allingham discreetly validates his role as an attentive listener to Tennyson and is not ashamed of inscribing his own vulnerability when interacting with the Laureate. In his biographical endeavour, Allingham very subtly traces his own presence among the Victorian intelligentsia, capturing and memorialising Tennyson in a lifelike, direct fashion, abstaining from the sentimental lingo that characterised the published reminiscences and 'At Home' reports discussed elsewhere in this study. His diary can thus be seen to bear testimony to the very personal meaning that real, as well as imagined, interactions with an admired person could have for a Victorian 'fan', and reflects the immense pressure to conform to accepted forms of celebrity-worship.

Conclusion

Allingham and Dodgson were ardent admirers of Tennyson's work and, like many of their contemporaries, sought to substantiate their imagined relationship with the poet through collecting and cherishing real-life interactions. Their diaries were vital tools not only for the construction of a mental anticipatory relationship to Tennyson, but, after meeting him, functioned as auto/biographical repositories of the living poet for posterity. While diaries are generally considered to be autobiographical texts, generically, these accounts of Tennyson must be situated at the intersection of 'private' diarising, 'public' retrospective autobiography and formal biography, constantly reacting to journalistic habits of representation and conventions of fandom. The diaries in question are characterised by a museum agenda because they privilege the collection of experiences over introspection: their object is less to trace the vicissitudes of daily life, but rather to showcase its highlights. Intimate emotion functions as an indicator of the value of specific events; with Allingham impressing through his candour and Dodgson leaning towards the abstraction of excitement through symbols rather than verbalisation, and the omission of low-spiritedness. The semi-private nature of the diaries demonstrates that, due to the overbearing influence of the Victorian press, the private veneration of a public figure inevitably became a public act. The diaries also show, that, conversely, the poet played an important part in these writers' consciousness, from which we can infer that the meaning that an autograph-seeker derived from Tennyson's response must have gone far beyond the mere thrill of possession. The emotional value of a collector's object relating to Tennyson, or a glimpse of him caught outside the gates of Farringford, was not simply something to show off, but also a trigger to substantiate an imagined but deeply personal relationship with the poet.

Notes

1. Theodore Watts-Dunton, 'Emily, Lady Tennyson', *Athenaeum*, 15 August 1896, 227–28 (p. 227), in *ProQuest British Periodicals* <http://www.proquest.co.uk> [accessed 12 April 2013].
2. Ibid.
3. *Fandom: Identities and Communities in a Mediated World*, ed. by Jonathan Gray, Cornel Sandvoss and C. Lee Harrington (New York and London: New York University Press, 2007), p. 2; Tom Mole, *Byron's Romantic Celebrity: Industrial Culture and the Hermeneutic of Intimacy* (Basingstoke: Palgrave Macmillan, 2007), p. xi.
4. Eric Eisner, *Nineteenth-Century Poetry and Literary Celebrity* (Basingstoke: Palgrave Macmillan, 2009), p. 1.
5. Susan Stewart, *On Longing: Narratives of the Miniature, the Gigantic, the Souvenir, the Collection* (Durham, NC: Duke University Press, 1984), p. 154.
6. Barbara J. Black, *On Exhibit: Victorians and Their Museums* (Charlottesville, VA: University Press of Virginia, 2000), p. 4.
7. Ibid.
8. Ibid., p. 3.
9. Judith Pascoe, *The Hummingbird in the Cabinet: a Rare and Curious History of Romantic Collectors* (Ithaca: Cornell University Press, 2006), p. 5.
10. Susan M. Pearce, Rosemary Flanders, Mark Hall and Fiona Morton, *The Collector's Voice: Critical Readings in the Practice of Collecting: Imperial Voices*, 3 vols (Aldershot: Ashgate, 2002), III, 86.
11. Pascoe, p. 4.
12. Ibid., p. 5.

13. Asa Briggs, *Victorian Things* (London: B. T. Batsford, 1988), p. 54.
14. *William Allingham's Diary 1847–1889*, ed. by H. Allingham and D. Radford (London: Centaur Press, 2000), p. 63; *The Diaries of Lewis Carroll*, ed. by Roger Lancelyn Green, 2 vols (Westport: Greenwood Press, 1971), I, 124.
15. Rebecca B. Rubin and Alan M. Rubin, 'Attribution in Social and Parasocial Relationships', in *Attribution, Communication Behaviour, and Close Relationships*, ed. by Valerie L. Manusov and John Harvey (Cambridge: Cambridge University Press, 2001), pp. 320–37 (p. 327).
16. David Giles, *Illusions of Immortality: a Psychology of Fame and Celebrity* (Basingstoke: Macmillan, 2000), p. 4.
17. John Pudney, *Lewis Carroll and His World* (London: Thames and Hudson, 1976), p. 17.
18. Wendy Wiener and George C. Rosenblatt, 'A Moment's Monument: the Psychology of Keeping a Diary', in *The Narrative Study of Lives*, ed. by Ruthellen Josselson and Amia Lieblich (London: Sage, 1993), pp. 30–58 (p. 30).
19. Stewart, *On Longing*, p. 138.
20. Ibid., p. xii.
21. Helmut Gernsheim, *Lewis Carroll: Photographer* (London: Max Parrish & Co., 1949), p. 25.
22. Peter Hamilton and Roger Hargreaves, *The Beautiful and the Damned: the Creation of Identity in Nineteenth-Century Photography* (Aldershot: Lund Humphries, 2001), p. 11.
23. John Plunkett, 'Celebrity and Community: the Poetics of the Carte-de-Visite', *Journal of Victorian Culture*, 8 (2003), 55–79 (p. 72).
24. Ibid.
25. 'The Philosophy of Yourself', *All the Year Round*, 9 (1963), 391–94 (p. 393), in *ProQuest British Periodicals* <http://www.proquest.co.uk> [accessed 12 April 2013].
26. Robin and Carol Wichard, *Victorian Cartes-de-Visite* (Princes Risborough: Shire, 1999), p. 79.
27. Mole, *Byron's Romantic Celebrity*, p. 4.
28. Rather than to express joyful emotion, Dodgson credits days of national importance, such as 'The Wedding Day of the Prince of Wales' (10 March 1863) (*The Diaries of Lewis Carroll*, I, 194), professional satisfactions – '*Dies notandus*. Discovered rule for dividing a number by 9, by mere addition and subtraction' (27 September 1897) – and extraordinary achievements: 'Dies cretâ notandus. I have actually superseded the rules discovered yesterday' (28 September 1897) (Stuart Dodgson Collingwood, *The Life and Letters of Lewis Carroll* (London: T. Fisher Unwin, 1898), p. 167).
29. Pudney, *Lewis Carroll and His World*, p. 67.
30. Ibid., p. 17; *The Diaries of Lewis Carroll*, I, 83, 224.
31. *The Diaries of Lewis Carroll*, I, 128–29.
32. Ibid., p. 129.
33. Derek Hudson, *Lewis Carroll: An Illustrated Biography* (New York: Clarkson N. Potter, 1977), p. 91.
34. Ibid., p. 127.
35. Ibid., p. 118.
36. Ibid.

37. Ibid., p. 119.
38. Pudney, *Lewis Carroll and His World*, p. 61.
39. *The Diaries of Lewis Carroll*, I, 124.
40. John Urry, *The Tourist Gaze*, 2nd edn (London: Sage, 2002), p. 13.
41. *The Diaries of Lewis Carroll*, I, 124.
42. Ibid.
43. Ibid.
44. Ibid.
45. Ibid.
46. Ibid.
47. Ibid.
48. Ibid., (22 September 1857).
49. Ibid., p. 126.
50. *The Letters of Lewis Carroll*, ed. by Morton N. Cohen and Roger Lancelyn Green, 2 vols (New York: Oxford University Press, 1979), I, 35.
51. Ibid.; *The Diaries of Lewis Carroll*, I, 124.
52. *The Letters of Lewis Carroll*, I, 36.
53. Edmund Yates, *Celebrities At Home*, repr. from *The World*, 3 vols (London: Office of *The World*, 1877–9); 'Interviewers and Interviewing', *All the Year Round*, 8 (1892), 422–26, in *ProQuest British Periodicals* <http://www.proquest.co.uk> [accessed 12 April 2013].
54. James Buzard, *The Beaten Track: European Tourism, Literature, and the Ways to Culture, 1800–1918* (Oxford: Clarendon Press, 1993), p. 159.
55. *The Letters of Lewis Carroll*, I, 36.
56. Ibid.
57. *The Letters of Lewis Carroll*, I, 53 (19 April 1862).
58. *William Allingham's Diary 1847–1889*, pp. 2, 7.
59. Juliette Atkinson, *Victorian Biography Reconsidered: a Study of Nineteenth-Century 'Hidden' Lives* (Oxford: Oxford University Press, 2010), p. 47.
60. *William Allingham's Diary 1847–1889*, p. 60.
61. Ibid.
62. Ibid., p. 31.
63. Ibid., p. 33.
64. Ibid.
65. Rubin and Rubin, p. 327.
66. Sharon Marcus, *Between Women: Friendship, Desire, and Marriage in Victorian England* (Princeton: Princeton University Press, 2007), p. 86.
67. *William Allingham's Diary 1847–1889*, p. 45.
68. Ibid.
69. Rubin and Rubin, p. 327; *William Allingham's Diary 1847–1889*, p. 45.
70. *William Allingham's Diary 1847–1889*, p. 51.
71. Ibid.
72. Ibid., p. 54 (5 August 1849).
73. Ibid.
74. Ibid.
75. Ibid.
76. Harald Hendrix, 'Writers' Houses as Media of Expression and Remembrance: From Self-Fashioning to Cultural Memory', in *Writers' Houses and the Making*

of Memory, ed. by Harald Hendrix (London and New York: Routledge, 2008), pp. 1–12 (p. 1).

77. *William Allingham's Diary 1847–1889*, p. 54.
78. Harold Nicholson, *Tennyson: Aspects of his Life, Character and Poetry* (London: Constable, 1949); A. N. L. Munby, *The Cult of the Autograph Letter in England* (London: Athlone Press, 1962), p. 6.
79. *William Allingham's Diary 1847–1889*, p. 54.
80. Ibid.
81. Ibid.
82. Ibid.
83. Ibid., p. 61.
84. Ibid., p. 62.
85. Ibid.
86. Ibid.
87. Ibid., p. 84 (28 June 1863).
88. Ibid.
89. Ibid.
90. Ibid.
91. Ibid.
92. Ibid., p. 145.
93. Thomas Carlyle, *On Heroes, Hero-Worship and the Heroic in History*, ed. by Archibald MacMechan (London: Ginn, 1901), p. 2.
94. *William Allingham's Diary 1847–1889*, p. 149 (1 February 1868).
95. Carlyle, p. 15; 'Lord Tennyson', *The Saturday Review*, 8 October 1892, pp. 405–06, in *ProQuest British Periodicals* <http://www.proquest.co.uk> [accessed 12 April 2013].
96. Nicholson, p. 3.
97. *William Allingham's Diary 1847–1889*, p. 189 (17 October 1868).
98. Ibid., p. x.
99. Ibid., p. 117.
100. Ibid., p. 137.
101. Ibid., p. 158.
102. Ibid., p. 94 (28 December 1863).
103. Ibid., p. 87.
104. Ibid., p. 117.
105. Ibid.
106. Ibid., p. 152.
107. Ibid.
108. Ibid., p. 151 (3 April 1867); p. 148 (24 January 1867).
109. Ibid., p. 151.
110. Ibid., p. 189 (17 October 1868).
111. Ibid.
112. Ibid.

5
'Troops of Unrecording Friends': Vicarious Celebrity in the *Memoir*

Anne-Marie Millim

Tennyson's 1849 poem 'To – , After Reading a Life and Letters' renders the poet's irritated reaction to the publication of Keats's love letters in 1848 and exemplifies the dismissive attitude to biography that he would maintain all his life. The poem's speaker – clearly Tennyson himself – condemns the public's tendency to 'break lock and seal; betray the trust; / Keep nothing sacred' and to frantically unearth the fictional celebrity poet's 'faults he would not show', 'ere he scarce be cold'.[1] The commemorative frenzy staged by the public means that after his death, 'the Poet cannot die', because his heart is torn and distributed 'before the crowd'.[2] Even before the spectacular rise in popularity that came with the Laureateship, Tennyson sought to deter future biographers from '[moving his] bones' when he asked the *Examiner*'s editor John Forster to publish this poem.[3] For the duration of his office, Tennyson was acutely aware of the fact that the coveted lot of the bird 'that dies unheard within his tree' would not be his, but he still took pains to encourage the public's reluctance to biographise him.[4] As is well known, Tennyson commissioned and directed his son Hallam's composition of an official biography in order to gain and maintain control over the 'transmission of meaning' of his poems and his person.[5] For Hallam, the compilation of this biographical account was a complicated task as he had to accommodate multiple expectations: he had to please his father, family and friends and educate the readers on the facts of the poet's life whilst trying to quench their curiosity on his private self. As this chapter shows, Hallam catered to the differing functions attributed to biography by Victorian society through creating a collage-type text to commemorate his father. The conception of this supposedly legitimate textual monument had an additional outcome that Tennyson probably did not expect when commissioning his biography: the text not only instituted a definite image of the Laureate for posterity, but it also gave Hallam, Tennyson's friends and even the reviewers of the *Memoir* the opportunity to establish themselves as vicarious celebrities whose proximity to and knowledge of Tennyson marked them as superior to the readers. It thus fuelled the cult of celebrity, expanding the idolisation of the poet to his social circle – the 'troops of unrecording friends' – who, unlike Tennyson himself, embraced public visibility.

While Hallam backed up and complemented his accounts by referring to the reminiscences of family friends, there is also reason to believe that he was eager to limit the number of accounts of his father's life circulating in the press because he anticipated that his friends and acquaintances would compete for visibility in the literary sphere. In order to avoid the dissemination of multiple portraits in an avid and lucrative celebrity market, he engineered the collective appearance of Tennyson's entourage and created a quasi-unified monument. This strategy, although intended to regulate the multiplication of meanings attributed to the poet and his works, still allowed the reminiscers to accentuate their own relevance in Tennyson's life, because they could enter the public limelight as celebrities through association since their contributions would be rephrased in the press and, consequently, in conversation. Because of their repeated insistence on their own importance as biographical sources, their reminiscences consistently blur the boundaries between biography and autobiography. The *Memoir* must therefore not be seen as a univocal tribute but rather as a multi-author project that establishes the unique proximity to the poet that Tennyson's biographers enjoyed as an indicator of a personal merit deserving of celebrity status. Although he allows room for incongruity in the inscription of the reminiscers' individuality, Hallam ultimately retains complete control over the project, refusing to make Tennyson an example of emulable behaviour and opposing the social improvement ethic that characterises a lot of Victorian biographies.[6] He made sure that Tennyson retained the exceptionality of a historically located individual whose like would never be seen again.

In the context of Victorian biography, Hallam's prominent role in the compilation of the *Memoir* is not surprising. As A. O. J. Cockshut has noted, 'the majority of nineteenth-century biographies were written by people to whom the subject had been intimately known'.[7] In most of these texts, the biographer's presence is clearly palpable and the authorial point of view is accentuated. What is quite unique about the *Memoir* is not only the fact that Hallam appointed reminiscers as fellow biographers in order to strengthen the image of the poet that he wanted to publicise, but that the book presents itself as a gathering of the select few who had access to Tennyson's private sphere. The agenda of the *Memoir* reflects the hierarchy inherent in celebrity culture: through establishing a permanent legacy for Tennyson, Hallam and the reminiscers positioned themselves above the masses of lionisers and created parameters for the legitimacy and value of fandom. As Christopher Ricks has remarked, 'a memoir is defined as "a biography or biographical notice" (*OED* 4, from 1826); but this ignores the fact that a memoir carries some implication of personal knowledge, and that like memoirs it engages with persons whom you have known'.[8] Insisting on personal knowledge as a prerequisite for legitimate biography, many of these biographers, in and through their reports, reinforce the gap between touristy fans and authorised friends as they self-consciously stress their crucial role in shaping Tennyson's posterity. By thus inserting themselves into the poet's history, they tend to claim the status of vicarious celebrities, asserting themselves as superior to those relying on the press for information about the poet.

The pressure to praise: the *Memoir's* generic context

Because Hallam, as editor, was responsible for both the distribution and creation of knowledge about his father, he was subjected to the dual pressure of praising and protecting his father and of offering a pedagogical and objective account to society. Since Victorian theorisations of the task and execution of biography consistently struggled to reconcile the interests of what we might call the biographical triad – the subject, the biographer and the reader – Hallam found himself at the centre of a vortex of often conflicting expectation. While most Victorian critics viewed the reader's curiosity about an author's life as an inborn interest, debates about the amount and nature of the knowledge that the reader deserved were ongoing. Perhaps as a consequence of the commercialisation of biography that came with the progression of celebrity culture and the 'instantaneous', furious 'backlash' that followed James Anthony Froude's *Life of Carlyle* (1882–4), few later critics would have agreed with the enthusiasm for deconstructing the boundaries between the constituents of the biographical triad that Thomas Carlyle displays in 1832:[9]

> How inexpressibly comfortable to know your fellow creature; to see into him, understand his goings forth, decipher the whole heart of his mystery: nay, not only to see into him, but even to see out of

him, to view the world altogether as he views it; so that we can theo-retically construe him, and could almost practically personate him.[10]

The described convergence of the biographical triad allows 'the earnest Lover of Biography' to 'expand himself on all sides, and indefinitely enrich himself'.[11] For Carlyle, the task of the biographer is to merge with the subject, adopt his or her gaze and, through narrative, transform the reader's position from that of a detached spectator to that of an involved participant in a shared consciousness. As Chapter 2 has shown, Watts's *Hall of Fame* allowed viewers to imagine becoming like the distin-guished individual depicted; a process of cultural reproduction that he considered essential for the nation. To some extent, the reminiscers do exactly this: they see the world through the poet's eyes and, through their privileged knowledge of him, they become celebrities themselves. Their desire to be celebrities, is, however, stronger than their wish to enlighten the public, which is why, ultimately, the *Memoir* refuses to let the reader adopt the subject's perspective and limits him or her to the biographers' viewpoint.

While in the first part of the nineteenth century, the reader's emotional involvement was considered instrumental in his or her understanding of biography, the discourse of the latter half primarily tends to discuss both the necessity and the disadvantages of regulating the audience's animation through stylistic tactics. *Blackwood's Edinburgh Magazine* of 1851 rejoices in biography's ability to render truth by conveying 'the value of history, without the tedium, [and] the interest of romance, without the unsubstantiality'.[12] This article's inclusive attitude seems characteristic of mid-century attitudes, when, as Richard Altick has noted, biographies generally 'coupled' 'instruction [with] amusement', and were 'acceptable to the strictest consciousness', often '[serving] as a substitute for the forbidden novel'.[13] In the latter half of the century, biography became an increasingly serious matter and the constituents of the biographical triad were constantly matched against each other. In the debate about the public's proper attitude to celebri-ties, commentators tended to side either with the biographer or the reader, demanding less concealment or less curiosity, respectively. The Victorian journalist Robert Goodbrand thus describes the period after 1850 as 'an age when, whatever happens to a man while living, there is nothing permissible to his biographer, but praise of the dead'.[14] As a reader, Goodbrand is profoundly 'wearied of this way of writing people's lives' and advocates 'biography with a passionate love and an enthusias-tic admiration of the subject, in which, nevertheless, there should be an equally strong feeling not only of failure in the close, but of imperfection'.[15] Many subsequent critics were convinced of the damaging effects of the biographer's flattery of the subject on the reader's understanding – George Bentley, for instance, abhorred idealisation as displayed in John Gibson Lockhart's (1794–1854) biography of Walter Scott and exclaimed: 'we want Carlyle the man ... we want him good and bad, brightness and shadow'.[16] Bentley deplores that biography 'cooked ... from family affection' refuses to reveal the subject's 'qualifying colours' to the reader and thus deprives him or her of an 'honest portrait'.[17] Margaret Oliphant, on the other hand, is sympathetic to the biographer when she deems the praise of the dead as 'entirely justified by the instincts of human nature'.[18] However, for that very reason, she dismisses family members as biographers: 'it is not from such witnesses that we can expect the uncoloured chronicle of absolute truth,' which further helps to explain Hallam's decision to bolster his account by numerous reminiscers' views.[19]

Other critics, such as T. E. Kebbel, were sceptical of the readers' interest in the poet's self and condemned the public's 'appetite for scandal' as a 'vulgar' incentive to the biographer 'to minister' to it.[20] Wilfrid Ward, unsurprisingly, insists that 'one who is not a friend' cannot understand 'those remarkable traits which make a man worth writing about' and that the resulting 'idealised portrait ... is still juster to the dead'.[21] Not only did the biographer have to justify his choice of subject, but he or she also needed to earn the right to render the eminent person's life. Such exclusive and possessive attitudes were in turn criticised by fellow critics. Edmund Purcell, for instance, demonstrates a more respectful attitude to the British reading public, when he describes it as one 'which loves truth and hates suppression of facts and documents, no matter what the motive, as almost a lie' and thus accuses the biographer of dispossessing the public of 'historic truth'.[22] The *Memoir* thus inserted itself into a heterogeneous context in which the nature and limits of knowledge were the constant subject of heated debate.

The calculated exclusiveness that Hallam and the reminiscers practise goes against the grain of much of nineteenth-century biography, which generally aimed to enlighten and accommodate an expanding reading public. As Joseph W. Reed has noted, in the 1820s, 'references to the "average reader" and the "mass of mankind" turn up in reviews again and again', because writers felt that 'unsophisticated minds' could not distinguish 'virtue unless it was adequately applauded'.[23] Although Hallam and his network of biographers did try to teach the public the correct way of worshipping the poet, their agenda was generally more egotistical than philanthropic. They refrained from strengthening the relationship between hero worship and social improvement, which, according to recent critics, was an important concern for many Victorian biographers. As the biographical ideology of the day leaned towards '[prompting] emulation' through praise, Juliette Atkinson has argued, 'the lives of great men were often reduced to lessons about hard work and perseverance'.[24] Adopting such an approach and presenting Tennyson's life as an inspirational model for success would thus have banalised his superhuman talent and demoted the biographers' role to that of educators and reformers rather than celebrities in their own right.

Hallam and his colleagues recognised biography's power as a 'productive discursive event', to use David Amigoni's term, but, despite their relentless praise of the poet's intellectual brilliance, unpretentiousness and kind-heartedness, they were barely interested in furthering the public's education.[25] Unlike social reformers such as Samuel Smiles, who used biography to 'push individuals towards action', the majority of Tennyson's biographers, with the exception of Benjamin Jowett, sought to arrest their readers' inquisitive and acquisitive impulses rather than to promote them.[26] Their efforts to provide a 'complete' picture of the poet were intended to make readers feel like they had obtained ownership of Tennyson through purchasing the *Memoir*, thus stifling their curiosity about the 'real Tennyson'. Much like the authors of the 'Tennyson at Home' articles, discussed in Chapter 1, who align themselves and their middle-class readers closely with Tennyson's 'ideal', Hallam's text attracts its readers through donning biography's educational impetus by foregrounding 'Alfred Tennyson' in the title. In fact, however, it constitutes a series of consciously exclusive private memoirs that deny those readers the levelling insight they hope for. It is particularly Jowett's contribution, added as a supplementary reminiscence, which ensures the variety of perspectives on the poet.

In order to construct the *Memoir* as 'final and full enough' to render 'further and unauthentic biographers' unwelcome and unnecessary, and to deter readers from further violating the family's privacy, Hallam claims to have answered all the questions a reader may legitimately have.[27] Defining 'what people naturally wish to know' as information about 'birth, homes, school, college, friendships', Hallam pledges that he has provided 'enough to present the sort of insight into [Tennyson's] history and pursuits which one wants, if one desires to make a companion of a man'.[28] Though Hallam thus promises his readers intimate knowledge of the poet, he immediately withdraws his word by reminding them of the limits of the insight that he grants them: 'I have quoted from many manuscripts never intended for the public eye, many of which I have burnt according to [Tennyson's] instructions'.[29] By stressing the immense 'difficulty' of '[choosing] and [throwing] aside from the mass of material' at his disposal and by accentuating the absence of annihilated documents, Hallam guarantees the propriety of his biographical endeavour. Unlike the interviewers that Chapter 1 presents, he flaunts the insuperable gaps in his readers' knowledge and parades this element of personal mystery as central to celebrity.[30]

The biographical persona: Hallam and his reminiscers

Although the *Memoir*'s biographers were almost unanimously convinced of their supremely important role in preserving the memory of the living poet and in conveying it to the less fortunate masses, they had to establish their authority very carefully as self-elevation through knowledge could easily be read as betrayal. Because of the written and unwritten laws of biography and Tennyson's explicit wishes to be spared misrepresentation by posterity, his biographers tended to adopt an awed, idealising and stiffly apologetic attitude in their construction of the poet's image. While critics at the time understood the importance of privacy in biography, they also realised that Hallam and his reminiscers in fact veiled the real Tennyson in the 'baffles of protective conceal-ment', to use Michael Millgate's phrase, as I show in my final section.[31]

As I have indicated, Hallam's *Memoir* is motivated by a multiple agenda that celebrates his father's uniqueness but also his own and that of his reminiscers. From the beginning, Hallam establishes himself as a direct extension of Tennyson, acting 'according to my father's wish', advertising and then refusing to share the immensity of his knowledge:

> For my own part, I have generally refrained from attempting to pronounce judgment either on his poems or on his personal quali-ties and characteristics; although more than any living man I have had reason to appreciate his splendid truth and trustfulness, his varied creative imagination, and love of beauty, his rich humour, his strength of purpose, the largeness of his nature, and the wide range of his genius.[32]

With this list of admirable qualities, Hallam institutes his father as a hermetically sealed, impenetrable monument, consciously foregoing the biographer's task of merging with his subject and passing on his interpretation to the reader. Christopher Ricks's astute paraphrase demonstrates that Hallam's attitude towards his readers is exclusive rather than inclusive: 'you are not going to know my father; you would not *know* him even if you had lived with him as I did; and you must not suppose that the promise made (a preface is a promise) is that you will *know* him'.[33] Indeed, for Hallam and the reminiscers, who 'backed up' his project of exclusion, the composition of the *Memoir* was not solely an effort to fix and democratise Tennyson's legacy, but also an opportunity for self-elevation.[34]

Having established his authorial stance in the preface, Hallam tends to refrain from using the first-person singular and adopts a collective persona, constructing his narrative through combining a multiplicity of eulogising voices. The text is 'suffused with decorous domesticity', which, Altick has argued, is due to its rigorous omission of the 'idiosyncrasies that made [Tennyson] the engaging and often formidable character he was – his vanity, his atrabiliousness [and] his shaggy Lincolnshire abruptness'.[35] Hallam's choice of anecdote is limited to the poet blowing bubbles on feast days, receiving honorary awards and gracefully dealing with annoying requests and unbidden visitors. Hallam draws his supportive material from an extensive variety of sources, such as his mother's diary, flattering letters by Charles Kingsley, the Duke of Argyll and Thomas Woolner, Mrs Bradley's vivid notes and Frederick Locker-Lampson's possessive reminiscence. As he inserts considerably long reminiscences into his text, his function changes from that of the biographer to that of an editor tailoring a persuasive biographical pastiche. Thus using the reminiscers' elation as evidence of his father's charismatic presence, he endows his own narrative with the authority of further first-hand accounts. Some of these accounts appear to be taken directly from the reminiscers' diaries, others are edited and rewritten jottings from visits to Farringford and Aldworth, and still others are composed from memory.

Part of Hallam's strategy to contain and discourage his readers' invasive prying is his revelation that Emily Tennyson's diaristic documentations of the family's everyday life constitute the primary basis for his *Memoir*. By regularly referring to this major source, Hallam creates the impression that he entrusts his reader with private information directly drawn from the family archives. In the Preface, Hallam draws attention to the significance of Emily's diary through emphasising her report as one of the 'most interesting' manuscript sources 'to [himself]' and then minimises it to 'a simple record of daily something-nothings'.[36] Hallam feigns intimacy with the reader by simultaneously stressing and understating the importance of 'the journal of our home life', accentuating the relatable banality of the family's quotidian routine and thus justifying the readers' partial exclusion.[37] At the same time, through portraying Emily's journal as the family annals, Hallam promises the reader limited inclusion into the family circle. Hallam attributes varying levels of privacy to the diary, portraying it as a unified statement by the Tennysons, a strictly private record and as Tennyson's commissioned informal biography, thus requiring the readers to correspondingly adjust their position to the quoted documents. When, in his chapter on the years 1853–55, Hallam creates a distance between himself and his mother, he stresses the sanctity of the perused documents: '[throughout] the following chapters I have, with my mother's leave, made free use of her private journal'.[38] The biographer's uneasy respect passes over to the readers, whose allocated position changes from that of half-included, half-excluded participants in family life to that of semi-authorised spectators of a 'necessarily compressed' spousal life.[39] Generally, however, the *Memoir* retains a distinctly domestic backbone, presenting Tennyson's life as well as the creation of his biography as a family enterprise. This is evident in Hallam's documentation of the 1870s, in which he acknowledges his reliance on the 'regular journal, giving the bare facts of our daily life, which my father had wished my mother to keep for his private use' and which ends in 1874, meaning that he 'no longer [has] this on which to depend for the exact date as to days'.[40] While Hallam briefly considers Emily as a private person, he tends to portray her as the family's representative – the original biographer, acting according to her husband's wishes.

The relatively welcoming domestic atmosphere with which Hallam imbues his *Memoir* can be seen as a tactical ploy to veil his exclusive agenda. Although Hallam grants his readers superficial access to the family papers, he severely doubts their trustworthiness. His conviction that the readers' ignorance sullies Tennyson's art, shared by several of his reminiscers, inspires his repeated refusal to engage in his duties as an objective biographer. When documenting the years in which *Idylls of the King* was produced, for instance, Hallam positions himself above those who understand the poet's work as his true biography, thus undermining the attitude that he and his colleagues had been striving to inculcate in the public. Out of all of Tennyson's works, Hallam identifies 'The Holy Grail' as the poem that best reflects his father's 'highest self', basing his judgement on 'that far away rapt look on his face' during the writing process.[41] By detecting his father's 'genius' in his 'appearance, personal habits and private manners', Hallam can be seen to participate in the idea of 'original genius', which, as David Higgins has pointed out, developed in the late eighteenth and early nineteenth century.[42] Due to his unique proximity to the poet, Hallam 'saw him in the writing of his poem' and heard 'the *inspired* way in which he chanted to us the different parts of the poem as they were composed'.[43] In this passage, Hallam emphasises the importance of visual observation in the assessment of creativity, deliberately depriving his readers of the insight thus gained and refusing to explicate the relation between his subject and the poem: 'most explanations and analyses [of *Idylls*], although eagerly asked for by some readers, appeared to my father somewhat to dwarf and limit the life and scope of the great Arthurian tragedy; and therefore I will add no more'.[44] Having just insisted on the significance of *Idylls* for an informed understanding of his subject, Hallam has called attention to his own unparalleled insight into the poet's mind, yet, rather than elucidating his readers by sharing his knowledge, he explicitly chooses to let them grope around in a state of ignorance.

The reminiscers

While Hallam's position wavers between his adherence to the family persona and punctuated reclamations of control over his biography, he hands over his authorial agency to selected reminiscers with seeming generosity, giving them not only the chance to present their experience of the 'many-sided' Tennyson, which the book depends upon for authority, but also to bring about a rise in status.[45] By inserting selected reminiscences into his text, Hallam creates a chorus of voices to celebrate Tennyson's life, which is later reinforced by additional, separately appended recollections at the end of the second volume. Mrs Bradley, Frederick Locker-Lampson and W. E. H. Lecky's accounts are examples of reminiscers' self-construction as celebrities, because they, to varying extents, employ the genre's call for an authorial presence to perpetuate their superiority over their readers.[46] Their initiation stories are not primarily designed to improve the readers' knowledge of Tennyson, but rather to heighten the social profile of the writers, who, through adopting a tone of feigned reluctance, express their pride over having befriended the poet. Much like the celebrity circle in *Idylls* discussed in the last chapter, Tennyson's circle can be seen to re-produce a 'brand' of celebrity-behaviour, namely, self-reluctance mixed with self-promotion.

In order to complete his report of 1860–62 – Emily's journals for these years had been 'mislaid' – Hallam inserts the loose acquaintance Mrs Bradley's 'Reminiscences written by her during the visits she and the present Dean of Westminster paid to us at Farringford'.[47] The immediacy of this initiation account, which renders Bradley's excitement about becoming a celebrity through meeting a celebrity, fits into the chronological narrative that Hallam aims to create, supporting the impression of the *Memoir*'s completeness. In her private record, which seems prepared for publication, Bradley moves herself from the status of a vicarious onlooker to that of an habitué of the house by constructing two major bursts of revelation. She starts off by recounting her husband's memories, regaling in the former's experiences: 'Granville has had walks and talks with [Tennyson] and brings away memories full of pleasure and interest'.[48] Her exclamation: '[to] have come near the *man* and found in him all one could have desired in a great poet!' communicates a mixture of pride and envy of her husband that is rhetorically designed to heighten the surprise effect of her own presence in the account: 'I must write down my first sight of [Tennyson]'.[49] Her use of the indefinite pronoun 'one' indicates her identification with those unable to enjoy the 'rare treat [of being] in [Tennyson's] domestic circle, where he talks freely and brightly without shyness or a certain morbidity which oppresses him occasionally in society', but can also be seen as triumphant superiority.[50] Having penetrated the poet's private sphere, Bradley establishes herself not only as more privileged than those forced to merely 'desire' to interact with Tennyson, but also as superior to those who have been in his 'society.' Firstly admiring her husband for his conquest of Tennyson, she further claims admiration for herself.

While Mrs Bradley's reminiscences are imbued with her surprised delight of having risen in status through making Tennyson's acquaintance, Frederick Locker-Lampson portrays his connection to Tennyson as a permanent achievement: 'I am proud to have won the friendship of Alfred Tennyson'.[51] From their second meeting in 1865, Locker-Lampson and Tennyson 'were cordial [and] soon became intimate' and the reminiscer 'rejoices' that they 'have always remained so'.[52] Although the author insinuates that his friendly 'appropriation' of the poet is well-merited, he does not, like Dodgson and Allingham (Chapter 4), reveal the pains he took at deepening their acquaintance and developing their friendship, which implies that he seeks to portray the rise in status that came with the poet's friendship as an essentially deserved elevation. His report of Tennyson's dismissal of popularity as a 'bastard fame' from which he 'shrinks' seems designed to exclude the less respectable fans whom Tennyson did not care to befriend: '[he] maintains that the artist should spare no pains, that he should do his very best for the sake of his art, and for *that* only'.[53] Though Tennyson did not entirely refrain from creating art with the intention to sell, as Kathryn Ledbetter has shown, he had ethical reservations regarding the active cultivation of fame. However, beyond this reference to the poet's dislike of the limelight, Locker-Lampson's stress on 'that' implies that Tennyson created his art for its own sake, rather than for that of the public that generated its popularity, questioning the legitimacy of that public's engagement with Tennyson's work.

W. E. H. Lecky, whom Hallam consults in order to document the period from 1874 to 1881, for instance, ostentatiously insists on his duty to exclude the reader from his text whilst clearly embracing his exposure as a biographer as an opportunity to inscribe himself into Tennyson's legacy as his close friend. He constructs a correlation between the intimate knowledge of Tennyson and the absence of written memory, which is also characteristic of other elite members of the poet's circle: 'I knew too well his deep hatred of the common fashion of journalising in a great man's house, and writing down for future publication these careless utterances of free conversation, to be guilty of such an act.'[54] Paradoxically, Lecky embarrasses his readers, who evidently wish to learn about the poet's life through first-hand narration, by associating biography with lionising spies and trespassing journalists. He blames his readers for their interest in his necessarily inculpating text, which is, after all, intended for their consumption. Lecky disregards the fact that his text will form part of a published volume and thus writes the readers out of the report by addressing it solely to Hallam: 'you asked me to put down a few recollections of your father'.[55] Although he has just established biographical silence as a virtue, he apologises for '[relying] wholly on [his] memory' and expresses his concern that 'to you [Hallam], who knew him so much better than I did, these few notes can be of little use'.[56] By portraying his manifold, artfully presented memories of Tennyson as insignificant, Lecky elevates himself as infinitely superior to his readers, yet as incapable of competing with Hallam. It is clear that Hallam included this justificatory introduction in order to highlight the well of knowledge he shared with the reminiscers and to thus exclude the readers. Most importantly, however, this biographically unnecessary passage heightens the impression of the authors' objectivity and competence.

In order to accentuate his incontestable superiority as a legitimate fan and confidant of Tennyson's, Lecky establishes a contrast between himself and insensitive, invasive and damaging fans. Having gained 'much insight into [Tennyson's] ways of thinking and feeling' on 'long walks with him', Lecky metaphorically positions himself within the gates of

Farringford, witnessing the poet's 'alarm at a flock of sheep which he mistook for tourists' threatening from the outside.[57] In an accusatory tone, he follows up this anecdote by expounding the 'pathetic contrast between [Tennyson's] character and his position', claiming that

> Nature evidently intended him for the life of the quietest and most secluded of country gentlemen, for a life spent among books and flowers and a few intimate friends, and very remote from the noise and controversies of the great world. Few men valued more highly domestic privacy.[58]

Lecky portrays his connection to the poet as an organic and nurturing one, clashing with the vulgarity of the intruding world that threatens to sully the wholesome simplicity on which the poet thrives. He holds the 'troops of tourists, newspaper writers and interviewers' responsible for disrupting Tennyson's natural habitat, and making 'true privacy ... impossible', launching an indirect attack on the readers of the *Memoir*, who are likely to have been trying to substantiate their image of Tennyson through newspaper articles, literary tourism and by purchasing the biography that targets and excludes them.[59]

Interestingly, even very loquacious reminiscers tend to feign reluctance to engage in biographising and continuously stress the fact that, had Hallam not prompted them to contribute to his *Memoir*, they would have compliantly abstained not only from reducing Tennyson to a necessarily incomplete text, but also from offering him to the world. In order to keep the delicate balance between helpful biographer and treacherous friend, those reminiscers eager to present themselves as Tennyson's confidants are inclined to emphasise the uniqueness of their recollections while at the same time downplaying their desire to biographise. Hallam includes these justifications in order to convey his simultaneous belief in the need for and superfluity of biography and to heighten the readers' awareness of the ambiguous legitimacy of their interest in Tennyson.

Supplementary reminiscences

The *Memoir* comprises about 1000 pages and contains countless reminiscences inserted into the body of Hallam's text. In order to engineer a semblance of objectivity, Hallam inserts seventy pages of addenda of reminiscences by his father's friends at the end of volume II, which possess the status of a paratextual supplement to the official biography in that they complement his supposedly complete text and ward off external misrepresentations not only of the subject, but also of the biographer(s). Koenraad Claes has recently theorised the literary supplement as an obvious 'extension' of the parent periodical, which the editors of the latter employ to 'claim an additional authorial niche' and keep their readers from 'having to resort to rival publications'.[60] Claes examines the editorial decision to shift the obviously salient supplementary information 'to the paratextual threshold' and concludes that the supplement tends to function as a 'satellite' that '[broadens] the otherwise rather limited scope' of the parent periodical – it is 'conspicuously demarcated' so that it 'secures the integrity' of the latter, but still advertises and promulgates the editors' agenda.[61] Despite the differences in layout and reading practices that divide books and periodicals, Claes's work permits us to interrogate Hallam's choice to separate his own narrative and the invited reminiscences. The *Memoir* is clearly 'singled out as the text to be studied', to be affirmed by the reminiscences.[62] But although Hallam frames these accounts as separate studies by independent experts, he eliminates their supposed neutrality by grouping them together in his biography, thus preventing them from circulating freely and exerting their authority. In order to prevent the 'inescapable ephemerality' and uncontrollable dissemination to which accounts of his father would be exposed if issued separately, Hallam captures them within the confines of a bound volume.[63] He not only claims ownership over them, but, in a sense, even presents himself as their author, selling them as 'A Memoir by His Son', ignoring the reminiscers' contributions in the title and distinguishing their work from his own merely by a thin line in the table of contents.

Although all of the supplementary reminiscers support the idealising picture of Tennyson as a bright, entertaining and spirited man that Hallam constructs in the *Memoir*, their attitude towards the readers varies. The reminiscences of Benjamin Jowett and Francis Taylor Palgrave, the two most elaborately self-conscious reminiscers, are a striking example of clashing authorial agendas. While Benjamin Jowett validates the members of his audience, addressing them and correcting common misrepresentations of the poet, Palgrave represents his ideological counterpart, who, like many of the other reminiscers, tends to privatise biography and stages himself as a celebrity biographer, reinforcing the gap between legitimate and unwanted admirers.[64] Hallam does not comment on this clash, but uses it to piece together a text that is neither objective, nor overtly censored, thus evading the reproach of different ideological camps.

Within the largely uniform body of eulogies that Hallam assembles, Benjamin Jowett's reminiscence stands out from the others in its distinctly critical approach to exclusive biography. Jowett modestly disavows the connection between intimate knowledge of the poet and the ability to provide superior biographical insight that Hallam and most reminiscers assert so adamantly. While he knows that the world expects his biographical authority, he insists that 'anything which I or others may have to say of [Tennyson's] daily life must, necessarily, be fragmentary and disappointing'.[65] Unlike his colleagues, Jowett refrains from elevating his own importance as a close friend of the poet's, stating that '[a] great man's character rarely, if ever, appears in the jests which he makes with his friends at table, or in the good stories which he narrates'.[66] Thus deconstructing the other reminiscers' claim to fame, he contends that Tennyson's 'truest self must be estimated in his greatest efforts' and that his 'best and deepest nature' will be found in the works of his genius, such as *In Memoriam* – a move frequently encountered in press contributions on Tennyson (Chapter 1).[67] In the context of the self-aggrandising narratives that precede Jowett's account, his unassuming inclusiveness seems almost provocative: 'those who have read Tennyson attentively and consecutively know much more about him than can ever be learnt from passing observation'.[68] While Jowett does allude to tourists and fans lurking to get a momentary view of the poet, he primarily seems to question the usefulness of biographical writing, which is necessarily limited to representations of moments that are unrepresentative because they are unrepresentable. Rather than merely flaunting his privileged position through his narrative, Jowett uses his advanced insight to illuminate the readers, saving them from the falsifications engineered by the media. He patiently explicates that the 'peculiarities about [Tennyson], which have furnished endless material for gossip, and which have never been properly explained', were 'easier to understand when looked at a little more closely'.[69] From the standpoint of an intimate friend, Jowett helpfully clarifies, Tennyson's 'unmanly' '[sensitivity] to the opinions of the public' was 'not really a desire of praise, or fear of blame', but stemmed from his grief 'at the injustice and meanness of mankind'.[70] Jowett respectfully calls Tennyson's inquisitive fans 'persons' and abstains from the implied derision which represents an integral part of his fellow reminiscers' texts.

Although Jowett values the efforts that Tennyson's friends and readers have made in order to understand the relationship between the poet's private self and his public persona, and to befriend him socially and parasocially, he questions the possibility of any bilateral relationship between Tennyson and his private and public audiences.[71] While the reminiscers under examination document their attempts to inscribe themselves into Tennyson's domestic environment in the hope of being associated with the context that provided the poet's creative inspiration, Jowett confutes his co-biographers, such as Lecky, who construct themselves as Tennyson's 'natural' society: 'I never remember him receiving the least pleasure from the commendations of his friends'.[72] He plays down the effect of the most sincere flattery in counteracting the early 'pain from the attacks of [Tennyson's] enemies' and portrays Tennyson as detached from the societal world: '[the] truth seemed to be that, as his fame became established in the world, he hardly thought much of what was said of him. The feeling of pleasure, which was not wanting in him, was due to an appreciation of himself in his own breast'.[73] By representing Tennyson as a unilateral, self-contained generator of pleasure, Jowett does not simply dismiss the influence of the media on the poet's inner life, but, significantly, also denies that his co-biographers and himself hold any sway over Tennyson's self.

In light of Carlyle's definition of biography, Jowett is the only contributor who seeks to reveal, rather than to conceal, what one might call Tennyson's everyday self. With provocative modesty, he identifies a major flaw in general biographical practices – the frequent omission of marital life: '[if] it were possible, with propriety, I should like to say something about the wife who survives him, though I am aware that such a subject is beyond the proper limits of biography'.[74] Contemptuously mimicking the voice of convention, Jowett mocks the enterprise of contributing to a biography that is strictly committed to constructing half-truths about the subject. Jowett condemns the constrictions of 'propriety' that could, and, with the exception of the tribute chapter 'My Mother's Death', did, cause the mute absence of Tennyson's 'best critic'.[75] Though we cannot be sure that Jowett had read his co-biographers' contributions, his tone, structure and inherent self-elevation recall their tactics of self-construction as celebrities:

> The greatest influence of his life would have to be passed over in silence if I were to omit her name. These few lines I have ventured to insert without the permission of you, Hallam, lest by some inadvertence matters so important should pass out of remembrance.[76]

Jowett highlights the importance of his own intervention in order to covertly attack Hallam for letting propriety prevent him from doing justice to both his parents by practically writing their marriage out of his father's life. Through directly addressing Hallam and uncovering the *Memoir*'s strict constructedness, Jowett positions himself outside the volume's staged flattery and, implicitly, minimises the importance of biography. Jowett's subtly offensive denigration of Emily to a mere trifle that could inadvertently be forgotten in the compilation of Tennyson's life makes apparent Hallam's conditioning interference in the reminiscences that his father's friends produced. But, even more significantly, through destabilising the book's authority as a definitive biographical project by revealing its gaping omissions and embellishments – like its obsessive propriety – designed to mask them, Jowett's account affirms Hallam's objectivity as an editor.

Although Palgrave professes to be guided by an enlightening agenda that is similar to Jowett's in its desire to rectify 'the tales, which have painted Tennyson as a recluse', he pompously draws attention to the depth of his own insight and the magnitude of his influence as a friend and critic, clearly using the *Memoir* as a means of self-marketing.[77] Knowing as we do that in 1868 Palgrave had greatly displeased Tennyson in his inability 'to restrain his self-importance', which led him to show several manuscript poems to a third party, his assurances of absolute confidence seem staged to impress not only the readers of the *Memoir*, but also friends and colleagues who may have recalled this scandalous betrayal.[78] Palgrave's climactic conclusion to his report, which establishes 'the dominant note of Alfred Tennyson, – Loveableness', appears all the more theatrical when read in light of Robert Bernard Martin's assessment that 'Palgrave and Allingham willingly put up with rudeness and condescension for the pleasure of claiming his acquaintance'.[79] It is clear that Palgrave uses his reminiscence to durably efface his disloyalty and to construct a monument for himself as a celebrity biographer and friend.

Palgrave, like Lecky, paradoxically seeks to institute himself as an 'unrecording friend' by creating a biographical record. He laboriously constructs his biographical abstinence as an act of loyalty, inspired by Tennyson's gift of the poem 'To – , After Reading a Life and Letters' to him, which had just been printed in a newspaper. He cunningly uses this 1849 anecdote to stress that he received his directions for adequate fandom directly from the source and reacted accordingly, holding himself 'absolutely barred by the fealty of friendship, from the attempt to make any memorial of his words'.[80] Moreover, this story gives him the chance to emphasise his personal possession of the original poem and to distinguish himself from the masses of anonymous readers who read an impersonal, commodified version of the poem. He further delineates his position as a true friend of Tennyson's by ascertaining that he constantly prioritised the poet's wishes at the expense of fulfilling his own yearning to chronicle: '[deeply] and often indeed did I long for such record, thinking with pain, after hours often carried past midnight in long dialogue, how much that one would not willingly let die, that golden streams had flowed by to waste and Lethe'.[81] For Palgrave, the absence of a (historical) record serves as a rhetorical ploy in two ways: firstly, it establishes him as one of Tennyson's closest and most loyal friends, and secondly, it stimulates the readers' limitless respect for Palgrave's unnarrated conversations with the poet.

Although Palgrave claims to deplore this 'waste' of unrecorded memories for the sake of his readers, he generally tends to inscribe his oblivion as a marker of superiority. His recollections of his first meeting with Tennyson in 1847 trace his passage from being an anonymous fan to becoming one of the initiated. While before the meeting, he portrays himself as adoring *The Princess*, 'which had been given to [him], as to thousands more', this distant adulation turns into the 'pride of looking upon this great enchanter' afterward.[82] Although this event was obviously instrumental for Palgrave's advance into Tennyson's sphere, he purposefully minimises its effect in order to accentuate the quality and frequency of subsequent meetings:

> But I was here in the circle of his own friends, Thackeray amongst others; and except recognition of the features and abundant hair (familiar through the little print from S. Laurence's fine monochromatic portrait), and of a few words upon our common friendship with the Hallam family, I have preserved no memory of Tennyson during this evening.[83]

Compared to other initiation reports, such as Edmund Gosse's or Mrs Bradley's, Palgrave's is strikingly sparse in detail and culminates in a disappointing admission of his lack of memory. Inscribed oblivion here functions as an anticlimactic climax that substantiates Palgrave's status of an habitué whose relationship with the poet consisted of 'long talks, and gay laughter, and things comic and serious discussed' from their second meeting (in Twickenham) onwards.[84]

Palgrave's definition of biography differs fundamentally from Jowett's because he believes that the biographer's close proximity determines his or her ability to capture 'the man'. His interpretation of the genre conveniently allows him to accentuate the importance of his contribution to the *Memoir*, which shows the audience that 'like all eminently true men, Tennyson was a far simpler problem than some have fancied'.[85] Setting up a contrast between those who 'read' the 'tales ... ascribing to Tennyson now vanity, now rudeness' and himself, who knows the poet's shyness, Palgrave helpfully exposes the distorting representational practices employed by celebrity culture, but then offers his own, heavily idealised version of Tennyson as the only alternative.[86] Palgrave blames society's adulation of the poet for 'the stress of nervous impulse' that the 'terror of leonisation' inflicted on the latter, causing his 'cold unsympathetic exterior' and building up to his triumphant conclusion that he himself had no reason to find Tennyson anything but 'loveable'.[87]

Palgrave thus cunningly embeds a discussion of biography into his reminiscence in order to parade his authority as a celebrity biographer – not only to prove his enviable friendship with the poet, but also to demonstrate his influence on literary criticism. Thanks to his first-hand experience of the poet, Palgrave considers himself qualified and entitled to reassess common public misconceptions: 'Tennyson asked me to be his companion [on several summer journeys]: – equally a privilege and a pleasure. Travelling together is said to bring out the whole man, in his natural gifts, his manners, his good sense and temper, or otherwise'.[88] Palgrave highlights Tennyson's invitation to leave the familiar grounds of Farringford together as an indicator of his inestimably high status, thus lending authority to his evaluation of the poet's character.

For Palgrave, the equation of the poet with his work undercuts his own authority as a friend, biographer and critic, as his poetry was widely disseminated commercially and easily accessible to millions of readers. Emphasising that the poet's living presence heightens the value of his art, Palgrave supports Hallam's cliquish approach to literary and biographical criticism when he describes Tennyson's poems as having somewhat deflated after the poet died: 'something of their music, some part of their very essence, has passed with the Maker'.[89] In his eagerness to distinguish between legitimate admirers and the reading masses Hallam had adamantly insisted on the fact that Tennyson's poetry could only develop its true meaning if read out loud by the poet himself, quoting Dr Mann's *Maud Vindicated* to highlight and permanently establish the inequality between those who heard the poet read his work and those who merely stared at his words in print: 'with organ-tones of great power and range, [Tennyson's voice] thoroughly brought out the drama of [*Maud*]. You were at once put in sympathy with the hero'.[90] Hallam further insists that the printed *Maud* was 'wholly misapprehended' by 'such appreciative critics as Mr Gladstone and Dr Van Dyke', until they had 'heard my father read it'.[91] The majority of readers found their reading devalued as insuperably superficial and were permanently excluded from the poet's intellectual sphere. While Jowett's account tends to adopt a plural authorial voice, supplanting the first-person singular with 'most of Tennyson's friends' or 'we', Palgrave, mimicking Hallam, is not only eager to set himself apart from the readers but also from the other biographers by constructing himself as an 'unrecording' celebrity friend of unparalleled insight.[92] We see that the *Memoir* displays interactions between contributors who employ their reminiscences as a means of auto/biographical appropriation, and those who wish to empower the readers.

Reviewers as biographers

The newspaper reviewers that commented on the *Memoir*'s effectiveness on the day of its appearance – 6 October 1897 – tend to either advocate, like Jowett, or discourage, like Palgrave, the biographer's sustained transparency. Portraying their task of mediating between the biographer/subject and their audience as an essential, additional feature of biography, reviewers invented themselves as a separate, integral part of the biographical triad deserving of celebrity status. Although the individual reviewers are not identifiable in the newspaper articles, their selective re-phrasings of or quotations from the *Memoir* suggest an imagined participation in the celebrity circle as well as an active contribution to Tennyson's textual monumentalisation, which reached a much wider audience than the biography itself.

Hallam Tennyson's decision to fragment his father's life, rather than to render it in a seamless narrative, has earned him an abundance of criticism. His reluctance to educate the reader may account for the fact that 'it is often said or implied that Hallam Tennyson was a dullard and couldn't possibly have shaped a book well or written it well', to refer to Christopher Ricks's assessment of the *Memoir*'s critical legacy.[93] However, like Ricks, I contest that Hallam is an 'unimaginative' writer, as he, quite successfully, managed to write a biography that showed a distinct awareness of the demands posed by celebrity culture. Considering the Victorian reviewers' response to Hallam's work, it seems that Richard Altick exaggerates when he describes the *Memoir*'s reception as 'cool'.[94] Although most reviewers assess Hallam's work as 'more a sort of *log-book*', 'not a formal biography', 'materials for a life rather than the life itself', or even 'nothing in the nature of biography', they almost unanimously praise its 'completeness'.[95] For the *Memoir*'s reviewers, however, 'completeness' seems to designate the wealth of material provided, rather than the depiction of the 'whole' Tennyson. They tend to applaud the abundance of documents and facts included because they seem to associate the disclosure of the latter as the biographer's fundamental duty to the readers. After judging whether Hallam has accomplished this primary task, they evaluate his work based on their own position in contemporary debates on the genre, either demanding more insight for their readers, or acclaiming their exclusion for the benefit of the subject's privacy.

Despite the touch of inherent contradictoriness that characterises most reviews, they are generally appreciative of Hallam's achievement and, through praising and mimicking the biographer's craft, seek to portray themselves as essential authorities on the subject to the readers. *The Standard*, in two reviews on the same day, applauds Hallam's dispensation of knowledge 'of Tennyson's private life' as well calculated and therefore 'gratifying'.[96] Defining successful biography as that which 'does not compel us to draw unwelcome contrasts between the Poet and the Man', like Froude's *Carlyle* had done, the first reviewer believes that, thanks to the *Memoir*, 'the world has now before it all that can be known – or, at least, all that it has any title to know'.[97] According to *The Standard's* reviewer, the reader and the subject are equally in need of protection from biographies 'that show us the hero in ignominious undress'.[98] While the reviewer acknowledges Tennyson's dislike of the 'unwelcome attentions' of the 'general public', he or she does not blame the fans for dragging 'names we are eager to reverence ... in the mire of squalid trivialities', but instead holds biographers responsible for revealing their subjects' moral imperfections.[99] Based on the *Memoir's* ability to 'deepen and strengthen the general conception of the noble purpose and moral elevation of Tennyson's life', the second review attributes an enormous educational value to Hallam's work because of its reticence: 'there is not a line or a word of malice, pettiness, or ill-natured gossip'.[100] Though Hallam's agenda is not primarily instructive, the reviewer 'thanks' him for '[enhancing] respect and affection for the poet and the man', thus 'engineering reception' and constructing him- or herself as the authoritative mediator between biographer/subject and the readers.[101]

The *Pall Mall Gazette* condemns the wilful deception of the readers inherent in Hallam's eulogistic approach and reveals its damaging consequences for the thus belittled subject. Acceding that 'the present Lord Tennyson has had a peculiarly difficult task' and was successful in his 'duty' of showing the reader that 'Tennyson's personality was one of the most majestic of the century', the review calls for a re-thinking of biographical tactics when it asserts that '[perhaps] the selection of conversations which Lord Tennyson gives have a slight tendency to ide-alisation'.[102] Using his review to correct the image that Hallam constructs of his father and to educate the reader, the reviewer respectfully explains his objection, which is based on the reports of 'many of [Tennyson's] auditors': '[the] great poet had a strong physical nature [and] a certain boisterous and forceful virility of talk which is certainly not represented here'.[103] By contrasting the *Memoir*'s deliberate maiming of the poet's true self with more reliable sources, the reviewer claims authority for his superior complementary knowledge. He advocates that since Tennyson was a much less docile type of hero than the *Memoir* makes out, he deserves a Boswellian biography to represent his true intellectual and rhetorical firepower: '[we] should be sorry if we were obliged to think that Lord Tennyson's daily talk only resembled the kind of talk he would have put into the lips of his blameless King Arthur'.[104] Promoting biographical candour as the proper form of hero worship, the reviewer presents Tennyson as the ultimate victim of protective concealment and the common equation of work and biography, as both approaches tend to accentuate his feebleness rather than his strength.

In order to highlight the importance of their mediatory task, the *Memoir*'s reviewers tend to impersonate the part of the biographer, mimicking Hallam's difficulties in selecting and assembling the materials for his work. They accentuate their own meta-biographical activity to establish themselves as involved in writing Tennyson's life. *The Standard*, for instance, having quoted from Hallam's text abundantly, deplores that it 'can but suggest rather than describe the content of the Memoir' and limits its task to '[sending] the reader to the book itself'.[105] Evidently, the reviewer imagines himself as a supplementary biographer, connect-ing the reader to both the original biographer and the subject by making the *Memoir* accessible to a wider audience. T. P. O'Connor, in *The Graphic*, seems to completely identify with the biographer:

> How I am, in the brief space at my command, to give an idea of the vast and opulent mine of material for forming an idea of the poet and of his temperament and life which is to be found within the covers of these two copious volumes? It is vain to try and give a connected narrative; the reader must be satisfied with a dip here and there – a specimen taken almost at random out of this lode and then out of that.[106]

O'Connor presents himself as exasperated at the difficulty of his self-imposed task of presenting the biographer's work to his readers by re-portraying the poet. Through aggressively giving voice to the pressure exerted by each of the members of the biographical triad, reviewers generally draw attention to the importance of their role in framing the poet's celebrity, thus inserting themselves into Tennyson's legacy.

Conclusion

While the *Memoir* may itself not be altogether representative of Victorian biographical practices, the volume and variety of texts it engendered certainly reflect the process of turning a celebrity into a hero as well as the consequent celebrification of his or her entourage. The reviews and reminiscences under examination demonstrate that Hallam Tennyson's *Memoir* is less to be seen as a biography that portrays Tennyson as a 'many-sided man', than as a multi-author project that reveals the complications of defining the purposes of biography and of reconciling the individual concerns of the biographical triad.[107] The *Memoir*'s private ideology prescribes an adulatory depiction of the poet, but the juxtaposition of multiple voices inherent in its narrative fabric also allows the readers to discern the reminiscers' individual approaches to the biographical enterprise.

The *Memoir* not only set the tone for the posthumous remembrance of Tennyson, but it also began the practice of privileging Tennyson's celebrity over that of his circle which would continue well into the twentieth and twenty-first centuries, at times obscuring Cameron's and Watts's contribution to the circle. Despite the very frequent interactions between the Cameron and Tennyson families and Julia Margaret's prominence in other reminiscences (such as Allingham's or Lear's), the *Memoir* barely touches on this aspect of life at Farringford. Wilfrid Ward, when recalling Hallam's editorial agenda for *Tennyson and his Friends*, indicates that the strict parameters of remembrance he conceived shaped not only the legacy of the poet, but also the idea of the extraordinary, self-contained and almost superhuman celebrity: 'I have contributed some recollections of my own to the volume, but my contribution was limited by the scope marked out for it in the editor's invitation. The present article [published in the *Dublin Review*] is an attempt to supplement what was therein set down'.[108] Ward then proceeds to talk about the *circle* rather than just Tennyson, insisting on and re-inscribing the networks of friendship, inspiration and opportunity that underlie the reality of celebrity. What Ward's article ultimately makes clear is that, in his desire to control and circumscribe the accounts of his father in circulation, Hallam established guidelines

for commemorative writing that made his father into a disembod-
ied icon. Ironically, Hallam's very plan to prevent a proliferation of
accounts had the opposite effect and generated complementary and
explanatory paratexts.

In contrast with these public recollections, commissioned, collected
and publicised by Hallam, the private diaristic testimonies of the two
recording friends William Allingham and Charles Dodgson (Lewis
Carroll) accentuate the importance of writing in the construction of a
personal relationship with a well-known celebrity such as Tennyson.
Both used their diaries as a means of positioning themselves within the
poet's circle, audience and media following. The reminiscers exploit
their biographical possibilities and actively realise their very personal
desire for autobiographical inscription, which shows that celebrity
culture is shaped by individuals.

Notes

1. *The Poetical Works of Alfred Tennyson, Poet Laureate* (Boston: Ticknor and
   Fields, 1856), pp. 163–64 (ll. 18–19, 17, 15).
2. Ibid., ll. 13, 36.
3. Epitaph to the poem; see Kathryn Ledbetter, *Tennyson and Victorian
   Periodicals: Commodities in Context* (Aldershot: Ashgate, 2007), p. 51.
4. *The Poetical Works of Alfred Tennyson*, p. 164 (l. 32).
5. Ledbetter, p. 45.
6. This chapter strictly focuses on definitions of biography created in and by
   Hallam's *Memoir*, as well as the immediate press response, and can therefore not consider book-length biographies such as Andrew Lang's *Alfred
   Tennyson* (1901) and Alfred Lyall's *Tennyson* (1902), or magazine articles
   by Tennyson's friends, such as James Knowles's 'Aspects of Tennyson' or
   Francis Thompson's 'The Life of Tennyson', which, no doubt, played a
   crucial role in constructing the poet's posthumous image, but appeared
   either before or considerably after the *Memoir* (see Alfred Lyall, *Tennyson*
   (London: Macmillan, 1902); Andrew Lang, *Alfred Tennyson* (Edinburgh and
   London: Blackwood & Sons, 1901); James T. Knowles, 'Aspects of Tennyson',
   Nineteenth Century, 33 (1893), 164–88).
7. A. O. J. Cockshut, *Truth to Life: the Art of Biography in the Nineteenth Century*
   (London: Collins, 1974), p. 13.
8. Christopher Ricks, *Essays in Appreciation* (Oxford: Clarendon, 1996), p. 175.
9. Trev Lynn Broughton, *Men of Letters, Writing Lives: Masculinity and Literary
   Auto/Biography in the Late-Victorian Period* (London: Routledge, 1999), p. 87.
10. 'Biography', *Fraser's Magazine*, 5 (1832), 253–60 (p. 253), in *ProQuest British
    Periodicals* <http://www.proquest.co.uk> [accessed 12 April 2013].
11. Ibid.
12. 'Biography', *Blackwood's Edinburgh Magazine*, 69 (1851), 40–53 (p. 42), in
    ProQuest British Periodicals <http://www.proquest.co.uk> [accessed 12 April
    2013].

13. Richard D. Altick, *Lives and Letters: a History of Literary Biography in England and America* (New York: Alfred A. Knopf, 1965), p. 89.
14. Robert Goodbrand, 'A Suggestion for a New Kind of Biography', *Contemporary Review*, 14 (1870), 20–28 (p. 23), in *ProQuest British Periodicals* <http://www.proquest.co.uk> [accessed 12 April 2013].
15. Ibid., p. 24.
16. George Bentley, 'Sincerity in Biography', *Temple Bar*, 62 (1881), 329–36 (p. 330), in *ProQuest British Periodicals* <http://www.proquest.co.uk> [accessed 12 April 2013].
17. Ibid., pp. 330, 329.
18. Margaret Oliphant, 'The Ethics of Biography', *Contemporary Review*, 44 (1883), 76–93 (p. 78), in *ProQuest British Periodicals* <http://www.proquest.co.uk> [accessed 12 April 2013].
19. Ibid., p. 80.
20. T. E. Kebbel, 'Biography', *Cornhill Magazine*, 47 (1883), 601–07 (p. 601), in *ProQuest British Periodicals* <http://www.proquest.co.uk> [accessed 12 April 2013].
21. William Ward, 'Candour in Biography', *The New Review*, 14 (1896), 445–52 (p. 52), in *ProQuest British Periodicals* <http://www.proquest.co.uk> [accessed 12 April 2013].
22. Edmund Purcell, 'On the Ethics of Suppression in Biography', *Nineteenth Century*, 40 (1896), 533–42 (p. 534), in *ProQuest British Periodicals* <http://www.proquest.co.uk> [accessed 12 April 2013].
23. Joseph W. Reed, *English Biography in the Early Nineteenth Century: 1801–1838* (New Haven and London: Yale University Press, 1966), p. 63.
24. Juliette Atkinson, *Victorian Biography Reconsidered: a Study of Nineteenth-Century 'Hidden' Lives* (Oxford: Oxford University Press, 2010), p. 47.
25. David Amigoni, *Victorian Biography: Intellectuals and the Ordering of Discourse* (New York and London: Harvester Wheatsheaf, 1993), p. 24.
26. Atkinson, p. 66.
27. *Alfred Lord Tennyson: a Memoir by His Son*, ed. by Hallam Tennyson, 2 vols (London: Macmillan & Co., 1897), I, p. xv.
28. Ibid.
29. Ibid, p. xvi.
30. Ibid.
31. Michael Millgate, *Testamentary Acts: Browning, Tennyson, James, Hardy* (Oxford: Clarendon Press, 1992), p. 54.
32. *Memoir*, I, p. xvi.
33. Ricks, *Essays in Appreciation*, p. 192.
34. Millgate, p. 54.
35. Altick, p. 239.
36. *Memoir*, I, p. xvi.
37. Ibid.
38. Ibid., p. 368.
39. Ibid.
40. *Memoir*, II, 208.
41. Ibid., p. 92.
42. David Higgins, *Romantic Genius and the Literary Magazine: Biography, Celebrity and Politics* (London and New York: Routledge, 2005).

43. *Memoir*, II, 92.
44. Ibid., p. 134.
45. *Memoir*, I, p. xvi
46. Marian Bradley (née Philpot) (1831–1910) was the wife of George Granville Bradley (1821–1903), who first met Tennyson in the early 1840s. From a master at Rugby in 1845–58, he had an impressive career and became the Dean of Westminster in 1881. Sharon Marcus has read Marian's diaries as primarily interested in documenting her 'outer life', which may indicate that she considered them as images of, and potential participants in, the public sphere. See Marcus, *Between Women: Friendship, Desire, and Marriage in Victorian England* (Princeton: Princeton University Press, 2007), p. 35. Frederick Locker-Lampson (1821–95) was a book-collector and poet, who could be seen as a 'lioniser,' as he 'was friends with many of the most important writers of his time – Tennyson, Thackeray, George Eliot, Dickens, Trollope and Bulwer-Lytton. It was said there was nobody significant in London whom he had not at least met'. See *The Victorians: An Anthology of Poetry and Poetics*, ed. by Valentine Cunningham (Oxford: Wiley-Blackwell, 2000), p. 516. William Edward Hartpole Lecky (1838–1903) was a historian and poet.
47. *Memoir*, I, 467.
48. Ibid.
49. Ibid.
50. Ibid., p. 469.
51. *Memoir*, II, 66.
52. Ibid.
53. Ibid., p. 79.
54. Ibid., p. 200.
55. Ibid.
56. Ibid.
57. Ibid., pp. 200–01.
58. Ibid., p. 201.
59. Ibid.
60. Koenraad Claes, 'Supplements and Paratext: the Rhetoric of Space', *Victorian Periodicals Review*, 43 (2010), 196–210 (pp. 206, 205).
61. Ibid., p. 205.
62. Ibid., p. 202.
63. Ibid., p. 208.
64. Benjamin Jowett (1817–93) was a renowned educator and the master of Balliol College, Oxford.
65. *Memoir*, II, 460.
66. Ibid.
67. Ibid.
68. Ibid.
69. Ibid., p. 465.
70. Ibid., p. 466.
71. Ibid., p. 465.
72. Ibid., p. 466.
73. 'He never allowed himself to be puffed in the newspapers if he could possibly prevent it. B. J.' Footnote in *Memoir*, II, 465.
74. Ibid., p. 466.

75. Ibid., p. 465.
76. Ibid., p. 467.
77. Ibid., p. 487.
78. Robert Bernard Martin, *Tennyson: the Unquiet Heart* (Oxford: Clarendon Press, 1983), p. 469.
79. *Memoir*, II, 509.
80. Ibid., p. 484.
81. Ibid.
82. Ibid., 485.
83. Ibid.
84. Ibid., p. 487.
85. Ibid.
86. Ibid., p. 494.
87. Ibid.
88. Ibid.
89. *Memoir*, II, 494.
90. Cited in *Memoir*, II, 396.
91. Ibid., p. 398.
92. Ibid., p. 461.
93. Ricks, p. 189
94. Altick, p. 240.
95. 'Tennyson', *Pall Mall Gazette*, 6 October 1897, p. 1; 'Alfred Lord Tennyson', *Daily News*, 6 October 1897, p. 6; 'The Life of Tennyson', *Glasgow Herald*, 6 October 1897, p. 4; 'Tennyson', *Morning Post*, 6 October 1897, p. 6, all in *Gale 19th Century British Library Newspapers* <http://gale.cengage.co.uk> [accessed 12 April 2013].
96. *The Standard*, 6 October 1897, p. 4, in *Gale 19th Century British Library Newspapers* <http://gale.cengage.co.uk> [accessed 12 April 2013].
97. Ibid.
98. Ibid.
99. Ibid.
100. 'The Tennyson Biography', *The Standard*, 6 October 1897, p. 2, in *Gale 19th Century U.S. Newspapers* <http://gale.cengage.co.uk> [accessed 12 April 2013]
101. Andrew Franta, *Romanticism and the Rise of the Mass Public* (Cambridge: Cambridge University Press, 2007), p. 93.
102. 'Tennyson', *Pall Mall Gazette*, p. 1.
103. Ibid.
104. Ibid.
105. 'The Tennyson Biography', p. 2.
106. T. P. O'Connor, 'Books Worth Reading', *The Graphic*, 7 October 1897, p. 484, in *Gale 19th Century British Library Newspapers* <http://gale.cengage.co.uk> [accessed 12 April 2013].
107. *Memoir*, I, p. xi.
108. Wilfrid Ward, 'Tennyson at Freshwater', *Dublin Review*, 150 (1912), 68–85 (p. 68).

6
'Much Honour and Much Fame Were Lost': *Idylls of the King* and Camelot's Celebrity Circle

Páraic Finnerty

In 'Lancelot and Elaine', the seventh of the twelve idylls that comprise Tennyson's *Idylls of the King* (1859–85), while on their way to a field near Camelot where the tournament of the diamond is about to take place, Sir Lavaine of Astolat is told by his anonymous travelling companion: 'you ride with Lancelot of the Lake'.[1] On hearing this, 'Abash'd Lavaine, whose instant reverence, / Dearer to true hearts than their own praise, / But left him leave to stammer, "Is it indeed?"' (416–18). After catching his breath, the still muttering and shocked young man contrasts this unexpected brush with 'the great Lancelot' with his expectation of seeing at the tourney, 'our liege lord / The dread Pendragon, Britain's King of kings, / Of whom the people talk mysteriously' (419, 421–23). On his arrival at the lists, Lavaine 'let his eyes / Run thro' the peopled gallery' until he found the 'clear-faced King, who sat / Robed in red samite, easily to be known' (427–28, 430–31). As Lavaine 'gaped upon [King Arthur] / As on a thing miraculous', Lancelot tells him:

> Me you call great: mine is the firmer seat,
> The truer lance: but there is many a youth
> Now crescent, who will come to all I am
> And overcome it; and in me there dwells
> No greatness, save it be some far-off touch
> Of greatness to know well I am not great:
> There is the man.
>
> (444–50)

Idylls of the King abounds with similar scenes presenting close encounters between well-known Camelot personalities and their awe-struck admirers; involving the distant scrutiny of mysterious but visibly

191

recognisable figures; describing the illustrious Camelot, its public spectacles and citizens on display; recounting the reproduction and replication of a brand of knightliness; and demarking a hierarchy of eminence
in which an individual's fame is created or increased according to his
or her proximity to a more famous person, to 'some far-off touch of
greatness'. In so doing, this poem evokes aspects of Victorian celebrity
culture that have already been discussed in previous chapters.

Tennyson's poem is one of the most famous and influential manifestations of what has been termed Victorian medievalism, which
describes not merely the popularity of medieval culture at this time, but
a powerful and pervasive discourse that affected practical, conceptual
and cultural life in the period.[2] Emerging out of the late eighteenth-
century revival of interest in and fascination with medieval history
and culture, Victorian medievalism was a means of unifying the British
nation in the celebration and valorisation of courtly love and chivalry;
it offered a spiritual, class-inflected and value-laden belief system to a
materialistic and sceptical age in which traditional social and moral
values were in a state of flux.[3] Updating Thomas Malory's *Le Morte
d'Arthur* (1485), Tennyson used King Arthur's Britain to evoke features
of Queen Victoria's and highlighted this in his 1862 'Dedication' of
the poem to Prince Albert and, again, in his 1872 postscript 'To the
Queen'. Although some of his contemporaries condemned the way,
as Algernon Charles Swinburne put it, Tennyson 'lowered the note
and deformed the outline of the Arthurian Story', others approvingly
announced that '"The Round Table" is the world of to-day' and praised
the way Tennyson '[fixed] on the legend of Arthur, as that which most
readily lent itself to imposing accessories and details charged with
enough of the ideal element to relieve the baldness of modern ideas'.[4]
Unsurprisingly, much recent scholarship has focused on the many ways
in which Tennyson's Arthurian epic explores the effects on Victorian
society of 'modern' concerns such as imperial expansion, democracy,
urbanisation, scientific and technological advances, religious scepticism, industrial power and the disruption of traditional gender roles.[5]
What has not yet been discussed is that this poem, written and revised
over the course of his long career and published serially at the height
of his fame, represents Tennyson's most sustained response to celebrity
culture, reflecting his simultaneous aversion to and entanglement in its
complex mechanisms and processes. This chapter argues that his adap-
tation of the stories of Arthur and his Round Table reveals much about
his experience of being, along with Charles Dickens, Thomas Carlyle
and Florence Nightingale, 'one of the first generation [after Byron] to

experience the pressures of being mediated personalities' and the disintegration of the traditional separation of public and private life.[6]

Tennyson inherited a conception of King Arthur as a legendary figure who represented masculine honour and public service, and whose alleged achievements eclipsed his personal history to the point that it remained mysterious and unrecoverable.[7] At its very essence, then, King Arthur's renown is antithetical to the post-eighteenth-century democratisation and feminisation of fame that subordinated merit, genius and achievement to the fascination with individual personality and biography, and concomitantly popularised the ephemeral, commercial and sensational and its transient human embodiments.[8] What made *Idylls* commercially successful and popular, and eventually opened it up to criticism, particularly in the final decades of the century, was Tennyson's decision to '[pull] legend down to the level of reality' and humanise Arthur, making him 'Ideal manhood closed in real man' ('To the Queen', 38).[9] As Linda Hughes notes, '*Idylls of the King* meant from the start a human-centered, accessible, vivid set of stories and attractive characters' that was seen, despite 'metaphysical themes and heavily symbolic patterns', 'within a framework of identifiable and lively human interest'.[10] The reception history of the poem and Tennyson's comments on *Idylls*, however, suggest a continual tension between allegorical readings in which the poem's characters are treated as symbolic or archetypal, and literal readings in which they are regarded as human beings, each with 'subtle differences of voice, appearance, manner'.[11] Tennyson's characters, in so far as they are at once symbolic and real, ideal and human, are analogous to nineteenth-century celebrities, who were, at the time, paragons of masculinity and femininity, as well as being highly individualistic figures.[12] Moreover, as this chapter will show, the overriding focus of *Idylls* is on the communal dissemination of the much-discussed, publicly observed and physically recognisable figures of Camelot; the intellectual and emotional consumption of these personalities by a heterogeneous audience; and the propagation and celebration of present as opposed to posthumous fame. While critics have emphasised the connection *Idylls* makes between private immorality and political and social apocalypse,[13] what has been less discussed is the poem's concentration on figures who are on perpetual display, who are denied the haven of privacy and whose personal lives are subject to persistent public scrutiny.[14] *Idylls* presents a rumour-fuelled world, very much like Tennyson's own, in which public figures desire privacy and anonymity, while private individuals covet publicity and fame.[15] This, of course, reflects the intrusion of the workings of a publicity-driven

Victorian culture and its newly emerging practices of fandom into the world of Arthurian romance. When Tennyson was writing about them, however, these Arthurian personalities also corresponded to what Chris Rojek calls 'celeactors': Arthur, Guinevere and Lancelot, despite much speculation about their historical reality, were essentially fictional characters that were, at the time, 'accepted as "real" people who embody and reflect [cultural] tensions'.[16] In a similar manner to Sherlock Holmes or Robin Hood, these Arthurian characters existed beyond their original medium and were integrated into Victorian literary, visual and popular culture. Becoming part of the national consciousness, these figures gained a level of autonomy and were treated by audiences and mass media in a similar way to real celebrities.[17] The popularity of Tennyson's poem, then, stems, in part, from the fact that he offered psychologically revealing portraits of figures who were household names and appealed to the functional nature of personal revelation, moral transgression and scandal in celebrity culture.

Poetics of renown

The first idyll, 'The Coming of Arthur', begins by describing a war-torn land swarmed by 'the heathen host', a place 'Wherein the beast was ever more and more, / But man was less and less' (8, 11–12). Arthur's achievement is then clarified: he 'for a space / ... thro' the puissance of his Table Round / Drew all their petty princedoms under him, / Their king and head, and made a realm, and reign'd' (16–19). This idyll goes on to explicate Arthur's accomplishment as, primarily, the careful branding, marketing and reproduction of his exceptional personality.[18] Tennyson's Arthur possesses charisma, which Max Weber defines as:

> a certain quality of an individual personality by virtue of which he is set apart from ordinary men and treated as endowed with super-natural, superhuman, or at least specifically exceptional powers or qualities. These are such as are not accessible to the ordinary person, but are regarded as of divine origin or as exemplary, and on the basis of them the individual concerned is treated as a leader.[19]

Divinely inspired and supernaturally validated, Arthur has the charis-matic power to attract followers and inspire loyalty to 'the normative patterns or order revealed or ordained by him'.[20] Rather than confirming that Arthur is King Uther's true heir, as Malory does, Tennyson focuses on the way Arthur's legitimacy derives not from his birth or lineage, but from his military prowess and moral virtue, or, more precisely, from the manner in which his remarkability is promulgated through rumour.[21] From the beginning, Arthur's renown does not originate from his position as king, but rather from forms of cultural circulation and mediation that recall the mechanisms of nineteenth-century celebrity that have been discussed in previous chapters.[22] This is first made apparent when Leodogran, before giving consent to a marriage between his daughter, Guinevere, and Arthur, asks for information about Arthur's origins. Sir Bedivere supplies the following overview of Arthur's position:

> Sir, there be many rumours on his head:
> For there be those who hate him in their hearts,
> Call him baseborn, and since his ways are sweet,
> And theirs are bestial, hold him less than man:
> And there be those who deem him more than man,
> And dream he dropt from heaven.

> (177–82)

The implication here and elsewhere in *Idylls* is that the transmission of Arthur's unprecedented and baffling characteristics enables his conversion of military triumph into stable political authority and social power. When Leodogran asks Queen Bellicent about Arthur, her half-brother, she agrees to reveal 'secret things', but only once her sons Gawain and Modred have left the room (317). Modred, however, remains unobserved with his ear to the door and 'half-heard' what she divulges (323). This marks the first instance of eavesdropping in the poem, an activity whose ubiquity clarifies how information and anecdotes about Camelot's public figures are spread. Queen Bellicent tells Leodogran that Arthur is 'fair / Beyond the race of Britons and of men' (329–30), and reveals one tale of his origin that associates him with a dragon-shaped ship and 'shining people' and describes him being thrown as a 'naked babe' by a wave at Merlin's feet (375, 383). Leodogran is also offered her prediction that Arthur will become 'so great [that] bards of him will sing' and that his story will reverberate and bring 'comfort' in times to come, 'Ranging and ringing thro' the minds of men, / And echo'd by old folk beside their fires' (413, 417, 415–16). Bellicent notes that:

> Merlin in our time
> Hath spoken also, not in jest, and sworn
> Tho' men may wound him that he will not die,
> But pass, again to come; and then or now

> Utterly smite the heathen underfoot,
> Till these and all men hail him for their king.
>
> (418–23)

Bellicent's Arthur is a time-defying figure whose political and military power will be as much a reality in the future as in the present; he is a Christ-like individual who cannot die and who comes from, and will return to, an otherworldly place. Later idylls confirm Bellicent's prophecy by presenting Arthur as a living legend and showing that her 'secret things' have become common knowledge. In 'Guinevere', for example, the novice recalls that her father, who was present at the founding of the Round Table, told her of a bard whose songs of 'Arthur's glorious wars' presented the king as a being 'wellnigh more than man', who was found as 'a naked child upon the sands / Of dark Tintagil by the Cornish sea', and whose 'grave should be a mystery / From all men, like his birth' (284, 285, 291–92, 295–96). In a similar manner, in 'The Last Tournament', Sir Tristram notes the way the knights were, at first, in awe of Arthur's otherworldly physical appearance and amazed by 'the weird legend of his birth, / With Merlin's mystic babble about his end' (664–65); eying Arthur as a 'God', each knight was 'lifted up beyond himself / Did mightier deeds than elsewhere he had done' (673, 674–75). *Idylls*, then, implies that the production and maintenance of Arthur's regal legitimacy is the result of the manner in which his personal uniqueness and exceptional deeds are culturally distributed by a medieval form of Victorian publicity.

If Arthur's distinctiveness is circulated through gossip and songs, then the first idyll underlines that, from his birth, supernatural forces intervened in the shaping of his charisma and extraordinary destiny. Arthur overcame the 'heathen hordes, and made a realm and reign'd' ('The Coming of Arthur', 518) not only because of his ability to unleash the power of the battleaxe and brand and 'follow Christ', but also because, as his knights triumphantly sing, 'God hath told the King a secret word' and 'breathed [in Arthur] a secret thing' (499, 488, 500). Arthur's earlier military victory over those in his realm who doubted his right to rule is, similarly, made possible because 'the Powers who walk the world / Made lightnings and great thunders over him, / And dazed all eyes, till Arthur by main might' overthrew his enemies (106–08). Likewise, at the moment Arthur founded the Round Table, Queen Bellicent witnessed otherworldly intervention that allowed him to speak 'large, divine and comfortable words / Beyond [the] tongue to tell' (267–68). These powers created a visual spectacle of blinding light followed by a 'Flame-colour, vert and azure' display, as Arthur publicly bound his knights 'by so strait vows to his own self' (274, 261). As each knight rose 'some / Were pale as at the passing of a ghost, / Some flush'd, and others dazed, as one who wakes / Half-blinded at the coming of a light' (262–65). Overseeing this ceremony, too, were the numinous figures who authenticated and authorised Arthur's sovereignty: the mysterious 'three fair queens' 'who will help him at his need' (275, 278); the 'mage Merlin' who used 'his craft' to make him king (279, 233); and 'the Lady of the Lake', who 'knows a subtler magic than [Merlin]' and gave Arthur the legendary sword Excalibur, a spectacular object that '[bewilders] heart and eye' (282–83, 299). The novice, again, relaying what she heard from her father, describes the founding of the Round Table as a golden time 'full of signs / And wonders', of 'strange music', of elves, spirits, and even a mermaiden, and of a magical feast provided by 'hands unseen' ('Guinevere', 230–31, 237, 264).

The level of intervention involved in the creation and circulation of Arthur's mysterious personality corresponds to the way an individual's celebrity was produced and sustained in the Victorian period. Here *Idylls* reflects what Eric Eisner has identified as a recurring motif in nineteenth-century poetry whereby 'unique subjectivity' is elevated to 'a position of transcendence', while, at the same time, being 'increasingly visible' as the mediated, impermanent product of a set of impersonal structures and forces.[23] Although Tennyson was very concerned about his own commodification, for example, by publishers, periodicals and photographers, his representation of Arthur suggests that the poet, like his contemporaries, was also fascinated by the mass-media marketing and fashioning of individuals as charismatic objects of wonder, whose exceptionality, like Arthur's, inspired admiration and trepidation. This context makes especially provocative the spectacular founding of the Round Table that involves the reproduction of the king's distinctiveness. According to Bellicent, as Arthur's knights vowed to imitate him, they literally became his replicas: 'From eye to eye thro' all their Order flash / A momentary likeness of the King' ('The Coming of Arthur', 269–70). This is the moment, as Guinevere, later explains, that Arthur, 'Rapt in this fancy of his Table Round', made his men swear 'vows impossible, / To make them like himself' ('Lancelot and Elaine', 129–31). The decline of Arthur's order will stem from his knights' inability to be 'all of one mind with him' ('The Coming of Arthur', 254), or, more precisely, their failure to be him.

Throughout *Idylls*, the knights of the Round Table are instantly recognisable to others, not, at first, as identifiable individuals, but as having the manner and appearance of one of Arthur's knights. For example, in 'The Holy Grail', Ambrosius guesses that his fellow monk Percivale used to be one of Arthur's men because

> such a courtesy
> Spake thro' the limbs and in the voice – I knew [you]
> For one of those who eat in Arthur's hall;
> For good ye are and bad, and like to coins,
> Some true, some light, but every one of you
> Stamp'd with the image of the King.
>
> (22–27)

The poem's emphasis on Arthur's remarkableness, therefore, coexists with and is unsettled by a persistent theme of identity duplication and imitation.[24] This moulding or fashioning of celebrity identities through an association with great men, a recurring feature in Tennyson's circle, confirms Leo Braudy's assertion in *The Frenzy of Renown* that in part Western culture 'celebrates uniqueness, and in part it requires that uniqueness be exemplary and reproducible'.[25] After the founding of the Round Table, such reproducibility becomes essential to the maintenance of Arthur's order and power. For example, when many of his knights fail to return to Camelot after the quest for the Holy Grail, Arthur is forced to make new knights to replace them. In 'Pelleas and Ettarre', Sir Pelleas, one of these new knights, expresses his wish to be like Arthur and to use 'spear and sword' to make a fair woman '[a]s famous' as Guinevere; he calls out, 'O my Queen, my Guinevere, / For I will be thine Arthur when we meet' (43, 44–45). These lines suggest that in Camelot, as in Victorian celebrity culture, the normalisation of the pursuit of fame often blurred the boundary between personal aspiration and the re-enactment of valorised but unexceptional motifs. The imagery of replication also evokes the industrialised and institutionalised process whereby objects associated with and visual images depicting the likenesses of celebrated Victorian personalities were mechanically reproduced and turned into commodities, which were, in turn, central to the attainment and preservation of celebrity. These sections call to mind one of the poem's central paradoxes: despite its initial and ongoing celebration of the individuality and uniqueness of Arthur, *Idylls* textually marginalises the king, partly to preserve and confirm his enigma. Indeed, the poem prioritises the stories of the replica-knights, copies that, at first, propagate the original's aura, but, later, call attention to faults within the Arthurian brand.

Sketches of the king

Like 'The Coming of Arthur', most of the idylls present King Arthur indirectly by examining how he is represented in the thoughts, discussions and lives of his subjects; they offer sketches of a mystical, 'ghostlike' figure who fascinates a personality-driven community ('Guinevere', 601). Arthur is central but peripheral, present yet absent; he occupies an incongruous position in the text comparable to that occupied by reluctant nineteenth-century celebrities such as Tennyson, for whom the 'rejection of the marketplace became very marketable'.[26] When the elusive Arthur does appear in the poem, it is usually in his capacity as king, suggesting that, to a large extent, his personal identity has disappeared behind his public role. He is the sum of the stock anecdotes, rumours and ideas circulating about him that precede his public appearances, speeches and actions as king. As such, in *Idylls*, as in Victorian culture, there is a continual drive, using various means, to discover the private person behind the public personality. Arthur's knights, for instance, are frequently asked by those they encounter about the king and Camelot. These conversations closely resemble reminiscences about celebrated figures – for example, those contained in Hallam Tennyson's *Alfred Lord Tennyson: a Memoir* (1897) – and the type of published interviews with celebrities and armchair tourism that began to proliferate in the second half of the nineteenth century to meet the public's demand for such information.[27] In 'Lancelot and Elaine', for example, Lancelot, during his stay at Astolat, is 'ask'd of court and Table Round' and offers his delighted listeners a unique eyewitness account of 'Arthur's glorious wars' (267, 284), as well as, confidentially, revealing that

> However mild [Arthur] seems at home, nor cares
> For triumph in our mimic wars, the jousts –
> For if his own knight cast him down, he laughs
> Saying, his knights are better men than he –
> Yet in this heathen war the fire of God
> Fills him: I never saw his like: there lives
> No greater leader.

(310–16)

In a similar manner, in 'The Holy Grail', Ambrosius questions Sir Percivale about why he renounced his life as a famous knight, as well as asking for a first-hand report of the significant events that took place in Camelot. During what amounts to a celebrity interview, Ambrosius is offered privileged information about Camelot's celebrity circle, including about the pivotal moment, when, during Arthur's absence, his knights vow to search for the Holy Grail, abandoning the king and causing the 'chance of noble deeds [to] come and go / Unchallenged' (318–19). At various points, the monk interrupts Percivale's account to seek clarification and specific information, asking, for instance, 'Tell me, and what said each, and what the King?' (707); to which Percivale responds:

> And that can I,
> Brother, and truly; since the living words
> Of so great men as Lancelot and our King
> Pass not from door to door and out again,
> But sit within the house.

(708–12)

The words of great men are 'living' because they publicly circulate and also penetrate the domestic realm, where they have an important and lasting effect. Percivale's authoritative reiteration of these words not only elevates him, who originally heard them, but also his listener, Ambrosius, who can now with second-hand authority repeat them. These words also imply that although 'he that told the tale' inevitably changes ('Gareth and Lynette', 1392), there is always an implicit hierarchy of those closest to 'great men'. Like the reminiscers in the previous chapter, those in closest proximity to Arthur, especially his knights, vicariously experienced his celebrity, accepting the cultural accessibility and visibility that the king, like Tennyson, rejected in favour of a personal style associated with enigma and remoteness. Percivale's comment about the proliferation of the words of great men intriguingly evokes one incident, representative of many, in which Tennyson's private words became public knowledge. On this occasion, Tennyson's words were, first, recorded in an 1862 letter from Julia Margaret Cameron to a mutual friend, Henry Taylor; then, published in Taylor's *Autobiography* (1885); and, finally, reprinted in *The Times*. Furious at this violation of his privacy, Tennyson regarded this as symptomatic of the 'bad taste of the age'.[28] Ironically, what Cameron had originally transcribed was Tennyson's diatribe against his society's 'passion for autographs and anecdotes and records' and his opinion that the desire for anecdotes about and an 'acquaintance with the lives of great men was treating them like pigs to be ripped open for the public'.[29] Tennyson's opinions would have been no great surprise to their original hearer, Cameron, nor for that matter to anyone in his circle; moreover, by the time they were published in *The Times* his views were hardly even newsworthy. In fact, as previous chapters have demonstrated, Tennyson's dislike of these intrusive features of celebrity culture became an essential part of his self-fashioned brand of celebrity.

Although Tennyson was increasingly protective of his own privacy and fearful of its violation, he makes the key points of his poem those that intrusively offer access to the evasive king. Pointedly, the first idyll directly depicts the musings of the recently crowned, yet untested and virtually unknown Arthur. Dressed as a simple knight without the 'golden symbol of his kinglihood' ('The Coming of Arthur', 50), he arrives in King Leodogran's land to drive the heathens out and kill the beasts; here he felt 'the light of [Guinevere's] eyes into his life' (56). Having succeeded in his task and on his way to do battle with the rebellious lords and barons in his own land, Arthur reflects on his desire to be 'join'd with Guinevere' and to rule 'side by side' with her, making it clear that without her, his purposes, victories and sovereignty mean 'nothing' (76, 80):

> What happiness to reign a lonely king,
> Vext – O ye stars that shudder over me,
> O earth that soundest hollow under me,
> Vext with waste dreams? for saving I be join'd
> To her that is the fairest under heaven,
> I seem as nothing in the mighty world,
> And cannot will my will, nor work my work
> Wholly, nor make myself in mine own realm
> Victor and lord. But were I join'd with her,
> Then might we live together as one life,
> And reigning with one will in everything
> Have power on this dark land to lighten it,
> And power on this dead world to make it live.

> (81–93)

Arthur's contemplation implies that, for him, love and marriage offer a type of personal satisfaction that is far superior to public recognition, or even civic accomplishments. This belief corresponds to the Victorian idealisation of the domestic space, namely, the idea that '[h]ome and family anchored and fulfilled a man, tempered his passions, and renewed his spirit'.[30] Arthur's love for Guinevere gives him perspective: it makes the world 'all so clear about him' as he goes into battle and allows him to triumph over his foes (97). This internal monologue suggests the important influence of the private on the public sphere and provides a context for understanding Arthur's sorrow and anger at Guinevere's infidelity with Lancelot. But Arthur's words also anticipate the very public position that he and Guinevere will occupy once they are joined as 'one life' and 'one will in everything' and have power over 'this dark land' and 'this dead world'. Their status is later confirmed by their very public marriage before the 'stateliest of [Britain's] altar-shrines' (454) and by Dubric, the high saint and chief of the church, who links the couple's vows to the 'boundless purpose' of Arthur and his Round Table (474). From this point onwards, the king and queen are public figures whose actions, hidden or overt, have communal implications; their position is underlined in the poem by the fact that it, for the most part, conceals their domestic interactions.[31] The direct representation of Arthur's interiority in the first idyll, therefore, provides another explanation as to why such moments of introspection are foreclosed in the rest of the poem: the now-famous and publicly significant king's right to privacy has been absolved and his true self has been eclipsed by his public role.

As with their Victorian counterparts, access to the hidden selfhood of Camelot's most famous personalities takes on a valued status, inspiring and authorising strategies of intrusion and invasion on the part of other characters and on the part of Tennyson himself. Consequently, although Arthur's thoughts and feelings, in general, remain impenetrable, Tennyson ensures they can be gleaned from his public or private interactions with others.[32] In this regard, the final two idylls are particularly significant because they present the much-discussed but mysterious king as a self-expressive, passionate man. Although the association of Arthur with what at the time were regarded as culturally feminine attributes was condemned by some reviewers as making him, as Henry Crabb Robinson puts it, 'unfit to be an epic-hero', the feminisation of the king was central to the poem's success.[33] If Tennyson's Arthur fell short of Victorian standards of manliness, especially because of his inability to exert authority over the domestic sphere, then it is the king's articulation of his own failures and inadequacies that humanises and personalises him and makes him a more interesting biographical subject. As David Staines suggests, the scene between the betrayed king and the adulterous queen in the penultimate idyll, 'Guinevere', offers 'the fullest and most direct presentation of the King in Tennyson's poetry'; here, the warrior leader reveals his personal vulnerability and all-encompassing sorrow in the aftermath of the collapse of his marriage and of the fellowship of knights he established.[34] Guinevere's actions, Arthur tells her, have destroyed everything he holds dear: 'high thought, ... amiable words / ... courtliness, ... the desire of fame, / And love of truth and all that makes a man' (478–80). By the end of the scene, when Arthur forgives Guinevere, Tennyson expects his readers, like the queen, to see the flesh-and-blood Arthur, who is 'the highest and most human too' (644), and not merely the saintly, chaste figure without that 'touch of earth' ('Lancelot and Elaine', 133).

Similarly, the final idyll, 'The Passing of Arthur', going even further than its earlier incarnation, 'Morte d'Arthur' (1842), opens with Arthur's last remaining knight, Sir Bedivere, overhearing the 'moanings of the King' (8). Assuming that he is unheard, Arthur presents himself as a self-doubting and insecure individual who believes that he has failed to live up to his destiny and has been abandoned and forgotten by God and the supernatural forces that made him king (22–28). Attending the distraught king, Sir Bedivere tries to reassure Arthur that his 'name and glory cling / To all high places like a golden cloud' (53–54) and tells the king 'conquer as of old' (64); however, Arthur admits: 'on my heart hath fall'n / Confusion, till I know not what I am / Nor whence I am, nor whether I be King', adding that 'The sequel of to-day unsolders all / The goodliest fellowship of famous knights / Whereof this world holds record' (143–45, 182–84). After the final battle, the wounded king, as he expresses similar apprehensions as well as faith in the future, is served and comforted by Sir Bedivere.[35] Tennyson's representation of the personal exchanges between these two men simultaneously consecrates and violates the privacy and intimacy being depicted. In these invasive scenes, as in the final scene between Arthur and Guinevere, Tennyson is 'ripping [Arthur] open for the public', giving readers the illusion of access to the celebrity king's authentic, unmediated selfhood.[36] This strategy is made all the more conspicuous by earlier idylls that present Arthur as a self-conscious public performer careful to ensure that his every word and action reinforce the ongoing mythologisation of himself and his order.[37]

The hall of fame

If the first idyll details how Arthur's political and social power are established through the communal circulation of his unique selfhood, renowned deeds and supernatural associations, later idylls elaborate on how these same forms of publicity, at first, sustain and, then, destroy the validity of Arthur and his order. The second idyll, 'Gareth and Lynette', offers the most detailed account of the features of Camelot that ensured the stability of Arthur's reign and unified his realm; it demonstrates, in particular, the importance of Camelot's alluring and attractive personalities, who are recognised, observed, talked about, encountered and emulated by a diverse audience. An examination of this idyll also exposes contradictions within Camelot's celebrity culture that point to fault lines in its Victorian counterpart. The idyll begins with Prince Gareth, son of Queen Bellicent and nephew of Arthur, telling his overly protective mother that only by becoming one of Arthur's knights can he do 'man's work', namely, 'follow the Christ, the King, / Live pure, speak true, right wrong' (115–17). More specifically, what Gareth wants is the public recognition that comes from being a knight and circling up 'To the great Sun of Glory', and from there 'swoop[ing] / Down upon all things base, and dash[ing] them dead' (22–23). The implication is that the 'mere gold' of his princely name and noble position will not bring Gareth true masculine fulfilment (65). With Arthur and his knights as implicit models, Gareth seeks the 'true steel' of honour based on publicly validated prowess and a type of fame 'won by force' and desired by 'many men' (65, 104–05). Bellicent relents and allows her son to go to Camelot, but only if he agrees to her degrading condition that he go there in disguise to work as a scullion in Arthur's kitchen. Fascinated by the allure of Camelot, Gareth replies, 'The thrall in person may be free in soul, / And I shall see the jousts' (162–63).

Evoking nineteenth-century travel literature and the emerging discourse of celebrity tourism discussed in Chapter 1, Gareth and two of his servants describe their journey to Camelot to see the 'glories of [the] King' (240). The young men offer the poem's first account of the magical city with its large spires and turrets that seem to disappear in the mists, while reiterating the commonplace myths and rumours, which have shaped their gaze, such as the idea that Camelot is a 'city of Enchanters, built / By fairy Kings' and that 'this King is not the King, / But only changeling out of Fairyland, / Who drave the heathen hence by sorcery / And Merlin's glamour' (196–97, 199–202). Unafraid, Gareth spurs his companions onwards to the gates on which 'The Lady of the Lake stood' and the 'three Queens', and where Arthur's wars were represented 'in weird devices' (212, 225, 221). This iconography made 'New things and old co-twisted, as if Time / Were nothing, so inveterately, that [the visitors] / Were giddy gazing there' (222–24).[38] To the men, moreover, it appears that the 'dragon-boughts and elvish emblemings / Began to move, seethe, twine and curl' (229–300). Reinforcing the ongoing work of rumours and the bards' songs in recording Arthur's achievements, the visual imagery on the 'gateway [seems] alive' (231).

The animated gateway symbolises the fact that the fame of Arthur and his knights must be, in order to sustain itself, an immediate, organic reality; the images depicted are alive because they have been internalised by admirers such as Gareth and, as a result, they unsettle distinctions between past and present victory, historical and contemporary authority. When Gareth, a proto-tourist, asks a native of Camelot about the veracity of the rumours that abound about the city and the king, he is given an ambiguous reply. What the old man does imply is that the celebrity of a place or person is not tied to physicality or materiality, but to what he calls 'the Riddling of the Bards', namely, the discursive formations that accentuate 'Confusion, and illusion, and relation, / Elusion, and occasion, and evasion', and so heighten fascination and mystery (280–82).

Once within the city, the sightseers describe it as a place of 'shadowy palaces', 'rich in emblem', where 'a healthful people stept / As in the presence of a gracious king' (296, 297, 308–09). Gareth, as the poem's first characterisation of the figure of the fan, delights in seeing 'pure women' and hearing the sound as knights passed in the hall; he is 'half beyond himself for ecstasy' when these same knights 'Clash like the coming and retiring wave, / And the spear spring, and good horse reel' (307, 514, 512–13). The notion that fame in Camelot is a living thing is further demonstrated in the conversations Gareth overhears during his time working as a scullion in Arthur's kitchen. His lower-class companions reiterate the standard anecdotes about Arthur's birth and mysterious nature (492–93) and, tellingly, express their own personal investment in the mythology of Camelot and its celebrities:

> the thralls had talk among themselves,
> And one would praise the love that linkt the King
> And Lancelot – how the King had saved his life
> In battle twice, and Lancelot once the King's –
> For Lancelot was the first in Tournament,
> But Arthur mightiest on the battle-field.

> (481–86)

Not only are the 'thralls' interested in Arthur's military victories, but their conversations reveal that Arthur and his knights are public figures whose private and intimate relationships are of communal significance.

What Gareth also witnesses and participates in is the process whereby the king establishes the Arthurian brand of kingliness and knightliness. Watching 'the splendour of the presence of the King / Throned and delivering doom', Gareth hears the way Arthur distinguishes himself from the 'kings of old' by offering justice and help to the 'wrong'd / Thro' all [the] realm' (313–14, 366, 363–64). During these formal proceedings, Arthur clarifies that the virtuous characters and deeds of his knights make them different from all other men of noble birth within the realm (416–18). The presence down one side of Arthur's hall of 'A stately pile' (398) of shields on which his knights' achievements are publicly displayed also emphasises that Arthurian knightliness is an ongoing public performance of virtuous actions:

> Some blazon'd, some but carven, and some blank,
> There ran a treble range of stony shields, –
> Rose, and high-arching overbrow'd the hearth.
> And under every shield a knight was named:
> For this was Arthur's custom in his hall;
> When some good knight had done one noble deed,
> His arms were carven only; but if twain
> His arms were blazon'd also; but if none,
> The shield was blank and bare without a sign
> Saving the name beneath.

> (399–408)

Functioning in a similar way to the portraits of distinguished Victorians in G. F. Watts's *Hall of Fame,* these 'stately shields' establish the names and qualities (although not the faces) of those most worthy of renown. Despite this gallery's evocation of Victorian middle-class ideology, noble rank still is the basic entry requirement to be one of Arthur's knights. Having discovered Gareth's true identity and questioned his nephew briefly about his ability to practise 'hardihood', 'gentleness', fidelity in love, and 'uttermost obedience', Arthur willingly makes Gareth a knight (542–44). Although it is his nobility that allows Gareth to move from being a mere fan to becoming one of Camelot's celebrities, Gareth wishes to keep his princely identity a secret, telling Arthur: 'Let be my name until I make my name! / My deeds will speak' (562–63). As a result, when Arthur gives Gareth the quest of saving Lynette's sister, Lyonors, from the four brother-knights who hold her captive, Gareth's lower-class associates cheer him on as one of their own, whose advancement confirms the possibility, implicitly opened up by Arthur's own 'baseborn' sovereignty, of their own upward mobility (678–83). Tennyson's circle, in an analogous manner, gives the illusion of inclusiveness, allowing entry to every reader of the poet, while, at the same time, making its Freshwater centre a site of privileged exclusivity, which only the poet's true admirers, namely the unobtrusive ones, would venerate rather than violate.

Sceptical and derogative about his abilities, Lynette accuses Gareth of merely imitating knightliness: 'how like a noble knight he talks! / The listening rogue hath caught the manner of it' (757–58). She changes her mind, however, once she witnesses Gareth's bravery and constancy, and realises the truth of his assertion: 'The knave that doth thee service as full knight / Is all as good, meseems, as any knight' (991–92). Unlike Gareth, who wants his worthy deeds to establish his knightly identity, the brother-knights, whom he easily defeats, are concerned with fashioning their public identities as fierce, 'mighty men' through self-promotion, performance and display, and enjoying the empowering benefits of such renown (628). Gareth's adversaries, who are associated with parable, allegory and mere 'form' (1170), kidnap Lyonors with the expectation that Arthur will send his 'chief man / Sir Lancelot whom [they trust] to overthrow' and, in this way, gain greater 'glory' (604–06). The idyll, then, differentiates an Arthurian brand of knightliness, represented by Gareth, from the flawed version adopted by his antagonists, who 'do but what they will; / Courteous or bestial from the moment, such / As have nor law nor king' (615–17).

Before arriving in Camelot, Gareth also associated knightliness with the pursuit of personal glory; however, Arthur, before he makes Gareth a knight, clarifies that it is 'for the sake of me, their King, / And the deed's sake my knighthood do the deed, / Than to be noised of' (558–60). During the quest, Gareth rescues a Baron, a friend of Arthur, who is being assaulted; when the Baron offers him a reward, Gareth, echoing Arthur's words, refuses, saying 'for the deed's sake have I done the deed', to which the Baron responds, 'I well believe / You be of Arthur's Table' (814–15). In 'Merlin and Vivien', Merlin also emphasises that the Round Table was founded not for worldly fame, but for 'love of God and men / And noble deeds' and to be the 'flower of all the world' (409–10). The 'fire for fame', which Merlin associates with the noise of 'trumpet-blowings', merely distracts knights from their true purpose (415–16). As a result, Merlin, like Arthur, prefers 'use' to 'fame', noting:

> but Fame with men,
> Being but ampler means to serve mankind,
> Should have small rest or pleasure in herself,
> But work as vassal to the larger love,
> That dwarfs the petty love of one to one.

> (486–90)

The ideal promoted here, of course, denies the forces of medieval publicity that popularised Arthur and his knights as those who 'crush / All wrongers of the Realm' and make the margins of land as safe as 'the centre of this hall' ('Gareth and Lynette', 610–11, 590). It is, of course, this 'noising of' knightly deeds that literally and symbolically expands Arthur's land and maintains his order, inspiring men such as Gareth to aspire to the famed manliness and glory associated with the Round Table. Gareth's initial opinions about knightliness are confirmed in Camelot where he sees that the 'Clear honour' that shone from the king made his knights seek 'the light of victory, / And glory gain'd, and evermore to gain' (322, 324–25).

Even more blatantly, Arthur's and Merlin's comments disregard the elaborate iconography of Camelot, including Arthur's 'Hall of Fame', which concretises the achievement of Arthur and his knights.[39] Adding to Gareth's earlier account of such memorialisations in Camelot, Sir Percivale, in 'The Holy Grail', describes Arthur's hall, built by Merlin, as the 'stateliest under heaven' with 'twelve great windows [that] blazon Arthur's wars, / And all the light that falls upon the board / Streams thro' the twelve great battles of our King' (224, 248–50). The hall contains 'four great zones of sculpture' charting human development from beast-slaying men to 'warriors, perfect men' to men 'with growing wings' (232, 236–37); and 'over all':

> one statue in the mould
> Of Arthur, made by Merlin, with a crown,
> And peak'd wings pointed to the Northern Star.
> And eastward fronts the statue, and the crown
> And both the wings are made of gold, and flame
> At sunrise till the people in far fields,
> Wasted so often by the heathen hordes,
> Behold it, crying, 'We have still a King.'
>
> (238–45)

As in Farringford and elsewhere in Victorian Britain, celebrity in Camelot is produced and reproduced by such images that connote power and personality, as well as by public spectacles. In Camelot, for instance, jousts, tournaments and parades allow Camelot's citizens and visitors to catch a glimpse, or call out the names, of their favourite knights. Percivale recalls that the most elaborate of such displays was instigated by Arthur, who, before his knights left Camelot on their quest for the

Grail, suggested there should be one last show of 'The yet-unbroken strength of all his knights, / Rejoicing in that Order which he made' (326–27). Although happy in reminiscing about Camelot, Percivale summarises the 'practices of the court' as 'vainglories, rivalries, / And earthly heats that spring and sparkle out / Among us in the jousts, while women watch / Who wins, who falls' (32–35). While these are the words of a man who has renounced a worldly life for a monastic one, his comments highlight the hierarchical and renown-orientated order that Arthur inaugurated, validated and, perhaps, egotistically enjoyed. Supporting this idea, Guinevere remarks:

> for to speak [Arthur] true,
> Ye know right well, how meek soe'er he seem,
> No keener hunter after glory breathes.
> He loves it in his knights more than himself:
> They prove to him his work: win and return.
>
> ('Lancelot and Elaine', 153–57)

Similarly, Sir Tristram notes the way that, from the beginning, the knights sought to have 'each new glory, set [Arthur's] name / High on all hills, and in the signs of heaven' ('The Last Tournament', 336–37). These opinions show that the order Arthur created was a cult of personality, established 'according to the designs of one being'.[40] In this context, although seemingly antithetical to the brother-knights whom Gareth conquers, Arthur and his knights also establish and maintain their power and importance through a comparable use of rumour, spectacle and iconography.

In *Idylls*, knightliness is associated with public glory derived from civic deeds, on the one hand; and with pure altruism and inner virtue that comes from actions done for the greater good, on the other. These contradictory ideas evoke what Leo Braudy has identified as the two competing ideals at the heart of Western fame: 'Roman and classical ideals of public service, civic virtue and national glory' and 'Judeo-Christian ideals of humbleness, modesty, spirituality, and private virtue'.[41] The Arthurian ideal of doing the deed for 'the deed's sake' corresponds to a comment Tennyson made about his own writing. According to Frederick Locker-Lampson, Tennyson, although initially interested in 'popularity', eventually regarded it as a 'bastard fame' and, instead, thought a poet should 'spare no pains, that he should do his very best for the sake of his art, and for *that* only'.[42] Just as Arthur and Merlin discount the mechanisms that ensure their own renown,

Tennyson, here, is disingenuously distancing himself from his own highly successful strategies of self-publicity and self-promotion, which were increasingly necessary for poets working in the highly competitive nineteenth-century literary marketplace. Like Arthur in *Idylls*, who creates and promotes a distinctive type of kingliness and knightliness, easily differentiated from other earlier forms, Tennyson, too, successfully branded himself and his works, making that which could be called 'Tennysonian' a selling point. 'Gareth and Lynette', therefore, taps into the need in Arthur's and Victoria's Britain to categorise and discriminate between various types of renown to counter the often indiscriminate workings of celebrity and publicity; but it also captures the reality that famous men such as Tennyson, like Arthur and his knights, could, despite their own rhetoric to the contrary, easily become indistinguishable from those from whom they sought to differentiate themselves and whom they deemed less worthy.[43]

Brushes with disfame

In 'Merlin and Vivien', Vivien reminds Merlin of the pointlessness of attempts to control the mechanisms of fame because 'The Fame that follows death is nothing to us; / And what is Fame in life but half-disfame' (462–63). She gives as an example the fact that he is derogatively called the 'Devil's son' and the 'Master of all vice' (465, 467). Agreeing with her, Merlin goes on to say, 'Sweet were the days when I was all unknown' (499). If the first two idylls are concerned with the poetics of renown, the other ten show the workings of 'disfame' that eventually cause the downfall of Arthur's moral and social order. Medieval publicity, like its nineteenth-century equivalent, is shown to be an uncontrollable and unmanageable force that facilitates and permits the scrutiny of personal privacy for hidden truth or secret shame. It can transform rumour and public opinion into fact and turn on those who seek to use its mechanisms.[44] *Idylls*, in this regard, shows the relationship between forms of publicity and their influence on the 'voice of the public' and its creation of 'consensus', reflecting Tennyson's fears about the rise of political democracy, but also the consequences of the interrelationship between a democratised market place and a culture of publicity that specialised in gossip, rumour, and scandal.[45] If Arthur's uniqueness first attracted his followers and facilitated the establishment of his realm, then, as rumours begin to circulate about Guinevere's adulterous relationship with Sir Lancelot, the once-praised qualities that differentiated Arthur from all others become increasingly problematic. The scandal undermines Arthur's authority, as those around him, such as Sir Tristram, 'babble[d] about him, all to show [their] wit – / [asking] whether [Arthur] were King by courtesy, / Or King by right'? ('The Last Tournament', 340–42). Such questions, spread by 'the tonguesters of the court', mean that Arthur is no longer seen as a figure 'Dropt down from heaven', but as an anomaly with no 'trace' of 'the flesh and blood' of 'old kings' (392, 680–82); he becomes, thus, 'a doubtful lord / To bind [others] by inviolable vows, / Which flesh and blood perforce would violate' (682–84). The poem, in this regard, plays out what Nicholas Dames identifies as the central dynamic and practice of Victorian celebrity culture: 'the dual gesture of enlarging the image of the celebrity in question, combined with the pleasure of puncturing this enlarged image'.[46] The relationship between the process of deifying and debunking also manifests itself in the idylls 'The Marriage of Geraint', 'Geraint and Enid', 'Balin and Balan' and 'Merlin and Vivien'. Each idyll elaborates on the mechanisms of rumour and the consequences of disfame: the first two focus on the vulnerability of Camelot's public figures, the third on the susceptibility of their admirers and the fourth on the vindictiveness of one of the key proliferators of scandal in the poem.

In 'The Marriage of Geraint', when Enid and her parents first meet Geraint, he is a well-known figure. Enid's father, Earl Yniol, instantly recognises Geraint by his movement, state and presence as 'one of those / That eat in Arthur's hall at Camelot' (431–32). On hearing Geraint's actual name, Yniol adds that it is a celebrated name 'far-sounded among men / For noble deeds' and that his daughter 'ever loved to hear' the 'noise' of knightly deeds and 'feats of arms' (427, 435–37). The rest of the scene represents a diluted version of lionism, as Yniol and his family, despite their poverty, ensure that their celebrity guest is attentively entertained and fittingly worshipped. Such celebrity encounters frequently occur in *Idylls,* reflecting the significance of nineteenth-century 'brushes with fame' that, according to Dames, structure consciousness, organise memory and provide a sense of personal distinctiveness for those who experience them.[47] The consequences of the family's encounter with Geraint are even more significant, as he restores their social and economic fortunes and marries Enid. When a 'rumour' circulates about Guinevere's 'guilty love for Lancelot' (24–25), Prince Geraint immediately abandons Arthur's court to prevent the reputation of his wife being tainted by her close friendship with Guinevere. Returning to his realm in Devon, Geraint prioritises his private relationship with Enid and neglects his public role as a participant in communal events such as hunts and tournaments. His indifference to his position as a public figure, whose actions are scrutinised by an anonymous audience, jeopardises his reputation: for 'when [his subjects] met / In twos and threes, or fuller companies / [they] Began to scoff and jeer and babble of him / As of a prince whose manhood was all gone' (56–59). This growing disfame affects his marital relationship because Enid, seeing the censure in 'the people's eyes' and hearing the 'people's talk' and men 'slur[ring] him, and saying all his force / Is melted into mere effeminacy', believes that she 'cannot love [her] lord and not his name' (61, 82, 106–07, 92).

Realising on some level the connection between his public reputation and private life, in 'Geraint and Enid', Geraint attempts to demonstrate that '[his] vigour is not lost' (82) by riding anonymously, accompanied only by Enid, into the 'wilds', which are full of 'bandit-haunted holds' and 'perilous paths' (28, 30, 32). Although attacked, sporadically, by robbers because of his wretched, pathetic appearance (60–61), Geraint is also recognised by a youth as a man 'of mark', a celebrity-knight (229). When Geraint asks the boy to find him lodgings for the night, this brush with fame causes the boy to hold 'his head high, and [think] himself a knight' (242). The boy's contemplation confirms, again, that Arthur's knights are not merely talked about, admired and identifiable figures, but also men who inspire identification and imitation, even for those, like the rustic boy or the thralls who cheer on Gareth before his knightly quest, for whom such a rise in rank is impossible. During his time in the wilderness, Geraint, by killing various groups of bandits and their leaders, fulfils Arthur's mission of 'clear[ing] the dark places and let[ting] in the law / And [breaking] the bandit holds and cleans[ing] the land' (942–43). These deeds, along with his renewed participation in tournaments and hunts, restore Geraint's reputation: 'all hearts / Applauded [him], and the spiteful whisper died' (956–57). In fact, Geraint and Enid become embodiments of ideal masculinity and femininity:

> They call'd him the great Prince and man of men.
> But Enid, whom her ladies loved to call
> Enid the Fair, a grateful people named
> Enid the Good.

> (960–63)

Despite this happy ending, this idyll makes clear that fame and disfame in an Arthurian or Victorian context affect the innermost being of celebrities and those who encounter them. Additionally, despite the indifference of public figures such as Geraint to their celebrity, their reputations are at the bestowal of a publicity-led audience that judges and scrutinises what it sees and has the power to create, destroy and re-create reputations.

Unlike Geraint, the eponymous brothers in the idyll 'Balin and Balan' self-consciously use the mechanisms of rumour to regain the glory they once had as Arthur's knights, before being banished from Camelot because of Balin's violent assault on one of the king's servants. These brothers, like the brother-knights in 'Gareth and Lynette', seek public attention through spectacular displays of strength, hurling 'to the ground what knight soever spurr'd / Against [them]' to show that they are 'ten-times worthier to be [Arthur's knights]' (64–66). Having heard of this, Arthur, with the 'spirit of his youth' returning to his heart, travels incognito to the brothers, challenges and overthrows them, proving that his skills as a warrior rest on his deeds rather than his name (19–20). Arthur, like Geraint and later Lancelot, seeks temporary personal obscurity and desires also to assert a core identity untrammelled by his empowering and imprisoning reputation. This is, however, the only instance in which the masquerade of anonymity is not revealed and exists merely as another elaboration, for the reader's benefit, of Arthur's inner nature.[48] Having been admitted back into Arthur's court, while his brother has been given the quest of hunting the 'demon in the woods', Balin attempts to subdue his 'fierce manhood' by following the example of Lancelot's 'worship of the Queen', and wearing Guinevere's cognisance on his shield to 'help him of his violences' (121, 71, 175, 201). However, whereas Gareth develops and grows by using Lancelot as his model, Balin is doomed by his participation in Camelot's cult of personality, owing to Lancelot's and Guinevere's disfame.[49]

When he accidentally observes a private meeting between the Queen and Lancelot, Balin believes his corrupt nature allows him to misinterpret this as a tryst between a 'Damsel and lover' (277). As a result, he flees to the court of Pellam, where he is taunted for his worship of the impure and shameful queen; he then escapes to the forest, where Vivien tells him, untruthfully, that her squire has witnessed the adultery of Guinevere and Lancelot. Upon the realisation that those he idolised are false, Balin begins stamping on his once-prized shield; on seeing him the passing Balan mistakes his brother for the 'Wood Demon' and the helmeted brothers, unknowingly, kill each other. This makes clear that it is Balin's personal investment in Camelotian celebrity that causes tragedy. In a similar manner, in 'Pelleas and Ettarre', the idealistic knight Pelleas, having been betrayed by his beloved Ettarre and another of Arthur's knights, Sir Gawain, is enraged at hearing about the scandalous relationship of

Lancelot and Guinevere (558). He rails against the emptiness and hollowness of reputed names and desires no name himself. Instead he seeks to become 'a scourge' 'To lash the treasons of the Table Round' and as 'wrath and shame and hate and evil fame' to 'like a poisonous wind', 'blast / And blaze the crime of Lancelot and the Queen' (553–58). Here *Idylls* draws attention to the fluctuating nature of reputation and its wider effects, and, in particular, to the anger of fans when their idols fail to live up to the ideals projected upon them.[50] Like the 'Wood Demon', Pelleas and Balin have become enraged figures owing to rumours spread by 'evil tongues' ('Balin and Balan', 122). Pelleas, moreover, resembles the 'Wood Demon' because he, too, goes on to take revenge on the world by 'Strik[ing] from behind' (128); he becomes the disreputable and treacherous Red Knight, who, along with his followers, flaunts the personal vices that Camelot's knights hypocritically conceal.

When she meets Balin in the woods, Vivien, like the Red Knight, is determined to spread disfame by exposing the scandals behind Camelot's much-lauded celebration of 'knightlike purity' ('Merlin and Vivien', 11). Her intention is to go to Camelot to stir the 'snakes within the grass' 'till they sting'; to ferret 'out [the knights'] burrowings'; to uncover 'That old true filth, and bottom of the well / Where Truth is hidden' (33, 36, 55, 47–48).[51] In a golden time in Camelot, when all was 'joust and play', Vivien 'heard, watch'd / And whisper'd' and sowed 'one ill hint from ear to ear' and then departed as an enemy who has left 'Death in the living waters' (143, 136–37, 141, 146). Recent scholars have connected Vivien's spreading of disfame with the emergence in the mid-nineteenth century of scandalmongering journalists and biographers, who sought to uncover truth or fabricate dishonour, and who, from Tennyson's perspective, were despicable invaders of the privacy of public figures.[52] The legal right to privacy that came into place in 1890 was, as James Eli Adams notes, a reaction against this level of invasiveness and intrusiveness.[53] When Vivien reveals to Merlin the scandals she has uncovered, he condemns her equally for her 'vast and vague' accusations against Sir Valence, Sir Sagramore and Sir Percivale, and her reference to the actual adultery of Lancelot and Guinevere (699). Using Merlin as his mouthpiece, Tennyson implies that Vivien and her Victorian descendents aim to please the gossip-hungry crowd and to use the proliferation of disfame to cover their personal depravity, reducing that which is noble and spiritual to the level of materialism, sensuality and sexuality. Merlin accuses Vivien of searching to find 'Some stain or blemish in a name of note, / Not grieving that their greatest are so small, / Inflate themselves with some insane delight, / And judge all nature from her feet of clay' (830–33). The implication is that insidious dishonour-hunters such as Vivien empower themselves by attacking the great, and, in democratically 'level[ing] all', create an 'equal baseness' (826, 828).[54] Yet, provocatively, Merlin also suggests that Vivien's delight in scandal, 'that foul bird of rapine whose whole prey / Is man's good name' (726–27), does not mean that she has not been its victim. He reminds her of her anger at the knights who 'babble[d]' about her unsuccessful attempt to seduce Arthur and made it 'the laughter of an afternoon' (688, 161). In this regard, Vivien is also a vengeful 'base interpreter', who, like the 'Wood Demon', strikes from behind, 'Rag[ing] like a fire among the noblest names / Polluting, and imputing her whole self, / Defaming and defacing, till she left / Not even Lancelot brave, nor Galahad clean' (793, 800–03). These idylls, therefore, suggest that Arthurian celebrity, like its Victorian equivalent, is a system of provisional and fluctuating commendation, whose mechanisms, which can be manipulated, are finally unmanageable and always reversible. Whereas 'Gareth and Lynette' explored the correlation between celebrity-worship and personal development, the idyll 'Balin and Balan' points to a link between fandom and death.

Female fandom

Although the figures of Vivien and Elaine are usually interpreted as diametrically opposed, they are connected by their love for famous men. Their respective interactions with Merlin and Lancelot evoke a nineteenth-century context in which relationships between celebrities and fans were 'dangerously eroticized' and celebrity was associated with sexual power and allure.[55] As David Giles notes, although the term 'fan' was not coined until the 1890s, 'the origins of fandom stretch as far back as the origins of fame'; the word 'fan' had religious origins that 'gradually acquired a more negative connotation, indicating inappropriate or erroneous enthusiasm usually for a disapproved activity'.[56] As a result of the Byromania of the early nineteenth century, female fans were specifically associated with uncontrollable and unregulated energy, frenzy, hysteria, political fanaticism, revolution and the unruly mob.[57] These depreciatory associations reflect, in part, male anxiety about the new importance and power of women as consumers that feminised the mass market, and also manifest concerns about the ways in which female fans empowered and liberated themselves through their enthusiasm and complicated the boundaries between admirers and idols.[58] Tapping into such fears about gender-inflected power reversals and fandom more generally, *Idyll*'s Vivien sets out to make her name by beguiling Merlin into revealing his 'secret' charm, which she uses to imprison him in a death-like state, while Elaine empowers herself through her unrequited love for Lancelot, employing elaborate strategies, including her own death, to guarantee her immortal place in the history of Camelot and Lancelot's story. Both women are extreme embodiments of the system of ritualised admiration that Arthur's order puts in place, while sharing features of the male-centred fandom discussed in Chapter 4.

In 'Merlin and Vivien', Vivien enters Camelot as an awe-filled admirer, who orchestrates a meeting with Guinevere and addresses her as a devoted worshipper:

> Save, save me thou – Woman of women – thine
> The wreath of beauty, thine the crown of power,
> Be thine the balm of pity, O Heaven's own white
> Earth-angel, stainless bride of stainless King –
>
> (77–80)

This level of obsequiousness and deification fails to impress Guinevere, who tells Vivien, 'Peace, child! of overpraise and overblame / We choose the last' (89–90); however, such a display of expected devotion facilitates Vivien's integration into life in Camelot. Unlike the previously mentioned brushes with fame, Vivien's encounter with the queen is carefully orchestrated and highly self-conscious, and, accordingly, similar to the engineered Victorian encounters discussed in previous chapters. Resembling the careful self-fashioning strategies of Tennyson's admirers in Chapter 4, the character of Vivien shows that fans were as constructed as the celebrities they venerated. Proving correct Merlin's comment that the 'Face-flattered and backbiter are the same' (822), from the time of her arrival, Vivien spies on Lancelot and Guinevere, noting 'That glance of theirs, but for the street, had been / A clinging kiss – how hand lingers in hand!' (103–04). In the guise of a fan, Vivien aims to empower herself by uncovering the couple's secrets; then, as she asserts, 'Lancelot will be gracious to the rat, / And our wise Queen, if knowing that I know, / Will hate, loathe, fear – but honour me the more' (118–20). One of her strategies for having 'The hearts of all this Order in mine hand' (56) is to seduce its key male personalities. Having failed with Arthur, she decides to pursue and stalk Merlin, 'the most famous man of all those times', as she 'fanc[ies] that her glory [will] be great / According to his greatness whom she quench'd' (164, 215–16).

Like a Victorian celebrity interviewer, Vivien establishes an intimate relationship with Merlin in order to have him reveal his secrets to her. Merlin is, at first, amused by her 'pretty tricks and fooleries', but also senses that she is slowly draining away his power; he sees her as a wave that will break upon him and 'sweep [him] from [his] hold upon the world, / [his] use and name and fame' (263, 301–02). Vivien's psychological vampirism is disguised as a display of submissiveness and reverence; for instance, she tells him:

> Trample me,
> Dear feet, that I have follow'd thro' the world,
> And I will pay you worship; tread me down
> And I will kiss you for it[.]
>
> (224–27)

Although she rails against others, she seductively lifts her eyes and looks at Merlin as if his head were 'godlike', 'crown'd with spiritual fire, / And touching other worlds' (835–36). 'Glowing on him, like a bride' (614), she flatters him into believing that her low opinion of others in Camelot is a result of her high opinion of him. She tells him:

> The knights, the court, the King, dark in your light,
> Who loved to make men darker than they are,
> Because of that high pleasure which I had
> To seat you sole upon my pedestal
> Of worship.
>
> (873–77)

Hearing her admiringly call him 'lord and liege, / Her seer, her bard, her silver star of eve, / Her God, her Merlin, the one passionate love / Of her whole life' (951–54), and to demonstrate he trusts her, Merlin tells her the charm; she uses it to enclose him 'in the four walls of a hollow tower, / From which was no escape for evermore ... And [he became] lost to life and use and name and fame' (207–12). In doing so, Vivien does not merely locate Merlin where he says he wants to be, namely in 'some vast charm concluded in [a] star' which makes 'fame nothing', but makes his fame contiguous with hers (510–11). Her actions confirm the close relationship between worship and usurpation, tapping into a post-eighteenth-century conception of fans as those who do not merely admire and want to be 'like [their] idols', but actually want to replace them.[59] As well as connoting the biographer, journalist or interviewer, Vivien also corresponds to the Victorian lion-hunter who, combining the roles of 'admiring' fan and 'manipulative collector', transforms distinguished men into passive objects and trophies that demonstrate her power.[60] In constructing Vivien, Tennyson may be drawing on his apprehension about the similarity between flattering fame-worshippers and manipulative shame-hunters. Just as Vivien followed the melancholic Merlin, in retreat from the scandals of Arthur's court, to the 'wild woods of Broceliande' (202), as the first chapter of this study shows, Tennyson's admirers tracked him to his comparable withdrawal from London to Freshwater; and, perhaps, the paranoid poet wondered if his fans shared Vivien's ulterior motives.

Although Elaine does not aim to assume her idol's position, as Vivien does, she, too, gains cultural authority and personal autonomy by partaking in and shaping the reputation of a famous man.[61] Through the figure of Elaine, Tennyson explores the obsessive, excessive and extreme passions that were stereotypically associated with the female fan. When Elaine first meets Lancelot she doesn't know his name because he has decided to conceal it, following Guinevere's suggestion that he compete anonymously in the last of the nine diamond tournaments. When Lancelot arrives at Elaine's Astolat home, her father instantly recognises him as one of Arthur's knights, declaring, in a manner similar to Yniol on seeing Geraint, 'I might guess thee chief of those, / After the King, who eat in Arthur's halls / Him have I seen: the rest, his Table Round / Known as they are, to me they are unknown' ('Lancelot and Elaine', 182–85). Confirming this but refusing to reveal his actual identity, Lancelot is, as Geraint was, fittingly lionised by the Astolat family and fallen in love with by the daughter of the house. Elaine is enamoured, first, by his 'mellow' voice (242), as it describes Camelot, Arthur and the activities of the Round Table; then, with his 'marr'd' and 'mark'd' face (246); and, finally, with his noble manner, the fact 'he seem'd the goodliest man / That ever among ladies ate in hall' (253–54). Like a nineteenth-century fan, Elaine seeks to get to the life and mind of the mysterious celebrity-knight through a painter-like scrutiny of his face:

> And all night long his face before her lived,
> As when a painter, poring on a face,
> Divinely thro' all hindrance finds the man
> Behind it, and so paints him that his face,
> The shape and colour of a mind and life,
> Lives for his children, ever at its best

And fullest; so the face before her lived,
Dark-splendid, speaking in the silence, full
Of noble things, and held her from her sleep.

(329–37)

The portraitist Elaine, like the interviewing Vivien, is determined to get at the secret essence of this famous man. Lancelot is embarrassed by Elaine's public worship of him: the way she 'Rapt on his face as if it were a God's' (354). Before he leaves Astolat he gives her his 'sacred shield' to look after, and she, in turn, gets him to agree to enhance his anonymity at the tournament by wearing her favours, something Lancelot would never usually do (4). Once Elaine has the shield in her possession, she fetishises it, doing homage to it in the unsupervised privacy of the eastern tower. Elaine's excessive veneration of this metonymic object, for which she fashions an elaborate silk case, involves her searching the shield for 'hidden meanings' and making a 'pretty history to herself / Of every dint a sword had beaten in it, / And every scratch a lance had made upon it, / Conjecturing when and where' (17–21). Through this ritualistic worship, she differentiates herself from her family and establishes a private space in which to assert her personal and creative fan identity. Her behaviour is an extreme version of that of Victorian fans who enriched their private lives by collecting and personalising objects associated with the public figures they admired. Using a visual and tactile memento to get psychologically closer to her idol, Elaine, like her nineteenth-century counterparts, 'lived in fantasy' (27, 396).[62] The shield, thus, functions in a similar way to nineteenth-century autographs, photographs or portraits, the study of which was believed to offer biographical insight into a celebrity's inner life.[63]

Having discovered that Lancelot was the mysterious victor of the diamond tournament and implied much about his fellow knight's time in Astolat, Sir Gawain 'buzz'd abroad / About the maid of Astolat, and her love. / All ears were prick'd at once, all tongues were loosed' (717–19). This part of *Idylls* shows the way in which Elaine becomes incorporated into Camelot as a new celebrity: the workings of rumour transform the unknown Elaine into a figure of curiosity. What is very apparent is the level of scrutiny to which Camelot's public figures are put, as if it is their reactions that can validate the rumours and confirm Elaine's new status. As the rumour that 'The maid of Astolat loves Sir Lancelot, [and] Sir Lancelot loves the maid of Astolat' proliferated (720–21): 'Some read the King's face, some the Queen's, and all / Had marvel what the maid might be, but most / Predoom'd her as unworthy' (722–24). This 'tale', which spread for nine days, alters hierarchies, for 'at banquet twice or thrice, / [knights] Forgot to drink to Lancelot and the Queen / [Instead] ... pledging Lancelot and the lily maid' (729, 731–33). Maintaining her public persona throughout, the queen must express her pain and jealousy covertly: '[her] lips severely placid, felt the knot / Climb in her throat, and with her feet unseen / Crush'd the wild passion out against the floor / Beneath the banquet, where the meats became / As wormwood, and she hated all who pledged' (735–39). These overt and covert responses to Elaine's new-found fame signify the possible effects – in particular celebrity rivalry – of the arrival of a new luminary within coteries of fame such as Camelot and Freshwater.

When Elaine is told by Sir Gawain that her knight is Lancelot, 'the greatest knight of all' (663), she begins to express what her father describes as her wilfulness (745, 772) and moves beyond the familial, domestic and gender constraints imposed upon her. 'Lest [she] be found as faithless in the quest' as Sir Gawain was, 'who left the quest to [her]' (756–57), knight-like Elaine finds Lancelot and then, maid-like, she nurses him back to health. The role which Elaine refuses to play, however, is that of sister which Lancelot offers her. Instead she proposes a passionate, erotic relationship that transcends traditional marriage, telling him, 'I care not to be wife, / But to be with you still, to see your face, / To serve you, and to follow you thro' the world' (932–34). When Lancelot rejects Elaine's love, believing it to be not love, but 'love's first flash in youth', she makes it clear that if she cannot have him, she is determined to die (944).[64] His absence from Astolat makes Lancelot seem all the more present to Elaine; this suggests that the potency of her obsession increases as it takes on a parasocial character. Elaine still 'heard him, still his picture form'd / And grew between her and the pictured wall' (985–86); moreover, she transforms her story into a plaintive song, 'The Song of Love and Death' (998–1011). The potential for self-empowerment born out of a situation of powerlessness is evident as Elaine, before she dies, carefully plans and organises her own funeral that involves the journey of her corpse by barge from Astolat to Camelot. Having 'live[d] apart' (283) and perhaps been envious of her brothers' journeys to Camelot as prospective knights, Elaine imagines, in death, fulfilling her fantasy:

> There will I enter in among them all,
> And no man there will dare to mock at me;
> But there the fine Gawain will wonder at me,
> And there the great Sir Lancelot muse at me;

> Gawain, who bad a thousand farewells to me,
> Lancelot, who coldly went, nor bad me one:
> And there the King will know me and my love,
> And there the Queen herself will pity me,
> And all the gentle court will welcome me,
> And after my long voyage I shall rest!
>
> (1045–54)

Perfectly anticipating her reception in Camelot, Elaine has carefully stylised herself into an inexplicable, attention-seeking spectacle that is greeted by 'mouths that gaped' and 'babbled' (1241, 1252); some in Camelot even believe that Elaine is the Fairy Queen who has come to take Arthur to Fairyland (1251). When Arthur reads aloud Elaine's carefully worded letter 'For Lancelot and the Queen and all', the story of her unrequited love for Lancelot causes the lords and dames of Camelot to cry; and Lancelot to declare it 'a love beyond all love' (1284). Not only do Elaine's actions ensure she floats into the annals of Camelot celebrity, they also guarantee her participation in the construction of Lancelot and allow her to add nuances to his reputation. Having presented herself as a queen, Elaine is 'buried worshipfully' (1318) in a 'costly' tomb with her 'image thereupon' and 'the shield of Lancelot [carved] at her feet ... and her lily in her hand' and her name 'be blazon'd on her tomb / In letters gold and azure' (1329, 1330–34).[65] Tennyson's Elaine confirms Braudy's suggestion that fame in Western culture is 'inseparable from the ideal of personal freedom'; she is the fan who seeks to 'move outside the blare of publicity by using it for [herself], to be an object of attention rather than one of the mob of attention payers'.[66] Elaine's act of posthumous self-fashioning transforms her from the domesticated 'lily maid', daughter, sister and unrequited lover, to an iconic figure whose tomb immortalises her image, name and story.

The scandal of selfhood

When Swinburne criticised Tennyson for reducing 'Arthur to the level of a wittol, Guenevere to the level of a woman of intrigue, and Launcelot to the level of a "co-respondent"', he underlined one of the causes of the poem's popularity: it tapped into the Victorian fascination with sex scandals.[67] Like sensational novels, melodramas and other forms of literature, the poem dealt with one of Victorian culture's most generic topics, highlighting the way 'private subjectivity', in this period, was consolidated 'around a core of sexual identity' and was liable to be disseminated more widely by the workings of mass media.[68] Tennyson's poem, of course, features not merely a sex scandal but one involving figures who function as celebrities in the Arthurian epic and were treated as celebrities in the Victorian period. Even more so than he does with Arthur, Tennyson offers his readers exclusive access to the intimate scenes and private conversations between Guinevere and Lancelot and presents the subjectivity of each of these characters.[69] The effect is that Lancelot and Guinevere are represented as multifaceted, tragic figures who are 'plagued by divided loyalties', fail to live up to their public personae, and experience, what Tennyson calls, the 'war of Sense and Soul'.[70] Through close attention to and scrutiny of these figures, Tennyson's poem, then, attempts to garner a level of sympathy for the adulterous lovers, giving them a depth of character and moral complexity not afforded to the other adulterous characters in *Idylls*.[71] This is made explicit in the poem when Vivien, who alludes to the scandalous relationship, is told by Merlin to 'let them be' (775); he tells her a 'rumour runs' that when Guinevere first saw Lancelot she mistook him for the king ('Merlin and Vivien', 774–75). This idea, confirmed by the poem's access to Guinevere's memories ('Guinevere', 375–97), is supplemented by her claim that she found Arthur 'cold / High, self-contain'd, and passionless, not like him, / Not like [her] Lancelot' ('Guinevere', 402–04). In 'Guinevere', Tennyson reminds readers of the dangers of judging others without due attention to human complexity and an acknowledgment of 'the world, and all its lights / And shadows, all the wealth and all the woe' (341–42). Finally, once the lovers acknowledge their guilt and renounce their shameful love, Tennyson makes it clear that both are granted a level of forgiveness: Guinevere becomes a saintly abbess and Lancelot dies a 'holy man' ('Lancelot and Elaine', 1417–18).[72]

It is significant, though, that their atonement grants the characters the opportunity of moving beyond the fame-obsessed public realm to a cloistered life of obscurity, privacy and holiness. Tennyson's representation of these characters allows him to explore what he regarded as the real scandal of celebrity culture: its dissolution of the distinction between public and private life and the psychological effects of this on public figures such as himself. More than any other figures in the poem, Guinevere and Lancelot are shaped internally and externally by a constant threat of public exposure and an awareness of being continually in the public eye. Through these figures, Tennyson hints at his feeling of always being watched and the effects of this on his sense of self. As Julia Margaret Cameron summarised: 'the visitors look at him – Tourists seek him – Americans visit him – Ladies pester and pursue him – Enthusiasts dun him for a bit of stone off his gate – These things make life a burden and his great soul suffers from these insect stings', noting 'The *looking* at him would be the most capital offence of all if he were Ruler of the Universe'.[73] Like Guinevere and Lancelot, Tennyson, especially in public, attempted to avoid being recognised, evade the scrutiny of others and deny their attempts 'to pluck out the heart of [his] mystery'.[74]

In the beginning, Lancelot's devotion to Guinevere, because it was so public, was above suspicion; he tells the queen, 'many a bard, without offence, / Has link'd our names together in his lay, / Lancelot, the flower of bravery, Guinevere, / The pearl of beauty' ('Lancelot and Elaine', 111–14). Yet, it is this level of celebrity that means, as Guinevere reminds him, they must be careful owing to their ever-watchful enemies among the knights and the ever-vigilant crowd always ready to 'murmur' about the 'shameless ones' (100). The painful price of their illicit love is that it only takes one 'meddling rogue' to arouse a 'vague suspicion' in the king (127); as Guinevere intimates:

> The tiny-trumpeting gnat can break our dream
> When sweetest; and the vermin voices here
> May buzz so loud – we scorn them, but they sting.
>
> (137–39)

So, although, at times, the lovers carelessly disregard their predicament, because, as Lancelot puts it, 'let rumours be: / When did not rumours fly?' (1186–87), the poem highlights the detrimental psychological effects of this type of unvarying observation on the couple. Guinevere and Lancelot are hounded celebrities watched by 'the crowd' (105) and pursued by figures such as Vivien and Modred, who, like nineteenth-century journalists and biographers, seek the truth but are always hoping to find scandal. Such permanent surveillance means that Guinevere, in Sir Modred, 'half-foresaw that he, the subtle beast, / Would track her guilt until he found [it]' ('Guinevere', 58–59). The 'Heart-hiding smile, and gray persistent eye' of such an enemy make Guinevere become even more self-conscious in public (63). For instance, when the queen hears rumours about Lancelot's relationship with the maid of Astolat, she must maintain a 'pale tranquillity' and appear 'so unmoved a majesty / She might have seem'd her statue' ('Lancelot and Elaine', 728, 1163–64). For, as she explains later to Lancelot, she 'Would shun to break those bounds of courtesy / In which as Arthur's Queen I move and rule: / So cannot speak my mind' (1213–15). In contrast, in her private chambers she 'writhe[s]', clenches 'her fingers till they bit the palm', shrieks at the 'unhearing wall, / Then flash[es] into wild tears'; after which she 'ris[es] again, / And move[s] about her palace, proud and pale' (606–10). Although Guinevere can retreat to her 'bower' to express her pain ('The Last Tournament', 238–39), even here she is haunted (or hunted) by the threat of scrutiny and the possibility of exposure:

> In the dead night, grim faces came and went
> Before her, or a vague spiritual fear –
> Like to some doubtful noise of creaking doors,
> Heard by the watcher in a haunted house,
> That keeps the rust of murder on the walls –
> Held her awake: or if she slept, she dream'd
> An awful dream[.]
>
> ('Guinevere', 69–75)

When the shame of the lovers is publicised throughout Camelot, Guinevere pleads, 'Would God that thou couldst hide me from myself! / Mine is the shame' (117–18), and is plagued by the idea that the revelation of her shame would mean that 'hers / Would be for evermore a name of scorn' (59–60).

Lancelot, like Guinevere, also expresses his desire not 'to be known' and his sense that his great name has been sullied because '[h]e loves the Queen, and in open shame' ('Lancelot and Elaine', 159, 1075). Although he competes anonymously in the diamond tournament ostensibly to disprove the 'common talk' that 'men went down before his spear at a touch, / But knowing he was Lancelot' (575–77), his decision also allows him to escape, temporarily, his shameful identity. It is only when he is wounded and retires to the hermit's cave that he is, at last, 'Hid[den] from the wide world's rumour' (520), evoking the desire of Victorian celebrities such as Tennyson for self-effacement and a personal space or sanctuary outside the celebrity apparatus.[75] At the end of 'Lancelot and Elaine', Lancelot privately reflects on the impossibility of escaping his reputation:

> For what am I? what profits me my name
> Of greatest knight? I fought for it, and have it:
> Pleasure to have it, none; to lose it, pain;
> Now grown a part of me: but what use in it?
> To make men worse by making my sin known?
>
> (1402–06)

The speech implies that Lancelot's fame, even though it brings him no pleasure, has subsumed his identity and 'grown part of [him]'. These preoccupations are revisited by Lancelot in his public statement on why he failed in his quest for the Holy Grail. The reason, according to Lancelot, was:

> in me lived a sin
> So strange, of such a kind, that all of pure,
> Noble, and knightly in me twined and clung
> Round that one sin, until the wholesome flower
> And poisonous grew together, each as each,
> Not to be pluck'd asunder[.]
>
> ('The Holy Grail', 769–74).

The speech acknowledges what his listeners, with the exception of Arthur, already know, namely, that Lancelot's immorality has become inextricably connected with his hard-won reputation. As in his earlier inner monologue, here, Lancelot is not expressing his horror at finding a discrepancy between his public and private self, but openly accepting that, for him, no such divergence is possible. In both speeches, Tennyson captures something of his own position as a public figure whose reputation complexly affected his self-understanding to the extent that, as Tom Mole argues, 'neither self nor celebrity can be conceptually quarantined from the other' and there is no 'kernel of subjectivity that appears to be untouched by celebrity'.[76]

In her attempt to become 'unknown' ('Guinevere', 145) and escape her own reputation and name, Guinevere takes refuge as a nameless lady in the nunnery at Almesbury. However, even here, through the novice's 'gadding tongue' (311), she hears all the news and opinions from Camelot '[a]bout the good King' (207) and the 'evil work of Lancelot and the Queen' (305). The novice, unaware exactly to whom she is speaking, interviews Guinevere about her time at Camelot. She asks about Arthur and Lancelot and even inquires about who is the noblest of these men. Unhappy with the novice's line of questioning, Guinevere accuses her of being a spy: 'thou their tool, set on to plague / And play upon, and harry me, petty spy / And traitress' (357–59). Prior to this moment, Tennyson, through the novice, articulates the idea that for the 'great ones' of society, their 'grief' is exacerbated by the fact that they must bear their pain in public 'howsoever much they may desire / Silence, they cannot weep behind a cloud' (202–05). Tennyson's representation of Lancelot and

Guinevere, then, allows him to dramatise his comparable experience of constant surveillance and of a continual threat to his privacy. In so doing, perhaps, he hoped that his reader might move intellectually and emotionally, like the novice, beyond 'narrowing nunnery-walls' to understand the intricacy of a selfhood marked by celebrity (340).[77]

Conclusion

While readings of *Idylls*, typically, contrast Guinevere's shameful sin with Arthur's famed purity, or her flawed humanity with his inhuman and restrictive idealism, this chapter has suggested that Tennyson used Camelot's celebrity circle to explore features of Victorian celebrity: its obsession with exceptional personalities that obfuscates the manu-factured, mediated and duplicated nature of celebrities; its veneration and simultaneous violation of personal privacy; its blurring of distinc-tions between self-effacement and self-promotion; its mechanisms that oscillate between the construction and deconstruction of celebrated individuals; and its empowerment of worshipping fans. It is hardly surprising, then, that Tennyson's son, Hallam, noted that *Idylls of the King* 'regarded as a whole, gives [his father's] innermost being more fully, though not more truly, than "In Memoriam"'.[78] Even the words of the reprehensible Vivien, in her comments on the omnipresence of rumour, capture something of Tennyson's position, from 1850 onwards, as a man acutely self-aware of himself as an object of scrutiny in his Farringford garden, in the privacy of his house, on his walks on the downs, at social occasions or events and when a guest at hotels. She tells Balin:

> And even in this lone wood,
> Sweet lord, ye do right well to whisper this.
> Fools prate, and perish traitors. Woods have tongues,
> As walls have ears.

> ('Balin and Balan', 520–23)

Disappearing behind this level of self-consciousness, Tennyson's real self, like Arthur's, was reserved for his innermost circle of family and friends. Yet, the final idyll, perhaps, provides a revealing glimpse at the poet's attitude to fame. Along with 'Guinevere', 'The Passing of Arthur' consoli-dates the previously fragmented and marginalised king, ironically, at the moment of his personal and political effacement. Although the final idyll begins, as already noted, with Arthur's personal self-doubt, it then focuses on his concerns about his posthumous reputation, what Merlin dismissed as 'The cackle of the unborn about the grave' ('Merlin and Vivien', 505).[79] Aware that whatever he does will be included 'wheresoever I am sung or told / In aftertime, this also shall be known' ('The Passing of Arthur', 202–03) – and to fulfil Merlin's words ('The Coming of Arthur', 305–08) and the iconography in the hall in Camelot ('The Holy Grail', 252–57) – Arthur commands Bedivere to throw the sword Excalibur into the lake. At first, Bedivere is reluctant to do so, owing to the sword's beauty and the fact that it will be a 'relic of [his] lord', which, stored in 'some treasure-house of mighty kings', would in 'aftertime' authenticate Arthur and win him reverence; otherwise, 'much honour and much fame were lost' ('The Passing of Arthur', 266, 269, 275, 277). Disagreeing, Arthur insists that his instruction be obeyed. This implies that, for Arthur, fame and honour are not produced only by physical objects, but by the power of words and the imagination, what Bedivere disparagingly calls 'empty breath / And rumours of a doubt' (267–68).[80] In the rest of the idyll, the implication is that it is only by renouncing physicality that Arthur can 'pass' from the quotidian and material life of things to the intangibility of legend – to become, Camelot-like, 'never built at all, / And therefore built for ever' ('Gareth and Lynette', 273–74) – in whose region he can become the emblem of chivalry and male heroism.[81] Here, Tennyson expresses something of his own ongoing concern about his place in posterity, which was particularly accentuated in his final years.[82] As early as 1858, as he completed 'Guinevere', he complained to his wife of 'the want of reverence now-a-days for great men, whose brightness, like that of the luminous bodies in the Heaven, makes the dark spaces look the darker'.[83] Here, as in the idyll that was composed first and yet which closes the entire poem, Tennyson indicates his belief that true fame comes when one passes, like Arthur, beyond the transience of popularity and worldly success to join the ranks of 'great men', when one is no longer a celebrity and one has become a star.

Notes

1. Alfred Lord Tennyson, *Idylls of the King*, ed. by J. M. Gray (London: Penguin, 1996), p. 179, 'Lancelot and Elaine', (l. 415). All subsequent references to this text are taken from this edition and given as line numbers in parentheses in the essay.
2. Antony H. Harrison, 'Arthurian Poetry and Medievalism', in *A Companion to Victorian Poetry*, ed. by Richard Cronin, Alison Chapman and Antony H. Harrison (Oxford: Blackwell, 2002), pp. 246–61.

3. See Mark Girouard, *The Return to Camelot: Chivalry and the English Gentleman* (New Haven: Yale University Press, 1981); Stephanie Barczewski, *Myth and National Identity in Nineteenth-Century Britain: the Legend of King Arthur and Robin Hood* (Oxford: Oxford University Press, 1997); Laura Cooner Lambdin and Robert Thomas Lambdin, *Camelot in the Nineteenth Century: Arthurian Characters in the Poems of Tennyson, Arnold, Morris and Swinburne* (Westport: Greenwood Publishing, 2000); Inga Bryden, *Reinventing King Arthur: the Arthurian Legends in Victorian Culture* (Aldershot: Ashgate, 2005); David Matthews, 'Scholarship and Popular Culture in the Nineteenth Century', in *A Companion to Arthurian Literature*, ed. by Helen Fulton (Oxford: Blackwell, 2009), pp. 355–67; Inga Bryden, 'Arthur in Victorian Poetry', in *A Companion to Arthurian Literature*, ed. by Fulton, pp. 368–80.

4. Algernon Charles Swinburne, 'A. C. Swinburne on the *Idylls*', in *Tennyson: the Critical Heritage*, ed. by John D. Jump (London: Routledge and Kegan Paul, 1967), pp. 318–21 (p. 319); 'Mr. Tennyson and the Round Table', *British Quarterly Review*, 51 (1870), 200–14 (p. 203), in *ProQuest British Periodicals* <http://www.proquest.co.uk> [accessed 12 April 2013]. For an overview of the generally positive critical responses to *Idylls* throughout the 1860s and 1870s, see Laurence W. Mazzeno, *Alfred Tennyson: the Critical Legacy* (Rochester: Camden House, 2004), pp. 18–22. In his discussion of the creation of *Idylls*, Hallam Tennyson adds the following comment: 'Most explanations and analyses, although eagerly asked for by some readers, appeared to my father somewhat to dwarf and limit the life and scope of the great Arthurian tragedy; and therefore I will add no more except what Jowett wrote in 1893: "Tennyson has made the Arthur legend a great revelation of human experience, and of the thoughts of many hearts"' (Hallam Tennyson, *Alfred Lord Tennyson: a Memoir by His Son*, 2 vols (London: Macmillan & Co., 1897), II, 134).

5. See, for example, Elliot L. Gilbert, 'The Female King: Tennyson's Arthurian Apocalypse', *PMLA*, 98 (1983), 869–78; Margaret Linley, 'Sexuality and Nationality in Tennyson's *Idylls of the King*', *Victorian Poetry*, 30 (1992), 365–86; Jeffrey E. Jackson, 'The Once and Future Sword: Excalibur and the Poetics of Imperial Heroism in *Idylls of the King*', *Victorian Poetry*, 46 (2008), 207–29; Linda M. Shires, 'Patriarchy, Dead Men, and Tennyson's *Idylls of the King*', *Victorian Poetry*, 30 (1992), 401–19; Debra N. Mancoff, 'To Take Excalibur: King Arthur and the Construction of Victorian Manhood', in *King Arthur: a Casebook*, ed. by Donald Kennedy (New York: Garland, 1996), pp. 256–80; Ian McGuire, 'Epistemology and Empire in *Idylls of the King*', *Victorian Poetry*, 30 (1992), 387–400.

6. Peter Hamilton and Roger Hargreaves, *The Beautiful and the Damned: the Creation of Identity in Nineteenth-Century Photography* (Aldershot: Lund Humphries, 2001), p. 19.

7. See Bryden, *Reinventing King Arthur*, pp. 6–18.

8. According to Tennyson, readers should not 'press too hardly on details whether for history or for allegory'; Arthur is 'meant to be a man who spent himself in the cause of honour, duty and self-sacrifice, who felt and aspired with his nobler knights, though with a stronger and a clearer conscience ... There was no such perfect man since Adam' (*Memoir*, I, 194). Hallam Tennyson noted that: 'My father felt strongly that only under the inspiration

of ideals, and with his "sword bathed in heaven", can a man combat the cynical indifference, the intellectual selfishness, the sloth of will, the utilitarian materialism of a transition age' (*Memoir*, II, 129). According to William Gladstone, Tennyson's Arthur was 'the great pillar of the moral order, and the resplendent top of moral excellence', and 'a nobler and more overpowering conception of man' would be difficult to find in literature ('Tennyson's Poems', *London Quarterly Review*, 106 (1859), 250–67 (pp. 263, 262), in *ProQuest British Periodicals* <http://www.proquest.co.uk> [accessed 12 April 2013]).

9. Mancoff, p. 274. For an example of this backlash against *Idylls*, see Leslie Stephen, *Studies of a Biographer*, 4 vols (London: Duckworth & Co., 1898), II, 200–06.

10. Linda Hughes, 'Tennyson's Urban Arthurians: Victorian Audiences and the City Built to Music', in *King Arthur Through the Ages*, ed. by Valerie M. Lagorio and Mildred Leake Day, 2 vols (New York: Garland, 1990), II, 39–61 (p. 48).

11. J. M. Gray, *Through the Vision of the Night: a Study of Source, Evolution and Structure in Tennyson's Idylls of the King* (Edinburgh: Edinburgh University Press, 1980), p. 119. For an excellent discussion of this tension between the allegorical and the real, see Margaret Homans, *Royal Representations: Queen Victoria and British Culture 1837–1876* (Chicago: Chicago University Press, 1998), pp. 183–91.

12. See Alexis Easley, *Literary Celebrity, Gender, and Victorian Authorship, 1850–1914* (Newark: University of Delaware Press, 2011), pp. 13–14, 16, 18.

13. For a representative example of this approach, see Linley, pp. 377–78.

14. My work builds on recent research on Tennyson's relationship to commodity culture, mass media and publicity: see James Eli Adams, 'Harlots and Base Interpreters: Scandal and Slander in *Idylls of the King*', *Victorian Poetry*, 30 (1992), 421–39; Gerhard Joseph, 'Commodifying Tennyson: the Historical Transformation of "Brand Loyalty"', *Victorian Poetry*, 34 (1996), 133–47; Dino Franco Felluga, 'Tennyson's *Idylls*, Pure Poetry, and the Market', *Studies in English Literature*, 37 (1997), 783–803; Anna Barton, *Tennyson's Name: Identity and Responsibility in the Poetry of Alfred Lord Tennyson* (Aldershot: Ashgate, 2008), pp. 105–28.

15. Representative of Tennyson's many complaints about public intrusion into his private life is the following one recorded by his son Hallam: 'my father often felt oppressed by the compliments and curiosity of undiscerning critics, and would say: "I hate the blare and blaze of so-called fame"' (*Memoir*, II, 164–65). On another occasion Tennyson said he felt 'sick of this publicity – all this fulsome adulation makes me miserable and inclined to vomit morally' (*The Letters of Alfred Lord Tennyson*, ed. by Cecil Y. Lang and Edgar F. Shannon, Jr, 3 vols (Oxford: Clarendon Press, 1982–90), III (1990), 399). In letters, Tennyson expressed his hatred of what he called the 'pen-punctures of those parasitic animalcules of the press', wishing, as he put it, 'they kept themselves to what I write, and did not glance spitefully and personally at myself'. See *The Letters of Alfred Lord Tennyson*, II (1987), 236. See also *Tennyson: Interviews and Recollections*, ed. by Norman Page (Basingstoke: Macmillan, 1983), p. 117; Robert Bernard Martin, *Tennyson: the Unquiet Heart* (Oxford: Clarendon Press, 1983), pp. 410–12, 456, 466–70, 564.

16. Chris Rojek, *Celebrity* (London: Reaktion Books, 2001), pp. 23, 27.

17. See Simon Morgan, 'Celebrity: Academic "Pseudo Event" or a Useful Concept for Historians?', *Cultural and Social History*, 8 (2011), 95–114 (p. 97). For evidence of the integration of Arthurian legends into nineteenth-century culture, see Barczewski, pp. 53–72; Mancoff, pp. 262–78, 281.

18. See Barton, p. 106.

19. Max Weber, *On Charisma and Institution Building: Selected Papers*, ed. by S. N. Eisenstadt (Chicago and London: University of Chicago Press, 1968), p. 48.

20. Ibid., p. 46.

21. See David Staines, *Tennyson's Camelot: the Idylls of the King and its Medieval Sources* (Waterloo: Wilfred Laurier University Press, 1982), p. 81.

22. For a brief discussion of pre-eighteenth-century renown, see Fred Inglis, *A Short History of Celebrity* (Princeton and Oxford: Princeton University Press, 2010), p. 6.

23. Eric Eisner, *Nineteenth-Century Poetry and Literary Celebrity* (Basingstoke: Palgrave Macmillan, 2009), pp. 9–10.

24. In addition, other characters in *Idylls* become hyperbolic versions of Arthur. King Pellam, on 'seeing that [Arthur's] realm / Hath prosper'd in the name of Christ', takes 'in rival heat, to holy things', promoting excessive and boastful abstemiousness and religiosity among his people ('Balin and Balan', 95–97). The Red Knight becomes the moral antithesis of Arthur, creating a court made up of adulterous knights and harlots who in 'profess[ing] / To be none other than themselves' are truer than Arthur's knights, who are 'all adulterers' ('The Last Tournament', 82–83, 84).

25. Leo Braudy, *The Frenzy of Renown: Fame and its History* (New York: Vintage, 1997), p. 5.

26. David Higgins, 'Celebrity, Politics and the Rhetoric of Genius', in *Romanticism and Celebrity Culture, 1750–1850*, ed. by Tom Mole (Cambridge: Cambridge University Press, 2009), pp. 41–59 (p. 56). See also Braudy, pp. 375, 417–25; Staines, pp. 68, 85.

27. See Richard Salmon, 'Signs of Intimacy: the Literary Celebrity in the "Age of Interviewing"', *Victorian Literature and Culture*, 25 (1997), 159–77.

28. *Letters of Alfred Lord Tennyson*, III (1990), 313.

29. Ibid., II (1987), 319.

30. Mancoff, p. 266.

31. For exceptions to this sidelining of their domestic life, see 'Lancelot and Elaine', 565–610; 'The Last Tournament', 33–50.

32. For other examples of such direct access to Arthur's thoughts, see 'Lancelot and Elaine', 562–66; 'The Passing of Arthur', 29–49.

33. *Henry Crabb Robinson on Books and Their Writers*, ed. by E. J. Marley, 2 vols (London: J. M. Dent, 1938), II, 792. In *Idylls*, the Red Knight accuses Arthur of being a 'woman worshipper' and a 'eunuch-hearted king / Who fain had clipt free manhood from the world' ('The Last Tournament', 444–45). See Gilbert, pp. 869–70. For an alternative reading that emphasises Arthur's manliness, see Clinton Machann, 'Tennyson's King Arthur and the Violence of Manliness', *Victorian Poetry*, 38 (2000), 199–226, (p. 208).

34. Staines, p. 46. Other scenes also humanise Arthur and offer readers a clear sense of the king's personality: see, for example, the private exchanges between Arthur and Guinevere in 'Lancelot and Elaine', 568–610, and

between Arthur and Lancelot in 'The Coming of Arthur', 124–33; 'Lancelot and Elaine', 1345–75; and 'The Last Tournament', 112–25.

35. See Shires, p. 405; Linley, pp. 372, 378.
36. *Letters of Alfred Lord Tennyson*, II (1987), 319.
37. See Gilbert, pp. 865, 873; Mancoff, p. 268.
38. For another description of the gate, see 'Lancelot and Elaine', 795–96.
39. For an indication of Tennyson's attempt to navigate between his cultivation of the role of 'isolated poet-priest' and his success as a financially aggrandised writer, see Kathryn Ledbetter, *Tennyson and Victorian Periodicals: Commodities in Context* (Aldershot: Ashgate, 2007), pp. 5, 45–46, 144–47; Alan Sinfield, *Alfred Tennyson* (Oxford: Basil Blackwell, 1986), pp. 154–85.
40. Staines, p. 48
41. Braudy, p. 10. *Idylls* explicitly draws attention to this clash between Christian humility and public fame in 'The Holy Grail', in which 'true humility / is the highest virtue' and only by losing oneself can one save oneself (445–46, 178, 456).
42. *Memoir*, II, 79–80.
43. The success of *Idylls* is certainly the result of Tennyson's position as Poet Laureate, whose brand name guaranteed quality and sales, and the relationship he had established with his readers. As Tom Mole puts it, nineteenth-century poets such as Tennyson needed to 'mitigate [a] sense of information overload' in the literary marketplace by branding their personalities and making their brand 'amenable to commercial promotion'. By personalising the commodities associated with himself, Tennyson could relieve the feeling of 'alienation between cultural producers and consumers by constructing a sense of intimacy' (*Byron's Romantic Celebrity: Industrial Culture and the Hermeneutic of Intimacy* (Basingstoke: Palgrave Macmillan, 2007), p. 16).
44. See Adams, pp. 421–23.
45. Herbert F. Tucker, 'The Epic Plight of Troth in *Idylls of the King*', *English Literary History*, 58 (1991), 701–20 (p. 705); see Felluga, p. 796.
46. Nicholas Dames, 'Brushes with Fame: Thackeray and the Work of Celebrity', *Nineteenth-Century Literature*, 56 (2001), 23–51 (p. 40).
47. Ibid., p. 44; see also Inglis, p. 41.
48. Tennyson insisted on travelling anonymously to prevent publicity and the possible intrusion by the public into his private life; he also published his poems anonymously or using pseudonyms when he wanted to express ideas, sentiments or opinions without connecting them to his public role as Poet Laureate. See Leonée Ormond, *Alfred Tennyson: a Literary Life* (Basingstoke: Macmillan, 1993), pp. 150–51; Ledbetter, pp. 103–04.
49. See Staines, p. 139.
50. Particularly after the publication of *Maud*, in 1855, Tennyson experienced at first hand the consequence of falling out of favour with those who idolised him; one admirer wrote to him, 'Sir, I used to worship you, but now I hate you. I loathe and detest you. You beast!' (*Letters of Alfred Lord Tennyson*, II (1987), 119).
51. For an early discussion of this idyll, see 'Review of Idylls of the King, by Alfred Tennyson', *British Quarterly Review*, 30 (1859), 481–510 (pp. 481, 488, 508), in *ProQuest British Periodicals* <http://www.proquest.co.uk> [accessed 12 April 2013].

52. See Catherine R. Harland, 'Interpretation and Rumor in Tennyson's "Merlin and Vivien"', *Victorian Poetry*, 35 (1996), 57–69.

53. See Adams, pp. 430–33.

54. See Linley, p. 369.

55. Eisner, p. 47. For an indication of how Elaine and Vivien have been interpreted by previous scholars, see Arthur L. Simpson Jr, 'Elaine the Unfair, Elaine the Unlovable: the Socially Destructive Artist/Woman in *Idylls of the King*', *Modern Philology*, 89 (1992), 341–62.

56. David Giles, *Illusions of Immortality: a Psychology of Fame and Celebrity* (Basingstoke: Macmillan, 2000), pp. 129–30.

57. Ghislaine McDayter, *Byromania and the Birth of Celebrity Culture* (Albany: State University of New York Press, 2009), pp. 2–8, 23–25, 49–50.

58. Ibid., pp. 108–18.

59. Braudy, pp. 382–83.

60. Richard Salmon, 'The Physiognomy of the Lion: Encountering Literary Celebrity in the Nineteenth Century', in *Romanticism and Celebrity Culture, 1750–1850*, ed. by Mole, pp. 60–78 (p. 71).

61. See Braudy, pp. 380–81.

62. See McDayter, pp. 102–03.

63. See Hamilton and Hargreaves, p. 21. For an example of Tennyson's admirers fetishising objects associated with him, see Edith Nicholl Ellison, *A Child's Recollections of Tennyson* (London: J. Dent, 1907), p. 87; Martin, p. 467.

64. While Lancelot is concerned with how this would be perceived by the world, 'All ear and eye, with such a stupid heart / To interpret ear and eye, and such a tongue / To blare its own interpretations' ('Lancelot and Elaine', 936–68), Elaine dismisses as 'ignoble talk' her father's suggestion that 'all the people know' of Lancelot and Guinevere's 'open shame' (1081, 1074–77).

65. For an alternative reading of this idyll, see Barton, pp. 116, 124.

66. Braudy, pp. 7, 6.

67. Swinburne, p. 319.

68. William A. Cohen, *Sex Scandals: the Private Part of Victorian Fiction* (Durham: Duke University Press, 1995), p. 9. See also June Steffensen Hagen, *Tennyson and His Publishers* (London: Macmillan, 1979), pp. 112–13.

69. For examples, see private conversations between Lancelot and Guinevere: 'Lancelot and Elaine', 97–157, 1173–1235; 'Guinevere', 87–97, 107–21. For examples of access to Lancelot's thoughts, see 'Lancelot and Elaine', 1382–1416; for access to Guinevere's, see 'Guinevere', 607–56.

70. Staines, p. 55; *Memoir*, II, 130.

71. See Staines, pp. 59–61.

72. For a discussion of how such discussion of scandal can give the illusion of psychological depth to characters, see Adams, pp. 421–22, 437; Linley, p. 370.

73. *Letters of Alfred Lord Tennyson*, II (1987), 257–58. See also William Holman Hunt, *Pre-Raphaelitism and the Pre-Raphaelite Brotherhood*, 2 vols (New York and London: Macmillan, 1905–6), II (1906), 174.

74. *Tennyson: Interviews*, p. 88; *Letters of Alfred Lord Tennyson*, II (1987), 500.

75. Tom Mole, 'Introduction', in *Romanticism and Celebrity Culture, 1750–1850*, ed. by Mole, pp. 1–18 (p. 12).

76. Mole, *Bryon's Romantic Celebrity*, p. 3.

77. Tennyson contrasts these noble sinners with those in *Idylls* who are concerned with fame for its own sake such as Ettarre, Sir Gawain and Sir Tristram. For instance, although Ettarre thinks Pelleas is 'a fool', she flatters him so that he will win the list and circlet for her, as 'her mind was bent / On hearing, after trumpet blown, her name / And title, "Queen of Beauty," in the lists' ('Pelleas and Ettarre', 108–11). Similarly, Sir Gawain is more concerned about the public image of the Round Table than his own inner virtue. He chastises Pelleas for 'defame[ing] [his] brotherhood' (313–14) by allowing himself to be manhandled by Ettarre's servants, yet Gawain betrays Pelleas even though he 'pledged [his] troth ... by the honour of the Table Round' to help him (333–34). In like manner, in the idyll 'The Last Tournament' the diamonds which should be won by 'the purest [the] knights [might] win' are won by the most cynical and worldly, Sir Tristram; he, in turn, gives them to his married lover Queen Isolt, the wife of King Mark, who is not 'the purest of [the] maids' (49–50). Tristram's victory in 'The Tournament of the Dead Innocence' marks the demise of purity and virtue and the degeneration of Camelot. Like Ettarre and Sir Gawain, Sir Tristram is only interested in public reputation; he is victorious because of his 'Strength of heart / And might of limb, but mainly use and skill' (197–98). Interestingly, Tristram equates his illicit relationship with Isolt with that of Lancelot and Guinevere (202–04). But Tristram's victory is not applauded by those who attend; instead 'most of these were mute, some anger'd, one / Murmuring, "All courtesy is dead," and one, / "The glory of our Round Table is no more"' (210–12). Moreover, despite this level of opposition to Tristram's triumph, to gladden their 'sad eyes' it is decided to celebrate, and 'dame and damsel glitter'd at the feast / Variously gay' and revelled 'with mirth so loud / Beyond all use' (222, 225–26, 235–36).
78. *Memoir*, II, 128.
79. Staines, p. 130
80. See Jackson, p. 217.
81. See Shires, pp. 402, 407.
82. Provocatively, a published account of Tennyson's death suggested that it 'irresistibly brought to our minds his own "Passing of Arthur"' (see *Memoir*, II, 429). For a discussion of Tennyson's concerns about his posthumous reputation, see Michael Millgate, *Testamentary Acts: Browning, Tennyson, James, Hardy* (Oxford: Clarendon Press, 1992), pp. 39–67. See also *Tennyson: Interviews*, pp. 159–60; Martin, pp. 552–53.
83. *Memoir*, I, 424.

Bibliography

Adams, James Eli, 'Harlots and Base Interpreters: Scandal and Slander in *Idylls of the King*', *Victorian Poetry*, 30 (1992), 421–39

—— 'The Hero as Spectacle: Carlyle and the Persistence of Dandyism', in Christ and Jordan, eds, *Victorian Literature and the Victorian Visual Imagination*, pp. 213–32

Adams, W. H. Davenport, *Nelson's Handbook to the Isle of Wight* (London: T. Nelson and Sons, 1873)

Alexander, Christine, 'Myth and Memory: Reading the Brontë Parsonage', in Hendrix, ed., *Writers' Houses and the Making of Memory*, pp. 93–110

'Alfred Lord Tennyson', *Daily News*, 6 October 1897, p. 6, in *Gale 19th Century British Library Newspapers* <http://gale.cengage.co.uk> [accessed 12 April 2013]

Allen, Grant, 'Tennyson's Homes at Aldworth and Farringford', *English Illustrated Magazine*, 10 (1892), 147–56

Allingham, H., and D. Radford, eds, *William Allingham's Diary 1847–1889* (London: Centaur Press, 2000)

[Allingham, William], 'Mrs. Cameron's Photographs', *Pall Mall Gazette*, 29 January 1868, p. 10, in *Gale 19th Century British Library Newspapers* <http://gale.cengage.co.uk> [accessed 8 April 2013]

Altick, Richard D., *Lives and Letters: a History of Literary Biography in England and America* (New York: Alfred A. Knopf, 1965)

Amigoni, David, *Victorian Biography: Intellectuals and the Ordering of Discourse* (New York and London: Harvester Wheatsheaf, 1993)

'Anecdotal Photographs VIII. – The Laureate', *Truth*, 20 February 1879, pp. 234–35

Anning, Adeline, 'A Profession for Women: Photography', *The Woman's Signal*, 7 March 1895, p. 149, in *Gale 19th Century UK Periodicals* <http://gale.cengage.co.uk> [accessed 8 April 2013]

Armstrong, Isobel, *Victorian Poetry: Poetry, Poetics and Politics* (London: Routledge, 1993)

'Art in Photography', *Illustrated London News*, 15 July 1865, p. 50, in *The Illustrated London News Historical Archive 1842–2003* <http://gale.cengage.co.uk> [accessed 8 April 2013]

Atkin, Polly, 'Ghosting Grasmere: the Musealisation of Dove Cottage', in Watson, ed., *Literary Tourism and Nineteenth-Century Culture*, pp. 84–94

Atkinson, Juliette, *Victorian Biography Reconsidered: a Study of Nineteenth-Century 'Hidden' Lives* (Oxford: Oxford University Press, 2010)

Auerbach, Nina, *Ellen Terry: Player in Her Time* (London and Melbourne: J. M. Dent & Sons Ltd., 1987)

Bagehot, Walter, 'W. Bagehot on the *Idylls of the King*', in John D. Jump, ed., *Tennyson: the Critical Heritage* (London: Routledge and Kegan Paul, 1967), pp. 215–40

Baker, William, 'T. S. Eliot on Edward Lear: An Unnoted Attribution', *English Studies*, 64 (1983), 564–66

Banta, Martha, *Barbaric Intercourse: Caricature and the Culture of Conduct, 1841–1936* (Chicago: Chicago University Press, 2003)

Barczewski, Stephanie, *Myth and National Identity in Nineteenth-Century Britain: the Legend of King Arthur and Robin Hood* (Oxford: Oxford University Press, 1997)

Barlow, Paul, 'Facing the Past and Present: the National Portrait Gallery and the Search for "Authentic" Portraiture', in Joanna Woodall, ed., *Portraiture: Facing the Subject* (Manchester: Manchester University Press, 1997), pp. 219–38

Barrett, Elizabeth, 'Letter to Mary Russell Mitford (1843)', in Black, Conolly, Flint and others, eds, *The Broadview Anthology of British Literature: the Victorian Era*, p. 381

Barton, Anna, 'Delirious Bulldogs and Nasty Crockery: Tennyson as Nonsense Poet', *Victorian Poetry*, 47 (2009), 313–30

—— *Tennyson's Name: Identity and Responsibility in the Poetry of Alfred Lord Tennyson* (Aldershot: Ashgate, 2008)

Benjamin, Walter, 'A Small History of Photography', in *One Way Street and Other Writings*, trans. by Edmund Jephcott and Kingsley Shorter (London: Verso, 1985), pp. 240–57

Bennett, Andrew, *Romantic Poets and the Culture of Posterity* (Cambridge: Cambridge University Press, 1999)

Bentley, George, 'Sincerity in Biography', *Temple Bar*, 62 (1881), 329–36, in *ProQuest British Periodicals* <http://www.proquest.co.uk> [accessed 12 April 2013]

Berlanstein, Lenard R., 'Historicizing and Gendering Celebrity Culture: Famous Women in Nineteenth-Century France', *Journal of Women's History*, 16 (2004), 65–91

Bills, Mark, and Barbara Bryant, eds, *G. F. Watts: Victorian Visionary* (New Haven: Yale University Press, 2008)

'Biography', *Blackwood's Edinburgh Magazine*, 69 (1851), 40–53, in *ProQuest British Periodicals* <http://www.proquest.co.uk> [accessed 12 April 2013]

'Biography', *Fraser's Magazine*, 5 (1832), 253–60, in *ProQuest British Periodicals* <http://www.proquest.co.uk> [accessed 12 April 2013]

Black, Barbara J., *On Exhibit: Victorians and Their Museums* (Charlottesville, VA: University Press of Virginia, 2000)

Black, Joseph, Leonard Conolly, Kate Flint and others, eds, *The Broadview Anthology of British Literature: the Victorian Era* (Peterborough, Ontario: Broadview Press, 2006)

Blathwayt, Raymond, 'How Celebrities Have Been Photographed', *Windsor Magazine*, 2 (1895), 639–48, in *ProQuest British Periodicals* <http://www.proquest.co.uk> [accessed 8 April 2013]

Blunt, Wilfrid, *'England's Michelangelo': a Biography of George Frederic Watts* (London: Hamish Hamilton, 1975)

'Book Review', *London Review of Politics, Society, Literature, Art, and Science*, 27 February 1864, p. 226, in *ProQuest British Periodicals* <http://www.proquest.co.uk> [accessed 12 April 2013]

Booth, Alison, 'Author Country: Longfellow, the Brontës, and Anglophone Homes and Haunts', *Romanticism and Victorianism on the Net*, Special Issue: Victorian Internationalisms, 48 (2007), DOI:10.7202/017438ar

—— *How to Make It as a Woman: Collective Biographical History from Victoria to the Present* (Chicago and London: University of Chicago Press, 2004)

Boyce, Charlotte, and Páraic Finnerty, *Tennyson's Celebrity Circle* (Portsmouth: Tricorn Books, 2011)

Braudy, Leo, *The Frenzy of Renown: Fame and Its History* (New York: Vintage, 1997)

Briddon's Illustrated Handbook to the Isle of Wight, Containing Everything Necessary to the Tourist (Ryde: J. Briddon, 1862)

Briggs, Asa, *Victorian Things* (London: B.T. Batsford, 1988)

Brock, Claire, *The Feminization of Fame, 1750–1830* (Basingstoke: Palgrave Macmillan, 2006)

Broughton, Trev Lynn, *Men of Letters, Writing Lives: Masculinity and Literary Auto/ Biography in the Late-Victorian Period* (London: Routledge, 1999)

Browning, Elizabeth Barrett, *Aurora Leigh and Other Poems* (London: Penguin, 1995)

—— *Letters to Mrs. David Ogilvy, 1849–1861* (Quadrangle: New York Times Book Company and The Browning Institute, 1973)

Bryant, Barbara, *G F Watts Portraits: Fame and Beauty in Victorian Society* (London: National Portrait Gallery, 2004)

—— 'Invention and Reinvention: the Art and Life of G. F. Watts', in Bills and Bryant, eds, *G. F. Watts: Victorian Visionary*, pp. 19–49

Bryden, Inga, 'Arthur in Victorian Poetry', in Fulton, ed., *A Companion to Arthurian Literature*, pp. 368–80

—— *Reinventing King Arthur: the Arthurian Legends in Victorian Culture* (Aldershot: Ashgate, 2005)

Buzard, James, *The Beaten Track: European Tourism, Literature, and the Ways to Culture, 1800–1918* (Oxford: Clarendon Press, 1993)

Cameron, H. H. H., 'Introduction', in Cameron and Ritchie, eds, *Alfred, Lord Tennyson and his Friends*, pp. 7–8

Cameron, H. H. H., and Anne Thackeray Ritchie, eds, *Alfred, Lord Tennyson and his Friends: a Series of 25 Portraits and Frontispiece in Photogravure from the Negatives of Mrs. Julia Margaret Cameron and H. H. H. Cameron* (London: T. Fisher Unwin, 1893)

Cameron, Julia Margaret, 'Annals of My Glass House', in Hamilton, ed., *Annals of My Glass House: Photographs by Julia Margaret Cameron*, pp. 11–16

Carlyle, Thomas, *On Heroes, Hero-Worship and the Heroic in History*, ed. by Archibald MacMechan (London: Ginn, 1901)

'Cartes de Visite of Celebrities', *The Saturday Review*, 27 September 1862, pp. 372–73, *ProQuest British Periodicals* <http://www.proquest.co.uk> [accessed 8 April 2013]

'Celebrity: Its Pains and Penalties', *The Sixpenny Magazine*, 3 (1862), 82–83, in *ProQuest British Periodicals* <http://www.proquest.co.uk> [accessed 4 April 2013]

Cheshire, Jim, 'Introduction', in *Tennyson Transformed*, ed. by Cheshire, pp. 8–19

—— ed., *Tennyson Transformed: Alfred Lord Tennyson and Visual Culture* (Farnham: Lund Humphries, 2009)

Chesterton, G. K., *The Defendant* (London: E. Brimley Johnson, 1902)

—— *G. F. Watts* (London: Duckworth, 1904)

——'The Literary Portraits of G. F. Watts, R. A.', *The Bookman*, 19 (1900), 80–83, in *ProQuest British Periodicals* <http://www.proquest.co.uk> [accessed 12 April 2013]

Chitty, Susan, *That Singular Person Called Lear* (Stroud: Tempus, 2007)

Christ, Carol, 'Painting the Dead: Portraiture and Necrophilia in Victorian Art and Poetry', in Sarah Goodwin and Elisabeth Bronfen, eds, *Death and Representation* (Baltimore: The Johns Hopkins University Press, 1993), pp. 133–51

Christ, Carol T., and John O. Jordan, eds, *Victorian Literature and the Victorian Visual Imagination* (Berkeley, CA, and London: University of California Press, 1995)

Claes, Koenraad, 'Supplements and Paratext: the Rhetoric of Space', *Victorian Periodicals Review*, 43 (2010), 196–210

Clark, Anne, *Lewis Carroll: a Biography* (London: J. M. Dent & Sons Ltd, 1979)

Cockshut, A. O. J., *Truth to Life: the Art of Biography in the Nineteenth Century* (London: Collins, 1974)

Codell, Julie F., 'Victorian Artists' Family Biographies: Domestic Authority, the Marketplace and the Artist's Body', in Jo Law and Linda K. Hughes, eds, *Biographical Passages: Essays on Victorian and Modernist Biography* (Columbia: University of Missouri Press, 2000), pp. 65–108

Cohen, Morton N., *Lewis Carroll: a Biography* (New York: Alfred A. Knopf, 1995)

Cohen, Morton N., and Roger Lancelyn Green, eds, *The Letters of Lewis Carroll*, 2 vols (New York: Oxford University Press, 1979)

Cohen, William A., *Sex Scandals: the Private Part of Victorian Fiction* (Durham: Duke University Press, 1995)

Cole, Sarah Rose, 'The Recovery of Friendship: Male Love and Developmental Narrative in Tennyson's *In Memoriam*', *Victorian Poetry*, 50 (2010), 43–66

Colley, Ann C., *Edward Lear and the Critics* (Columbia, SC: Camden House, 1993)

—— 'Edward Lear's Anti-Colonial Bestiary', *Victorian Poetry*, 30 (1992), 109–20

—— 'Edward Lear's Limericks and the Reversals of Nonsense', *Victorian Poetry*, 26 (1988), 285–99

Collingwood, Stuart Dodgson, *The Life and Letters of Lewis Carroll* (London: T. Fisher Unwin, 1898)

Colvin, Sidney, 'English Painters and Paintings in 1867', *Fortnightly Review*, 2 (1867), 464–76, in *ProQuest British Periodicals* <http://www.proquest.co.uk> [accessed 12 April 2013]

—— *Memories and Notes of Persons and Places, 1852–1912* (London: Edward Arnold, 1921)

—— 'Review of *More Nonsense, Pictures, Rhymes, Botany, &c.*', *The Academy*, 3 (1872), 23–24, in *ProQuest British Periodicals* <http://www.proquest.co.uk> [accessed 12 April 2013]

Conway, M. D., 'South-Coast Saunterings in England: Saunter V – The Isle of Wight II', *Harper's New Monthly Magazine*, 40 (1870), 523–42, in *Cornell University Library Making of America Collection* <http://ebooks.library.cornell.edu/m/moa/> [accessed 3 April 2013]

Couldry, Nick, 'On the Set of *The Sopranos*: "Inside" a Fan's Construction of Nearness', in Gray, Sandvoss and Harrington, eds, *Fandom: Identities and Communities in a Mediated World*, pp. 139–48

Cox, Julian, and Colin Ford, eds, 'Introduction', in Cox and Ford, eds, *Julia Margaret Cameron*, pp. 1–5

—— *Julia Margaret Cameron, the Complete Photographs* (London: Thames & Hudson, 2003)

Craig, Edith, and Christopher St. John, eds, *Ellen Terry's Memoirs* (London: Victor Gollancz, 1933)

Craton, Lillian, *The Victorian Freak Show: the Significance of Disability and Physical Differences in 19th-Century Fiction* (Amherst: Cambria Press, 2009)

Cronin, Richard, 'Edward Lear and Tennyson's Nonsense', in Robert Douglas-Fairhurst and Seamus Perry, eds, *Tennyson Among the Poets: Bicentenary Essays* (Oxford: Oxford University Press, 2009), pp. 259–75

Crump, Beverly, 'Lord Tennyson: the Poet-Laureate's Picturesque Home', *The Sentinel* (Milwaukee, WI), 22 January 1888, p. 12, in *Gale 19th Century U. S. Newspapers* <http://gale.cengage.co.uk> [accessed 24 February 2012]

Cunningham, Valentine, ed., *The Victorians: An Anthology of Poetry and Poetics* (Oxford: Wiley–Blackwell, 2000)

Dakers, Caroline, *The Holland Park Circle: Artists and Victorian Society* (New Haven: Yale University Press, 1999)

Dames, Nicholas, 'Brushes with Fame: Thackeray and the Work of Celebrity', *Nineteenth-Century Literature*, 56 (2001), 23–51

Davidson, Angus, *Edward Lear: Landscape Painter and Nonsense Poet* (London: John Murray, 1938)

Demoor, Marysa, ed., *Marketing the Author: Authorial Personae, Narrative Selves and Self-Fashioning, 1880–1930* (Basingstoke: Palgrave Macmillan, 2004)

De Nie, Michael, *The Eternal Paddy: Irish Identity and the British Press, 1798–1882* (Madison: University of Wisconsin Press, 2004)

D. W., 'The Surrey Home of Mr G F Watts RA,' *Illustrated London News*, 29 July 1893, p. 135, in *The Illustrated London News Historical Archive 1842–2003* <http://gale.cengage.co.uk> [accessed 12 April 2013]

Easley, Alexis, *Literary Celebrity, Gender, and Victorian Authorship, 1850–1914* (Newark: University of Delaware Press, 2011)

[Eastlake, Lady Elizabeth], 'Art. V.', *The Quarterly Review*, 101 (1857), 442–68, in *ProQuest British Periodicals* <http://www.proquest.co.uk> [accessed 8 April 2013]

'Edward Lear', *Athenaeum*, 2 December 1911, p. 687, in *ProQuest British Periodicals* <http://www.proquest.co.uk> [accessed 12 April 2013]

Edward Lear Diaries (MS Eng 797.3). Houghton Library, Harvard University

Edward Lear's Diaries: the Private Journals of a Landscape Painter. <http://www.nonsenselit.org/diaries/> Transcript of Houghton Library MS Eng. 797.3 [accessed 12 April 2013]

Eisner, Eric, *Nineteenth-Century Poetry and Literary Celebrity* (Basingstoke: Palgrave Macmillan, 2009)

Elfenbein, Andrew, *Byron and the Victorians* (Cambridge: Cambridge University Press, 1995)

Elliot, Philip L., *The Making of the Memoir* (Furman University Press, 1978)

Ellison, Edith Nicholl, *A Child's Recollections of Tennyson* (London: J. Dent, 1907)

Emerson, P. H., 'Mrs. Cameron', *Sun Artists*, 5 (1890), 33–42

Erickson, Lee, *The Economy of Literary Form: English Literature and the Industrialization of Publishing, 1800–1850* (Baltimore: Johns Hopkins University Press, 1996)

Felluga, Dino Franco, 'Tennyson's *Idylls*, Pure Poetry, and the Market', *Studies in English Literature*, 37 (1997), 783–803

Fields, Annie, 'Tennyson', *Harper's New Monthly Magazine*, 86 (1893), 309–12, in *Cornell University Library Making of America Collection* <http://ebooks.library.cornell.edu/m/moa/> [accessed 4 April 2013]

'Fine Arts', *Illustrated London News*, 22 July 1865, p. 71, in *The Illustrated London News Historical Archive 1842–2003* <http://gale.cengage.co.uk> [accessed 8 April 2013]

'Fine Arts', *Illustrated London News*, 11 November 1865, pp. 462–63, in *The Illustrated London News Historical Archive 1842–2003* <http://gale.cengage.co.uk> [accessed 8 April 2013]

'Fine Arts', *Illustrated London News*, 18 November 1865, p. 486, in *The Illustrated London News Historical Archive 1842–2003* <http://gale.cengage.co.uk> [accessed 8 April 2013]

'Fine Arts', *Illustrated London News*, 9 December 1865, p. 566, in *The Illustrated London News Historical Archive 1842–2003* <http://gale.cengage.co.uk> [accessed 8 April 2013]

'Fine Arts', *Illustrated London News*, 28 April 1866, p. 411, in *The Illustrated London News Historical Archive 1842–2003* <http://gale.cengage.co.uk> [accessed 8 April 2013]

'Fine Arts', *Illustrated London News*, 27 December 1873, p. 619, in *The Illustrated London News Historical Archive 1842–2003* <http://gale.cengage.co.uk> [accessed 8 April 2013]

'Fine-Art Gossip', *Athenaeum*, 25 May 1861, p. 700, in *ProQuest British Periodicals* <http://www.proquest.co.uk> [accessed 12 April 2013]

'Fine-Art Gossip', *Athenaeum*, 2 November 1889, p. 604, in *ProQuest British Periodicals* <http://www.proquest.co.uk> [accessed 12 April 2013]

Ford, Colin, *Julia Margaret Cameron: a Critical Biography* (Los Angeles: J. Paul Getty Museum, 2003)

Fortescue, Chichester, *And Mr. Fortescue: a Selection from the Diaries from 1851 to 1862 of Chichester Fortescue, Lord Carlingford, K. P. P.* (London: J. Murray, 1958)

Franta, Andrew, *Romanticism and the Rise of the Mass Public* (Cambridge: Cambridge University Press, 2007)

Fuller, Hester Thackeray, *Three Freshwater Friends: Tennyson, Watts and Mrs. Cameron* (Newport: Isle of Wight County Press, 1933)

Fulton, Helen, ed., *A Companion to Arthurian Literature* (Oxford: Blackwell, 2009)

G. F. Watts Correspondence, Box 3, National Portrait Gallery, London

Galatea, 'Tennyson's Home', *The Daily Inter-Ocean* (Chicago, IL), 4 March 1875, p. 3, in *Gale 19th Century U. S. Newspapers* <http://gale.cengage.co.uk> [accessed 24 February 2012]

Garvey, Ellen Gruber, 'Scissorizing and Scrapbooks: Nineteenth-Century Reading, Remaking and Recirculating', in Lisa Gitelman and Geoffrey B. Pingree, eds, *New Media, 1740–1915* (Cambridge, MA and London: MIT Press, 2003), pp. 207–27

Gernsheim, Helmut, *Julia Margaret Cameron: Her Life and Photographic Work* (London: Gordon Fraser, 1975)

—— *Lewis Carroll: Photographer* (London: Max Parrish & Co., 1949)

Gernsheim, Helmut, and Alison Gernsheim, *The History of Photography: From the Earliest Use of the Camera Obscura in the Eleventh Century up to 1914* (London: Oxford University Press, 1955)

Gilbert, Elliot L., 'The Female King: Tennyson's Arthurian Apocalypse', *PMLA*, 98 (1983), 869–78

Giles, David, *Illusions of Immortality: a Psychology of Fame and Celebrity* (Basingstoke: Macmillan, 2000)

Girouard, Mark, *The Return to Camelot: Chivalry and the English Gentleman* (New Haven: Yale University Press, 1981)

Gladstone, William, 'Tennyson's Poems', *London Quarterly Review*, 106 (1859), 250–67, in *ProQuest British Periodicals* <http://www.proquest.co.uk> [accessed 12 April 2013]

Goodbrand, Robert, 'A Suggestion for a New Kind of Biography', *Contemporary Review*, 14 (1870), 20–28, in *ProQuest British Periodicals* <http://www.proquest.co.uk> [accessed 12 April 2013]

Gosse, Edmund, *Books on the Table* (New York: Charles Scribner's Sons, 1921)

—— 'A First Sight of Tennyson', in Page, ed., *Tennyson: Interviews and Recollections*, pp. 124–26

Gould, Veronica Franklin, 'G. F. Watts and Ellen Terry', in Katherine Cockin, ed., *Ellen Terry, Spheres of Influence* (London: Pickering & Chatto, 2011), pp. 33–47

—— *G. F. Watts: the Last Great Victorian* (New Haven and London: Yale University Press, 2004)

Gray, J. M., *Through the Vision of the Night: a Study of Source, Evolution and Structure in Tennyson's Idylls of the King* (Edinburgh: Edinburgh University Press, 1980)

Gray, Jonathan, Cornel Sandvoss and C. Lee Harrington, eds, *Fandom: Identities and Communities in a Mediated World* (New York and London: New York University Press, 2007)

Green, Roger Lancelyn, ed., *The Diaries of Lewis Carroll*, 2 vols (Westport: Greenwood Press, 1971)

Groth, Helen, *Victorian Photography and Literary Nostalgia* (Oxford: Oxford University Press, 2003)

Hagen, June Steffensen, *Tennyson and His Publishers* (London: Macmillan, 1979)

Halsey, Katie, '"Faultless Herself, As Nearly As Human Nature Can Be": the Construction of Jane Austen's Public Image, 1817–1917', in Hawkins and Ives, eds, *Women Writers and the Artifacts of Celebrity*, pp. 33–37

Hamilton, Peter, and Roger Hargreaves, *The Beautiful and the Damned: the Creation of Identity in Nineteenth-Century Photography* (Aldershot: Lund Humphries, 2001)

Hamilton, Violet, ed., *Annals of My Glass House: Photographs by Julia Margaret Cameron* (Seattle and London: University of Washington Press, 1996)

Hansard, 165 (1862), 1890–91

Hark, Ina Rae, *Edward Lear* (Boston: Twayne Publishers, 1982)

Harland, Catherine R., 'Interpretation and Rumor in Tennyson's Merlin and Vivien', *Victorian Poetry*, 35 (1996), 57–69

Harrison, Antony H., 'Arthurian Poetry and Medievalism', in Richard Cronin, Alison Chapman and Antony H. Harrison, eds, *A Companion to Victorian Poetry* (Oxford: Blackwell, 2002), pp. 246–61

Hartmann, C. Sadakichi, 'Tennyson at Home', *The Sunday Inter Ocean* (Chicago, IL), 22 November 1891, p. 31, in *Gale 19th Century U. S. Newspapers* <http://gale.cengage.co.uk> [accessed 13 March 2012]

Hawkins, Ann R., and Maura Ives, eds, *Women Writers and the Artifacts of Celebrity in the Long Nineteenth Century* (Farnham: Ashgate, 2012)

Hazard, Erin, 'The Author's House: Abbotsford and Wayside', in Watson, ed., *Literary Tourism and Nineteenth-Century Culture*, pp. 63–72

—— '"A Realized Day-Dream": Excursions to Nineteenth-Century Authors' Homes', *Nineteenth Century Studies*, 20 (2006), 13–34

Hazlitt, William, *Lectures on the English Poets, and the English Comic Writers* (London: George Bell & Sons, 1876)

Henderson, Philip, *Tennyson: Poet and Prophet* (London and Henley: Routledge and Kegan Paul 1978)

Hendrix, Harald, 'Epilogue', in Hendrix, ed., *Writers' Houses and the Making of Memory*, pp. 235–43

—— ed., *Writers' Houses and the Making of Memory* (London and New York: Routledge, 2008)

—— 'Writers' Houses as Media of Expression and Remembrance: From Self-Fashioning to Cultural Memory', in Hendrix, ed., *Writers' Houses and the Making of Memory*, pp. 1–12

Henry Cole Correspondence and Papers, 55.BB Box 8, Victoria and Albert Museum, London

Higgins, David, 'Celebrity, Politics and the Rhetoric of Genius', in Mole, ed., *Romanticism and Celebrity Culture, 1750–1850*, pp. 41–59

—— *Romantic Genius and the Literary Magazine: Biography, Celebrity and Politics* (London and New York: Routledge, 2005)

Hill, Emily, 'Photography for Women: An Interview with Mrs. Weed Ward', *The Woman's Signal*, 28 April 1898, 259–60, in *Gale 19th Century UK Periodicals* <http://gale.cengage.co.uk> [accessed 8 April 2013]

Hill, J. W., *Historical and Commercial Directory of the Isle of Wight* (London: T. Danks, 1879)

Hoge, James O., ed., *The Letters of Emily Lady Tennyson* (University Park and London: Pennsylvania State University Press, 1974)

[Hollingshead, John], 'A Counterfeit Presentment', *Household Words*, 18 (1858), 71–72, in *ProQuest British Periodicals* <http://www.proquest.co.uk> [accessed 12 April 2013]

Homans, Margaret, *Royal Representations: Queen Victoria and British Culture 1837–1876* (Chicago: Chicago University Press, 1998)

'Home of Alfred Tennyson', *Daily Evening Bulletin* (San Francisco, CA), 13 June 1868, column H, in *Gale 19th Century U. S. Newspapers* <http://gale.cengage.co.uk> [accessed 24 February 2012]

'Home Miscellany', *North Wales Chronicle*, 24 July 1858, [p. 3], in *Gale 19th Century British Library Newspapers* <http://gale.cengage.co.uk> [accessed 11 April 2013]

Hudson, Derek, *Lewis Carroll: An Illustrated Biography* (New York: Clarkson N. Potter, 1977)

Hughes, Linda, 'Tennyson's Urban Arthurians: Victorian Audiences and the City Built to Music', in Valerie M. Lagorio and Mildred Leake Day, eds, *King Arthur Through the Ages*, 2 vols (New York: Garland, 1990), II, 39–61

Hunt, William Holman, *Pre-Raphaelitism and the Pre-Raphaelite Brotherhood*, 2 vols (New York and London: Macmillan, 1905–06)

Hutchings, Richard J., and Brian Hinton, *The Farringford Journal of Emily Tennyson: 1853–1864* (Newport: Isle of Wight County Press, 1986)

Huxley, Leonard, ed., *Elizabeth Barrett Browning: Letters to her Sister, 1846–1859* (London: John Murray, 1929)

Inglis, Fred, *A Short History of Celebrity* (Princeton and Oxford: Princeton University Press, 2010)

'Interviewers and Interviewing', *All the Year Round*, 8 (1892), 422–26, in *ProQuest British Periodicals* <http://www.proquest.co.uk> [accessed 12 April 2013]

Ives, Maura, 'Introduction: Women Writers and the Artifacts of Celebrity', in Hawkins and Ives, eds, *Women Writers and the Artifacts of Celebrity*, pp. 1–12

Jackson, Jeffrey E., 'The Once and Future Sword: Excalibur and the Poetics of Imperial Heroism in *Idylls of the King*', *Victorian Poetry*, 46 (2008), 207–29

Jaffe, Aaron, *Modernism and the Culture of Celebrity* (Cambridge: Cambridge University Press, 2005)

Joseph, Gerhard, 'Commodifying Tennyson: the Historical Transformation of "Brand Loyalty"', *Victorian Poetry*, 34 (1996), 133–47

'Julia Cameron and her Work: the Story of a Remarkable Woman', *Woman's Herald*, 6 July 1893, p. 318, in *Gale 19th Century UK Periodicals* <http://gale.cengage.co.uk> [accessed 8 April 2013]

Kebbel, T. E., 'Biography', *Cornhill Magazine*, 47 (1883), 601–07, in *ProQuest British Periodicals* <http://www.proquest.co.uk> [accessed 12 April 2013]

Khasawneh, Hana F., 'The Dynamics of Nonsense Literature: 1840–1940', (unpublished doctoral thesis, University of Sussex, 2009)

Kitton, F. G., 'Tennyson at Aldworth: a Reminiscence', *Gentleman's Magazine*, 278 (1895), 53–59

Knowles, James T., 'Aspects of Tennyson', *Nineteenth Century*, 33 (1893), 164–88

Lambdin, Laura Cooner, and Robert Thomas Lambdin, *Camelot in the Nineteenth Century: Arthurian Characters in the Poems of Tennyson, Arnold, Morris and Swinburne* (Westport: Greenwood Publishing, 2000)

Lang, Andrew, *Alfred Tennyson* (Edinburgh and London: Blackwood & Sons, 1901)

Lang, Cecil Y., and Edgar F. Shannon, Jr, eds, *The Letters of Alfred Lord Tennyson*, 3 vols (Oxford: Clarendon Press, 1982–90)

Langford, Michael J., *Story of Photography: From Its Beginnings to the Present Day* (London: Focal Press, 1997)

Lear, Edward, *The Complete Nonsense and Other Verse*, ed. by Vivian Noakes (London: Penguin, 2002)

——— *More Nonsense, Pictures, Rhymes, Botany Etc.* (London: Robert John Bush, 1872)

'Lear's Book of Nonsense', *The Saturday Review,* 24 March 1888, p. 361, in *ProQuest British Periodicals* <http://www.proquest.co.uk> [accessed 12 April 2013]

'Lear's Nonsense Books', *The Spectator*, 17 September 1887, pp. 1251–52

Ledbetter, Kathryn, *Tennyson and Victorian Periodicals: Commodities in Context* (Aldershot: Ashgate, 2007)

Levi, Peter, *Edward Lear* (London: Taylor and Francis, 1995)

'The Life of Tennyson', *Glasgow Herald*, 6 October 1897, p. 4, in *Gale 19th Century British Library Newspapers* <http://gale.cengage.co.uk> [accessed 12 April 2013]

Linley, Margaret, 'Sexuality and Nationality in Tennyson's *Idylls of the King*', *Victorian Poetry*, 30 (1992), 365–86

'Lions of the Day in their Dens', *Judy*, 12 February 1890, p. 77, in *Gale 19th Century UK Periodicals* <http://gale.cengage.co.uk> [accessed 3 April 2013]

'Lions of the Day in their Dens', *Judy*, 19 March 1890, p. 141, in *Gale 19th Century UK Periodicals* <http://gale.cengage.co.uk> [accessed 3 April 2013]

Lippincott, Louise, 'Expanding on Portraiture: the Market, the Public, and the Hierarchy of Genres in Eighteenth-Century Britain', in Ann Bermingham and John Brewer, eds, *The Consumption of Culture, 1600–1800: Image, Object, Text* (London: Routledge, 1995), pp. 75–88

'London', *Orchestra*, 14 January 1865, p. 248, in *ProQuest British Periodicals* <http://www.proquest.co.uk> [accessed 12 April 2013]

'Lord Tennyson', *The Graphic*, 22 March 1884, p. 290, in *Gale 19th Century UK Periodicals* <http://gale.cengage.co.uk> [accessed 12 April 2013]

'Lord Tennyson', *The Saturday Review*, 8 October 1892, pp. 405–06, in *ProQuest British Periodicals* <http://www.proquest.co.uk> [accessed 12 April 2013]

Lukitsh, Joanne, *Cameron: Her Work and Career* (Rochester, NY: International Museum of Photography at George Eastman House, 1986)

—— 'Julia Margaret Cameron and the "Enoblement" of Photographic Portraiture', in Kristine Ottesen Garrigan, ed., *Victorian Scandals: Representations of Gender and Class* (Athens, OH: Ohio University Press, 1992), pp. 207–32

—— 'The Thackeray Album: Looking at Julia Margaret Cameron's Gift to Her Friend Annie Thackeray', *The Library Chronicle of the University of Texas at Austin*, 26.4 (1996), 33–61

Lyall, Alfred, *Tennyson* (London: Macmillan, 1902)

M., 'A Spring Day at Farringford: An Afternoon with Tennyson', *Temple Bar*, 126 (1902), 216–21

MacCarthy, Fiona, *William Morris: a Life for Our Time* (London: Faber and Faber, 1994)

McDayter, Ghislaine, *Byromania and the Birth of Celebrity Culture* (Albany: State University of New York Press, 2009)

McGill, Meredith L., *American Literature and the Culture of Reprinting, 1834–1853* (Philadelphia: University of Pennsylvania Press, 2003)

McGuire, Ian, 'Epistemology and Empire in *Idylls of the King*', *Victorian Poetry*, 30 (1992), 387–400

Machann, Clinton, 'Tennyson's King Arthur and the Violence of Manliness', *Victorian Poetry*, 38 (2000), 199–226

MacKay, Carol Hanbery, *Creative Negativity: Four Victorian Exemplars of the Female Quest* (Stanford: Stanford University Press, 2001)

Mancoff, Debra N., 'To Take Excalibur: King Arthur and the Construction of Victorian Manhood', in Donald Kennedy, ed., *King Arthur: a Casebook.* (New York: Garland, 1996), pp. 256–80

Marcus, Sharon, *Between Women: Friendship, Desire, and Marriage in Victorian England* (Princeton: Princeton University Press, 2007)

Marsh, Joss, 'The Rise of Celebrity Culture', in Sally Ledger and Holly Furneaux, eds, *Charles Dickens in Context* (Cambridge: Cambridge University Press, 2011), pp. 98–108

Marshall, Gail, *Actresses on the Victorian Stage: Feminine Performances and the Galatea Myth* (Cambridge: Cambridge University Press, 1998)

Martin, Robert Bernard, *Tennyson: the Unquiet Heart* (Oxford: Clarendon Press, 1983)

Mary Watts's Diary. Watts Gallery Archive, Surrey

Matthew, H. C. G., *Leslie Stephen and the New Dictionary of National Biography* (Cambridge: Cambridge University Press, 1997)

Matthews, David, 'Scholarship and Popular Culture in the Nineteenth Century', in Fulton, ed., *A Companion to Arthurian Literature*, pp. 355–67

Maxwell, Richard, 'Palms and Temples: Edward Lear's Topographies', *Victorian Poetry*, 48 (2010), 73–94

Mazzeno, Laurence W., *Alfred Tennyson: the Critical Legacy* (Rochester: Camden House, 2004)

Mill, John Stuart, 'A System of Logic Ratiocinative and Inductive', in *Collected Works of John Stuart Mill*, 33 vols, ed. J. M. Robson (London: Routledge and Kegan Paul, 1973)

Millais, John Guille, ed., *The Life and Letters of Sir John Everett Millais*, 2 vols (London: Methuen & Co., 1899)

Millgate, Michael, *Testamentary Acts: Browning, Tennyson, James, Hardy* (Oxford: Clarendon Press, 1992)

Milton, John, *The Major Works*, ed. by Stephen Orgel and Jonathan Goldberg (Oxford: Oxford University Press, 2003)

Mole, Tom, *Byron's Romantic Celebrity: Industrial Culture and the Hermeneutic of Intimacy* (Basingstoke: Palgrave Macmillan, 2007)

—— 'Introduction', in Mole, ed., *Romanticism and Celebrity Culture, 1750–1850*, pp. 1–18

—— ed., *Romanticism and Celebrity Culture, 1750–1850* (Cambridge: Cambridge University Press, 2009)

Monkhouse, William Cosmo, *British Contemporary Artists* (New York: Scribner's Sons, 1899)

Morgan, Simon, 'Celebrity: Academic "Pseudo Event" or a Useful Concept for Historians?', *Cultural and Social History*, 8 (2011), 95–114

'Mr. Alfred Tennyson', *Daily News*, 19 July 1858, p. 4, in *Gale 19th Century British Library Newspapers* <http://gale.cengage.co.uk> [accessed 11 April 2013]

'Mr. Alfred Tennyson', *Morning Post*, 17 July 1858, p. 5, in *Gale 19th Century British Library Newspapers* <http://gale.cengage.co.uk> [accessed 11 April 2013]

'Mr Lear's Drawings', *The Saturday Review*, 31 May 1890, p. 684, in *ProQuest British Periodicals* <http://www.proquest.co.uk> [accessed 12 April 2013]

'Mr. Lear's New Nonsense', *The Spectator*, 23 December 1871, pp. 1570–71

'Mr. Tennyson and the Round Table', *British Quarterly Review*, 51 (1870), 200–14, in *ProQuest British Periodicals* <http://www.proquest.co.uk> [accessed 12 April 2013]

'Mr. Tennyson's Garibaldian Tree', *The London Review*, 8 (1864), 406–07, in *ProQuest British Periodicals* <http://www.proquest.co.uk> [accessed 3 April 2013]

'Mrs. Julia Margaret Cameron', *Woman's Herald*, 4 April 1891, pp. 369–70, in *Gale 19th Century UK Periodicals* <http://gale.cengage.co.uk> [accessed 8 April 2013]

Munby, A. N. L., *The Cult of the Autograph Letter in England* (London: Athlone Press, 1962)

Napier, George G., *The Homes and Haunts of Alfred Lord Tennyson, Poet Laureate* (Glasgow: James Maclehose & Sons, 1892)

'A National Gallery', *The Gentleman's Magazine*, 45 (1856), 367–71, in *ProQuest British Periodicals* <http://www.proquest.co.uk> [accessed 12 April 2013]

'National Portrait Gallery', *Art Journal*, 16 (1856), 99–100, in *ProQuest British Periodicals* <http://www.proquest.co.uk> [accessed 8 April 2013]

Nicholson, Harold, *Tennyson: Aspects of his Life, Character and Poetry* (London: Constable, 1949)

Noakes, Vivian, *Edward Lear: the Life of a Wanderer*, rev. edn (Stroud: Sutton Publishing, 2004)

—— ed., *Selected Letters of Edward Lear* (Oxford: Oxford University Press, 1988)

Novak, Daniel A., *Realism, Photography and Nineteenth-Century Fiction* (Cambridge: Cambridge University Press, 2008)

O'Connor, Erin, *Raw Materials: Producing Pathology in Victorian Culture* (Durham: Duke University Press, 2000)

O'Connor, T. P., 'Books Worth Reading', *The Graphic*, 7 October 1897, p. 484, in *Gale 19th Century British Library Newspapers* <http://gale.cengage.co.uk> [accessed 12 April 2013].

O'Connor, V. C. Scott, 'Mrs. Cameron, Her Friends, and Her Photographs', *Century Magazine*, 55 (1897), 3–10, in *Cornell University Library Making of America Collection* <http://ebooks.library.cornell.edu/m/moa/> [accessed 8 April 2013]

—— 'Tennyson and his Friends at Freshwater', *The Century*, 55 (1897), 240–68, in *Cornell University Library Making of America Collection* <http://ebooks.library.cornell.edu/m/moa/> [accessed 3 April 2013]

Oliphant, Margaret, 'The Ethics of Biography,' *Contemporary Review*, 44 (1883), 76–93, in *ProQuest British Periodicals* <http://www.proquest.co.uk> [accessed 12 April 2013]

Olson, Kirby, 'Edward Lear: Deleuzian Landscape Painter', *Victorian Poetry*, 31 (1993), 347–62

'On Some of the Inconveniences of Celebrity', *The Sixpenny Magazine*, 4 (1862), 260–61, in *ProQuest British Periodicals* <http://www.proquest.co.uk> [accessed 12 April 2013]

Ormond, Leonée, *Alfred Tennyson: a Literary Life* (Basingstoke: Macmillan, 1993)

—— 'Tennyson and the Artists', in Cheshire, ed., *Tennyson Transformed*, pp. 42–61.

Ormond, Leonée, and Richard Ormond, *G. F. Watts: the Hall of Fame, Portraits of his Famous Contemporaries* (Compton: Watts Gallery, 2012)

Ormond, Richard, *G. F. Watts, the Hall of Fame: Portraits of his Famous Contemporaries* (London, National Portrait Gallery, 1975)

Page, Norman, ed., *Tennyson: Interviews and Recollections* (Basingstoke: Macmillan, 1983)

Pascoe, Judith, *The Hummingbird in the Cabinet: a Rare and Curious History of Romantic Collectors* (Ithaca: Cornell University Press, 2006)

[Patmore, Coventry], 'Mrs. Cameron's Photographs', *Macmillan's Magazine*, 13 (1866), 230–31, in *ProQuest British Periodicals* <http://www.proquest.co.uk> [accessed 8 April 2013]

Pearce, Susan M., Rosemary Flanders, Mark Hall and Fiona Morton, *The Collector's Voice: Critical Readings in the Practice of Collecting: Imperial Voices*, 3 vols (Aldershot: Ashgate, 2002)

Peattie, Roger W., ed., *Selected Letters of William Michael Rossetti* (University Park, PA: Pennsylvania State University Press, 1990)

Perry, Lara, 'Nationalizing Watts: the *Hall of Fame* and the National Portrait Gallery', in Trodd and Brown, eds, *Representations of G. F. Watts*, pp. 121–33

Phegley, Jennifer, 'Motherhood, Authorship, and Rivalry: Sons' Memoirs of the Lives of Ellen Price Wood and Mary Elizabeth Braddon', in Hawkins and Ives, eds, *Women Writers and the Artifacts of Celebrity*, pp. 189–204

'The Philosophy of Yourself', *All the Year Round*, 9 (1863), 391–94, in *ProQuest British Periodicals* <http://www.proquest.co.uk> [accessed 12 April 2013]

'Photography as an Employment for Women', *The Englishwoman's Review*, [1 July 1867], pp. 219–23, in *Gale 19th Century UK Periodicals* <http://gale.cengage.co.uk> [accessed 5 April 2013]

Piper, David, *The Image of the Poet: British Poets and their Portraits* (Oxford: Clarendon Press, 1982)

Pitman, Ruth, *Edward Lear's Tennyson* (Manchester: Carcanet, 1988)

Plunkett, John, 'Celebrity and Community: the Poetics of the Carte-de-Visite', *Journal of Victorian Culture*, 8 (2003), 55–79

—— *Queen Victoria: First Media Monarch* (Oxford: Oxford University Press, 2003)

'The Poet Laureate at Home', *Hampshire Telegraph and Sussex Chronicle*, 23 January 1869, p. 7, in *Gale 19th Century British Library Newspapers* <http://gale.cengage.co.uk> [accessed 3 April 2013]

'The Poet's Island Home', *New York Times*, 31 August 1878, p. 5, in *The New York Times Article Archive* <http://www.nytimes.com/ref/membercenter/nytarchive. html> [accessed 4 April 2013]

Pointon, Marcia, *Hanging the Head: Portraiture and Social Formation in Eighteenth-Century England* (New Haven: Yale University Press, 1997)

Pollock, Sir Frederick, '"Presidential Address", Photographic Society (1855)', in Black, Conolly, Flint and others, eds, *The Broadview Anthology of British Literature: the Victorian Era*, p. 381

Powell, Tristram, 'Editor's Note', in Virginia Woolf and Roger Fry, *Victorian Photographs of Famous Men and Fair Women*, ed. by Tristram Powell (London: Hogarth Press, 1973), pp. 21–2

Price, John, '"Heroism in Everyday Life": the Watts Memorial for Heroic Self Sacrifice', *History Workshop Journal*, 63 (2007), 254–78

Price, Kenneth M., and Susan Belasco Smith, eds, *Periodical Literature in Nineteenth-Century America* (Charlottesville and London: University Press of Virginia, 1995)

Pudney, John, *Lewis Carroll and His World* (London: Thames and Hudson, 1976)

Purcell, Edmund, 'On the Ethics of Suppression in Biography', *Nineteenth Century*, 40 (1896), 533–42, in *ProQuest British Periodicals* <http://www.proquest.co.uk> [accessed 12 April 2013]

Quarles, Geoffrey, 'Tennyson at Home', *The Sunday Inter Ocean* (Chicago, IL), 27 November 1887, p. 21, in *Gale 19th Century U. S. Newspapers* <http://gale. cengage.co.uk> [accessed 13 March 2012]

Quilter, Harry, 'The Art of Watts', *The Times*, 6 January 1882, p. 8, in *The Times Digital Archive* <http://gale.cengage.co.uk> [accessed 12 April 2012]

Rawnsley, H. D., 'Memories of Farringford', in Page, ed., *Tennyson: Interviews and Recollections*, pp. 60–75

Reed, Joseph W., *English Biography in the Early Nineteenth Century: 1801–1838* (New Haven and London: Yale University Press, 1966)

'A Reminiscence of Mrs. Cameron by a Lady Amateur', *Photographic News*, 1 January 1886, pp. 2–4

'Review of Idylls of the King, by Alfred Tennyson', *British Quarterly Review*, 30 (1859), 481–510, in *ProQuest British Periodicals* <http://www.proquest.co.uk> [accessed 12 April 2013]

Richards, Jeffrey, *Sir Henry Irving* (Hambledon: Continuum, 2005), pp. 259–81

Ricks, Christopher, *Essays in Appreciation* (Oxford: Clarendon, 1996)

—— ed., *The Poems of Tennyson* (London: Longmans, Green and Co., 1969)

—— ed., *Selected Poems of Alfred Tennyson* (London: Penguin, 2008)

Rideing, William H., 'Tennyson in the Isle of Wight', *North American Review*, 165 (1897), 701–10, in *Cornell University Library Making of America Collection* <http://ebooks.library.cornell.edu/m/moa/> [accessed 3 April 2013]

Rigney, Ann, 'Abbotsford: Dislocation and Cultural Remembrance', in Hendrix, ed., *Writers' Houses and the Making of Memory*, pp. 75–92

Ritchie, Anne Thackeray, 'Alfred Tennyson', *Harper's New Monthly Magazine*, 68 (1883), 21–41, in *Cornell University Library Making of America Collection* <http://ebooks.library.cornell.edu/m/moa/> [accessed 4 April 2013]

—— *From Friend to Friend*, ed. Emily Ritchie (London: John Murray, 1919)

—— 'Reminiscences', in Cameron and Ritchie, eds, *Alfred, Lord Tennyson and His Friends*, pp. 9–16

Ritchie, Hester, ed., *Letters of Anne Thackeray Ritchie* (London: John Murray, 1924)

Robinson, Henry Crabb, *Henry Crabb Robinson on Books and Their Writers*, ed. by E. J. Marley, 2 vols (London: J. M. Dent, 1938)

Robson, Catherine, *Men in Wonderland: the Lost Girlhood of the Victorian Gentleman* (Princeton: Princeton University Press, 2001)

Rojek, Chris, *Celebrity* (London: Reaktion Books, 2001)

Rossetti, W[illiam] M[ichael], 'Essays on Art by Francis Palgrave Turner', *Fine Arts Quarterly Review*, 1 (October 1866), 302–11, in *ProQuest British Periodicals* <http://www.proquest.co.uk> [accessed 8 April 2013]

—— 'Mrs. Cameron's Photographs', *Chronicle*, 31 August 1867, pp. 546–47

Rubin, Rebecca B., and Alan M. Rubin, 'Attribution in Social and Parasocial Relationships', in Valerie L. Manusov and John Harvey, eds, *Attribution, Communication Behaviour, and Close Relationships* (Cambridge: Cambridge University Press, 2001), pp. 320–37

Salmon, Richard, *Henry James and the Culture of Publicity* (Cambridge: Cambridge University Press, 1997)

—— 'The Physiognomy of the Lion: Encountering Literary Celebrity in the Nineteenth Century', in Mole, ed. *Romanticism and Celebrity Culture, 1750–1850*, pp. 60–78

—— 'Signs of Intimacy: the Literary Celebrity in the "Age of Interviewing"', *Victorian Literature and Culture, 25* (1997), 159–77

Shires, Linda M., 'The Author as Spectacle and Commodity: Elizabeth Barrett Browning and Thomas Hardy', in Christ and Jordan, eds, *Victorian Literature and the Victorian Visual Imagination*, pp. 198–212

—— 'Patriarchy, Dead Men, and Tennyson's *Idylls of the King*', *Victorian Poetry*, 30 (1992), 401–19

Simpson Jr, Arthur L., 'Elaine the Unfair, Elaine the Unlovable: the Socially Destructive Artist/Woman in *Idylls of the King*', *Modern Philology*, 89 (1992), 341–62

Sinfield, Alan, *Alfred Tennyson* (Oxford: Basil Blackwell, 1986)

Smith, Charles Saumarez, *The National Portrait Gallery* (London: National Portrait Gallery, 1997)

Smith, Lindsay, 'Further Thoughts on "The Politics of Focus"', *The Library Chronicle of the University of Texas at Austin*, 26 (1996), 13–31

—— 'The Politics of Focus: Feminism and Photographic Theory', in Isobel Armstrong, ed., *New Feminist Discourses* (London: Routledge, 1992), pp. 238–62

Snider, Clifton, 'Victorian Trickster: a Jungian Consideration of Edward Lear's Nonsense Verse', *Psychological Perspectives*, 24 (1991), 90–110

Somerset, Lady Henry, 'Books Worth Reading', *The Woman's Signal*, 24 May 1894, pp. 361–62, in *Gale 19th Century UK Periodicals* <http://gale.cengage.co.uk> [accessed 8 April 2013]

Sontag, Susan, *On Photography* (New York: Farrar, Straus & Giroux, 1977)

Spielmann, M. H., 'The Works of Mr George F. Watts, R. A. with a complete catalogue of his Pictures', *Pall Mall Gazette*, 22 (1886), 1–32, in *Gale 19th Century British Library Newspapers* <http://gale.cengage.co.uk> [accessed 12 April 2013]

Staines, David, *Tennyson's Camelot: the Idylls of the King and its Medieval Sources* (Waterloo: Wilfred Laurier University Press, 1982)

The Standard, 6 October 1897, p. 4, in *Gale 19th Century British Library Newspapers* <http://gale.cengage.co.uk> [accessed 12 April 2013]

Stephen, Julia, 'Cameron, Julia Margaret', in Leslie Stephen, ed., *Dictionary of National Biography*, series 1, 63 vols (London: Smith, Elder, & Co., 1885–1900), VIII (1886), 300

Stephen, Leslie, *Studies of a Biographer*, 4 vols (London: Duckworth & Co., 1898)

[Stephens, Frederic George], 'Fine-Art Gossip', *Athenaeum*, 20 May 1865, p. 690, in *ProQuest British Periodicals* <http://www.proquest.co.uk> [accessed 8 April 2013]

Stetz, Margaret D., *Facing the Late Victorians: Portraits of Writers and Artists from the Mark Samuels Lasner Collection* (Newark: University of Delaware Press, 2007)

Stewart, Susan, *On Longing: Narratives of the Miniature, the Gigantic, the Souvenir, the Collection* (Durham, NC: Duke University Press, 1984)

Stoker, Ben, 'Alfred: Informal Portraits of a Poet', in Cheshire, ed., *Tennyson Transformed*, pp. 62–67

[Strachey, Edward], 'Nonsense as a Fine Art', *Quarterly Review*, 167 (1888), 335–65, in *ProQuest British Periodicals* <http://www.proquest.co.uk> [accessed 8 April 2013]

Strachey, Lady, ed., *Later Letters of Edward Lear, Author of 'The Book of Nonsense', to Chichester Fortescue, Lord Carlingford, Frances Countess Waldegrave and others* (London: T. Fisher Unwin, 1911)

—— ed., *Letters of Edward Lear, Author of 'The Book of Nonsense', To Chichester Fortescue, Lord Carlingford, and Frances Countess Waldegrave* (London: T. Fisher Unwin, 1907)

'A Summer Ramble', *Leisure Hour*, 448 (1860), 476–78, in *ProQuest British Periodicals* <http://www.proquest.co.uk> [accessed 3 April 2013]

'The Surrey Hills: the Scenes around the Home of Tennyson', *Boston Daily Advertiser* (Boston, MA), 13 January 1883, p. 2, in *Gale 19th Century U. S. Newspapers* <http://gale.cengage.co.uk> [accessed 24 February 2012]

Swinburne, Algernon Charles, 'A. C. Swinburne on the *Idylls*', in *Tennyson: the Critical Heritage*, ed. by John D. Jump (London: Routledge and Kegan Paul, 1967), pp. 318–21

Symons, Arthur, 'The Art of Watts', *Fortnightly Review*, 74 (1900), 188–97, in *ProQuest British Periodicals* <http://www.proquest.co.uk> [accessed 12 April 2013]

Taylor, Sir Henry, *Autobiography of Henry Taylor, 1800–1875*, 2 vols (New York: Harper & Brothers, 1885)

'Tennyson', *Morning Post*, 6 October 1897, p. 6, in *Gale 19th Century British Library Newspapers* <http://gale.cengage.co.uk> [accessed 12 April 2013]

'Tennyson', *Pall Mall Gazette*, 6 October 1897, p. 1, in *Gale 19th Century British Library Newspapers* <http://gale.cengage.co.uk> [accessed 12 April 2013]

Tennyson, Alfred Lord, *Idylls of the King*, ed. by J. M. Gray (London: Penguin, 1996)

—— *The Poetical Works of Alfred Tennyson, Poet Laureate* (Boston: Ticknor and Fields, 1856)

'The Tennyson Biography', *The Standard*, 6 October 1897, p. 2, in *Gale 19th Century British Library Newspapers* <http://gale.cengage.co.uk> [accessed 12 April 2013]

Tennyson, Charles, *Alfred Tennyson* (London: Macmillan & Co., 1949)

'Tennyson Enraged', *Rocky Mountain News* (Denver, CO), 17 February 1884, p. 14, in *Gale 19th Century U. S. Newspapers* <http://gale.cengage.co.uk> [accessed 13 March 2012]

Tennyson, Hallam, *Alfred Lord Tennyson: a Memoir by His Son*, 2 vols (London: Macmillan & Co., 1897)

'Tennyson at Home', *Daily Evening Bulletin* (San Francisco, CA), 18 September 1876, column C, in *Gale 19th Century U. S. Newspapers* <http://gale.cengage.co.uk> [accessed 24 February 2012]

'Tennyson at Home', *Frank Leslie's Illustrated Newspaper* (New York), 7 November 1885, p. 190, in *Gale 19th Century U. S. Newspapers* <http://gale.cengage.co.uk> [accessed 24 February 2012]

'Tennyson at Home', *St. Louis Daily Globe-Democrat – Supplemental Sheet* (St Louis, MO), 10 September 1876, p. 11, in *Gale 19th Century U. S. Newspapers* <http://gale.cengage.co.uk> [accessed 24 February 2012]

'Tennyson at Home and Abroad', *Hawaiian Gazette* (Honolulu, HI), 14 May 1879, p. 4, in *Gale 19th Century U. S. Newspapers* <http://gale.cengage.co.uk> [accessed 24 February 2012]

'Tennyson at Home: Drinking, Smoking and Reading His Own Poetry', *The Sun* (New York), 28 December 1868, p. 1, in *Chronicling America: Historic American Newspapers* <http://chroniclingamerica.loc.gov> [accessed 4 April 2013]

'Tennyson and Sightseers', *Bismarck Daily Tribune* (Bismarck, ND), 13 December 1892, p. 4, in *Gale 19th Century U. S. Newspapers* <http://gale.cengage.co.uk> [accessed 13 March 2012]

'Tennyson's Aversion to Being Stared At', *Daily Evening Bulletin* (San Francisco, CA), 8 November 1873, column D, in *Gale 19th Century U. S. Newspapers* <http://gale.cengage.co.uk> [accessed 13 March 2012]

'Tennyson's Home', *New Hampshire Statesman* (Concord, NH), 14 June 1867, column G, in *Gale 19th Century U. S. Newspapers* <http://gale.cengage.co.uk> [accessed 24 February 2012]

[Thackeray, Anne], 'A Book of Photographs', *Pall Mall Gazette*, 10 April 1865, pp. 10–11, in *Gale 19th Century British Library Newspapers* <http://gale.cengage.co.uk> [accessed 8 April 2013]

Thwaite, Ann, *Emily Tennyson: the Poet's Wife* (London: Faber and Faber, 1996)

Tigges, Wim, *An Anatomy of Literary Nonsense* (Amsterdam: Rodopi, 1988)

Trodd, Colin, 'Illuminating Experience: Watts and the Subject of Portraiture', in Trodd and Brown, eds, *Representations of G. F. Watts*, pp. 135–52

Trodd, Colin, and Stephanie Brown, eds, *Representations of G. F. Watts: Art Making in Victorian Culture* (Aldershot: Ashgate Press, 2004)

Tromp, Marlene, with Karyn Valerius, 'Toward Situating the Victorian Freak', in Marlene Tromp, ed., *Victorian Freaks: the Social Context of Freakery in Britain* (Columbus: Ohio State University Press, 2008), pp. 1–18

Troubridge, Laura, *Memories and Reflections* (London: William Heinemann, 1925)

Tucker, Herbert F., 'The Epic Plight of Troth in *Idylls of the King*', *English Literary History*, 58 (1991), 701–20

—— *Tennyson and the Doom of Romanticism* (Cambridge, MA: Harvard University Press, 1988)

Urry, John, *The Tourist Gaze*, 2nd edn (London: Sage, 2002)

Vaughan, John, 'Jane Austen at Lyme', *The Monthly Packet*, n.s., 6 (1893), 271–79

Ward, Wilfrid, 'Tennyson at Freshwater', *Dublin Review,* 150 (1912), 68–85

Ward, William, 'Candour in Biography', *The New Review*, 14 (1896), 445–52, in *ProQuest British Periodicals* <http://www.proquest.co.uk> [accessed 12 April 2013]

Warre-Cornish, Blanche, 'Memories of Tennyson', in Page, ed., *Tennyson: Interviews and Recollections*, pp. 110–21

Watson, Nicola J., 'Introduction', in Watson, ed., *Literary Tourism and Nineteenth-Century Culture*, pp. 1–12

—— ed., *Literary Tourism and Nineteenth-Century Culture* (Basingstoke: Palgrave Macmillan, 2009)

—— *The Literary Tourist* (Basingstoke: Palgrave Macmillan, 2006)

Watts, G. F., 'The Present Conditions of Art', in Watts, *George Frederic Watts*, III, 147–90

Watts, M. S., *George Frederic Watts: the Annals of an Artist's Life*, 3 vols (London: Macmillan and Co., 1912)

Watts-Dunton, Theodore, 'Emily, Lady Tennyson', *Athenaeum*, 15 August 1896, pp. 227–28, in *ProQuest British Periodicals* <http://www.proquest.co.uk> [accessed 12 April 2013]

Weaver, Mike, *Whisper of the Muse: the Overstone Album and Other Photographs by Julia Margaret Cameron* (Malibu: J. Paul Getty Museum, 1986)

Weber, Brenda R., *Women and Literary Celebrity in the Nineteenth Century: the Transatlantic Production of Fame and Gender* (Farnham: Ashgate, 2012)

Weber, Max, *On Charisma and Institution Building: Selected Papers*, ed. by S. N. Eisenstadt (Chicago and London: University of Chicago Press, 1968)

Weld, Agnes Grace, *Glimpses of Tennyson and of Some of His Relations and Friends* (London and Oxford: Williams & Norgate, 1903)

Wermuth, Paul C. ed., *Selected Letters of Bayard Taylor* (Lewisburg and London: Bucknell University Press/Associated University Presses, 1997)

West, W. K., *G. F. Watts* (London: George Newnes, 1904)

Wichard, Robin, and Carol Wichard, *Victorian Cartes-de-Visite* (Princes Risborough: Shire, 1999)

Wiener, Wendy, and George C. Rosenblatt, 'A Moment's Monument: the Psychology of Keeping a Diary', in Ruthellen Josselson and Amia Lieblich, eds, *The Narrative Study of Lives* (London: Sage, 1993), pp. 30–58

Wolf, Sylvia, *Julia Margaret Cameron's Women* (New Haven and London: Yale University Press, 1998)

Woolf, Virginia, *Freshwater: a Comedy*, ed. by Lucio P. Ruotolo (London: Harcourt, 1985)

—— 'The New Biography', in *Selected Essays*, ed. by David Bradshaw (Oxford: Oxford University Press, 2008), pp. 95–100

Woolf, Virginia and Roger Fry, *Victorian Photographs of Famous Men and Fair Women* (London: Hogarth Press, 1926)

Wordsworth, William, *The Complete Poetical Works of William Wordsworth* (London: Edward Moxon, Son, and Co., 1869)

Wright, Philippa, 'Little Pictures: Julia Margaret Cameron and Small-Format Photography', in Cox and Ford, eds, *Julia Margaret Cameron: the Complete Photographs*, pp. 81–93

Wullschläger, Jackie, *Inventing Wonderland: the Lives and Fantasies of Lewis Carroll, Edward Lear, J. M. Barrie, Kenneth Grahame, and A. A. Milne* (London: Methuen, 1995)

Wynter, A[ndrew], 'Cartes de Visite', *Once a Week*, 25 January 1862, pp. 134–37, *ProQuest British Periodicals* <http://www.proquest.co.uk> [accessed 8 April 2013]

'A Yankee Visit to Tennyson', *The Derby Mercury*, 20 January 1869, p. 6, in *Gale 19th Century British Library Newspapers* <http://gale.cengage.co.uk> [accessed 3 April 2013]

'A Yankee's Visit to Tennyson', *The Hull Packet and East Riding Times*, 22 January 1869, p. 3, in *Gale 19th Century British Library Newspapers* <http://gale.cengage.co.uk> [accessed 3 April 2013]

Yates, Edmund, *Celebrities At Home*, repr. from *The World*, 3 vols (London: Office of *The World*, 1877–79)

—— *His Recollections and Experiences*, 2 vols (London: Richard Bentley and Son, 1884)

Index

Printed and bound in Great Britain by
CPI Group (UK) Ltd, Croydon, CR0 4YY